The World Wildlife Fund Guide to Extinct Species of Modern Times

Volume 1

Birds of the Pacific Islands and North America

Plants of the Hawaiian Islands

Fishes of North America

Mammals of North and South Africa

Mammals of North America and the Atlantic Islands

 BEACHAM PUBLISHING CORP.

The World Wildlife Fund Guide
to Extinct Species of Modern Times

Editor
Walton Beacham

Consulting Editor
Loyal A. Mehrhoff, Ph.D.
U.S. Fish & Wildlife Service
Portland, Oregon

Photo Editor
Deborah Beacham

Species Text Articles
The introduction to and all articles on Hawaiian plants were written by Loyal A. Mehrhoff; some of the other articles were adapted from data compiled by the Threatened and Endangered Species Information Institute (Golden, CO) for *Beacham's International Threatened, Endangered and Extinct Species* on CD-ROM, available from Beacham Publishing Corp.

Library of Congress
Cataloging-in-Publication Data

The World Wildlife Fund Guide to Extinct Species of Modern Times / editor, Walton Beacham
Includes bibliographical references and index
ISBN 0-933833-40-7
Describes 211 species that are believed to have become extinct since 1570 and discusses their probable causes of extinction.
1. Endangered species. 2. Endangered plants. 3. Extinct animals. 4. Extinct plants. I. Beacham, Walton, 1943- . II. World Wildlife Fund (U.S.)
QH75.W675 1996   574.5'29—dc20   96-29170

Printed in the United States of America
First Printing, January 1997

Contents—Volume 1

About World Wildlife Fund

World Wildlife Fund (WWF) is the leading private U.S. organization working worldwide to protect endangered wildlife and wildlands. Its top priority is conservation of the tropical forests of Latin America, Asia, and Africa — places that are home to most of the world's species and thus uniquely important in protecting the Earth's biological diversity.

Since its founding in 1961, WWF has worked in more than 100 countries to implement over 1,400 projects involving a comprehensive array of conservation methods. WWF has created or supported more than 300 national parks on five continents.

With WWF's help, species throughout the world have been saved from extinction. For example, the last few surviving Arabian oryx were brought to the U.S. for captive breeding; their progeny are now being reintroduced into the wild in Oman and Jordan. Major WWF efforts have safeguarded other threatened species such as India's Bengal tiger, Brazil's golden lion tamarin, America's peregrine falcon, and China's giant panda, which is WWF's organizational symbol.

WWF is unique among U.S. conservation organizations because of its affiliation with the international WWF network, which includes national organizations and associate groups in 26 countries around the world and an international secretariat in Gland, Switzerland. The U.S. headquarters of World Wildlife Fund are located at 1250 Twenty-fourth Street, N.W., Washington, D.C. 20037.

Color Photo Credits

Many of the images in the color insert are photos of hand-colored lithographs published in the nineteenth and early twentieth centuries.

From *The Mammals of Australia*
By John Gould
Illustrated by John Gould and H. C. Richter
London 1863
  Eastern Hare-Wallaby, C-2
  Western Barred Bandicoot, C-2

From *The Birds of New Zealand*
By W. L. Buller
Illustrated by J. G. Keulemans
London 1905
  New Zealand Quail, C-2
  Auckland Island Merganser, C-3
  Huia, C-3

From *The Birds of Norfolk and Lord Howe Islands*
By Gregory Macalister Mathews
Illustrated by Gregory Macalister Mathews
London 1928
  Lord Howe Purple Gallinule, C-2
  Norfolk Island Starling, C-3

From *The Birds of Europe*
By John Gould
Illustrated by Edward Lear
London 1832-37
  Great Auk, C-1

From *Avifauna of Laysan and the Neighboring Islands*
By Walter Rothschild
Illustrated by J. G. Keulmans
London 1893-1900
  Laysan Rail, C-3
  Greater Amakihi, C-5
  Laysan Millerbird, C-5
  Hawaii O'o, C-5
  Kioea, C-5
  Laysan Honeycreeper, C-6
  Hawaii Akialoa, C-6

Greater Koa Finch, C-6
Black Mamo, C-6
Kona Finch, C-7

From *Aves Hawaiiensis*
By S. B. Wilson and A. H. Evans
Illustrated by F. W. Frohawk
London 1893-1900
  Ula-ai-hawane, C-6
  Oahu 'Akepa, C-3

From *Ornithological Miscellany*
By G. D. Rowleg
Illustrated by J. G. Keulemans
London 1875
  Laughing Owl, C-4

From *New and Heretofore Unfigured Species of the Birds of North America*
By D. G. Elliott
Illustrated by Joseph Wolf
New York 1869
  Steller's Spectacled Cormorant, C-1

Other Images

Amistad Gambusia
  photo by James E. Johnson, C-1
Dodo
  illustrated by Richard Roelots, C-1
Bali Tiger
  illustrated by Helmut Diller, C-2
Black-Fronted Parakeet
  illustrated by William T. Cooper, C-3
Raiatea Parakeet
  illustrated by William T. Cooper, C-3
New Caldonia Lorikeet
  illustrated by William T. Cooper, C-4
Charmosyna wilhelminae
  illustrated by William T. Cooper, C-4
Norfolk Island Kaka
  illustrated by William T. Cooper, C-4
N.m. meridionalis
  illustrated by William T. Cooper, C-4

Wake Island Rail
  illustrated by J. Fenwick Lansdowne, C-4
Tahitian Red-Billed Rail
  illustrated by J. Fenwick Lansdowne, C-4
Kosrae Rail
  illustrated by J. Fenwick Lansdowne, C-4
Black Crake
  illustrated by J. Fenwick Lansdowne, C-4
Heath Hen
  photo by Charles R. Belinky, C-7
Carolina Parakeet
  photo by Charles R. Belinky, C-7
Labrador Duck
  photo by Charles R. Belinky, C-7
Newfoundland White Wolf
  photo by Tom McHugh, C-8
Texas Red Wolf
  photo by WWF, C-8
Passenger Pigeon
  photo by Charles R. Belinky, C-8
Dusky Seaside Sparrow
  photo by P. W. Sykes, USFWS, C-8

Ready Reference Index

Dieffenbach's rail	*Rallus dieffenbachii*	mid-1800s	74
dodo	*Raphus cucullatus*	1680	19
dusky seaside sparrow	*Ammospiza maritima nigrescens*	1990	178
eastern barred bandicoot	*Perameles fasciata*	c.1940	332
eastern hare-wallaby	*Lagorchestes leporides*	c.1890	328
Florida black wolf	*Canis rufus floridanus*	1917	357
gelada baboon	*Theropithecus darti*	unknown	312
Gilbert's potoroo	*Potorous gilberti*	c.1900	336
Grass Valley speckled dace	*Rhinichthys osculus reliquus*	1938-1959	278
great auk	*Pinguinus impennis*	c.1844	191
Great Plains Lobo wolf	*Canis lupus nubilus*	1926	354
greater amakihi	*Hemignathus sagittirostris*	c.1950	144
greater broad-billed moa	*Euryapteryx gravis*	c.1850	57
greater koa finch	*Rhodacanthis palmeri*	1896	170
greater rabbit-bandicoot	*Macrotis lagotis grandis*	c.1930	330
green and yellow macaw	*Ara erythrocephala*	1842	198
Guadalupe caracara	*Polyborus lutosus*	1900-1906	176
Guadalupe storm-petrel	*Oceanodroma macrodactyla*	1912	174
Guadeloupe burrowing owl	*Speotyto cunicularia guadeloupensis*	early 1900s	204
harelip sucker	*Lagochila lacera*	1893	264
Hawaii o'o	*Moho nobilis*	c.1904	154
Hawaiian rail	*Porzana sandwichensis*	1844	166
heath hen	*Tympanuchus cupido cupido*	1933	186
Hollandais pigeon	*Alectroenas nitidissima*	after 1830	15
Huia	*Heteraloca acutirostris*	1907	63
Jamaican least pauraque	*Siphonorhis americanus*	c.1860	200
Kenai wolf	*Canis lupus alces*	1915	353
kioea	*Chaetoptila angustipluma*	c.1850	132
Kona finch	*Chloridops kona*	1894	134
Korean crested shelduck	*Tadorna cristata*	c.1916	88
Kosrae Mountain starling	*Aplonis corvina*	c.1827	96
Kosrae rail	*Porzana monasa*	by 1880	98
Labrador duck	*Camptorhynchus labradorius*	c.1875	189
Lake Titicaca Orestias	*Orestias cuvieri*	c.1950	300
Lanai akialoa	*Hemignathus obscurus lanaiensis*	c.1894	140
Lanai creeper (='alauwahio)	*Paroreomyza maculata montana*	1937	162
Lanai thrush	*Myadestes lanaiensis lanaiensis*	1930s	156
laughing owl	*Sceloglaux albifacies*	c.1900	66
Laysan millerbird	*Acrocephalus familiaris familiaris*	c.1923	130
Laysan rail	*Porzana palmeri*	c.1944	164

Leguat's rail	*Aphanapteryx leguati*	c.1700	27
lesser koa finch	*Rhodacanthis flaviceps*	1891	168
lesser megalapteryx	*Megalapteryx didinus*	c.1800	59
longjaw cisco	*Coregonus alpenae*	1967	257
Lord Howe Island Flycatcher	*Gerygone ignata insularis*	1920s	44
Lord Howe Island fantail	*Rhipidura fuliginosa cervina*	c.1924	50
Lord Howe purple gallinule	*Porphyrio albus*	c.1834	48
Madagascar serpent eagle	*Eutriorchis astur*	c.1950	13
Mauritius red rail	*Aphanapteryx bonasia*	c.1675	17
Mexican dace	*Evarra eigenmanni*	1983	280
Mexican dace	*Evarra tlahuacensis*	1983	280
Mexican silver grizzly	*Ursus arctos nelsoni*	1964	363
modest rail	*Gallirallus modestus*	mid-1800s	72
Molokai o'o	*Moho bishopi*	c.1837	152
mysterious starling	*Aplonis mavornata*	unknown	100
New Caledonia lorikeet	*Charmosyna diadema*	1860	109
New Mexican wolf	*Canis lupus mogollonensis*	1920	355
New Zealand Grayling	*Prototroctes oxyrhynchus*	c.1923	302
New Zealand quail	*Coturnix novaezelandiae*	1868	61
Newfoundland white wolf	*Canis lupus beothucus*	1911	356
No Common Name	*Achyranthes atollensis*	1964	241
No Common Name	*Argyroxiphium virescens*	1945	242
No Common Name	*Clermontia multiflora*	1870s	243
No Common Name	*Cyanea arborea*	1928	220
No Common Name	*Cyanea comata*	1880s	222
No Common Name	*Cyanea giffardii*	early 1900s	224
No Common Name	*Cyanea linearifolia*	early 1900s	226
No Common Name	*Cyanea longissima*	1927	227
No Common Name	*Cyanea parvifolia*	1909	228
No Common Name	*Cyanea pohaku*	1910	229
No Common Name	*Cyanea profuga*	1912	231
No Common Name	*Cyanea purpurellifolia*	1935	232
No Common Name	*Cyanea pycnocarpa*	1880s	234
No Common Name	*Cyanea quercifolia*	1880s	235
No Common Name	*Cyrtandra gracilis*	1880s	244
No Common Name	*Delissea fallax*	1880s	237
No Common Name	*Delissea laciniata*	1880s	238
No Common Name	*Delissea sinuata*	1937	239
No Common Name	*Eragrostis hosakai*	1937	245
No Common Name	*Haplostachys bryanii*	1918	246

St. Francis Island potoroo	*Potorous sp.*	c.1900	340
Steller's spectacled cormorant	*Phalacrocorax perspicillatus*	c.1850	91
Stephen's Island wren	*Xenicus lyalli*	1894	68
stumptooth minnow	*Stypodon signifer*	c.1930	296
Tahitian red-billed rail	*Rallus pacificus*	c.1900	108
Tahitian sandpiper	*Prosobonia leucoptera*	after 1777	106
Tecopa pupfish	*Cyprinodon nevadensis calidae*	c.1960s	282
Texas gray wolf	*Canis lupus monstrabilis*	c.1920	355
Texas red wolf	*Canis rufus rufus*	1950s	356
thicktail chub	*Gila crassicauda*	1970s	284
Tristan Island gallinule	*Gallinula nesiotis nesiotis*	after 1861	210
ula-ai-hawane	*Ciridops anna*	c.1892	136
Utah Lake sculpin	*Cottus echinatus*	1936	266
Wake Island rail	*Rallus wakensis*	c.1945	113
Warrah (= Antarctic) wolf	*Dusicyon australis*	1876	358
western barred bandicoot	*Perameles myosura*	c.1910	334

The World Wildlife Fund Guide
to Extinct Species of Modern Times

Introduction

There are three general reasons why species become extinct. The first is that some species are vulnerable to natural catastrophe. Bird species occurring on Pacific islands are menaced by typhoons and hurricanes that destroy habitat and kill whole populations; the interruption of nesting grounds and mating territory by natural causes is a serious threat to some species. A species that has been weakened by natural disaster is especially vulnerable to predators, often humans, who kill the last members of the population.

The second source of extinction involves those species that are well adapted to their environment but are threatened when humans add pressures to the habitat or food supply. The giant panda, for example, will eat only one variety of bamboo shoot, and as Chinese agriculture has displaced bamboo forests, the panda's food source has diminished. The more resources a species requires, or the more selective it is in its requirements, the more vulnerable it becomes to extinction. If the giant panda were as adaptable in its food source as the brown bear, it would have a better chance of survival.

Third, species that have no predisposition to extinction, which are highly adaptable, with no limiting habitat or other special requirements become vulnerable because of some introduced imbalance to their ecosystem. Usually, though not always, these species have become extinct because people invaded their territory and altered their natural process by hunting them, introducing predators, changing or destroying their habitat, or interfering with their breeding process. All species of bears, wolves, lions and tigers that survive fall into this third category. These species were prolific survivors. Ranging throughout vast territories, they were dominant until the world's conquerors discovered their lands, hunted the species for food or killed out of fear, and altered and destroyed their habitat.

By selecting species whose extinction began with the European exploration of the world in the seventeenth century, we hope to create a snapshot of the plight of many other extinct species, some of which succumbed to the pressure brought by people exploring and settling new territories. We have organized the sections by birds, plants, fishes, and mammals, and within those sections grouped the species geographically, moving from the islands off Africa eastward, through the South Pacific to Hawaii, the mainland U.S., and the Caribbean. We have focused our survey of plants on Hawaiian Islands species because of the relationship between the decline in bird life and the degradation of habitat that led to the decline in plant species.

Generally, we have selected smaller, less recognizable species that are often the signposts for dangers ahead. Birds and fishes in particular signal habitat degradation long before it becomes apparent through the demise of other species. For the most part, we have selected species indigenous to islands or remote continental areas where it was easier for explorers to observe the rapid decline of species. We have not included European and Asian species that became extinct as human populations expanded gradually over many centuries, displacing species from one habitat to another until there was no place left for them to go. We have also excluded South American species. The enormity of destruction and extinction in the rain forests requires more focus and will be covered in a separate volume. For information about endangered species on the brink of extinction in these areas, we refer you to *Beacham's*

International Threatened, Endangered and Extinct Species on CD ROM, available from Beacham Publishing (P.O. Box 830, Osprey, FL 34229).

Extinction raises moral and ethical questions that modern society realizes it must address. Do all species have some innate right to survive? Most developed, modern societies acknowledge that humans have the right to live, but for lower species, we accept the death of individuals if there is some benefit to society at large, especially if it benefits people. The controversy over whether a bird's habitat is more important than a person's timber job has ignited the debate over extinction. While some people think that the extinction of a species is a serious, sad event, other people believe that humankind should control its environment, which includes the eradication of undesirable species. Who, if anyone, would welcome the presence of rampant dinosaurs in the United States today, yet many African farmers feel the same way about elephants. In 1996, The Centers for Disease Control decided to destroy the last remaining individuals of the smallpox virus. Thus, the U.S. government has given its first approval for the official eradication of a species.

The questions, and moral consequences of the destruction of an entire species can be argued from many perspectives. Environmentalists have well demonstrated and documented the disruption caused to an ecosystem when just one presumably unimportant species is removed, or when natural fires are suppressed, or when water flows are diverted. If there has been no other benefit to environmental awareness in the U.S. during the last decade, the one clear message is that humans have exerted a powerful, and usually detrimental impact upon nature.

Today, there are many species on the brink of extinction. In the Brazilian rain forests alone, some authorities predict the extinction of 200,000 different species within the next decade. In the following article on illegal wildlife trade, Ginette Hemley of World Wildlife Fund explains pressure brought on a few of the larger species, the ones that have gained world attention and garnered efforts for preservation. Other environmental organizations work diligently to help conserve a particular species (e.g., The Crane Foundation), or species that are important in the food chain (mollusks), or obscure plants for potential medical purposes. No one knows the value of most species to humans or to lower life forms. From this ignorance should arise the importance of preservation.

Walton Beacham
January 1997

Illegal Trade in Endangered Species

Few people realize that some of the world's most spectacular species are threatened by trade. Sometimes animals are sold alive, for medical research, zoos, or pets, but often they are killed for their body parts. The tiger, for example, one of the rarest mammal species, is prized in the Orient for its organs as well as its skin. Most people also do not know how large, and potentially harmful, trade is in flower bulbs and plants.

In addition to habitat destruction and alteration, overcollecting brings additional pressures on many species that are commercially valuable. Thousands of species, from familiar animals such as the orang utan, to obscure creatures like the red-kneed tarantula, are captured or killed to satisfy an international appetite for the exotic and the unusual.

The world trade in wildlife and wildlife products amounts to several billion dollars annually. While much of the trade is comprised of non-endangered species, as much as one-fourth of it may be illegal. The U.S. alone imports at least a billion dollars worth of wildlife each year, twice as much as a decade ago. The American appetite for wildlife is huge.

Most of the wildlife arrives in commercial shipments either as live animals, or as consumer goods, such as snakeskin shoes. Tourists returning from trips abroad bring in thousands of wildlife souvenirs, like coral, shell, and ivory trinkets. Thousands of illegally imported items are sold in American stores every day.

Some illegally traded wildlife is smuggled into the country by concealing it from government authorities, but more often shipping documents are counterfeited to disguise the origin of the exporting country or the identity of the species, a process called "laundering."

Poaching and laundering complicate law enforcement at both the exporting and importing ends of the trade. It is difficult enough for authorities to recognize the large number of illegally traded species; when documents have also been altered to disguise the species' identification, it is almost impossible for officials to catch them.

There are some species whose illegal trade has commanded world attention, and others that are barely noticed. The caiman, a species of the alligator family, is exported for pet shops and hunted for its fine patterned hide. The illegal caiman trade is difficult and dangerous to combat, for poachers are sometimes heavily armed and linked to the drug trade. As with drugs, the skins are transported to a neutral port, "laundered" to Europe or Asia, manufactured into fine products, and legally imported into the U.S. for sale in boutiques.

Millions of snakes and lizards are harvested annually to supply materials for belts, shoes, watchstraps, and other leather goods. The U.S. imports as many as 2 million live reptiles, 4 million skins, and 30 million manufactured products. Worldwide, that number may double. Some 85 percent of imported reptile skins come from Asian snakes and South American tegu lizards.

Flower Bulb Trade

Flower bulbs comprise one of the largest segments of the ornamental plant trade. More than a million bulbs were imported into the U.S. in 1990, double the number in 1982. Major suppliers include The Netherlands (75-80%), France, Portugal, Spain, the U.K., Belgium, Turkey, South Africa, India, Israel, and Japan.

Many of these suppliers propagate bulbs, and there is little danger that genetic materials will be lost, but the growing trade in bulbs collected from the wild poses a serious threat to plants originating from the Mediterranean region. Turkey, Spain and Portugal, among the major suppliers, export tens of millions of bulbs to Holland, where they are auctioned to buyers for propagation. Some popular flower species that make their way to the U.S. via Turkey and The Netherlands include Anemone, snowdrops, and Narcissus.

Overcollecting wild-collected bulbs depletes the gene pool and threatens a species' capability of propagating in the wild, especially for those species that are already under attack by habitat alteration, pollution, and human encroachment.

While many species of orchids and cacti are propagated artificially, unmanaged collection threatens hundreds of rare wild plants. The U.S. imports some 2 million orchids annually, about half of which are captive populated. Worldwide, as many as 10 million orchids may be traded annually; as much as 10 percent may be taken from the wild, improperly labeled as artificially propagated, and exported illegally. Wild-collected cacti continue to be smuggled out of Chile, Mexico, and the U.S. to Europe and Japan.

Tiger and Cat Trade

Although world attention and the refinement of synthetic animal skins have reduced the trade in fur coats, cats are still among the most exploited endangered animals. Because the larger spotted cats are better protected by law from trade, smaller cat species, such as the little spotted cat and lynx, have become prey to the fur trade.

In addition to the value of their pelts, the major profit in tiger trade is from the use of their body parts in oriental medicines. Tiger bone compounds are used to treat joint and back pain, muscular weakness, muscular spasms and paralysis. Tail compounds treat skin diseases; the brain treats acne; the penis sexual potency; and the whiskers become a good luck charm.

Although tigers are protected from trade by CITES, the U.S. Endangered Species Act, and protective laws in every country where tigers occur, the enforcement of tiger trade is difficult to enforce. The use of tiger parts for medicinal purposes has been practiced in Asian countries for centuries, and is deep-rooted in the culture. Because tiger pelts and parts bring such high prices, there is great incentive for poachers. A tiger pelt can fetch up to $8,000 and the bones up to $600 per pound (tiger bones can weight up to 23 pounds).

The world tiger population has declined from an estimated 100,000 during the early part of the century to fewer than 6,000 in the wild today. The Siberian tiger numbers 150-200; the South China tiger, 50; Bengal tiger, 2,900-4,500; Indo-Chinese tiger, 800-1,200; and the Sumatran tiger, 250-400. Most of the illegal trade in tiger parts occurs in the People's Republic of China, Korea, Taiwan, India, Thailand, Nepal, Cambodia, Laos, and Burma. The principal tiger-consuming countries are China, South Korea and Taiwan; South Korea and Taiwan do not have tiger populations. Two-thirds of the world's tigers occur in India, which loses 300-350 tigers to poaching every year.

Elephant Trade

Carved elephant ivory has been used as currency, for jewelry and figurines, religious icons, and musical instruments for centuries. By the mid-1980s the demand for ivory was so great that 90,000 African elephants were killed every year to satisfy the demand. The African elephant population declined from 1.2 million in the late 1970s to 600,000 today. Only 29,000-44,000 Asian elephants survive.

The availability of automatic weapons, political corruption, and unstable economies increased the efficiency and motives of poachers. Complicating the economic drive to kill elephants is the explosion of human population in Central African nations, which put man and elephant in competition for the same land, food and water resources. Of the tons of ivory tusks smuggled or laundered out of Africa, most went to Hong Kong or Japan where they were carved and exported throughout the world.

In 1988, a year in which the U.S. imported $20 million worth of ivory products, the U.S. Congress passed legislation to control illegal ivory imports, and in 1989 extended the legislation to ban all ivory imports into the U.S. In 1990 world trade in ivory was banned by CITES, which led to a dramatic decline in world ivory trade.

Rhinoceros Trade

As with elephants, rhinoceros are commercially valuable for their horns, hides, hooves and other body parts. In the Orient, rhino horn is used for fever reduction, and carved horns are used for ceremonial daggers. The profit from the sale of rhino horns is so enormous that it is almost impossible to stop rhino poaching: prices in Taiwan bring upwards of $30,000 per pound (a black rhino horn may weigh 5.5 pounds; a Javan rhino 1.5 pounds).

Black rhinos have disappeared in Chad, Ethiopia, Malawi, Somalia, and Sudan, and have nearly been extirpated from Angola, Mozambique, Rwanda, Zambia, and Tanzania. The only protection for rhino populations is in South Africa, Kenya and Namibia.

CITES and the U.S. Endangered Species Act prohibit trade in rhinos and rhino parts, with the exception of sport-hunting of southern white rhinos taken with permits in South Africa, where the population is controlled. Other emergency measures, such as dehorning rhinos to protect them from poachers, is helping reduce illegal trade, but rhino poaching is still out of control.

Bear Trade

Great pressure has been put on bears because of habitat loss and human persecution. As with elephants and rhinos, bears have been exploited for the medicinal Oriental trade. The bile salts in bear gall bladders are used to cure intestinal fever, liver, and heart illnesses. Gall blatters are also effective in relieving spasms, as a poison antidote, and as a cough suppressant. A bear gall bladder brings $800-3,000, while a bowl of bear paw soup sells for up to $1,500 in restaurants.

Eighteen Asian countries provide thriving markets for bear parts, and bears have been hunted to dangerously low levels. Habitat destruction in parts of Asia, eastern Europe, and

South America, combined with illegal trade, have caused the serious decline of bears worldwide. In the Russian republics, where bears were once plentiful, the breakdown in law enforcement has led to increased poaching of the brown bear. Even in North America poaching of black and brown bears has increased.

CITES has listed bear species in two categories. Appendix I, which prohibits all commercial trade, lists the Asiatic black bear, sun bear, sloth bear, giant panda, spectacled bear, and some populations of the brown bear. All other bear species are listed in Appendix II, which permits trade for species taken under a permit.

Only if the demand for bear gall bladders decreases will the lure of poachers diminish. Chemical substitutes for bile salts are available, but Asian consumers believe that the natural substance is more effective, and they continue to demand the animal product.

Primate Trade

Apes and monkeys are also in high demand for medical research, not for their body parts but because they are physically similar to humans. The rare species are sought by zoological parks, by pet traders, and by native people in some parts of the world as a food source. The species most in demand for medical research are the crab-eating macaque, pigtail macaque, rhesus macaque, and squirrel monkey. Baboons, savannah monkeys, owl monkeys, and capuchins are also used for medical research.

In the late 1980s, as many as 30,000 live primates may have been traded annually, but that number appears to have declined in the 1990s. The Philippines, Indonesia, Mauritius, and China are the principal suppliers for macaques. Kenya, Tanzania, Ethiopia, St. Kitts, and Barbados supply savannah monkeys and baboons. Guyana, Peru, and Brazil are the primary suppliers for squirrel, night, and capuchin monkeys. Species most often targeted by poachers include the chimpanzee, orang utan, golden lion tamarind, and drill.

The U.S. is the largest importer of primates, primarily for medical research. The U.S. imports 10,000-15,000 live animals annually, and the demand has increased because of AIDS research. Another 40,000 captive bred primates per year fill out the demand in the U.S. Other countries actively importing primates are Canada, France, Japan, The Netherlands, Taiwan, and the U.K.

Because the principal demand for primates is created by the medical industry in developed countries, there is less illegal trade with primates than with other endangered species. U.S. Public Health Service regulations have prohibited the importation of primates as pets since 1975, and the Endangered Species Act lists 58 primate species as threatened or endangered. But black market trading, especially in the Orient, continues to thrive, and better enforcement of trade and hunting laws is necessary to the survival of some primates.

Parrot Trade

Parrots are among the most widely sought animals for pets and for their plumage. At the end of the nineteenth century, feathers were in great demand for hats and other clothing apparel, and many birds with brightly colored plumage were exploited. Of the 330 parrot species, 40 are near extinction. The U.S., Japan, Belgium, The Netherlands, Germany, and the

U.K. are major importers of parrots. The U.S. alone imports some 450,000 birds annually, a third of which are parrots. Mortality among captured birds can be as high as 80 percent. Birds that survive capture and transit must also survive quarantine and caged bird diseases.

CITES lists the 40 near-extinct species under Appendix I, which prohibits all trade. All but 2 of the remaining parrot species are listed under Appendix II, which controls trade through a permit process. The illegal trade in parrots often involves a circuitous route, which increases the odds of death through transit. Birds captured in Australia, South America and Africa may be shipped to trade centers, such as Singapore, Argentina, and the Ivory Coast, where regulations against smuggling or laundering (falsification of papers) are not enforced. Even in the U.S., which does enforce strict import regulations, as many as 50,000 parrots may be smuggled across the Mexican border annually. To complicate the situation, wildlife trade laws in countries of origin change frequently, making enforcement more difficult.

Large parrots, which are most in demand as pets, do not produce large offspring, and their capability to replenish their numbers in the wild is diminishing because of habitat encroachment/alteration combined with overcollecting.

Consumers looking for pet parrots should make certain they purchase captive-bred species, which are usually healthier and tamer than wild-captured birds. The two species that are not endangered are the cockatiel and budgie. Some species that are captive-bred are the ring-necked parakeet, sun conure, blue and gold macaw, and peach-faced lovebird.

Diseases of Caged Parrots

When caged, parrots are susceptible to diseases they do not contract in the wild. With air sac infection, a discharge — caused by molds or mold-like bacteria — accumulates in the air sacs and may spread to the lungs or body cavity. Symptoms include weakness, shortness of breath, and lack of appetite.

Egg-binding is a phenomena in which females lay eggs that become lodged in the oviduct, possibly caused by a spasm of the oviduct. It causes the egg or yolk to spill into the body cavity, which in turn causes peritonitis. Obstipation results from the poor care of caged parrots. An accumulation of fecal materials and urates cause the cloaca to impact. The horn of the beak and claws may become overgrown because the bird lacks sufficient hard material on which to gnaw. Other well documented diseases are feather pulling, cardiovascular disease, arthritis, abscesses, liver disease, kidney disease, French molt, gout, mycosis, and a fever caused by a virus and bacteria.

Marine Species

Sea turtles have been relentlessly hunted for food and for their shells. Japan, once the largest commercial consumer, imported 30 metric tons of tortoise shell a year during the 1980s. That's the equivalent of 28,000 hawksbill turtles. Although Japan, under pressure from the U.S. government, has agreed to stop tortoiseshell imports, tortoiseshell jewelry and other sea turtle curios are very popular tourist souvenirs, and are among the most often seized items coming through U.S. customs.

Another sea creature traded in enormous numbers are tropical fish. Ninety-nine percent of the estimated 30 million marine fish representing 300 species traded internationally each year are not captive bred but are collected from tropical coral reefs in the Philippines and Indonesia. There are another 300 freshwater species of ornamental fish, mostly captive-bred in Southeast Asia. Most wild freshwater fish are imported from Brazil, Columbia, Peru, and Guyana. Altogether, in the early 1990s, the U.S. imported 200-250 million ornamental fish; worldwide 500-600 million were traded.

Mollusks are collected for shell collecting and products. The U.S. imports 10-15 million raw shells, and 45 million products. Most mollusks are imported from Asia for sale at U.S. beach resorts.

Coral reefs are under tremendous pressure, ecologically and from the jewelry and trinket trade. In the early 1990s, the U.S. imported 200,000-300,000 colonies of live coral, and up to a million items of raw coral, and 1-2 million manufactured products. Until the late 1980s coral could not survive in aquariums, but improved technology has generated a demand for live coral. Coral from the Philippines, the major exporter, has been banned in the U.S. because of illegal trade practices. Other southeast Asian countries supply most of the world demand, and as a result coral reefs are being destroyed. In addition to the plundering for trade, coral reefs are being distressed by dynamite fishing, pollution, and siltation.

Although trade in whales has been reduced as a result of the Marine Mammal Protection Act, whaling remains a politically explosive issue. Japan and Norway permit whaling, while seals and walruses continued to be taken in large numbers.

Controlling Wildlife Trade

Until CITES, the Convention on International Trade in Endangered Species of Wild Fauna and Flora, was formed in 1973, wildlife was traded on the world market with little interference. Since then, more than 120 countries have become signatories to the Convention. The United States was the first country to ratify CITES when the treaty entered into effect in 1975. The Endangered Species Act encompasses CITES; the Lacey Act prohibits the importation of wildlife products exported in violation of the wildlife laws of other countries; and the Marine Mammal Protection Act, the Migratory Bird Treaty Act, and the African Elephant Conservation Act restrict trade in certain wildlife species.

Upon accession to CITES, a country designates one or more government departments as its management authority for issuing permits and compiling annual trade reports. TRAFFIC (Trade Records Analysis of Flora and Fauna in Commerce) is the international network that monitors global trade in wildlife. There are 17 TRAFFIC offices worldwide. Through research, reports, investigation and scientific analysis, TRAFFIC provides an objective assessment on international wildlife trade for government agencies, private organizations, and CITES.

Ginette Hemley
World Wildlife Fund
Director of TRAFFIC USA

EXTINCT BIRDS OF MADAGASCAR, MASCARENE, AND THE SEYCHELLES

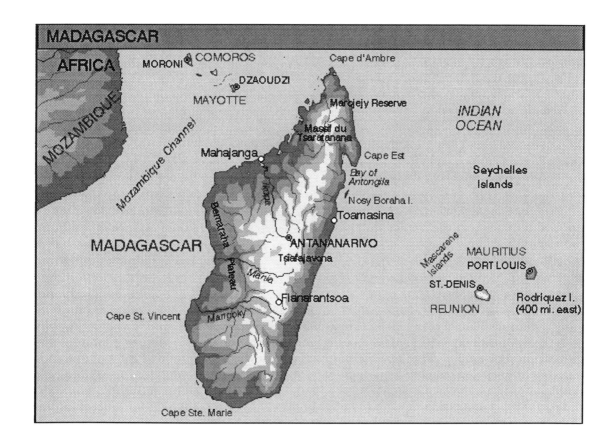

Madagascar

Madagascar is a large (226,658 square miles) island nation off the southeastern coast of Africa. The first humans arrived on the island 1,500 to 2,500 years ago, probably originating from a Malaysian-Indonesian homeland. These first colonists settled the highlands and began the process of clearing land by burning it, which, over the centuries of continuing this practice, has led to degraded landscapes. Although Madagascar has been known to Europeans for 400 years and much longer to the Arabs, the central portions of the island were not developed until modern times. Much of the island was once covered with evergreen and deciduous forests, but they were cut to clear rice fields, secure fuel, and to export valuable timber.

Madagascar was once connected to the African continent; 65 million years ago, it broke free and drifted eastward. As the eastward drift began at an early point in the evolutionary history of plants and animals, only a few of the existing fauna and flora are thought to have evolved from original African species. Without any interference from people for thousand of years, and with no mammal predators, wildlife developed on Madagascar as nowhere else on earth. Because of the island's isolation and size, many zoologically primitive primates have survived and evolved into unique forms. Three-quarters of all known lemurs are indigenous to Madagascar; several hedgehog-like insectivores have evolved; birds are bountiful; and there are 800 species of butterfly. Certain fish species, such as the spiny globefish that inflates when disturbed, and the cofferfish, are peculiar to Madagascar.

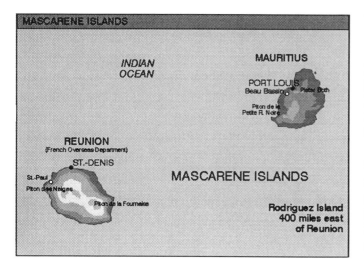

The Mascarene Islands

The Mascarene island group is located in the Indian Ocean 400 to 500 miles east of Madagascar. Mauritius, along with Réunion (or Bourbon) and Rodriguez make up this island group.

The Mascarene Islands are volcanic in origin with a moist climate. Geologic characteristics (i.e., a "continental" rock, clay-slate) indicate that the island of Mauritius was, at one time, larger and more rugged.

Mauritius

Mauritius (also called Cerne and Ile de France) is about 720 square miles in area. The mountains are now less rugged than those found on the island of Réunion. Because of this, the island appears to have provided a wider variety of habitats capable of supporting bird species. Historical accounts and skeletal remains confirm the presence of at least 19 avian species on Mauritius and 13 species on Réunion.

Réunion

Réunion is about 110 miles southwest of Mauritius. It is elliptically shaped, 40 miles long and 30 miles wide. Volcanic in origin, some of the cones rise to 10,000 feet and dominate the island. One of the volcanoes has erupted several times since 1925. There is abundant rainfall in the south and east of the island, while the north and west are almost rainless.

Réunion was settled in the 1660s as a layover station for ships rounding the Cape of Good Hope bound for India. African slaves were brought to work the coffee and sugar cane plantations.

Rodriguez

Rodriguez is about 400 miles east of Mauritius. It is the most isolated and the smallest (43 square miles in area) island in the Mascarenes. It is also volcanic in origin but now consists of low, rolling hills; the highest elevation on the island is 1,300 feet. The island is almost completely surrounded by a reef with many small cays or islets. Before the arrival of white men, the island was almost completely covered in forested habitats. The majority of the island was cleared for conversion to agriculture, primarily coffee and tobacco, and for human settlements. The only remaining forests are on the cays that surround Rodriguez. Only nine avian species are known to have existed on this island.

Causes for Extinction of Mascarene Bird Species

The dodos and solitaires, species of Columbiformes (pigeons and doves), were highly specialized island forms that probably arose in the Mascarene Islands and were peculiar to those islands. Three species are known: the dodo (*Raphus cucullatus*) on Mauritius, the Réunion solitaire (*Raphus solitarius*), and the Rodriguez solitaire (*Pezophaps solitaria*). A fourth species, the white dodo, may have existed on Réunion. These pigeon-like birds had lost the power of flight because there were no predators on the islands until explorers introduced exotic pigs, rats and other livestock. They had become large (the size of a turkey), heavily built birds with strong bills and feet.

Mauritius bird species were hunted for food by early explorers or sailors who stopped on Mauritius to replenish their food supply. A Dutch ship's captain's diary from 1602 described the crew's meals. The captain listed the vast number of birds from the islands (including the dodo) that were killed, brought on board and salted to stock the larder. The sailors hunted the island's birds with sticks, nets, guns, and any other equipment necessary to aid in the capture of the birds.

The introduction of exotic mammals to Mauritius, Réunion and Rodriguez islands had a devastating impact on the ground nesting and tree nesting avian species. Black rats (*Rattus rattus*) and brown rats (*R. norvegicus*) were reported as common in 1768. Their ability to climb trees allowed them to reach most or all bird nests where they probably ate and/or broke the eggs and possibly killed or injured young chicks. Swine, introduced soon after the Portuguese discovered the islands, were also fond of eggs and may have been, at least partially, responsible for the extirpation of the endemic land tortoises. Macaque monkeys (*Macaca cynomalogus*) were present as early as 1606. They inhabited the heavily forested areas in the hilly, rocky sections of the islands and were responsible for consuming, damaging, and/or injuring eggs and/or chicks. Other exotic mammals that have impacted the endemic vertebrate species on the Mascarene Islands include feral cats, goats, rabbits, and deer.

The Seychelles

The Seychelles islands rise from a shallow, crescent-shaped submarine plateau believed to be of the same continental origins as Madagascar. The picturesque islands are high, hanging gardens overlooking silver-white beaches and clear lagoons. The only remaining primary forests grow in protected reserves on Praslin and Curieuse islands. Aldabra Island is famed for its birdlife. The giant tortoise, once widely distributed, is almost extinct but now protected by law.

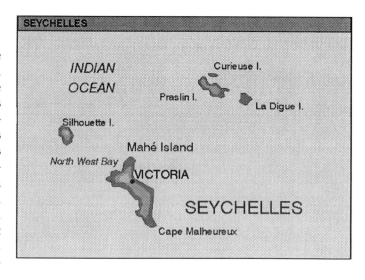

The Arabs were probably the first to discover The Seychelles but did not settle there. The Portuguese sighted the archipelago in the sixteenth century; the first recorded landings were made in 1609 by the English East India Company, which found the islands abundant in water, fish, birds and fruits. There were then and now few insects and no animals dangerous to man except for sharks in the seas.

In 1770 the first colonists arrived from Réunion, and they so depleted the forests and the giant tortoises for export that by 1789 they were forbidden to trade. The British were given control of the islands by the Treaty of Paris (1814), and after they abolished slavery in the 1830s, settlers changes from raising labor-intensive crops, such as cotton, to less-intensive crops such as coconuts and cinnamon, but the clearing of land had taken its inevitable destruction on wildlife by that time.

Madagascar Serpent Eagle

Eutriorchis astur

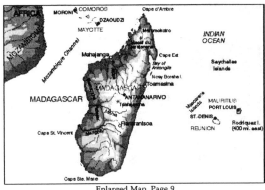

Enlarged Map, Page 9

Description

The Madagascar serpent eagle, *Eutriorchis astur,* was a medium-sized raptor with short, rounded wings and a long, rounded tail. The species was dark gray on the back and lighter grey on the throat, breast, and belly. The whole body was covered by dark barring. The beak was sharp and hooked, and the talons were well developed and strong. The eyes were yellow.

Behavior

The Madagascar serpent eagle was probably similar in behavior to the other African serpent eagles. These eagles were diurnal and carnivorous; their diet included snakes (some were venomous), lizards, and frogs. The serpent eagles hunted from high perches. When prey was sighted the bird would fly down and pounce on the animal, grasping it in its strong talons. Carrion was not eaten.

Habitat

The species inhabited the dense, humid,

Status	Possibly Extinct
Probable Extinction	c.1950
Family	Accipitridae (Eagles and Hawks)
Description	Medium-sized dark gray raptor with short rounded wings, a long rounded tail, and a lighter grey underside.
Habitat	Dense, humid, broadleaf evergreen forests.
Food	Snakes, lizards, frogs.
Reproduction	Possibly low reproductive rate.
Causes for Extinction	Destruction of habitat.
Range	Madagascar

broadleafed evergreen forests of northeastern and east-central Madagascar to an elevation of 550 meters (1,800 feet). The last confirmed sighting (see below) occurred in the Marojejy reserve. The lowest zone in the reserve, with altitudes of 165 to 2,600 feet, consists of lowland rainforests and a rich diversity of fauna that could serve as an unlimited food source for the serpent eagle.

Distribution

The species once occurred in the eastern broadleafed evergreen rainforests of the island of Madagascar.

The Madagascar serpent eagle is believed to have never been common. Until recently, the last definite sighting was over 50 years ago. Unconfirmed sightings were reported in 1977 from the northeast part of the island. In 1988, British ornithologists searching for other species sighted a single serpent eagle foraging beneath the canopy in the Marojejy reserve, located in the Diégo Suarez province in the northwest tip of the island.

Causes for Extinction

The species has become extinct due to the destruction of its habitat. It required a very specialized environment of humid rainforests. These have largely been destroyed on the island of Madagascar. It is assumed that the species had a low reproductive rate which, when combined with the destruction of habitat, caused the final decline in population.

Adapted from data compiled by the Threatened and Endangered Species Information Institute (Golden, CO) for *Beacham's International Threatened, Endangered, and Extinct Species* published on CD ROM, available from Beacham Publishing.

Hollandais Pigeon
Alectroenas nitidissima

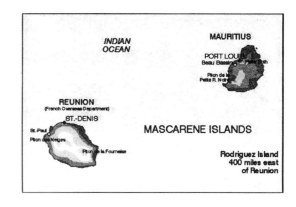

Description

The Hollandais pigeon, *Alectroenas nitidissima*, was a medium-sized (12 inches in length) pigeon with soft, long, white, pointed feathers on the head and neck, and a bluish back and breast. The area around the eye and on the forehead was bare and bright red. The upper tail coverts were a dark red color; the remainder of the tail was the same color interspersed with black markings.

This species is also called the Mauritius blue pigeon, colombe herissee, and pigeon hollandais. The name "Hollandais" was applied to the bird by Sonnerat, a naturalist who visited the island in 1774. He said the bird's red, white, and blue coloring reminded him of Holland's flag.

Behavior

Alectroenas sp. from Madagascar and the Seychelles were known to breed during most of the year (July through March). Observed nests in the Seychelles contained one pure white, symmetrical egg (40 millimeters by 26 millimeters).

Information of the food habits of this species are lacking, but it probably ate fruits, seeds, buds, and new-growth vegetation.

Status	Extinct
Probable Extinction	After 1830
Family	Columbidae (Doves and Pigeons)
Description	Medium-sized pigeon with soft, long, white, pointed feathers on the head and neck, and a bluish back and breast.
Habitat	Tropical forests.
Food	Probably fruits, seeds, buds, and new-growth vegetation.
Reproduction	Probably one egg per clutch.
Causes for Extinction	Habitat destruction/ alteration, overhunting, and the introduction of exotic birds and predators.
Range	Mauritius

Fruits may have made up a large percentage of this species' diet during certain times of the year. Mollusks may also have been eaten to some extent.

Although the periodicity is unknown for

this species, most pigeons and doves are primarily diurnal.

Habitat

One naturalist's notes from a visit to Mauritius indicate the Hollandais pigeon inhabited the edges of forested areas near streams. Closely related species on Madagascar and the Seychelles Islands appeared to be more closely associated with forest interiors. Birds were often observed perching in snags near the top of the forest canopy; they were also found in association with fruit-bearing trees (possibly a mainstay of their diet).

The Hollandais pigeon nests were most likely built in trees.

Distribution

The Hollandais pigeon was endemic to the island of Mauritius in the Mascarene Islands. Arabs most likely discovered the islands long before the Europeans but did not appear to settle the area or disrupt the natural processes.

Causes for Extinction

Habitat destruction/alteration, overhunting, and the introduction of exotic birds and predators were probably the primary factors responsible for the decline and extinction of the Hollandais pigeon.

The Hollandais pigeon was hunted for food by early settlers or sailors who stopped on Mauritius to replenish their food supply. This was probably one of the primary factors leading to the extinction of this species.

See also Causes for Extinction of Mascarene Bird Species, page 11.

Adapted from data compiled by the Threatened and Endangered Species Information Institute (Golden, CO) for *Beacham's International Threatened, Endangered, and Extinct Species* published on CD ROM, available from Beacham Publishing.

Mauritius Red Rail

Aphanapteryx bonasia

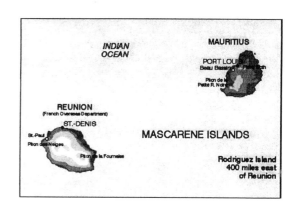

Description

The Mauritius red rail, *Aphanapteryx bonasia*, was about the same size as a domestic female chicken. The bill was long and slightly decurved and may have been a dark color. The entire body was a reddish brown color; the feathers may have been slightly plume-like (decomposed) in structure. The wings were much reduced indicating flightlessness. The legs were long and well developed.

Skeletal remains of a flightless rail were discovered in the Mare aux Songes Swamp on Mauritius in the nineteenth century. These bones show that this rail varied widely in size, indicating that the species may have been sexually dimorphic.

A. bonasia was a member of the rail, coot, and gallinule family, Rallidae. The species was described and named *Apterornis bonasia* by Selys-Longchamps in 1848. It is also referred to as *Aphanapteryx broeckii, Aphanapteryx broeckei, Didus herbertii, Didus broeckei, Aphanapteryx imperialis, Aphanapteryx imperatoris, Pezophaps broeckei, Pezophaps herbertii, Kuina mundyi,* and *Pezocrex herberti.* Other common names used in reference to this species include Van den Broecke's red rail, Peter Mundy's hen, Mauritian red rail, and red rail.

Status	Extinct
Probable Extinction	c.1675
Family	Rallidae (Rails, Gallinules and Coots)
Description	Bird with long slightly decurved bill which may have been a dark color; the entire body was a reddish brown color with small wings and long, well-developed legs.
Habitat	Moist climate of the Mascarene islands, volcanic in origin.
Food	Probably omnivorous.
Causes for Extinction	Introduction of exotic mammals, including black and brown rats.
Range	Mascarene Islands: Mauritius

Behavior

Like other rails, the Mauritius red rail was probably omnivorous but animal matter comprised the majority of the diet when available. Nothing is known about this species' reproductive habits.

Distribution

A. bonasia was endemic to the island of Mauritius in the Mascarene Islands. It is known only from skeletal remains and from drawings and descriptions by seventeenth century explorers. It apparently was fairly common when the islands were discovered but disappeared within 150 years (around 1675).

Because Mauritius lacked predators, a limiting factor for many large land mass species, evolution selected against characteristics necessary to avoid predation. This resulted in a fearless bird that was only capable of limited flight. When predators (including man) were introduced by sailors, the species was incapable of adapting to avoid predation.

The island's avian populations would have been limited by space and by food resources. Other limiting factors are unknown.

Causes for Extinction

The Mauritius red rail was hunted for food by early explorers or sailors who stopped on Mauritius to replenish their food supply. A Dutch ship's captain's diary from 1602 described the crew's meals. The captain listed the vast number of birds from the islands (including the dodo) that were killed, brought on board and salted to stock the larder. The sailors hunted the island's birds with sticks, nets, guns, and any other equipment necessary to aid in the capture of the birds. The species' gentle nature and flightlessness (or nearly so) left them vulnerable to hunters. It apparently was attracted to bright red objects, and hunters recounted the ease of catching this bird by waving a red object to attract the bird; when they were close enough the birds were clubbed on the head. Like the dodo of Mauritius, this was probably one of the primary factors leading to the extinction of this species.

An account in 1638 by Francois Cauche describes this rail and indicates that it was easy to catch and was quite tasty.

Adapted from data compiled by the Threatened and Endangered Species Information Institute (Golden, CO) for *Beacham's International Threatened, Endangered, and Extinct Species* published on CD ROM, available from Beacham Publishing.

Dodo
Raphus cucullatus

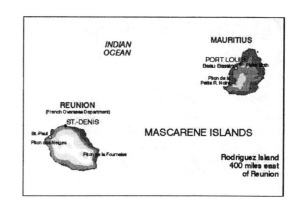

Description

The dodo, *Raphus cucullatus,* is one of the most widely recognized (at least in name) extinct species in the world. Physical and behavioral descriptions of this species are based on a limited number of skeletal remains and the accounts of early explorers. It was an extremely large bird, reaching weights of 50 pounds or more, with a strongly hooked bill up to 9 inches in length. The bill was a blackish color with some red above the tip. The irises were white. The eye, cheek, and forehead region of the head were featherless; the skin was a light ash color. The back feathers were an ash gray color fading to almost white on the breast. The thighs were a darker color, almost black. The short wings had yellowish-white primaries and black-tipped white coverts. The description of the tail (in words and drawings), as loose and curly feathers placed high on the rump, seems to describe upper tail coverts rather than the typical stiff flight feathers which had most likely been reduced or eliminated (as in the wings) through the evolutionary process. The legs and feet were featherless and a yellowish color.

Status	Extinct
Probable Extinction	1680
Family	Rhaphidae (Dodos and Solitaires)
Description	Extremely large with a strongly hooked blackish bill, white eyes, ash gray back feathers fading to white on the breast, short yellowish-white wings, and yellowish legs.
Habitat	Possibly the marsh regions of the Mauritius island, as well as its shrub forest community.
Food	Seeds and fruit.
Reproduction	Possibly one egg per clutch.
Causes for Extinction	Hunted for food; introduction of exotic animals; conversion of habitat for agricultural use.
Range	Mascarene Islands: Mauritius
Photo	See Color Insert, C-1

Behavior

Some accounts say the dodo built its nest in the forest and laid one white egg per clutch. The dodo was said to consume large pebbles which were found in its crop, a characteristic shared by many modern species. Members of the order Columbiformes (pigeons, doves, etc.) are primarily herbivorous. Seeds are the primary food items but fruit is consumed by some species.

Habitat

At least a portion of Mauritius supports a shrub forest community that the dodo was known to frequent. The species may have inhabited the marshy areas of the island. A large cache of this species' bones were found in the Mare-aux-Songes Marsh on Mauritius.

Distribution

The dodo was endemic to the island of Mauritius in the Mascarene Islands. It was probably extinct by 1680, about 175 years after the islands were "discovered" by Portuguese explorers.

Causes for Extinction

Large sections of the island of Mauritius have been converted to agricultural use. The extent of conversion in the 1600's is unknown but may have impacted this species' population.

The introduction of exotic mammals had a strongly negative impact on the ground nesting and tree nesting avian species found on these islands.

The dodo was hunted for food by early settlers or sailors who stopped on Mauritius to replenish their food supply. The bird's apparently curious nature and flightlessness (or nearly so) left them vulnerable to hunters. This was probably one of the primary factors leading to the extinction of this species.

See Causes for Extinction of Mascarene Bird Species, page 11, for additional information.

Adapted from data compiled by the Threatened and Endangered Species Information Institute (Golden, CO) for *Beacham's International Threatened, Endangered, and Extinct Species* published on CD ROM, available from Beacham Publishing.

Broad-Billed Parrot
Lophopsittacus mauritianus

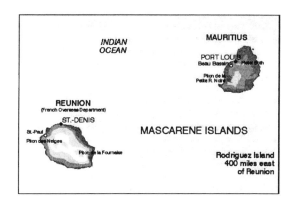

Description

The broad-billed parrot, *Lophopsittacus mauritianus*, was an extremely large, mostly flightless parrot with lengths averaging 70 centimeters (28 inches). These measurements are based on skeletal remains since no specimens of this species have survived. Skeletal remains indicate the species was distinctly sexually dimorphic but it is not known if it was the female or the male that was the much larger sex. The key distinguishing characteristic appears to have been this bird's huge bill. Despite its size, skeletal analyses indicate the bill was fairly thin and weak, and only capable of tearing fruit and other soft foods. The broad-billed parrot had a crest which started just above the upper mandible (between the eyes), a very long tail and short wings. Historical accounts that describe this species' color are contradictory. Accounts by Captain van der Hagen (1607) and Verhuffen (1611) report the presence of a gray parrot (most likely referring to the broad-billed parrot since all the other parrots known from this island are or were primarily green). Admiral van Neck described a blue parrot. The discrepancy may be explained by differences in coloration between sex and/or age classes or simply by variations in shading of a bluish-gray bird. The

Status	Extinct
Probable Extinction	1650
Family	Psittacidae (Parrot and Parakeets)
Description	Extremely large parrot with a huge bill that was thin and weak, a massive flat head, a crest, long tail and short wings.
Habitat	Shrub forest community of Mauritius Island.
Food	Fruit and other soft substances.
Causes for Extinction	Conversion of habitat to agricultural use; introduction of exotic mammals.
Range	Mascarene Islands: Mauritius

bird's small wings, reduced keel size, and large body size indicate it was only capable of extremely short flights or downhill glides. The species or its ancestors must have been capable of flight at one point in time to allow for the colonization of the island. The island's remoteness and lack of predators made flight to avoid predation unnecessary; thus the characteristics necessary for flight were slowly selected out, resulting in a flightless species.

Behavior

The weak, thin structure of this parrot's bill indicates it ate fruit and other soft substances.

Habitat/Distribution

The broad-billed parrot occurred in shrub and forest communities, and was endemic to the island of Mauritius. It was probably extinct by 1650.

Causes for Extinction

Because Mauritius lacked predators, a limiting factor for many large land mass species, evolution selected against characteristics necessary to avoid predation. This resulted in a fearless bird that was only capable of limited flight. When predators (including man) were introduced by man, the species was incapable of adapting to avoid predation.

See also Causes for Extinction of Mascarene Bird Species, page 11.

Adapted from data compiled by the Threatened and Endangered Species Information Institute (Golden, CO) for *Beacham's International Threatened, Endangered, and Extinct Species* published on CD ROM, available from Beacham Publishing.

Réunion Solitaire
Raphus solitarius

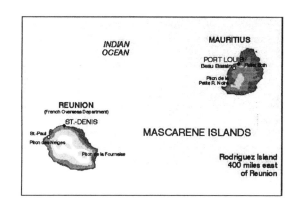

Description

The Réunion solitaire, *Raphus solitarius*, was apparently similar in appearance to its close relative, the dodo (*Raphus cucullatus*) of Mauritius. Its coloring was lighter, varying from a pale yellow to white with black tips to the wing and tail feathers. The dodo is one of the most widely recognized (at least in name) extinct species in the world. Physical and behavioral descriptions of this species are based on a limited number of skeletal remains and the accounts of early explorers.

The dodo was an extremely large bird, reaching weights of 50 pounds or more, with a strongly hooked bill up to 9 inches in length. The bill was a blackish color with some red above the tip. The irises were white. The eye, cheek, and forehead region of the head were featherless; the skin was a light ash color. The back feathers were an ash gray color fading to almost white on the breast. The thighs were a darker color, almost black. The short wings had yellowish-white primaries and black-tipped white coverts. The tail (in words and drawings), was described as loose with curly feathers placed high on the rump. This seems to describe upper tail coverts rather than the typical stiff flight feathers which had most

Status	Extinct
Probable Extinction	1750
Family	Raphidae (Dodos and Solitaires)
Description	Extremely large bird with a strongly hooked blackish bill with red above the tip; white irises; featherless eye, cheek, and forehead region; light ash color skin.
Habitat	Dense forests.
Food	Seeds and green vegetation.
Reproduction	One egg per clutch per year.
Causes for Extinction	Introduced rats.
Range	Mascarene Islands: Réunion

likely been reduced or eliminated (as in the wings) through the evolutionary process. The legs and feet were featherless and a yellowish color.

Behavior

The Réunion solitaire reportedly laid one

clutch per year with one egg per clutch.

The Réunion solitaire was said to consume large pebbles which were found in its crop, a characteristic shared by many modern species. Seeds and green vegetation probably comprised the majority of this species' diet.

Habitat

The Réunion solitaire may have nested in the island's forested habitats. Nests were built on the ground and were probably hidden in dense stands of grass or brush.

Distribution

The Réunion solitaire was endemic to the island of Réunion in the Mascarene Islands. It was probably extinct by 1750, about 250 years after the islands were "discovered" by Portuguese explorers. Arabs most likely discovered the islands long before the Europeans but did not appear to settle the area or disrupt the natural processes.

Causes for Extinction

Although more rugged than the other islands, much of Réunion had probably been cleared for agricultural uses. As a result, the island's avian populations would have been limited by space and by food resources.

The introduction of exotic mammals had a strongly negative impact on the ground nesting and tree nesting avian species found on these islands.

The Réunion solitaire was hunted for food by early settlers or sailors who stopped on Mauritius and Réunion to replenish their food supply. The bird's apparently curious nature and flightlessness (or nearly so) left it vulnerable to hunters. This was probably the primary factor leading to the extinction of this species.

See also Causes for Extinction of Mascarene Bird Species, page 11.

Adapted from data compiled by the Threatened and Endangered Species Information Institute (Golden, CO) for *Beacham's International Threatened, Endangered, and Extinct Species* published on CD ROM, available from Beacham Publishing.

Réunion Starling
Fregilupus varius

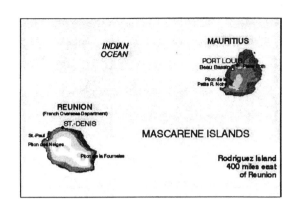

Description

The Réunion starling, *Fregilupus varius*, was a medium-sized (12 inches or 30 centimeters in length) bird with a prominent crest made up of pale ashy gray to white modified, plume-like (or decomposed) feathers. The head and neck were also a pale ashy gray, and the back, rump, and upper tail coverts were a dark ashy brown with a rufous overtone. The primary coverts were white with a brown tip. The cheeks, throat, breast and belly were white.

The Réunion starling has also been called Daubenton's starling, Bourbon crested starling (Réunion was once called Bourbon Island), huppe, and calandre (islander names for the bird).

Behavior

The Réunion starling was known to feed and move around in flocks. Food habits for this species are unknown but other members of this family are omnivorous, consuming a wide variety of insects, fruits, and seeds.

Distribution

The Réunion starling was endemic to the

Status	Extinct
Probable Extinction	c.1850
Family	Sturnidae (Starlings)
Description	Medium-sized bird with prominent crest of pale ashy gray to white plume-like feathers with white cheeks, throat, breast and belly.
Habitat	Specific habitat unknown; moist climate of Mascarene Islands.
Food	Unknown, but possibly a wide variety of insects, fruits, and seeds.
Causes for Extinction	Introduction of exotic mammals; habitat loss due to agricultural development.
Range	Mascarene Islands: Réunion

island of Réunion in the Mascarene Islands.

Causes for Extinction

The tameness of this species left it vulnerable to vandalism and overcollection. Some birds were collected by individuals to keep as pets. It is possible that the species was also collected for the commercial pet trade.

See also Causes for Extinction of Mascarene Bird Species, page 11.

Adapted from data compiled by the Threatened and Endangered Species Information Institute (Golden, CO) for *Beacham's International Threatened, Endangered, and Extinct Species* published on CD ROM, available from Beacham Publishing.

Leguat's Rail
Aphanapteryx leguati

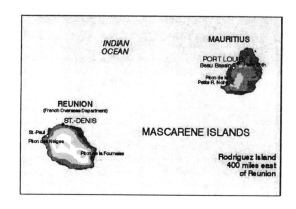

Description

Leguat's rail, *Aphanapteryx leguati*, was about the size of a domestic female chicken. Its red bill was about 2 inches (50 millimeters) long, and was slightly decurved. The eye's orbital ring was red. The body was a grayish or white with a grayish tinge color. The wings were much reduced in size indicating the species was flightless. The legs and feet were red.

A. leguati was a member of the rail, coot, and gallinule family, Rallidae. *A. leguati* was described and named *Erythromachus leguati* by Milne-Edwards in 1874. *A. leguati* is also referred to as *Miserythrus leguati*. Other common names for this species include Leguat's blue rail and Leguat's gelinote.

A. leguati and *A. bonasia* (Mauritius red rail, page 17) are thought to have evolved from the same species.

Behavior

Like other rails, Leguat's rail was probably omnivorous but animal matter probably made up the majority of the diet when available.

Status	Extinct
Probable Extinction	c.1700
Family	Rallidae (Rails, Gallinules and Coots)
Description	Flightless bird with a red orbital eye ring; the body was a grayish or white and the legs and feet were red.
Habitat	Volcanic forest with a moist climate.
Food	Probably omnivorous.
Causes for Extinction	Introduction of exotic mammals, including black and brown rats.
Range	Mascarene Islands: Rodriguez

Distribution

A. leguati is known from Francois Leguat's diary kept while he and six other Huguenots lived on Rodriguez and from skeletal remains. The species was probably fairly common when Leguat and his companions arrived on Rodriguez. The species is thought to have declined to extinction by 1700.

Causes for Extinction

See Causes for Extinction of Mascarene Bird Species, page 11.

Adapted from data compiled by the Threatened and Endangered Species Information Institute (Golden, CO) for *Beacham's International Threatened, Endangered, and Extinct Species* published on CD ROM, available from Beacham Publishing.

Rodriguez Little Owl
Athene murivora

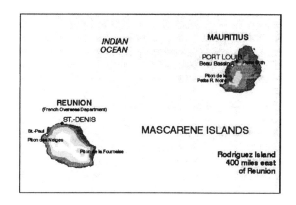

Description

Skeletal remains (leg and beak fragments, and a recent discovery of part of a cranium and pelvis) and one spartan account of the species are all that is known about the Rodriguez little owl, *Athene murivora*. This small owl was about 9 inches (23 centimeters) in length and may have been mostly brown.

A. murivora was a member of the owl family, Strigidae. It was described and named *Athene murivora* by Milne-Edwards in 1874 from bones found on Rodriguez and from one limited early account. The Rodriguez little owl is also referred to as Carine murivora.

Status	Extinct
Probable Extinction	c.1850
Family	Strigidae (Owls)
Description	Small owl that may have been mostly brown.
Habitat	Nested in and hunted from trees.
Food	Small birds and lizards.
Causes for Extinction	Hunted for food; introduction of exotic mammals, including black and brown rats.
Range	Mascarene Islands: Rodriguez

Behavior

The Rodriguez little owl was said to have eaten small birds and lizards. A relative, *Athene* sp., are primarily carnivorous. They feed on a wide variety of insects, small mammals, small birds, and reptiles. *Athene* sp. hunt from a perch. Once spotted, prey are pounced on, grasped in the talons, and carried back to the perch to be consumed.

Habitat

Accounts (the anonymous "Relation de l'ile de Rodrigue") indicate the species nested in and hunted from trees on Rodriguez Island.

Distribution

The Rodriguez little owl was endemic to Rodriguez Island. Arabs most likely discovered the islands long before the Europeans, but apparently did not settle the area or disrupt the natural processes. This species is believed extinct from Mauritius (Rodriguez Island) after approximately 1850.

Causes for Extinction

The Rodriguez little owl was probably hunted for food by early settlers or sailors who stopped on Rodriguez to replenish their food supply. This may have been one of the primary factors leading to the extinction of this species.

See also Causes for Extinction of Mascarene Bird Species, page 11.

Adapted from data compiled by the Threatened and Endangered Species Information Institute (Golden, CO) for *Beacham's International Threatened, Endangered, and Extinct Species* published on CD ROM, available from Beacham Publishing.

Rodriguez Starling
Necropsar rodricanus

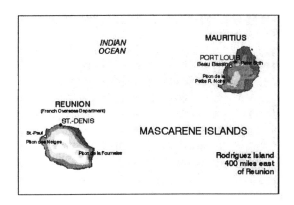

Description

The Rodriguez starling, *Necropsar rodricanus*, was closely related to the Réunion starling (*Fregilupus varius*, page 25). The Rodriguez starling is only known from skeletal remains. Measurements indicate it was somewhat smaller than *F. varius* (10 inches versus 12 inches in length) and a written description indicates the Rodriguez species did not have the distinctive crest found on *F. varius*; otherwise the two species are thought by some to be quite similar in appearance. *F. varius'* head and nape feathers were an ashy-gray with a white vein; the belly, throat, cheeks, lores, and eyebrows were white; the back, and the rump and upper tail coverts were brown. Another species account attributed to the Rodriguez starling describes the species as follows: "most of the body was white with the primary and secondary flight feathers and the tail being black; and the bill and feet were yellow." This description was supposedly of a bird from Islet au Mat, an islet near Rodriguez.

Distribution

The Rodriguez starling was endemic to the forests and rolling hills throughout the

Status	Extinct
Probable Extinction	1840
Family	Sturnidae (Starlings)
Description	Medium-sized bird with a crest made up of pale ashy gray to white modified, plume-like feathers; pale ashy gray head and neck; and dark ashy brown back, rump, and upper tail coverts.
Habitat	Forests and rolling hills
Food	Probably insects, fruits and seeds.
Causes for Extinction	Loss of habitat; introduced predators.
Range	Mascarene Islands: Rodriguez

island of Rodriguez.

Causes for Extinction

See Causes for Extinction of Mascarene Bird Species, page 11.

Rodriguez Solitaire

Pezophaps solitaria

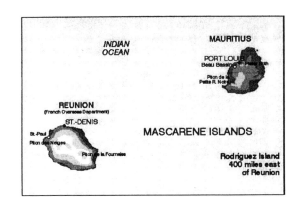

Description

The Rodriguez solitaire, *Pezophaps solitaria*, was a large, stocky bird, weighing 40 to 50 pounds. It had a shorter bill than its close relative, the dodo (*Raphus cucullatus*). Reports on the color of this species vary. These contradictions may be the result of variations between the sexes or age classes or simply color morphs. Described colors include brownish-gray, blonde or pale yellow, white, and grayish-white with a blackish upper back. The feet were large, scaly, and very strong; well-adapted to running over uneven, rocky surfaces. The wings were much reduced, indicating this species was flightless like the dodo.

Behavior

Some accounts indicate Rodriguez solitaire laid one clutch per year with one egg per clutch. Adults were said to aggressively protect their chicks; they were capable of inflicting serious bite wounds to individuals approaching the chicks.

The Rodriguez solitaire was said to consume large pebbles which were found in it's crop, a characteristic shared by many modern species. Seeds and green vegetation probably made up the largest percentage of this species' diet.

The Rodriguez solitaire was a ground nester; nests were probably placed in well-hidden sites in dense stands of grass or shrubs since naturalists visiting the island did not describe the nests or eggs in great detail.

Status	Extinct
Probable Extinction	1800
Family	Raphidae (Dodos and Solitaires)
Description	Large, stocky bird with a short beak and wings, and ranging in color from gray to white.
Habitat	Dense forests.
Food	Seeds and green vegetation.
Reproduction	One egg per clutch per year.
Cause for Extinction	Hunting.
Range	Mascarene Islands: Rodriguez

Distribution

The Rodriguez solitaire was endemic to the island of Rodriguez. It was probably extinct by 1800.

Causes for Extinction

The Rodriguez solitaire was hunted for food by early settlers or sailors who stopped on Mauritius to replenish their food supply.

See also Causes for Extinction of Mascarene Bird Species, page 11.

Adapted from data compiled by the Threatened and Endangered Species Information Institute (Golden, CO) for *Beacham's International Threatened, Endangered, and Extinct Species* published on CD ROM, available from Beacham Publishing.

Rodriguez Ring-Necked Parakeet

Psittacula exsul

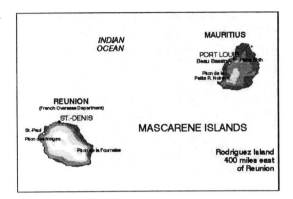

Description

The Rodriguez ring-necked parakeet, *Psittacula exsul*, was a medium sized (16 inches or 41 centimeters) member of the parrot family. The female's body was a bluish green color with darker patches on the chin and sides of the neck and along the inner edge of the flight feathers. The upper mandible was a dark red, the lower mandible was black, and the irises were yellowish. The tail was long and tapered. Male specimens were not collected but reports indicate the males may have had a red shoulder patch.

This species is also called Newton's parakeet and Newton's parrot.

Behavior

Information concerning the food habits of Rodriguez ring-necked parakeet is limited. Other members of the parrot family consume a wide variety of fruits and seeds. The Rodriguez ring-necked parakeet was observed eating the nuts from an olivaceous (olive-like) tree.

Habitat

The Rodriguez ring-necked parakeet

Status	Extinct
Probable Extinction	1880s
Family	Psittacidae (Parrots and parakeets)
Description	Medium-sized parrot with a bluish green body, darker patches on the chin and sides of the neck; a dark red upper mandible and black lower mandible; yellowish irises; and a long, tapered tail.
Habitat	Forests.
Food	Nuts, fruits and seeds.
Causes for Extinction	Loss of habitat; hunting; overcollecting.
Range	Mascarene Islands: Rodriguez

inhabited the forested areas on the island of Rodriguez.

Distribution

The species was thought to be fairly common in the eighteenth century. The last specimens of Rodriguez ring-necked parakeet were collected in 1875 and the last confirmed sighting in the field was in 1874. It was presumed to be extinct not long after 1875.

Causes for Extinction

See Causes for Extinction of Mascarene Bird Species, page 11.

Adapted from data compiled by the Threatened and Endangered Species Information Institute (Golden, CO) for *Beacham's International Threatened, Endangered, and Extinct Species* published on CD ROM, available from Beacham Publishing.

Seychelles Alexandrine Parrot

Psittacula wardi

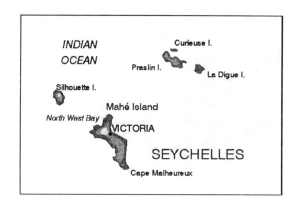

Description

The Seychelles Alexandrine parrot, *Psittacula wardi,* was a medium-sized (16 inches or 41 centimeters) member of the parrot family. It is similar in appearance to the Mascarene parrots but did not have a rose colored collar. The males did have a reduced black collar, a massive red bill, and a red shoulder patch. Both sexes were mostly green with bluish napes and long, tapering pale blue tails.

Behavior

Information concerning the food habits of the Seychelles Alexandrine parrot is limited. Other members of the parrot family consume a wide variety of fruits and seeds. This species showed a definite preference for maize.

Habitat

The Seychelles Alexandrine parrot probably inhabited the more densely forested areas and moved out into the open areas (primarily croplands) to feed.

Status	Extinct
Probable Extinction	1881
Family	Psittacidae (Parrots and parakeets)
Description	Medium-size mostly green parrot with a black collar, massive red bill, red shoulder patch, and long, tapering pale blue tails.
Habitat	Dense forests and croplands.
Food	Probably fruits and seeds.
Causes for Extinction	Hunting, overcollecting, persecution.
Range	Seychelles Islands

Distribution

The Seychelles Alexandrine parrot was considered rare by 1866. The last specimens were collected in 1881 by H. M. Warry.

Causes for Extinction

The Seychelles Alexandrine parrot was extensively trapped and shot in an effort to control its predation on the islanders' maize crops. The species was probably collected by commercial pet traders. These activities may have been the primary factor responsible for the decline and extinction of this species.

Large areas of forested land were also cleared for agricultural and urban development but the steepness of Mahe's terrain would have ensured that at least some forested areas would have been left intact.

Adapted from data compiled by the Threatened and Endangered Species Information Institute (Golden, CO) for *Beacham's International Threatened, Endangered, and Extinct Species* published on CD ROM, available from Beacham Publishing.

EXTINCT BIRDS OF AUSTRALIA, LORD HOWE AND NORFOLK ISLANDS

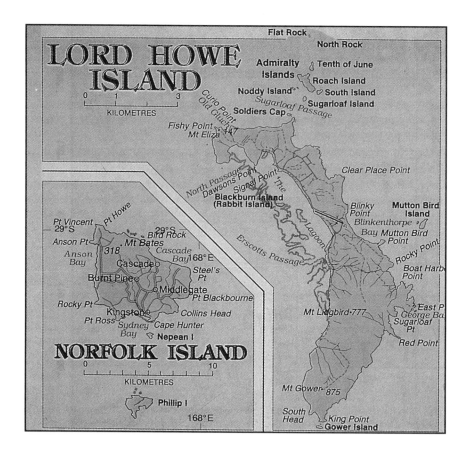

Lord Howe Island

Lord Howe Island is about 300 miles east of the coast of New South Wales, Australia and about 550 miles southwest of Norfolk Island. Norfolk Island is found about equidistant from Australia, New Zealand, and New Caledonia.

Lord Howe Island is about 5 square miles in area with two major, heavily forested peaks up to 2,800 feet in elevation. Below these summits are rainforests, wooded hills and pasturelands. In the westward lee of the island, a coral reef protects a lagoon that is rich with marine life. The island was uninhabited when it was discovered in 1788; the earliest settlers were British and American seamen, along with some Maori women and a chieftan's daughter from the Gilbert Islands. Originally, Lord Howe was used as a supply station for whaling ships, which contributed to the extinction of species. Sixteen, possibly seventeen, avian species were known to have colonized this island; eight of these species are now extinct. The only native mammal species is a bat.

Norfolk Island

Norfolk Island and the two nearby uninhabited islands of Phillip and Nepean together are only about 13 square miles in area. The highest point on each of the islands is about 400 feet. Although most of the island has been cleared for agriculture and pastures, the once dominant Norfolk Island pines (*Araucaria* sp.) are still a notable feature. The island possesses rich flora and fauna. There are 173 species of native plants and 250 introduced plant species. Fifty of those plants are endemic to the island. There are 55 indigenous species of birds (14 endemic).

Discovered by James Cook in 1774, the island was settled by the British from New South Wales, Australia, as a penal colony in 1788 for the purpose of propagating flax and exploiting timber. Introduced animals completely denuded the small islands of Phillip and Nepean. Abandoned as a penal colony after 26 years, it has been occupied variously as a whaling station, exile colony, and tourist attraction. Its tax-free economy has boosted the population to over 20,000, plus an influx of 20,000 visitors annually. The human presence has placed considerable pressure on the island's natural resources and wildlife.

Paradise Parrot
Psephotus pulcherrimus

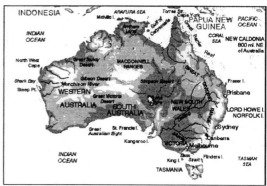

Enlarged Map, Page 326

Description

The male paradise parrot, *Psephotus pulcherrimus*, had a red forehead, a blackish brown nape and crown, and a greenish yellow eye ring. The cheeks, sides of the head, chin, throat and breast were greenish blue. The lower abdomen, thighs and under tail coverts were red. The underparts were mostly grayish brown but the rump was turquoise, with the outer tail feathers blue and the wing coverts red. The irises were brown and the feet greyish brown. The wingspan was 121-135 mm (4.7-5.3 inches) and the tail measured 143-182 mm (5.6-7.1 inches) long. The female was about the same size.

The female had a whitish yellow forehead with a brown crown and nape. The face, throat and breast were yellowish green with orange-brown markings. The abdomen was pale blue flecked with red.

The paradise parrot is similar and often confused with the golden-shouldered parrot (*Psephotus chrysopterygius*) and the Mulga parrot (*P. varius*).

Status	Extinct
Probable Extinction	c.1927
Family	Psittacidae (Parrots and parakeets)
Description	Parrot with a red forehead, a blackish brown nape and crown, and a greenish yellow eye ring; the cheeks, sides of the head, chin, throat and breast were greenish blue.
Habitat	River valleys, savannah woodland and scrub grassland.
Food	Grass seeds.
Reproduction	Nests were burrowed in termite mounds to produce a narrow tunnel ending in a hovel about a foot in diameter.
Causes for Extinction	Possibly depletion of food supply by habitat conversion and drought.
Range	Australia: southern Queensland and northern New South Wales.

Behavior

These parrots may have fed directly from standing stalks of grass, sliding the strands sideways through their beaks and stripping seeds. They did not appear to have eaten grass seed-by-seed, and they may have thus restricted themselves to certain varieties of grasses.

They were relatively tame birds that could be approached and captured with nets. They usually gathered in pairs or small groups, spending most of their time on the ground feeding. Their flight patterns were swift and undulating.

Breeding was recorded between September and March. Nests were sometimes hollowed out in steep or vertical river banks, and the birds often burrowed in termite mounds to produce a narrow tunnel ending in a hovel about a foot in diameter. No nesting materials were introduced. A clutch of 3-5 eggs was laid in the loose dirt. Incubation lasted for 3 weeks. Males did not enter the tunnel during incubation and the care of the young was the sole responsibility of the female. The male would come to the entrance of the tunnel and beckon his mate with soft chirps.

The call of the male was very animated. His whole body vibrated with the force and intensity of his song, imparting an agitated motion and intense emotion on his activity.

Habitat

The paradise parrot inhabited river valleys, savannah woodland and scrub grassland.

Distribution

John Gould first recorded the paradise parrot on the Darling Downs in 1844. This parrot was a well-known bird, and was distributed over a wide area of southern Queensland and northern New South Wales, from Rockhampton to Brisbane along the coast and inland to Darling Downs. Its decline was followed over several decades at the turn of the twentieth century. The bird became increasingly rare and by 1915 seems to have vanished completely. An effort was made in 1921 to locate the birds, and a small colony was verified by C. H. H. Jerrard in the Burnett River area of Queensland. Jerrard extensively photographed the colony, but they vanished again and were last sighted in 1927.

Causes for Extinction

This species had few natural enemies, and there is no clear evidence of the effect that introduced predators may have had. The grazing of cattle and sheep depleted their food stocks of grass seed. Several years of drought and brush fires further threatened the food supply, and the paradise parrot apparently was unable to adapt to new foods or new feeding grounds. They may have also been collected for caged bird export. Caged species were not uncommon during the nineteenth century, although there is no account of birds in captivity after 1894.

Norfolk Island Starling
Aplonis fusca

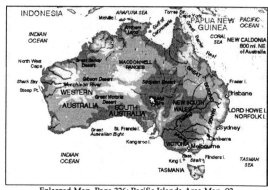

Enlarged Map, Page 326; Pacific Islands Area Map, 93

Description

The Norfolk Island starling, *Aplonis fusca*, was 7 to 7.75 inches (20 centimeters) in length. Males of the Norfolk Island subspecies, *A. f. fusca*, were a dark grayish color over much of the body. The head, throat, breast, scapulas, back, rump, and upper tail coverts produced a glossy iridescent green sheen in various lighting situations. The undertail coverts were white while the rest of the underside was a dark ashy gray color. The bill and feet were black and the irises were reddish-orange. Females were similar to males but a lighter shade of gray with a less obvious green sheen and a yellowish lower abdomen and undertail coverts. The Lord Howe Island subspecies, *A. f. hulliana*, was similar in appearance to *A. f. fusca* but with more of a brownish instead of gray body.

This species was also called the Norfolk & Lord Howe Starling, Lord Howe Island starling, red-eye, and cudgimaruk (this name refers to the bird's call).

Behavior

Information concerning the reproductive

Status	Extinct
Probable	
Extinction	c.1925
Family	Sturnidae (Starlings)
Description	Dark grayish color over much of the body, with the head, throat, breast, scapulas, back, rump, and upper tail coverts a glossy iridescent green sheen; white undertail coverts; black bill and feet; and reddish-orange irises.
Habitat	Pine forests.
Food	Probably insects, fruits and seeds.
Reproduction	Clutch of 2-5 eggs.
Causes	
for Extinction	Introduced rats.
Range	Norfolk and Lord Howe Islands
Photo	See Color Insert, C-3

characteristics of this species is limited. Clutches apparently contained from 2 to 5 eggs.

Food habits for this species are unknown but other members of this family are omnivorous, consuming a wide variety of insects, fruits, and seeds.

Habitat

The Norfolk Island starling was endemic to Norfolk and Lord Howe Island. This species was probably found most often in the islands' forested habitats. Nests were placed in tree cavities or deep depressions, often quite close to the ground.

Distribution

The Norfolk Island starling may have been quite abundant on Lord Howe Island prior to the introduction of rats. This starling may have been especially susceptible to rat predation because its nests were often placed near to the ground in easily accessible cavities or depressions. Individual birds would return to the same nest from year to year and would lay a second, and maybe a third clutch if the first clutch was lost. The species' population plummeted following the introduction of this predator and it was presumed to be extinct by 1925. The species was also assumed to have become extinct on Norfolk Island around the same time.

Causes for Extinction

Lord Howe Island's first permanent (European) settlement was established in the late 1700s. The four endemic passerine species listed as extinct became so between 1918 and 1925. Rats were introduced to Lord Howe Island in 1918 when a ship named the "Mokambo" ran ashore on Ned's Beach. These rats apparently destroyed the nests and eggs of these passerine species and by 1919 the population's reproductive rates had declined dramatically. Owls introduced to control the rat population probably preyed upon the local birds as well.

Norfolk Island was discovered in 1777 during one of James Cook's voyages. Around 1790 a penal colony was established on the islands. Island inhabitants were periodically forced to live off the land which meant that the island's avian fauna was hunted for food and the forested areas were probably cleared for fuel and shelter. Fifteen species are known to have inhabited this island group. At least three species (a parrot, pigeon, and Norfolk Island starling) are now extinct.

Adapted from data compiled by the Threatened and Endangered Species Information Institute (Golden, CO) for *Beacham's International Threatened, Endangered, and Extinct Species* published on CD ROM, available from Beacham Publishing.

Lord Howe Island Flycatcher

Gerygone ignata insularis

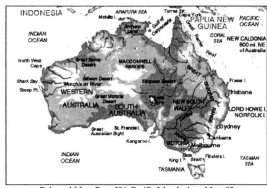

Enlarged Map, Page 326; Pacific Islands Area Map, 93

Description

The Lord Howe Island Flycatcher, *Gerygone ignata insularis*, despite its name, was not a member of the flycatcher family, Muscicapidae, but, instead, was a member of the Australian warbler family, *Acanthizidae*. *G. i. insularis* was a subspecies of *G. ignata,* a New Zealand warbler. *G. i. insularis* was a small, forest dwelling bird of about 12.7 centimeters (5 inches) in length with a white eyering, a subdued olive-green head, back, wings, and tail, a yellow belly, and a gray upper breast and throat. Portions of the outer tail feathers were white giving a spotted appearance. The Lord Howe Islanders referred to this subspecies as the "rainbird".

Status	Extinct
Probable	
Extinction	1920s
Family	Acanthizidae (Warblers)
Description	Small, forest-dwelling bird with a white eye-ring, an olive-green head, back, wings and tail, and a gray upper breast and throat.
Habitat	Forests of Lord Howe Island.
Food	Insects
Reproduction	Clutch of 3-6 eggs.
Causes for	
Extinction	Exotic rats.
Range	Australia: Lord Howe Island

Behavior

This subspecies' nest, as described by the islanders, was dome-shaped with the entrance placed on the side; the entrance was covered by a slight protuberance of the nest (e.g., a hood). Nests were placed from 5 to 25 feet above the ground. *G. ignata,* the New Zealand species, breeds from August through January and lays 3-6 eggs per clutch. Incubation lasts about 17-19 days and the chicks fledge in an additional 17-19 days.

Both sexes feed the chicks by providing them with grubs, caterpillars, and other small insects.

G. ignata is listed as being almost entirely insectivorous; its preferred diet is insects and spiders. It can only be assumed that *G. i. insularis* was also primarily insectivorous.

Habitat

G. i. insularis inhabited the forests on Lord Howe Island. It was often observed flying above the trees, chasing after insects. *G. ignata*, the New Zealand species, is also commonly seen feeding along the tops of the trees.

Distribution

G. i. insularis was considered to be a common bird prior to 1918. The introduction of the rat, and subsequently, the owl to Lord Howe Island, located about 500 miles east of New South Wales, Australia, precipitated the decline and extinction of this species within as little as 2 to 3 years.

Causes for Extinction

Rats were introduced to the island in 1918 when a ship named the "Mokambo" ran ashore on Ned's Beach. These rats apparently destroyed the nests and eggs of *G. i. insularis* and by 1919 the population's reproductive rate had declined dramatically. Owls introduced to control the rat population probably preyed upon the local birds as well. The subspecies was declared to be extinct around 1920.

Adapted from data compiled by the Threatened and Endangered Species Information Institute (Golden, CO) for *Beacham's International Threatened, Endangered, and Extinct Species* published on CD ROM, available from Beacham Publishing.

Norfolk Island Kaka
or Parrot
Nestor meridionalis productus

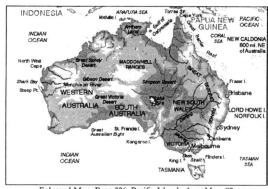

Enlarged Map, Page 326; Pacific Islands Area Map, 93

Description

The Norfolk Island Kaka, *Nestor meridionalis productus,* is considered by many to be a subspecies of *N. meridionalis,* a fairly common and extremely variable (many subspecies) species found on New Zealand's South, North, and Stewart Islands.

The Norfolk Island kaka was a large parrot (15 to 16 inches in length) with a brownish-gray head and neck, a yellow to orange chin, cheeks, and lores, a greenish yellow nape, a darker brownish-gray upper back, a red lower back and rump, greenish wing coverts, brown tail and wings, grayish-brown upper breast, bright yellow lower breast, and reddish-orange belly and thighs. These color patterns are said to have been widely variable. The upper, strongly decurved mandible appears to have been at least twice as long as the lower mandible.

Behavior

Reproductive characteristics are probably similar to New Zealand's *N. meridionalis.* Nests were probably placed in tree cavities; these same sites were used in successive years. The breeding season ran from October

Status	Extinct
Probable Extinction	1851
Family	Psittacidae (Parrots and Parakeets)
Description	Large parrot with a brownish-gray head and neck, yellow to orange chin, cheeks and lores, brownish-gray upper back, red lower back and rump, bright yellow lower breast, and reddish-orange belly and thighs.
Habitat	Native forests of New Zealand.
Food	Fruits, nectar and insects.
Reproduction	Clutch of 4-5 eggs laid October through February.
Causes for Extinction	Hunting, overcollecting, habitat loss.
Range	Australia: Norfolk, Phillip and Lord Howe Islands.
Photo	See Color Insert, C-4

through February. The 4 to 5 eggs in a clutch hatched in about 21 days. Chicks fledged in about 10 weeks.

The Norfolk Island kaka was non-migratory. *N. meridionalis*, the New Zealand species, is omnivorous, consuming a wide variety of fruits and insects, including grubs of wood-boring beetles and the leaves and nectar from *Metrosideros* spp.

Habitat

The Norfolk Island kaka appears to have been a forest dwelling species; its habitat requirements were probably similar to New Zealand's *N. meridionalis*. *N. meridionalis* inhabits fairly continuous areas of native forests on New Zealand. It has not spread into agricultural and urban areas as many other native forest species have done. It is occasionally sighted in urban gardens and other areas where fruit/nectar-bearing trees have been planted.

Distribution

Historic records indicate the Norfolk Island kaka was found on Norfolk Island, Phillip Island, and possibly Lord Howe Island. All these islands are a part of Australia. The Norfolk and Phillip Islands are found about equidistant from Australia, New Zealand, and New Caledonia. Lord Howe Island is off the coast of New South Wales, Australia.

Causes for Extinction

The last captive Norfolk Island kaka died in London around 1851. Although not confirmed, the species was assumed to have become extinct throughout its range in the wild around the same time. The species was probably widely hunted for food by the Maori and by European explorers, convicts, and settlers, and for the commercial pet bird trade.

Destruction of forest habitats inhabited by this species was widespread in the early to mid-1800s. This, along with overcollecting, led to the demise of the kaka on Norfolk Island in the early 1840s. The last of the species were found on Phillip Island, a small island (8 kilometers or 5 miles in circumference) about 4.8 km or 3 miles from Norfolk Island.

Adapted from data compiled by the Threatened and Endangered Species Information Institute (Golden, CO) for *Beacham's International Threatened, Endangered, and Extinct Species* published on CD ROM, available from Beacham Publishing.

Lord Howe
Purple Gallinule
Porphyrio albus

Enlarged Map, Page 326; Pacific Islands Area Map, 93

Description

The Lord Howe purple gallinule, *Porphyrio albus*, was similar in body shape to other gallinules. It was about 22 inches (55 centimeters) in length with reddish legs, feet, bill and frontal shield. The wings were reduced in size, the tail feathers modified (probably soft versus stiff) and the legs more developed than the mainland Australia species, *P. porphyrio*, indicating that *P. albus* was flightless or nearly so. The known specimens were almost pure white, one had a blue tinge on the wings. It is possible that the species varied in color and may have included white, blue and white, and blue birds. This presumption is based on excerpts from Surgeon Bowes' journal from 1788 where he describes a visit to Lord Howe Island.

P. albus was a member of the rail, gallinule, and coot family, Rallidae. This species was described and named Fulica alba by White in 1790. Two other species described from Lord Howe Island, *P. raperi* and *P. stanleyi*, are probably synonymous with *P. albus*.

Fuller states that there is enough evidence to support the presence of flightless-

Status	Extinct
Probable Extinction	c.1834
Family	Rallidae (Rails, Gallinules and Coots)
Description	White wading bird with reddish legs, feet, bill and frontal shield.
Habitat	Freshwater wetlands, and possibly brackish and salt-water wetlands.
Food	Seeds, including rice, and various grasses; also animal prey including aquatic beetles and bugs.
Reproduction	Nests were often placed on floating mats over deep water.
Causes for Extinction	Overhunting
Range	Australia: Lord Howe Island
Photo	See Color Insert, C-2

ness (soft retrices, reduced wing length, well developed legs) in *P. albus* and thus to support separating *P. albus* from *P. porphyrio*.

The Lord Howe purple gallinule is also referred to as the white swamp-hen, white gallinule, Lord Howe swamphen, and white takahe. Other scientific names applied to this species include *Gallinula alba*, *Notornis alba*, and *Notornis stanleyi*.

Behavior

The North American species, *Porphyrula martinica* (purple gallinule), is omnivorous with seeds making up a large percentage of its diet in the summer and fall. A wide variety of seeds are consumed by *P. martinica*, including rice, duckweed, wild millet, spikerush, and various grasses. Animal prey items include aquatic beetles and bugs, mollusks, ants, spiders, flies and fly larvae, caterpillars, and dragonfly/damselfly nymphs. *P. albus*' diet may have been similar to *P. martinica*'s.

Specific information concerning this species' activity patterns are unknown but it was probably diurnal.

Habitat

Gallinules, in general, inhabit freshwater emergent wetlands (and possibly brackish and saltwater wetlands to some extent). Nests are often placed on floating mats over deep water near the open water edge of dense stands of emergent vegetation.

Distribution

The species' population size when first discovered is not discussed, but it probably was not uncommon. The exact time of extinction is not known; it was probably prior to the establishment of the first settlement in 1834.

The Lord Howe purple gallinule was endemic to Lord Howe Island, and possibly, Norfolk Island.

Greenway considered *P. albus* to be a subspecies of *P. porphyrio* of New Zealand (now *P. melanotus*) and Australia, and considered that all these species or subspecies were closely related to the takahe, *Notornis mantelli*, of New Zealand. There have been sporadic sightings (some fairly recent, 1936) of *P. porphyrio* (Greenway's *P. p. melanotus*) on both Lord Howe Island and Norfolk Island and it is possible that there was intermixing of *P. albus* and *P. porphyrio* in the past. Because of this and because of the small sample size used to describe *P. albus*, Greenway states that it is possible that the measurements (possibly inaccurate) for *P. albus* could have fallen within the accepted variation in size and color phases for a species, indicating that *P. albus* may not have been a distinct species but simply a subspecies of *P. porphyrio*.

Causes for Extinction

The species is believed to have been extirpated from Lord Howe Island before the first settlement was established in 1834 since there was no mention of a "white fowl" by early settlers. *P. albus'* apparent flightlessness left it vulnerable to attack and harassment by sailors (whalers, naval vessels, and convict supply ships) who visited the island. Overcollecting by these sailors is believed to have been responsible for the decline and extinction of *P. albus*. Rats and other mammalian predators were not introduced to the island until after the species was presumed to be extinct.

Lord Howe Island Fantail

Rhipidura fuliginosa cervina

Enlarged Map, Page 326; Pacific Islands Area Map, 93

Description

The Lord Howe Island fantail, *Rhipidura fuliginosa cervina,* was a subspecies of *R. fuliginosa,* the gray fantail, an extant, more widespread species. *R. f. cervina* was a small bird averaging 5 inches in total length. The tail was long with a rounded tip. The name fantail comes from the bird's habit of fanning its long tail. The top of the head and the wings were a dark brown color; the wings had two white bars. The lower part of the body was a buffy or cinnamon-brown color. The outer tail feathers had white edges.

R. f. cervina was a member of the Old World flycatcher family, Muscicapidae. The gray fantail (*R. fuliginosa*) is still found in the Solomon Islands, New Guinea, New Zealand, Australia and New Caledonia.

R. f. cervina was described and named *Rhipidura cervina* by Ramsay in 1879. It has a designated status of extinct, as of approximately 1925, in Australia (Lord Howe Island).

Status	Extinct
Probable Extinction	c.1924
Family	Musicapidae (Old World Flycatchers)
Description	Small bird with a long tail; the top of the head and the wings were a dark brown color; the wings had two white bars; lower part of the body was a buffy or cinnamon-brown color; and the outer tail feathers had white edges.
Habitat	Forested habitats including woodlands adjacent to or in wetlands, mangrove swamps, and wetland scrub communities.
Food	Insects.
Causes for Extinction	Predation by rats.
Range	Australia: Lord Howe Island

Behavior

The Lord Howe Island fantail was observed flitting around among the trees after insects. Clutches for *R. fuliginosa* include 2-3 eggs.

Habitat

R. fuliginosa inhabits forested habitats including woodlands adjacent to or in wetlands, mangrove swamps, and wetland scrub communities. Cultivated areas are utilized for feeding. Nests are placed in trees or bushes.

Distribution

The Lord Howe Island fantail was endemic to Lord Howe Island which is about 300 miles (480 kilometers) east of the Australian mainland. The species was not uncommon before the introduction of rats in 1918. It was assumed to be extinct or near extinction by 1924.

Causes for Extinction

Rats were introduced to Lord Howe Island in 1918. As on other islands in the Pacific and Indian Oceans, rats were probably responsible for the decline of several endemic species. Both ground and tree nesting species were vulnerable to the rats. The rats raided nests, destroying the eggs and killing the young chicks. Adults may also have been preyed upon to some extent.

Adapted from data compiled by the Threatened and Endangered Species Information Institute (Golden, CO) for *Beacham's International Threatened, Endangered, and Extinct Species* published on CD ROM, available from Beacham Publishing.

EXTINCT BIRDS OF NEW ZEALAND

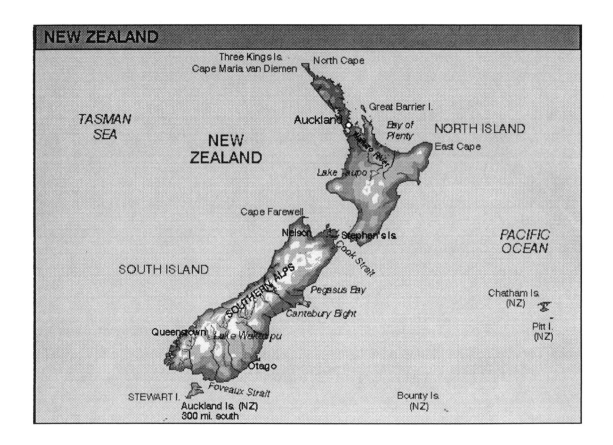

North and South Island, New Zealand

Although New Zealand is small, its geological history resembles that of a continent. During its formation, little of the island was above water; then warping occurred and the mountain building period created the backbone of the north and south islands. The major North Island mountains are volcanic in origin, and one is still active. On South Island, the eastern area has extensive alluvial plains that contrast with the precipitous slopes on the west coast.

The indigenous vegetation consisted of mixed evergreen forests that covered two thirds of the country, but today the dense bush occurs only in park lands. Because of New Zealand's isolation, there was no high animal life when the Maori arrived around 1,000 A.D. There were two species of lizards and a "beak-headed" reptile thought to be extinct for a hundred million years in the rest of the world. One of the most interesting native species was a flightless bird the Maori called "moa" (see below) that was quickly exterminated from the islands by the European explorers.

A Dutch sailor was the first European to arrive in New Zealand in 1642; James Cook charted the islands in his voyage of 1769-1770, and during the nineteenth century whalers used the islands to replenish their supplies. The European settlers who came in the first part of the nineteenth century brought domestic animals, red deer for hunting, and opossum for skins. These animals eventually became feral and damaged much of the avian habitat.

Auckland Islands, New Zealand

The Auckland Islands, an outlying group 290 miles south of New Zealand's South Island, comprises six islands and several islets. Volcanic in origin, they have a cool, humid, and windy climate. Soils are generally poor, and shrub forests cover lower elevations. A whaling station was established, then abandoned in 1852, and there was an unsuccessful effort to introduce cattle and sheep in the 1890s. The islands are currently without human inhabitants.

Chatham and Pitt Islands, New Zealand

Although of volcanic origin, there is evidence that the Chatham Islands group may once have been attached to New Zealand. Chatham Island, the largest in the group, is dominated by shallow lagoons, swamps, heath and dune; Pitt Island is the highest. There are no indigenous mammals, and the reptiles are of New Zealand species. The original forest vegetation has been significantly changed by fires and grazing since the arrival of Europeans in 1861, when whaling stations were established. Sheep were introduced in 1865, and the export of breeding stock and wool is the basis of the island's economy.

New Zealand Moas

Moa, the Maori name for extinct, ostrichlike, flightless birds native to New Zealand, constituted two families with 25 species, some as tall as 10 feet high. According to Maori tradition, moas were swift runners which, when cornered, defended themselves by kicking. Early Polynesians hunted moas for food, made spear points, hooks and ornaments from their bones, and water carriers from their eggs. Moas were chiefly browsers and grazers; they probably ate seeds, fruits, leaves, and grasses. Although most moas were probably extinct by the seventeenth century, a few of the smaller species might have survived until the nineteenth century. Some people believe a few may still exist in the remote parts of the islands.

The family included many genera and species, up to 37 species according to Rothschild. *Megalapteryx didinus, Euryapteryx gravis,* and *Dinornis torosus* appear to have become extinct since 1600; all the others have been extinct for more than 400 years.

Moas appear to have inhabited New Zealand for millions of years. How this family of birds made its way to this remote island chain is much debated. One theory is that a primitive moa inhabited this area of land when it splintered off of Gondwanaland (the ancient supercontinent) some 130 million years ago. Colonization after this land mass split would have required reaching the island by sea or air. Fossil remains do not indicate that the older species were capable of flight but undiscovered remains may yet prove the existence of a pre-historic moa capable of flight. These pre-historic moas evolved to fill niches normally filled by mammalian species. This led to the evolution of several moa species, some adapted to forest environments, others to more open habitats.

All members of this family were supposedly endemic to New Zealand. Fossil remains found in Queensland, Australia have been assigned to Dinornithidae by some but the limited number of fossil fragments available leaves many questions, and most experts do not believe there is enough evidence to say there were moas in Australia. Information concerning moas discusses the possibility that moas filled many niches on New Zealand in forested, shrub, wetland, and grassland habitats. Habitats utilized by this species are unknown.

The Maori recounted a tale of a small moa, possibly *M. didinus*, being captured at Preservation Inlet in 1868. Rumors that moas may still exist may be related to this species. Its smaller size may have made it easier for this moa to remain hidden from humans. If *M. didinus* inhabited some of the more remote, densely forested parts of the South Island and if it was a quiet, secretive, strictly nocturnal species, it could possibly exist in certain areas without contact with humans.

Moa Behavior

According to the Maori, female moas incubated the egg or eggs and were fed and guarded by the males. Moa eggs (species unknown) measured up to 10 inches (25 cm) in length and apparently had a rather fragile shell.

Moas appear to have been strictly herbivorous species. They probably grazed on grasses and forbs and consumed the leaves and berries of shrubby vegetation. Their strong feet and claws may have been used to dig up roots and tubers. They may have consumed insects uncovered during this activity. Large stones were also ingested along with food items. These stones are found along with the fossil remains.

Maori tales indicate that at least one of the larger moas was active at dusk and into the night. This may have been a response to hunting pressure and may not have applied to all species of moa. This is especially true since the birds apparently evolved to fill several niches; some were probably more nocturnal while others were more active during the day.

Moas were described as aggressive birds by the Maori. Males vigorously defended females as they incubated the egg or eggs.

Slender Moa
Dinornis torosus

Enlarged Map, Page 52

Description

The slender moa, *Dinornis torosus*, was believed to have been about 7 feet (215 centimeters) tall. All members of this bird family identified from fossils or more recent bone fragments were not only completely flightless but lacked even reduced humeral bones. The genus Dinornis included the largest of the moa species with *D. maximus* growing to a height of 13 feet (4 meters).

The external physical appearance of this species is completely conjectural; many pictures of moas depict a massive bird with long, robust legs and feet, a long slender neck, and a small head. The common name "slender moa" indicates this species' body may not have been as massive as some of the other species. *D. torosus* had deep pits along the top of the skull on some specimens indicating that either the males or females may have had a crest of some kind.

D. torosus was described and named by Hutton in 1891 from skeletal remains found on the South Island of New Zealand near Takaka. Other scientific names used in reference to this species include *Palapteryx plenus*, and *Dinornis strenuus*. The species is also referred to as the brawny great moa.

Status	Extinct
Probable Extinction	c.1600
Family	Dinornithidae (Moas)
Description	Flightless bird about 7 feet tall having deep pits along the top of the skull.
Habitat	Forested, shrub, wetland, and grassland habitats.
Food	Grasses, forbs, leaves and berries.
Reproduction	Females incubated the egg or eggs.
Causes for Extinction	Hunting; destruction of habitat due to fires.
Range	New Zealand: South Island

Behavior

See Moa Behavior, page 54.

Habitat

Information concerning moas suggests the possibility that moas filled many niches on New Zealand in forested, shrub, wetland, and grassland habitats.

Distribution

S. torosus was restricted to the South Island; the distribution of skeletal remains indicate that the species may have inhabited the higher elevation, hill country.

D. torosus was also restricted to the South Island. Fossil remains and bone fragments have been found near Canterbury, Otago, and Nelson.

Causes for Extinction

The Maori probably hunted this species extensively. Food resources on New Zealand were limited making this large bird a prime target for hunters.

Most moas disappeared during the Pleistocene era; humans did not reach New Zealand until much later. It is believed that most of the remaining moa species were in a population decline when the Maori arrived; their presence (hunting pressure) simply accelerated the species' decline. Fires set by the Maori may have destroyed the moa's breeding habitat.

Adapted from data compiled by the Threatened and Endangered Species Information Institute (Golden, CO) for *Beacham's International Threatened, Endangered, and Extinct Species* published on CD ROM, available from Beacham Publishing.

Greater
Broad-Billed Moa
Euryapteryx gravis

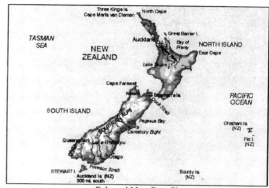

Enlarged Map, Page 52

Description

The greater broad-billed moa, *Euryapteryx gravis*, was believed to have been about 6 feet (190 centimeters) tall. Members of the genus Euryapteryx had broad bills with rounded tips and large, stout bodies. *E. gravis* may have been the largest of the Euryapteryx sp. All members of this family identified from fossil or more recent bone fragments were not only completely flightless but lacked even reduced humeral bones.

The external physical appearance of this species is completely conjectural; many pictures of moas depict a massive bird with long, robust legs and feet, a long slender neck, and a small head.

E. gravis was a member of the moa family, Dinornithidae. It was described and named *Dinornis gravis* by Owen in 1870 from skeletal remains found on the South Island of New Zealand near the Kakanui River.

Other scientific names used in reference to this species include *Emeus gravipes, Emeus parkeri, Emeus boothi, Emeus haasti,* and *Euryapteryx kuranui*. The species is also referred to as the burly lesser moa.

Status	Extinct
Probable Extinction	c.1850
Family	Dinornithidae (Moas)
Description	Flightless bird about 6 feet tall with broad bill with rounded tips and large, stout body with long, robust legs and feet, a long slender neck, and a small head.
Habitat	Forested, shrub, wetland, and grassland habitats of New Zealand.
Food	Probably grazed on grasses and forbs and consumed the leaves and berries of shrubby vegetation.
Reproduction	Females incubated the egg or eggs.
Causes for Extinction	Overhunted for food.
Range	New Zealand

Behavior

See Moa Behavior, page 54.

Habitat

This species' widespread distribution indicates it may have inhabited a variety of habitat types. Information concerning moas discusses the possibility that moas filled many niches on New Zealand in forested, shrub, wetland, and grassland habitats.

Distribution

All members of this family were supposedly endemic to New Zealand. Fossil remains found in Queensland, Australia have been assigned to Dinornithidae by some but the limited number of fossil fragments available leaves many questions, and most experts do not believe there is enough evidence to say there were moas in Australia.

E. gravis was possibly one of the most widespread members of this family. Its remains have been found throughout the North and South Islands as well as Stewart Island. *E. gravis* was considered extinct in New Zealand sometime after 1600, possibly as late as 1700.

Causes for Extinction

The Maori probably hunted this species extensively. Food resources on New Zealand were limited making this large bird a prime target for hunters.

Most moas disappeared during the Pleistocene era; humans did not reach New Zealand until much later. It is believed that most of the remaining moa species were in a population decline when the Maori arrived; hunting pressure simply accelerated the species' decline. Fires set by the Maori may have destroyed the moa's breeding habitat.

Adapted from data compiled by the Threatened and Endangered Species Information Institute (Golden, CO) for *Beacham's International Threatened, Endangered, and Extinct Species* published on CD ROM, available from Beacham Publishing.

Lesser Megalapteryx
Megalapteryx didinus

Enlarged Map, Page 52

Description

The lesser megalapteryx, *Megalapteryx didinus*, was believed to have been about 3.5 feet (110 centimeters) tall. All members of this family identified from fossil or more recent bone fragments were not only completely flightless but lacked even reduced humeral bones. The external physical appearance of this species is completely conjectural; many pictures of moas depict a massive bird with long, robust legs and feet, a long slender neck, and a small head. *M. didinus* may have been built along the same lines but on a smaller scale. Skeletal remains with dried skin and feathers probably have revealed more about this species than of any other moa. One set of remains found in a cave near Lake Wakatipu in 1878 included a dried head, neck and legs; all had some skin and feathers. Another leg found in a cave near the headwaters of the Waikaia River also had feathers attached. A third, almost complete, skeleton had dried skin on the head and neck and ligaments were still attached to the leg bones. This last set of remains indicated the species had small feathers on the top of the head and larger feathers on the neck. The feathers were hair-like in appearance, grayish brown, some

Status	Extinct
Probable	
Extinction	c.1800
Family	Dinorithidae (Moas)
Description	Flightless bird about 3.5 feet tall with small feathers on the top of its head and larger hair-like feathers on the neck colored grayish brown, some with a shade of rufous and others with white tips; also covered with feathers to the feet.
Habitat	Forested, shrub, wetland, and grassland habitats.
Food	Grasses, forbs, leaves and berries.
Reproduction	Females incubated the egg or eggs.
Causes for	
Extinction	Overhunting; destruction of habitat due to fires.
Range	New Zealand

with a shade of rufous and others with white tips. These remains indicate the species, unlike other moas, was covered with feathers to the feet.

M. didinus was a member of the moa family, Dinornithidae. *M. didinus* was described and named *Dinornis didinus* by Owen in 1883 from skeletal remains found on the South Island of New Zealand near Queenstown. Other scientific names used in reference to this species include *Megalapteryx hectori, Megalapteryx tenuipes, Megalapteryx hamiltoni,* and *Megalapteryx huttoni.* The species is also referred to as the South Island tokoweka.

Behavior

See Moa Behavior, page 54.

Habitat

Information concerning moas suggests the possibility that moas filled many niches on New Zealand in forested, shrub, wetland, and grassland habitats. Habitats utilized by this species are unknown.

Distribution

M. didinus probably was restricted to the South Island. It may have been most common at somewhat higher elevations on the Takaka tableland and in western Otago. *M. didinus* was considered extinct sometime after 1600, possibly as late as 1868.

Causes for Extinction

The Maori probably hunted this species extensively. Food resources on New Zealand were limited making this large bird a prime target for hunters.

Most moas disappeared during the Pleistocene era; humans did not reach New Zealand until much later, so it is believed that most of the remaining moa species were in a population decline when the Maori arrived; hunting pressure simply accelerated the species' decline. Fires set by the Maori may have destroyed the moa's breeding habitat.

Adapted from data compiled by the Threatened and Endangered Species Information Institute (Golden, CO) for *Beacham's International Threatened, Endangered, and Extinct Species* published on CD ROM, available from Beacham Publishing.

New Zealand Quail
Coturnix novaezelandiae

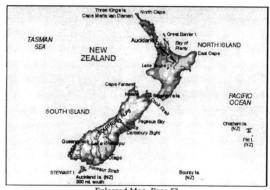

Enlarged Map, Page 52

Description

The New Zealand quail, *Coturnix novae-zelandiae*, was rust in color near the sides of the head, the throat, and between the eye and the upper edge of the bill, as well as the line over the eye. The crown and nape were dark brown edged with paler feathers running down the center and marked in the middle with a yellowish white. The shoulders, mantle, and all the upper surfaces were rust-colored with varying black and decorated with many lanceolate stripes of white. The primaries and outer secondaries were dark brown with the inner secondaries, the wing coverts, and the tail feathers a grayish brown varied with pale rust and shafted with white. The lower part of the neck was mottled with black and white with the sides and long plumage overlapping the thighs of rust-brown. Its feathers were margined and marked down the center with white and streaked on the webs with blackish brown. The abdomen was fulvous white with the under tail coverts barred with black. The iris was light hazel, bill black but pale at the tip, and the feet pale flesh brown.

Males and females were similar in ap-

Status	Extinct
Probable Extinction	1868
Family	Phasianidae (Pheasants and Quail)
Description	Rust color head and throat; dark brown crown and nape, edged with paler feathers running down the center.
Habitat	Scrubland
Food	Forbs, grasses, and invertebrates.
Reproduction	Clutch of 8-10 eggs laid in ground nests.
Causes for Extinction	Overhunting; introduced predators; agricultural development.
Range	New Zealand
Photo	See Color Insert, C-2

pearance but the female possessed no rust on the face or throat. Rather, they were whitish and varied with brown. The male wing measured 110 millimeters (4.3 inches) and its tail was 40 mm (1.56 inches) long. The culmen was 12 mm (.47 inches) while the tarsus was 25 mm (.98 inches) in length. The female was slightly larger.

Behavior

Nests were made in depressions in the ground and were lined with grass. Females laid from 8 to 10 eggs which were yellowish brown or buff and spotted with darker brown. Eggs measured about 31 mm by 24 mm (1.2 by .9 inches) and incubation took 21 days. The chicks were precocial. A chick grew quickly after hatching and appeared similar to their parents within 4 months of being born.

Quail, in general, consume the seeds of a wide variety of forbs and grasses with the percentage of invertebrates consumed increasing during the summer. The species was active during the day.

Habitat

New Zealand quail inhabited the scrubland areas of New Zealand. The species required areas of grass covered down with undulating ground where it would nest in depressions.

Distribution

The species ranged over the South Island of New Zealand.

Causes for Extinction

When the species was first reported in 1769, it was noted to be common. Yet, 100 years later, it was on the verge of extinction. The species was hunted by early European colonists who were reminded of the sport they had once enjoyed at home. In 1848, 42 individals were reported as being shot within a single day near the city of Nelson. Twenty years later, the species was gone.

Introduced mammalian predators may have had a negative impact on the species as well as a widespread procedure of burning off land in preparation for agriculture. Other reasons that have been suggested for extinction include an unidentified avian disease and the introduction of various closely related species including *Coturnix pectoralis*, *Synoicus australis*, *Synoicus ypsilophorus*, and various pheasant species. The exotic quails were not introduced until about 1865, which was not long before New Zealand quail was determined to be extinct, but the pheasants were brought to the islands as early as 1842. Competition and diseases from these species along with the introduction of mammalian predators (rats, dogs, cats, etc.), overcollecting, and habitat loss combined probably resulted in the extinction of New Zealand quail.

The species was valued by European colonists for hunting and was probably hunted by the Maori. Overcollecting for sport and food may have been an important contributing factor in the extinction of New Zealand quail.

Adapted from data compiled by the Threatened and Endangered Species Information Institute (Golden, CO) for *Beacham's International Threatened, Endangered, and Extinct Species* published on CD ROM, available from Beacham Publishing.

Huia
Heteraloca acutirostris

Description

The Huia, *Heteraloca acutirostris*, was a perching bird which grew to a length of 48 centimeters (19 inches). Its plumage was black with metallic green throughout and a broad, white terminal tail band. It possessed a large, rounded, fleshy and wrinkled piece of deep orange skin that hung from its chin (like a turkey). Its eyes were brown and its legs and feet bluish grey. Both males and females were colored alike except for the shape of the bill. In both sexes, the base of bill was ivory-white turning to blackish grey at the base. The whitish bills of the male and female were so different that the first specimens to reach Europe were considered distinct species. The male's bill was of medium length, stout, straight, chisel-like and sturdy. The female's was long, delicate, thinner and gracefully down-curved. Immature individuals possessed dull black plumage that was suffused with brown.

Male wingspans were from 210 to 220 millimeters (mm). Their tail was 20 mm (.78 in); culmen from 57 to 60 mm (2.3 to 2.34 in); and tarsus from 84 to 86 mm (3.28 to 3.35 in). The wingspan in the female extended from 200 to 205 mm (7.8 to 8 in). Female tail lengths were from 195 to 200 mm (7.6 to 7.8

Status	Extinct
Probable Extinction	1907
Family	Callaeidae
Description	Medium-sized perching bird with black and metallic green plumage, a white tail band, and a piece of deep orange skin that hung from its chin like a turkey.
Habitat	Mountain and lowland forests of New Zealand.
Food	Larvae and insects.
Reproduction	Nests located in hollow trees or in clumps in dense vegetation.
Causes for Extinction	Destruction of habitat, exotic predators, hunting.
Range	New Zealand
Photo	See Color Insert, C-3

in); culmen from 85 to 88 mm (3.3 to 3.4 in); and tarsus up to 78 mm (3 in).

Behavior

Nesting occurred in November. Clutch

sizes ranged from 2 to 4 eggs. Eggs were stone grey with brown and purple spots. The male/female pair bond was very strong. A number of records state how an individual would cry and show signs of distress at the shooting of its mate. It would often stay in the general area where the shooting took place and search for its partner rather than flee evident danger. The species migrated from its upper forest habitat in the mountains in the summer to its lower forest habitat of the lower elevations and valleys in the winter.

The species fed on larvae and insects living in rotten tree trunks. The male's thick, short beak allowed it to strip the bark off the trunk by pecking at it almost like a woodpecker. Once the bark was off the tree, males would take the insects that were the most accessible just beneath the bark while the female used her more delicate beak to pull out larvae from the deeper crevices of the trunk. This adaptation suggested that the sexes needed close cooperation.

The species preferred the Huhus (*Prionoplus reticularis*), a nocturnal beetle, and its larvae. Larvae of this species were large and plump, like a human finger.

Pairs of these large, glossy-black birds hunted together on or near the ground in deep forests for wood-boring grubs, the male chiseling away the bark and wood to expose the bores, the female probing the holes to extract the grubs.

After seizing their meal, Huia transported their prey to a perch were the victim would be secured with the foot. Hard parts of the larvae were ripped off and discarded. The larvae was then thrown up and caught in the species' bill and swallowed whole.

The species was active during the day when its nocturnal prey was in its nest.

Habitat

The species inhabited the mountain forests of New Zealand's North Island as well as adjacent stretches of lowland forest. It depended on old stands of upper and low land forests which provided nesting sites for its chief source of food, the nocturnal beetles and other insects. It may have been restricted to sections of the Rimutaka, Tararua, Ruahine and Kaimanawa Ranges.

Nests were located in hollow trees or in clumps of dense vegetation.

Distribution

The home range of this species included the Rimutaka, Tararua, Ruahine, and Kaimanawa Ranges along with their adjacent stretches, all of the lowland forest in the southern half of New Zealand's North Island. It was argued in the last century that the species also inhabited areas more to the north and even the South Island in the Marlborough and Nelson districts.

The species was limited by its habitat requirements. When these forests were cut down, the species upon which they preyed disappeared. In 1907, two males and a female were seen a few days after Christmas. This was the last time the species was seen alive. The last of the species probably were found in the rough, high mountain portions of its range.

Causes for Extinction

The species was sacred to the Maori, a Polynesian tribe native to New Zealand. They made pendants, amulets, and carved wooden boxes in the species' image. The species' feathers were worn in battle, given as tokens of friendship and marks of respect, and used during funeral rites.

When Europeans came to the islands, the skins of the species were objects of commercial trade. The species was stuffed and used to decorate colonial drawing rooms. Many were exported to museums and collectors.

Much of this species' habitat was destroyed beginning from the date the first humans set foot upon New Zealand. Much of the forests were converted to farm and grazing land and this process accelerated when the Europeans arrived.

Europeans also introduced exotic mammalian predators and diseases that proved fatal to Huia. Ticks (*Haemaphysalis leachi* and *Hyalomma aegyptiumwere*) and the diseases they transmitted were introduced, to which the species had no immunity.

Hunting may have also contributed to the species' decline. The Maoris were believed to have been careful not to hunt the species past its ability to sustain its numbers. When numbers fell low, local chieftains imposed bans. However, after war with the Europeans, their culture and society in shambles, many Maori were dispirited and hunted the species to sell to the Europeans.

Adapted from data compiled by the Threatened and Endangered Species Information Institute (Golden, CO) for *Beacham's International Threatened, Endangered, and Extinct Species* published on CD ROM, available from Beacham Publishing.

Laughing Owl
Sceloglaux albifacies

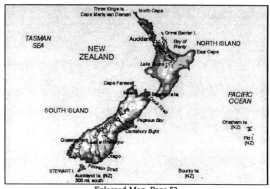

Enlarged Map, Page 52

Description

The laughing owl, *Sceloglaux albifacies*, was a large owl averaging 16-19 inches (45 centimeters) in length with wing measurements of 260-280 millimeters (10.1-10.9 in), tails 160-175 mm (6.2-6.8 in), culmen 25 mm (.98 in), and tarsus 65-68 mm (2.5-2.65 in). This hornless owl had a whitish facial disk with gray to dark rufous markings toward the center of the disk. The sides of the head, forehead, and throat were grayish-white while the sides of the neck were white (these feathers had a dark vein). The crown and nape feathers were a dark brown edged in yellowish-brown or white. The back and rump were dark brown with some streaking, spots and bars (tawny and white) on the lower back. The throat and breast were dark brown with a lighter margin to the feathers. The belly, sides, and undertail coverts were a yellowish-brown with a darker vein on each feather. The feathered legs were a lighter brown. The bill and nails were black, the irises were yellow-brown, and the feet brown with a thin covering of stiff, yellow hairs. The tail was dark brown with lighter barring and a terminal tail band. The wing feathers were dark brown with lighter spots

Status	Extinct
Probable Extinction	c.1900
Family	Strigidae (Owls)
Description	Large hornless owl with a whitish facial disk; the head and throat were grayish-white while the sides of the neck were white.
Habitat	Open or brushy habitats with rock outcrops (often limestone) and caves.
Food	Beetles, lizards, native rats.
Reproduction	Clutch size averaged 2 eggs and incubation lasted about 25 days.
Causes for Extinction	Introduced mammalian predators.
Range	New Zealand
Photo	See Color Insert, C-4

or bars along the edges.

The wings were somewhat reduced and

the legs were well developed, indicating that the species was probably a weak flier and spent a good percentage of the time on or near the ground.

The laughing owl was a member of the owl family, Strigidae. It was described and named *Athene albifacies* by G. R. Gray in 1844 from specimens collected by Percy Earl. Other scientific names applied to this species include *Sceloglaux rufifacies, Sceloglaux albifacies albifacies, Sceloglaux albifacies rubifacies, Ieraglaux albifacies,* and *Athene ejulans.* The Maoris named this owl "whekau."

Behavior

Eggs were laid in cavities beneath boulders; thin patches of grass were often found at the back of the cavity. Breeding commenced in September. Clutches included an average of 2 eggs and incubation lasted about 25 days. Females incubated the eggs most of the time but males did assist to some extent.

Chicks were fed worms. Based on analyzed casts or pellets, the adults consumed beetles, lizards, native rats (*Rattus exulans*) and probably a wide variety of other animal matter.

The laughing owl was apparently mostly nocturnal.

Habitat

The laughing owl inhabited more open or brushy habitats with rock outcrops (often limestone) and caves. Nests were placed under boulders; entrances were narrow and the cavities were often 5-6 yards (4.5-5.5 meters) deep.

Distribution

The laughing owl may have been in a population decline when discovered by white explorers; it was considered to be extremely rare by 1880 and was determined to have become extinct during the early part of the twentieth century, sometime after 1914.

The laughing owl was endemic to New Zealand. It occurred on both the North and South Islands, but appeared to be more common on the South Island.

Causes for Extinction

The laughing owl was collected and exported (dead and alive) to several European countries. Several live birds were known to have been sold as "pets" for prices exceeding 50 pounds. Collected birds were apparently easy to tame.

Although not confirmed, the introduction of the brown rat (*Rattus norvegicus*) may have precipitated the decline of this owl. Brown rats out-competed the native *R. exulans*, a primary food source of the laughing owl. Elimination of this food source may not have affected the owl; they probably switched to *R. norvegicus*. But the introduced rat's tendency to raid nests and destroy eggs or kill chicks probably did have a major impact on the species. They were especially vulnerable since they nested in ground level cavities or burrows that would have been preferred by the rats.

Other introduced mammalian predators (stoats and weasels) likely had a significant impact on this owl as well. The laughing owl was apparently a weak flier and would have been vulnerable to predation.

Stephen's Island Wren
Xenicus lyalli

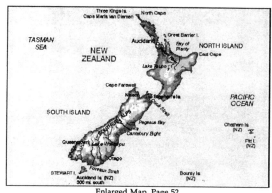

Enlarged Map, Page 52

Description

The Stephen's Island wren, *Xenicus lyalli,* was a small bird (4 inches or 10 centimeters) with a mottled brown upperside and a yellowish underside with a very short tail. Its bill was a bit thicker and the body a bit larger than the mainland members of this family (rifleman, *Acanthisitta chloris*; bush wren, *X. longipes* ssp.; and rock wren, *X. gilviventris*). The wings were reduced in size with rounded tips and soft feathers; this indicates that the species' flight capabilities were weak and some believe it may have been the only known flightless passerine.

Behavior

Reproductive habits for this species are unknown but they were probably similar to Stephen's Island Wren's close relatives on mainland New Zealand. *X. l. longipes* (South Island) apparently laid their clutches of 2 to 3 eggs in December; the Stewart Island birds laid eggs (2 to 3 per clutch) in November and December. Both sexes incubated the eggs and fed the chicks.

Food habits for Stephen's Island Wren are unknown. *X. l. longipes* is thought to

Status	Extinct
Probable Extinction	1894
Family	Acanthisittidae (Wrens)
Description	Small bird with a mottled brown upperside and a yellowish underside with a very short tail.
Habitat	Wooded or brushy areas within a rocky, rugged terrain.
Food	Perhaps insects foraged from bark.
Reproduction	Probably a clutch of 2-3 eggs hatched in December.
Causes for Extinction	A cat named Tibbles.
Range	New Zealand: Stephen's Island

have been primarily insectivorous. It fed most often in the foliage and on tree trunks, and sometimes on the ground, where it probed the bark and detritus for insects.

Behavioral data related to this species is limited but it appears that it may have been mostly crepuscular and even nocturnal, to some extent.

Reproductive habits are, again, mostly unknown. Mainland birds most likely nested above the ground more often; the Stewart Island and Stephen's Island birds may have nested in burrows (e.g., old petrel burrows), logs, or clumps of vegetation. *Acanthisitta chloris* (rifleman), another closely related species, nests on the ground and in trees up to 60 feet above the ground (average was 20 to 30 feet) in hollow limbs or crevices.

Habitat/Distribution

The Stephen's Island wren inhabited Stephen's (or Stephen) Island. This island is located between New Zealand's North and South Islands in the Cook Straight. The island is about one square mile (2.6 kilometers) in surface area with a peak elevation of 1,000 feet (305 meters). This wren most likely inhabited the wooded or brushy areas on this rocky, rugged island. Behavior and habitat preferences were, again, probably similar to *X. l. longipes* which inhabited the remote forests found on New Zealand's South Island, where it was observed running among or hiding in the bushes and rocks.

Causes for Extinction

A cat named Tibbles was credited and blamed for the discovery and subsequent dramatic decline and extinction of the Stephen's Island wren in 1894. This bird was, most likely, rare when discovered, and it was possibly the only passerine species to have lost (or nearly lost) its ability to fly. Additionally, Stephen's Island is very small. Many nests were located on or close to the ground where the birds were often observed feeding, making them easy prey.

Adapted from data compiled by the Threatened and Endangered Species Information Institute (Golden, CO) for *Beacham's International Threatened, Endangered, and Extinct Species* published on CD ROM, available from Beacham Publishing.

Auckland Islands Merganser
Mergus australis

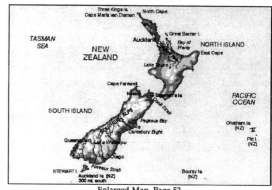

Enlarged Map, Page 52

Description

The Auckland Islands merganser, *Mergus australis,* was about 23 inches (58 cm) in length. Other measurements for males and females, respectively, were: wing - 192 mm (7.5 in), 180 mm (7 in); tail - 87 mm (3.4 in), 82 mm (3.2 in); culmen - 60 mm (2.34 in), 54 mm (2.1 in); and tarsus - 42 mm (1.64 in); 40 mm (1.56 in). It had a dark reddish-brown neck, head and crest with a lighter brown chin and throat. The back, scapulars, rump, and upper tail coverts were a dark bluish-black. The wings were a dark gray with black primaries and white tipped greater secondary coverts. The breast was a dull gray with a dark edged tip to the short, well-rounded feathers. The abdomen was a mottled gray and white. The legs and feet were orange to reddish brown. The lower mandible was yellow-orange with a dark tip and the upper mandible was mostly black. Females were similar to males but had a shorter crest and a grayish-red crown. The wings were reduced in size, but the species was still capable of limited flight.

Behavior

The breeding habits of *M. australis* are

Status	Extinct
Probable Extinction	c.1910
Family	Antidae (Ducks and Geese)
Description	Duck with a dark reddish-brown neck, head and crest with a lighter brown chin; bluish-black back and rump; and grey wings and breast.
Habitat	Freshwater streams and wetlands.
Food	Primarily fish, but also crustaceans, amphibians, insects and mollusks.
Reproduction	Probably nested in tree cavities.
Threats	Overcollecting; introduction of pigs, cats, mice, and rats.
Range	Auckland Islands
Photo	See Color Insert, C-3

unknown. Other mergansers often nest in tree cavities, but some do nest on the ground. Information concerning the food habits of *M. australis* is also limited. They were observed feeding on fish (*Galaxias* sp.) and freshwater shrimp. North American mergansers are primarily fish eaters but they also consume crustaceans, amphibians, insects and mollusks. Very little plant matter is consumed. Daily and seasonal activity patterns are unknown, but most waterfowl species are primarily diurnal.

Habitat

M. australis inhabited the Auckland Islands' freshwater streams and wetlands in the fjord-like inlets, and the upper portions (brackish) of the estuaries. The saltwater portions of the estuaries were probably utilized to some extent.

Distribution

M. australis inhabited the Auckland Islands (Auckland, Adams, and possibly Campbell), located about 200 miles (320 kilometers) south of the New Zealand mainland. The presence of the species on Campbell Island is thought to be doubtful. Fossil remains of *M. australis* have been found around Rangitoto, a volcano on New Zealand's North Island.

The Northern Hemisphere supports five species of merganser, most with widespread distributions. The Southern Hemisphere had two species, an extant species in Brazil and *M. australis*. This species, restricted to the Auckland Islands and New Zealand, was separated from its nearest relatives by several thousand miles and a large expanse of open ocean.

Causes for Extinction

Reasons for the decline and extinction of *M. australis* are undocumented but it is thought that the presence of humans (by overcollecting) and the introduction of pigs, cats, mice, and rats probably were the primary factors. This species' habit of hiding among the rocks instead of diving to avoid danger left it vulnerable to collection and predation. Rats undoubtedly raided and destroyed the mergansers' nests. *M. australis* was probably widely hunted for food by the Maori and by European explorers, convicts, and settlers.

Pigs were introduced to the islands in 1806 and rats probably colonized the islands long before that. *M. australis* was may have been uncommon by the time Hombron and Jacquinot collected and described the species in the late 1830s.

Adapted from data compiled by the Threatened and Endangered Species Information Institute (Golden, CO) for *Beacham's International Threatened, Endangered, and Extinct Species* published on CD ROM, available from Beacham Publishing.

Modest Rail
Gallirallus modestus

Enlarged Map, Page 52

Description

The modest rail, *Gallirallus modestus*, was a small rail, averaging 17.8 centimeters (7 inches) in length. Wing measurements taken from specimens were: male, 88 millimeters (3.43 in); female, 76 mm (2.96 in). It was pale brown with light barring on the breast. A more detailed description lists the bird as an olive-brown color above with a gray chin, gray-brown throat, breast, belly, and tail (these feathers were lightly edged in white, giving the bird a barred look), and the wings were brownish with barring. The legs and bill were light brown. The bill was fairly long and decurved. Chicks resembled the adults for the most part; they may have initially been a brownish black color. *G. modestus* was sexually dimorphic; the female was smaller, more heavily barred on the breast and its bill was much shorter. This dimorphism was quite possibly a result of the very narrow ecological niche filled by this rail; so narrow the males and females developed divergent feeding habits. *G. modestus* was completely or almost completely flightless.

Status	Extinct
Probable Extinction	Mid-1800s
Family	Rallidae (Rails, Gallinules, and Coots)
Description	Small, pale-brown bird with light barring on the breast and wings, gray chin, gray-brown throat, breast and belly and tail.
Habitat	Freshwater, brackish or saltwater marshes.
Food	Insects
Reproduction	Nested in burrows in the ground.
Threats	Competition from other rails; feral predators, habitat loss.
Range	New Zealand: Chatham, Pitt and Mangare Islands.

Behavior

Being flightless (or mostly so), the species was not migratory. *G. modestus* was known to consume insects. Remains of beetles and sand hoppers (crustaceans) were found in specimen stomachs.

Habitat

Members of the rail family, *Rallidae*, typically inhabit freshwater, brackish, or saltwater emergent marshes. Nests were placed in burrows in the ground; newly hatched chicks were moved to fallen, hollow trees.

Distribution

G. modestus inhabited three of the Chatham Islands group: Chatham Island; Pitt Island; and Mangare Island. The Chatham Islands are located several hundred miles off the east coast of New Zealand. By the time it was discovered by H. H. Travers in 1871, the species had already been extirpated from Chatham and Pitt Islands and was uncommon on Mangare Island (only 1.25 square kilometers or .43 square miles in area). It was eliminated from Mangare Island by 1900.

Causes for Extinction

Competition with the larger Dieffenbach's rail (*Gallirallus dieffenbachii* or *Rallus philippensis dieffenbachii*) may have led to the decline and extinction of *G. modestus* on the islands of Chatham and Pitt.

The widespread destruction of habitat on the island of Mangare following its discovery by Europeans and collecting of *G. modestus* were probably responsible for the species' extirpation on Mangare Island less than 30 years after its discovery. The introduction of feral cats, goats, and rabbits and frequent bush fires caused an incredible amount of damage to all habitats and species on the islands. Large sections of the island were converted to pasture for sheep.

Adapted from data compiled by the Threatened and Endangered Species Information Institute (Golden, CO) for *Beacham's International Threatened, Endangered, and Extinct Species* published on CD ROM, available from Beacham Publishing.

Dieffenbach's Rail
Rallus dieffenbachii

Enlarged Map, Page 52

Description

Dieffenbach's rail, *Rallus dieffenbachii*, is regarded by some experts as a subspecies of *R. philippensis dieffenbachii* (banded rail), a now rare New Zealand species. *R. dieffenbachii* was similar in appearance and probably in its habits to this New Zealand species. It was considered to be a medium sized rail, averaging 11 to 12 inches in length. *R. philippensis* is described as a bird with an olive-brown back with black and white spots, a white streak above the eye, a chestnut streak through the eye back to the hindneck, a chestnut band across the breast, a whitish chin, a gray foreneck and throat, and a black belly with narrow, irregular white barring. The feet were brown and the bill reddish-brown. *R. dieffenbachii* differed from *R. philippensis* in the following ways: the throat band was black and white; the breast was barred with brown and black; the bill was thicker and more recurved; the crown and hind neck were a reddish brown color; the streak above the eyes was gray; and the chin and throat were a pale gray.

The Maori name for this species is "meri-ki" or "moeriki". *R. dieffenbachii* is also called the Chatham Islands banded rail.

R. modestus (modest rail) and *R.*

Status	Extinct
Probable Extinction	Mid-1800s
Family	Rallidae (Rails, Gallinules, and Coots)
Description	Medium-sized bird with an olive-brown, white-spotted back, and a white streak above the eye.
Habitat	Mangrove swamps, salt and fresh water marshes, and inland creeks.
Food	Animal matter found in mud and other substrates.
Reproduction	Clutch of 4-7 eggs laid September-February.
Causes for Extinction	Habitat loss, exotic cats, goats and rabbits.
Range	Chatham, Pitt and Mangare Islands.

philippensis dieffenbachii (or *R. dieffenbachii*) (Dieffenbach's rail) are thought to be closely related. *R. modestus* evolved from a species which colonized the Chatham Islands from New Zealand. This New Zealand species (*Rallus philippensis*) is thought to have invaded (colonized) this island group in two waves. *R. p. dieffenbachii* probably evolved from the same New Zealand species during the second invasion (colonization).

Behavior

Being mostly flightless, the species was not migratory. This rail probed the mud and other substrates for prey items. Rails, in general, are somewhat omnivorous, but primarily consume animal matter. Nests were placed in thick stands of grasses or rushes adjacent to or over water. Eggs were laid from September through February; clutches contained 4 to 7 eggs. Incubation lasted about 18 days. Both sexes incubated. Two broods may have been completed per year.

Habitat

Members of the rail family, *Rallidae*, typically inhabit freshwater, brackish, or saltwater emergent marshes.

R. dieffenbachii was thought to be a subspecies of *R. philippensis* and apparently was similar in habit to this species. *R. philippensis* inhabits mangrove swamps, salt and freshwater emergent marshes, inland creeks, and open areas adjacent to these habitats.

R. dieffenbachii was thought to inhabit the tussock grass marshes on the Chatham Islands.

Distribution

This species once inhabited the Chatham Islands group which includes Chatham Island, Pitt Island, and Mangare Island. The Chatham Islands are located several hundred miles off the east coast of New Zealand. *R.*

dieffenbachii was extirpated from these islands by the mid 1800s, not long after its discovery.

Causes for Extinction

The widespread destruction of habitat on the islands following their discovery by Europeans was probably responsible for the species' extirpation from the islands less than 5 years after its discovery. The introduction of feral cats, goats, and rabbits and frequent bush fires caused an incredible amount of damage to all habitats and species on the islands. Large sections of the islands were converted to pasture for sheep.

Adapted from data compiled by the Threatened and Endangered Species Information Institute (Golden, CO) for *Beacham's International Threatened, Endangered, and Extinct Species* published on CD ROM, available from Beacham Publishing.

EXTINCT BIRDS OF THE FAR EAST ISLANDS

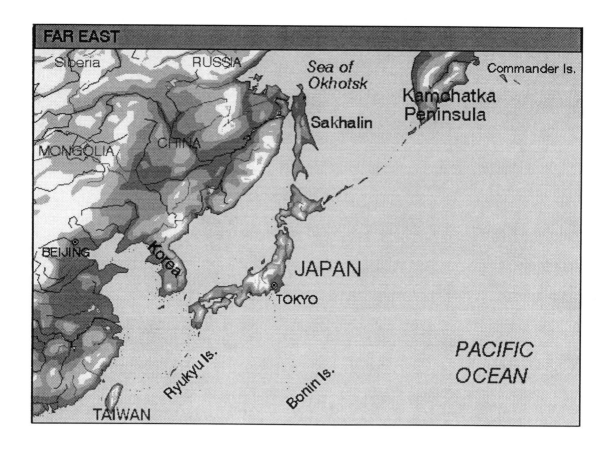

Bonin Islands

The Bonin Islands comprise about 30 volcanic islands in the central Pacific Ocean, 500 miles southeast of Japan; the chain of islands is about 50 miles long with a combined area of only 29 square miles. Situated in a strategic position to East Asia, the islands have historically been used for navigational and military purposes, and as a result have been subjected to the introduction of exotic species and military operations that disrupt native species and habitat. About 90 percent of the islands are hilly, and at one time were heavily forested with cedar, rosewood, ironwood, boxwood, sandalwood, and white oak. Valuable timber harvesting and offshore whaling constitute the basis of the economy.

The Peel or Beechey Island group is just south of the Parry group. Peel Island is the largest in the Bonin Island group about 9.5 by 4.5 miles. Peel Island is the type locality for most of the unique avian species found in this island group. The Bonin Islands are volcanic in origin and occur in a warm climate.

Ryukyu Islands

The Ryukyu Islands or Archipelago includes 55 islands with a total land area of 900 square miles. These islands are strung between Japan on the north and Formosa on the south. The islands fall into four major groups from north to south: 1) Satsunan Shoto — this group, which is about 20 miles south of Kiushu, Japan, includes 2 large islands, Yaku Shima and Tanega Shima; 2) Linshoten Islands; 3) an unnamed group which contains the islands of Amami and Okinawa; and 4) Sakishima Gunto — this group is about 75 miles northeast of Formosa. Temperatures in this area range from 60 to 80 degrees Fahrenheit, and more open pine forests typify the island's vegetation. The larger islands are volcanic, with mountainous terrain, while the smaller islands are coralline and relatively flat. With a semi-tropical climate, the Ryukyus are subject to annual typhoons that threaten avian wildlife. The Ryukyus are primarily rural. Agriculture, including sugar and pineapples, is the dominant occupation. Fishing, lacquer and pottery manufacturing, whaling, and some industrial plants are growing industries.

Bonin Island Grosbeak
Chaunoproctus ferreirostris

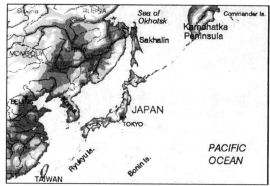

Enlarged Map, Page 76

Description

The Bonin Island grosbeak, *Chaunoproctus ferreirostris*, was about 8 inches (20 centimeters) in length. The male's throat, upper breast, chin, cheeks, lores, and forehead were an orangish-red color. The belly was a lighter shade of orange-red fading to a whitish color toward the tail. The crown, nape, back, rump, wings, and tail were an olive brown color. The bill was thick and short like a grosbeak's.

C. ferreirostris was a member of the finch family, Fringillidae. It was described and named *Coccothraustes ferreirostris* by Vigors in 1828. Other common names applied to this species include the Bonin finch.

Behavior

Von Kittlitz found small fruits and buds in the stomachs of specimens he collected.

Habitat

The warm volcanic, forested terrain of Peel Island would have provided dense cover and an ample food supply for this bird that was generally observed on the ground foraging for small fruits and buds.

Status	Extinct
Probable Extinction	c.1828
Family	Fringillidae (Finches)
Description	Bird about 8 inches in length; male's throat, upper breast, chin, cheeks, lores, and forehead were an orangish-red color; belly was a lighter shade of orange-red; the crown, nape, back, rump, wings, and tail were an olive brown color.
Habitat	Volcanic forests.
Food	Small fruits and buds.
Causes for Extinction	Predation by rats.
Range	Bonin Islands: Peel Island

Distribution

The Bonin Island grosbeak was endemic to Peel Island (Chichi-jima) in the Beechey Island group.

The species was generally observed alone or in pairs. The Bonin Island grosbeak was considered an uncommon species when it was discovered and soon succumbed to extinction (c. 1830).

Causes for Extinction

The Bonin Island grosbeak may have been collected for food by island residents. It is not known whether or not this occurred, and if so, to what extent it affected the stability of the population.

Peel Island was settled two years (1830) after von Kittlitz discovered *Z. terrestris* and saw the Bonin Island grosbeak, but von Kittlitz noted the presence of pigs, rats, and cats during his visit. The island was settled by American and British sailors, and a few Polynesians. Whalers began to use the island as a repairs stopover. Rats and cats most likely escaped from ships being repaired. As on other islands in the Pacific and Indian Oceans, rats were probably responsible for the decline of several endemic species. Both ground and tree nesting species were vulnerable to the rats. The rats raided nests, destroying the eggs and killing the young chicks. Adults may also have been preyed upon to some extent.

Adapted from data compiled by the Threatened and Endangered Species Information Institute (Golden, CO) for *Beacham's International Threatened, Endangered, and Extinct Species* published on CD ROM, available from Beacham Publishing.

Bonin Wood Pigeon
Columba versicolor

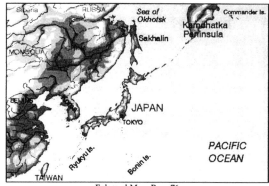

Enlarged Map, Page 76

Description

The Bonin wood pigeon, *Columba versicolor*, was a large bird (18 inches or 46 centimeters long) with the male having an iridescent grayish-black back, rump, upper wing coverts, crown and mantle; the iridescence appeared primarily as a bright amethyst, bright red-purple or golden-green except for the coverts which were a golden-green iridescence. The lower wing and tail were grayish-black but were not iridescent. The underparts and face were gray; the breast had a tinge of glossy golden-green. The bill was greenish yellow and the legs/feet were dark red.

This species is also called the Bonin black pigeon, Bonin fruit pigeon, and shining pigeon.

Status	Extinct
Probable Extinction	Early 1900s
Family	Columbidae (Doves and Pigeons).
Description	Large pigeon with an iridescent grayish-black back, rump, upper wing coverts, crown and mantle.
Habitat	Forests on warm volcanic islands.
Food	Probably fruits, seeds, buds, and new-growth vegetation.
Causes for Extinction	Habitat loss; introduced predators.
Range	Japan: Bonin Islands

Behavior

Information of the food habits of this species is lacking but it probably ate fruits, seeds, buds, and new-growth vegetation. Most pigeons and doves are primarily diurnal.

Habitat

The Bonin wood pigeon inhabited Nakondo Shima and Peel Island in the Bonin Island group. The pigeons nested in trees on Peel Island and probably on Nakondo Shima. These two islands may have been the only lands with enough forested habitat to support the species. Records are scarce so it is possible that Bonin wood pigeon occurred on some of the smaller forested islands.

Distribution

The Bonin wood pigeon was endemic to the Bonin Islands which are about 500+ miles (800 kilometers) southeast of Japan. It was known to inhabit Nakondo Shima and Peel Island and may have occurred on some of the smaller forested islands as well.

This species' population was probably never very large. It began to decline following the establishment of a permanent settlement in the 1830s. Logs from ships that stopped at the islands in the 1850s mentioned that all the birds were very rare. In 1889, the Bonin wood pigeon still occurred on Nakondo Shima in small numbers but was not found on Peel Island. By the early part of the 1900s all the rare birds were gone.

Causes for Extinction

Three of four species known to inhabit Peel Island are now extinct. All the populations appeared to decline dramatically following the establishment of a settlement on the island in the 1830s. The three extinct species were hunted extensively for food, especially following the severe typhoons that periodically hit the islands. Habitat loss caused by clearing and overgrazing/trampling by domestic livestock, and possibly the introduction of exotic birds and predators (e.g., rats) may have impacted the species. Competition from introduced species, the introduction of new diseases, and increases in predation led to the decline and extinction of other Pacific Island species. Shipwrecks were responsible for introducing rats, deer, goats, pigs, sheep, cats, and dogs to the islands.

Adapted from data compiled by the Threatened and Endangered Species Information Institute (Golden, CO) for *Beacham's International Threatened, Endangered, and Extinct Species* published on CD ROM, available from Beacham Publishing.

Bonin Island Thrush
Zoothera terrestris

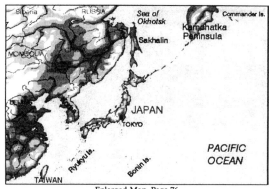

Enlarged Map, Page 76

Description

The Bonin Island thrush, *Zoothera terrestris*, was about 9 inches (23 cm) in length. The wing was 3.9 inches (99 mm) in length, the tail 2.6 inches (66 mm), the culmen .86 inch (22 mm), and the tarsus 1.1 inches (28 mm). *Z. terrestris* was olive-brown above with a rufous tinge to the rump and tail and dark streaks on the back and shoulders. The lores were a dark brown; the eye line was indistinct. The chin and central throat and belly were whitish, darkening to an olive-brown on the sides.

The Bonin Island thrush was a member of the thrush and chat family, Turdidae. It was described and named *Turdus terrestris* by F. H. von Kittlitz in 1830 from specimens he collected on Peel Island in 1829. Other scientific names applied to this species include *Geocichla terrestris, Cichlopasser terrestris,* and *Aegithocichla terrestris.* The Bonin Island thrush was also called the Bonin thrush and Kittlitz's thrush.

Status	Extinct
Probable Extinction	c.1850
Family	Turdidae (Thrushes)
Description	Thrush measuring about 9 inches in length; wings were olive-brown above with a rufous tinge to the rump and tail with dark streaks on the back and shoulders.
Habitat	Ground dweller.
Food	Probably consumed a variety of plant and animal matter.
Reproduction	Ground nester.
Causes for Extinction	Predation by rats.
Range	Bonin Islands: Peel Island

Behavior

Food habits for this species are unknown but they, like their relatives, probably consumed a variety of plant and animal matter. Nests were built on the ground.

Habitat

The Bonin Island thrush was a ground

dweller.

Distribution

The Bonin Island thrush inhabited (and may have been limited to) Peel Island in the Beechey Island group, a part of the Bonin Islands which are about 500+ miles (800 kilometers) southeast of Japan. The species may have occurred on other islands in the chain, but records only exist for Peel Island.

The last specimens of the Bonin Island thrush were collected in 1828. Naval expeditions visiting the island in the 1850s indicated that the species was rare at that time. Surveys in 1889, 1920, and 1930 failed to locate the species. This species is believed extinct from Bonin Islands (Peel Island) after approximately 1850.

Causes for Extinction

Peel Island was settled two years (1830) after von Kittlitz discovered the Bonin Island thrush, but von Kittlitz noted the presence of pigs, rats, and cats during his visit. The island was settled by American and British sailors, and a few Polynesians. Whalers began to use the island as a repairs stopover. Rats and cats most likely escaped from ships being repaired. As on other islands in the Pacific and Indian Oceans, rats were probably responsible for the decline of several endemic species. Both ground and tree nesting species were vulnerable to the rats. The rats raided nests, destroying the eggs and killing the young chicks. Adults may also have been preyed upon to some extent.

The Bonin Island thrush may have been collected for food by island residents. It is not known whether or not this occurred, and if so, to what extent it affected the stability of the population.

Adapted from data compiled by the Threatened and Endangered Species Information Institute (Golden, CO) for *Beacham's International Threatened, Endangered, and Extinct Species* published on CD ROM, available from Beacham Publishing.

Ryukyu Wood Pigeon
Columba jouyi

Enlarged Map, Page 76

Description

The Ryukyu wood pigeon, *Columba jouyi*, was a large (about 18 inches), mostly black pigeon with a purplish iridescence on the upper neck (back and sides) and a greenish iridescence on the lower back. A silvery crescent-shaped band divided the lower back part of the neck from the crown. The feet were purple and the bill was greenish blue with a lighter tip. Variations in plumage between the sex and age classes have not been documented.

This species is also called the silver-crescented pigeon and Riu-Kiu black wood pigeon.

Behavior

Information of the food habits of this species is lacking but it probably ate fruits, seeds, buds, and new-growth vegetation.

Most pigeons and doves are primarily diurnal.

Habitat

The Ryukyu wood pigeon inhabited the

Status	Extinct
Probable Extinction	Before 1945
Family	Columbidae (Doves and Pigeons)
Description	Large mostly black pigeon with a purplish iridescence on the upper neck (back and sides); a greenish iridescence on the lower back; and a silvery crescent-shaped band dividing the lower back part of the neck from the crown.
Habitat	Denser areas of pine forests.
Food	Probably fruits, seeds, buds, and new-growth vegetation.
Causes for Extinction	Habitat destruction.
Range	Japan: Ryukyu Islands

more densely forested habitats on Sheya Jima, Ijina (Izena) Shima, Yagaji Shima (Yagachi), Zamami Shima, and Okinawa. Similar habitats were probably utilized on the inhabited Borodino Islands (Minami and Kita Daito Jima).

Distribution

The Ryukyu wood pigeon inhabited the Ryukyu Islands (Nansei-shoto) of Sheya Jima, Ijina (Izena) Shima, Yagaji Shima (Yagachi), Zamami Shima, and Okinawa. It also was found on the Borodino Islands of Minami and Kita Daito Jima.

Surveys in the 1930s revealed the presence of Ryukyu wood pigeon within its known range. This species was not found during a 1945 survey.

Causes for Extinction

This species' decline and extinction is thought to have been caused, in part, by the widespread loss of forested habitats. Logging and clearing for urban and agricultural development resulted in the loss of a large percentage of the habitats required by the Ryukyu wood pigeon.

This species was probably hunted by island residents and may have provided an important source of food. Hunting for sport may also have occurred but this has not been documented.

The species was still present in the Ryukyu Islands in the 1930s but a 1945 survey failed to find the species. Activities related to World War II may have accelerated the demise of the species. Hunting pressures may have increased if island residents had a difficult time obtaining food from other sources. Habitat destruction or alterations would have increased during this period in association with the following: bombs dropped on the islands could have destroyed large areas of inhabited forests; increases in human activity (including bombing) near its nesting areas could have disrupted the reproductive cycle; and forest clearing for shelter and firewood may have increased.

Adapted from data compiled by the Threatened and Endangered Species Information Institute (Golden, CO) for *Beacham's International Threatened, Endangered, and Extinct Species* published on CD ROM, available from Beacham Publishing.

Ryukyu Kingfisher
Halcyon miyakoensis

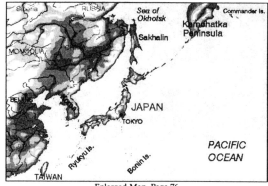

Enlarged Map, Page 76

Description

The Ryukyu kingfisher, *Halcyon miyakoensis*, possessed black lores and small patches over its bluish-white eyes. A stripe passed beneath the eye and extended to the side of the greenish-blue nape where it widened. The remainder of the head and neck were a deep cinnamon-chestnut color. Its back and scapulars were dark blue-green. Its lower back and upper tail coverts were a bright cobalt blue. The primaries were dull brownish-black, wing coverts and tail were ultramarine tinged with green, and the underparts were a uniform cinnamon. The feet were dark red and the claws were dark brown.

Ryukyu kingfisher's wing extended to 105 millimeters (4.1 in). Its tail was 80 mm (3.12 in) long, and its tarsus was 17 mm (.66 in) long.

Science has not established whether or not this is a valid species. The only specimen ever collected sits in the Tokyo museum, where it has been since 1887. It was taken in the Ryukyu Islands; however, this specimen was not described until 30 years later, in 1919, by Kuroda. Biologists treat with caution any species that has been described from only one specimen. This specimen may

Status	Extinct
Probable Extinction	c.1887
Family	Alcedinidae (Kingfishers)
Description	Small bird with a dark blue-green back, bright cobalt blue upper tail, wing coverts and lower tail ultamarine, and its underparts cinnamon.
Food	Probably fish, crustaceans reptiles, amphibians, and small invertebrates.
Range	Japan: Ryukyu Islands

be a hybrid of another species. And, since it was described so long after it was collected, there is room for many errors. Though the museum in Tokyo gives the collection locality as Miyako-shima which is one of the Ryukyu Islands, museum labels are commonly known to be incorrect.

Also throwing doubt on this species is the fact that the color of its beak cannot be determined. The mandibles lack their horny covering. Thus, the species' nearest extant relative possesses a beak which is mostly black except for a pale yellow area at the base of the lower mandible. This species is the Micronesian Kingfisher (*Halcyon cinnamomina*). *H. miyakoensis* may simply be a race of Cinnamomina.

The common name of this species is kingfisher. This comes from the Anglo-Saxon meaning "king of the fishes". The Belted Kingfisher comes from the belt of blue-gray feathers across its white breast. The name of this species, Ryukyu, comes from the locality the only specimen is believed to have come from.

This species is also referred to by the common name "Miyako kingfisher".

Behavior

Nothing is known of this species' reproductive phenology, or migration patterns. The food habits are not known but kingfishers, in general, consume fish, crustaceans, reptiles, amphibians, and small invertebrates.

Habitat

The only type specimen of this species was taken from the Ryukyu Islands south of Japan. Beyond this, nothing is known of its habitat or habitat requirements.

Distribution

The only known collection of the species occurred on Miyako-shima, on one of the Ryukyu Islands south of Japan. Yet, even this fact is doubted among biologists. Nothing else is known of the past distribution of this species.

Causes for Extinction

There are no apparent reasons for the decline of this species, since little is known about its occurrence.

Adapted from data compiled by the Threatened and Endangered Species Information Institute (Golden, CO) for *Beacham's International Threatened, Endangered, and Extinct Species* published on CD ROM.

Korean Crested Shelduck

Tadorna cristata

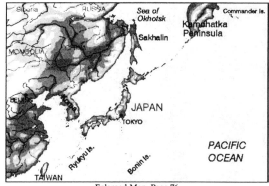

Enlarged Map, Page 76

Description

The Korean crested shelduck, *Tadorna cristata*, was about 25-28 inches (63-71 centimeters) long and slightly larger in body size than a mallard. Mature males had a black (greenish-black or metallic green crown (extending from the base of the upper mandible to the nape), breast, primaries, tail, and upper tail coverts. The remainder of the face, chin, and throat were a brownish black color. The belly, undertail coverts, and flanks were a dark gray with fine black striations. The upper wing coverts were white and the speculum was an iridescent green. The bill and legs were pinkish. Mature females had a white eye-ring, a black crest (from the eyes back to the nape), a white face, chin, throat, neck, and upper wing coverts, and a dark brown (with fine white striations) body. Immature plumages are not known.

Ruddy shelducks (*T. ferruginea*) breeding in Korea commence egg-laying in late April through June. Clutch sizes for the various shelduck species range from 6-14 eggs with 8-10 eggs being the average. Incubation lasts from 27-32 days and is the sole responsibility of the female but males do defend the breeding territory. The chicks are precocial and fledging occurs in about 7-10 weeks.

Status	Extinct
Probable Extinction	c.1916
Family	Anatidae (Ducks and Geese)
Description	Large duck with (males) a black (greenish-black or metallic green) crown, breast, primaries, tail, and upper tail coverts; the remainder of the face, chin, and throat were a brownish black color.
Habitat	Wide variety of wetland and deep-water habitats.
Food	Vegetation, agricultural crops, algae, invertebrates, garbage, and carrion.
Reproduction	Clutch sizes range from 6-14 eggs, averaging 8-10 eggs; incubation lasts from 27-32 days.
Causes for Extinction	Overcollecting; habitat loss.
Range	Russia (Siberia), Korea, and Japan

T. cristata may have been a migratory species, traveling to Siberia for breeding and wintering and/or breeding in Korea, southern Russia, and Japan.

T. cristata was a member of the duck, goose, and swan family, Anatidae, and the shelgoose and shelduck tribe, Tadornini. It was described and named *Pseudotadorna cristata* by Kuroda in 1917 from specimens collected along the Naktung River near Fusan, Korea. *T. cristata* was initially thought to be a hybrid and was named *Tadorna casarca x Querquedula falcata* by Sclater in 1890. Only three specimens exist: two are from Korea and the third was collected near Vladivostok in the former USSR.

This species is also referred to by the following common names: Korean shelduck; crested shelduck; Schopfkasarka (German); tadorna huppe (French); and oca de Corea (Spanish).

Behavior

Some shelduck species are primarily herbivorous while others are more dependent on animal matter. New, green vegetation, agricultural crops (cereal grains, millet), algae, invertebrates, garbage, and carrion (ruddy shelduck) are consumed.

The ruddy shelduck is more active at night, and in the late evening and early morning hours. Information on periodicity for other shelduck species is unknown.

Shelducks are almost always found in pairs and, generally, are part of a small or large flock. The largest flocks are usually observed during the post-breeding molt.

Habitat

Shelducks, in general, inhabit a wide variety of wetland and deep-water habitats from high elevation (4,000-4,500 meters) steppe lakes and rivers to lowland rivers, lakes, brackish and saltwater marshes (open areas) and tidal flats to the open ocean. Grains such as millet and wheat may constitute a portion of the fall diet so agricultural fields are important to some shelducks.

Other shelducks nest in burrows or cavities (natural and manmade).

Distribution

T. cristata may have been fairly common about 200 years ago when this shelduck was exported to Japan but apparently suffered a decline in population size between that time and the time of its description.

T. cristata occurred in Korea and Ussuriland, Russia. Specimens were collected near Vladivostok (Russia) and near Fusan and Kunsan (Kun-Kiang River), Korea. Greenway indicates the species' range may have included eastern Siberia (breeding habitat), and Korea and Japan (winter habitat and possibly breeding habitat).

T. cristata has a designated status of extinct, as of approximately 1916. In Korea and Russia, the species may have been sighted in 1943 near Chushinhokudo and in the Rimskii-Korsakov Archipelago (located southwest of Vladivostok) in 1964. The 1964 sighting was of two females and a male in a small flock of harlequin ducks (*Histrionicus histrionicus*).

Causes for Extinction

The specific reasons for extinction are unknown, but habitat loss and overcollecting may have contributed to the decline. This species was apparently collected and exported to Japan and possibly to China in the early 1700s or earlier. Japanese aviculturists referred to the species as the chosen-oshi or Korean mandarin duck. Old Chinese tapestries and paintings depict a duck much like *T. cristata*.

Adapted from data compiled by the Threatened and Endangered Species Information Institute (Golden, CO) for *Beacham's International Threatened, Endangered, and Extinct Species* published on CD ROM.

Steller's Spectacled Cormorant

Phalacrocorax perspicillatus

Enlarged Map, Page 76

Description

Steller's spectacled cormorant, *Phalacrocorax perspicillatus,* possessed a naked area around the base of the bill which varied in color from blue to white. It had thick skin and was white-spectacled around the eyes. Its double crest projected from the occiput of greenish blue. The remainder of the head was a dark greenish blue and was decorated with long, hair-like pale yellow feathers extending onto the upper part of the neck. The body and wings were a deep bronze-green color which showed steel-blue reflections on the neck. The species possessed a large whitish patch on each flank. Its tail was black. The male and females appeared similar, but the female was smaller and lacked the crest and spectacles. The species' wing measured 342 millimeters (13.3 inches). Its tail was 180 mm (7 inches) long, culmen 74 mm (2.88 inches), and its tarsus, 72 mm (2.81 inches).

The species, like other cormorants, usually nested in colonies and laid eggs of blue covered with a white chalky layer.

Status	Extinct
Probable Extinction	c.1850
Family	Phalacrocoracidae
Description	Medium-large bird with a dark greenish-blue head with a double crest and decorated with long, hair-like, pale-yellow feathers extending to the neck; body and wings were a deep bronze green and the tail was black.
Habitat	Coastal waters.
Food	Marine invertebrates.
Reproduction	Nested in colors and produced blue eggs with a white, chalky layer.
Causes for Extinction	Unknown. Hunting contributed to the decline.
Range	Bering and Commander Islands
Photo	See Color Insert, C-1

Behavior

The species fed on fish and marine invertebrates. They dove, possibly to great depths, from the surface of the water to catch their prey. The species was active during the day.

Habitat/Distribution

The species was known from Bering Island, Commander Island, and other smaller islands around the general vicinity of the Bering Sea. The species inhabited coastal waters and probably did not roam too far from land.

Causes for Extinction

In the century after Steller's description, the species was exterminated systematically by sealers and other hunters who caught and ate them. During the 1820s, the species was imported to the island of Aleuts by commercial interests. Occasionally, when the species roamed to Kamchatka, the natives cooked them whole in clay pots — feathers and all.

Adapted from data compiled by the Threatened and Endangered Species Information Institute (Golden, CO) for *Beacham's International Threatened, Endangered, and Extinct Species* published on CD ROM.

EXTINCT BIRDS OF THE SOUTH PACIFIC ISLANDS

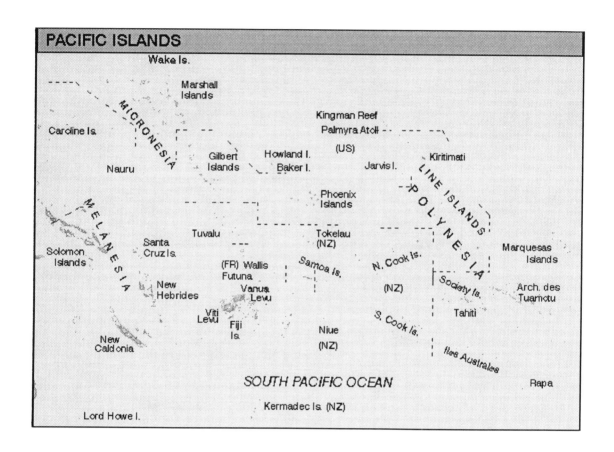

Caroline Islands

The Caroline Islands Archipelago spans a 2,000-mile east to west distance. The islands are north of Papua New Guinea, east of the Palau Islands and south of Guam. There are about 500 islands and islets in the archipelago but only four (Yap, Ponape, Truk, and Kusaie) are mountainous and large enough to support land and fresh-water avian species.

The Caroline Archipelago may be divided into two physiographic types: to the east, coral caps surmount mountains of volcanic origins; to the west, the islands are sections of the Earth's crust that have been folded and pushed above the ocean's surface. Island areas are: Yap — 80 square miles; Ponape (now Pohnpei) — 134 sq miles (highest elevation= 3,000 feet); Truk — 50 sq miles; and Kusaie (or Kosrae) — 42 sq miles (highest elevation= 2,064 feet). The eastern Carolines were probably settled earlier than the second century, and there is evidence of Chinese trade goods reaching the islands by the seventh century. The Carolines were seized by the Japanese in 1914 and during World War II were heavily fortified by the Japanese military. They are currently administered, along with Mariana and Marshall Island, by a U.S. high commissioner.

Society Islands

The Society Islands are southwest of the Tuamotu Archipelago and southeast of Samoa. This archipelago includes the islands of Tahiti (600 sq miles in area), Moorea (Eimeo) (50 sq. miles in area), the Leeward Islands (west of Tahiti) of Bora-Bora (less than 14 sq. miles in area), Huahine (less than 14 sq. miles in area), and Raiatea (Ulieta) (about 150 sq. miles of area), and three isolated atolls found further west (Mopiti, Mopelia, and Funua Ura). The western atolls are small and support only one species of land bird.

Six avian species endemic to these islands are extinct, and five others have been extirpated from Tahiti but still occur on the smaller islands and atolls. Tahiti is formed from two ancient volcanic cones which rise 7,300 feet above sea level. The terrain, apart from a narrow fertile coastal plain, is jagged and mountainous; the mountains contain no human settlements. Many swift streams descend to the coast; vegetation includes coconut palms, pandanus, lantana, hibiscus, and tropical fruit trees. The island, 33 miles long, is fringed by coral reefs and lagoons. Moorea, separated from Tahiti by a 12-mile wide channel, is also a high island and is encircled with very white coral sand beaches. Raiatea has a coastal plain with coconut groves where livestock are grazed.

The causes for extinction for Society Islands' birds can be attributed directly to the arrival of explorers and settlers. When Polynesians inhabited these islands, they brought several species of plants and animals with them including the Polynesian rat (*R. exulans*), pigs, dogs, exotic pet birds, and the guava bush. Whalers and other white explorers and settlers introduced the black and Norway rats (*R. rattus* and *R. norvegicus*) to the islands. The guava bush outcompeted native plant species in many areas and the exotic bird species may have introduced diseases that the native species were not adapted to deal with. Settlers also cleared many sections of land for agricultural and urban use. This loss of habitat, combined with competition from exotic species and predation were probably the primary causes leading to the extinction of the mysterious starling, the black-fronted parakeet, the Raiatea parakeet, and other endemic species.

New Caldonia

New Caldonia, 248 miles long and 31 miles wide, is encircled by the world's second largest barrier reef. The island rises to a double chain of high central mountains. The climate is mostly subtropical; forests occur on the east coast and in some valleys, and the west coast has savannas. Discovered by James Cook in 1774, the island was settled by a French Roman Catholic mission in 1843. It served as a penal colony from 1864 to 1894, during which time there were revolts by the indigenous people that may have contributed to the disruption of some avian species.

Samoa

The Samoan archipelago is divided into two parts: American Samoa and Western Samoa, which is governed by New Zealand. American Samoa comprises six islands, with a total area of 76 square miles. Western Samoa comprises nine islands, with an area of 1,100 square miles, and includes the inhabited islands of Upolu, Savai'i, Manono, and Apolima. Savai'i is the largest. There have been two eruptions from Savai'i's volcanoes in modern times, the most recent in 1905. The islands host 53 species of birds, at least 16 unique to the Samoas, including a rare toothed-billed pigeon. The only native mammals are the flying fox bat and smaller bats. There are several native lizards and two harmless snakes of the boa family. Rats, wild cattle and pigs were introduced by European explorers, and are the cause of avian extinction.

Wake Island

Wake Island, located 2,300 miles west of Honolulu, comprises three low-lying coral islets linked by causeways surrounding a lagoon. The atoll received little rainfall, and was not inhabited until 1899 when the U.S. established a cable station under naval jurisdiction. During World War II the island was overrun by the Japanese military.

Kosrae Mountain Starling

Aplonis corvina

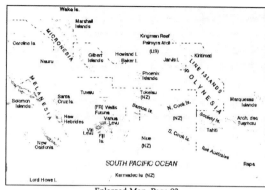

Enlarged Map, Page 93

Description

The Kosrae Mountain starling, *Aplonis corvina*, was a large (10 inches or 25 centimeters) starling with a long, somewhat slender, very slightly decurved, black bill; red irises; and a glossy black body. The tail was somewhat broad and long. Data on juvenile plumage are not available but in other starlings immature birds have a duller, browner color to their feathers.

This species is also referred to as Kittlitz' starling, Kusaie Mountain Starling, and Kusaie Island Starling.

Behavior

Food habits for this species are unknown, but other members of this family are omnivorous, consuming a wide variety of insects, fruits, and seeds.

Habitat

The Pohnpei Mountain starling, *A. pelzelni*, (a species closely related to Kosrae Mountain starling) inhabited the island's forested mountainous areas. It was most often found (or heard) in the forest canopy

Status	Extinct
Probable Extinction	c.1827
Family	Sturnidae (Starlings)
Description	Large starling with a long, somewhat slender, very slightly decurved, black bill; red irises; and a glossy black body.
Habitat	Mountainous forests.
Food	Probably insects, fruits and seeds.
Causes for Extinction	Probably introduced rats.
Range	Caroline Islands

but other habitats at lower elevations may have been utilized.

Distribution

The Kosrae Mountain starling was endemic to Kusaie or Kosrae Island in the Caroline Islands.

Causes for Extinction

The precise reasons for the extirpation of this species from Kusaie Island are not known. Many factors may have contributed to this bird's decline but similar factors affected the other islands in the chain without the resultant extinction of endemic species. The following describes some of these factors.

Kusaie Island is the smallest of the four islands inhabited by avian species. Its total area is not that much smaller than Truk which consists of a series of small islands surrounding a lagoon.

Kusaie Island supports a large rat population, both *Rattus rattus* and *R. norvegicus*. The other islands also have rat populations. It is postulated that repeated visits by whaling vessels to Kusaie Island for cleaning and repair may have repeatedly introduced the rats, resulting in large, periodic population increases. Avian populations able to withstand the initial influx of rats may have succumbed during subsequent invasions.

The Kosrae Mountain starling was not a particularly specialized species but it may have been a relict of the closely related starling on Pohnpei.

Competition from the late colonizer, the Micronesian starling (*A. opacus*), may have restricted the species' range to the higher, more densely forested areas of the island. The Micronesian starling is a smaller, more aggressive bird that nests in small cavities; this behavior may protect the birds, to some extent, from the rats. This species still inhabits the island.

Adapted from data compiled by the Threatened and Endangered Species Information Institute (Golden, CO) for *Beacham's International Threatened, Endangered, and Extinct Species* published on CD ROM, available from Beacham Publishing.

Kosrae Rail

Porzana monasa

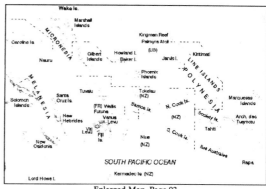

Enlarged Map, Page 93

Description

The Kosrae rail, *Porzana monasa*, was a very small (7 inches or 18 centimeters), stout-bodied, black rail; the black feathers had a bluish tinge. The tail and wing feathers were a bit browner. The irises and feet were red. The species was a weak flier at best and may have been mostly flightless.

Behavior

The Kosrae rail was non-migratory. Periodicity is unknown, but other related species are mostly diurnal or crepuscular.

Food habits for this species are unknown, but other members of this family are omnivorous. Rails consume a wide variety of insects, other invertebrates and seeds, but animal matter makes up the largest percentage of the diet.

Habitat

The Kosrae rail inhabited taro patches and wet, densely forested areas and other freshwater, brackish, and saltwater wetland areas (e.g., marshes, swamps).

Status	Extinct
Probable Extinction	By 1880
Family	Raillidae (Rail, Gallinules and Coots)
Description	Very small, stout-bodied, black rail.
Habitat	Wet, dense forests, freshwater, brackish, and saltwater wetlands.
Food	Probably insects, seeds, and animal matter.
Causes for Extinction	Introduced rats.
Range	Caroline Islands
Photo	See Color Insert, C-4

Distribution

The Kosrae rail was endemic to Kusaie or Kosrae Island in the Caroline Islands. The species was considered to be uncommon when first collected by Kittlitz in 1827 to 1828. Surveys of the coastal and inland forested areas in 1880 and 1931 failed to find the Kosrae rail.

Causes for Extinction

The precise reasons for the extirpation of this species from Kusaie Island are not known. Many factors may have contributed to this bird's decline but similar factors affected the other islands in the chain without the resultant extinction of endemic species.

Kusaie Island is the smallest of the four islands inhabited by avian species. Its total area is not that much smaller than Truk, which consists of a series of small islands surrounding a lagoon.

Kusaie Island supports a large rat population, both *Rattus rattus* and *R. norvegicus*. The other islands also have rat populations. It is postulated that repeated visits by whaling vessels to Kusaie Island for cleaning and repair may have repeatedly introduced the rats resulting in large, periodic population increases. Avian populations able to withstand the initial influx of rats may have succumbed during subsequent invasions.

Adapted from data compiled by the Threatened and Endangered Species Information Institute (Golden, CO) for *Beacham's International Threatened, Endangered, and Extinct Species* published on CD ROM, available from Beacham Publishing.

Mysterious Starling

Aplonis mavornata

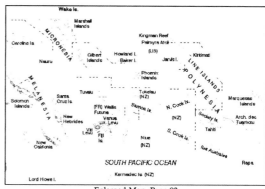

Enlarged Map, Page 93

Description

The mysterious starling, *Aplonis mavornata*, was a small (7 inches or 18 centimeters), bird, brown above and below with a slight bronzy glow on the head and a few hair-like whitish shafts on the breast. Its irises were yellow.

Behavior

Food habits for this species are unknown, but other members of this family are omnivorous, consuming a wide variety of insects, fruits, and seeds.

Habitat

The mysterious starling possibly inhabited Raiatea (Ulieta) Island in the Society Islands. Raiatea is the largest and most densely populated of the Society Islands. It has a large coastal plain suitable for farming and livestock grazing, which encouraged population development and the decline of some species. The only certain location for the species was the island of Mauke.

Status	Extinct
Probable	
Extinction	Unknown
Family	Sturnidae (Starlings)
Description	Small brown bird with glossy head feathers.
Food	Probably insects, fruits and seeds.
Causes for	
Extinction	Loss of habitat; low numbers.
Range	Society Islands

Distribution

In 1890, a British ornithologist, Richard B. Sharpe, noticed a skin in the British Museum which was very old. In 1888, Walter Buller had named this species *A. mavornata*, but the name Sharpe found inscribed on the stand of the mounted specimen was *A. inornata*. Sharpe assumed that a published description might exist that would supersede Buller, but his extensive research did not turn up any documents.

In the absence of information, it was assumed that the bird might have come from a Pacific Island, and that the specimen was collected from one of Captain Cook's voyages. Over the years various ornithologists examined the skin, comparing it unsuccessfully to *Turdus ulientensis* (Latham and Stresemann) and *A. tabuensis* (Mayr, 1951). In 1986, Storrs L. Olson published an article in which he correlated with certainty *A. mavornata* with a bird listed in a manuscript by Andrew Bloxham, who had sailed aboard the HMS *Blonde*, departing England on September 28, 1824. In May 1825, the ship arrived in the Hawaiian Islands, where Bloxham collected birds. The voyage then headed south. While in the South Pacific, the *Blonde* touched at the Cook Islands, and stopped at the island of Mauke, due south of Raiatae. On August 9, 1825, Bloxham shot three birds: a pigeon, a kingfisher, and a starling. These specimens eventually found their way into the British Museum.

No other attempts were made to locate this species until the 1970s, when D. T. Holyoak visited Mauke and found no trace of the bird. Other than the single skin in the British Museum, nothing is known of *A. mavornata* except that in Bloxham's account, it was "killed hopping about in a tree."

Causes for Extinction

Please see Society Islands, page 94.

Raiatea Parakeet

Cyanoramphus ulietanus

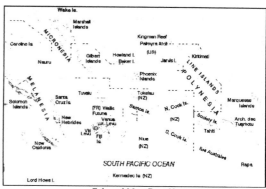

Enlarged Map, Page 93

Description

The Raiatea parakeet, *Cyanoramphus ulietanus*, was 10 inches (25 centimeters) in length. This parakeet had a dark chocolate brown head with an olive brown flecked with grayish-purple back and wings, a dusky yellowish-orange breast and abdomen, and a dark brownish-red rump and upper tail coverts. The long tail's inner flight feathers were olive green and the outer feathers were grayish purple. The bill was gray and the legs and feet were grayish brown.

This species is also called the Society parrot and Society parakeet.

Behavior

Information concerning the food habits of Raiatea parakeet is not known. Other members of the parrot family consume a wide variety of fruits and seeds.

Habitat/Distribution

The Raiatea parakeet probably inhabited the forested areas of Raiatea Island (Ulieta)

Status	Extinct
Probable Extinction	Unknown
Family	Psittacidae (Parrots and Parakeets)
Description	Parakeet with a dark chocolate brown head, olive brown flecked with grayish-purple back and wings, a dusky yellowish-orange breast and abdomen, and a dark brownish-red rump and upper tail coverts.
Habitat	Tropical forests.
Food	Probably fruits and berries.
Causes for Extinction	Predators
Range	Southeast of Samoa: Society Islands
Photo	See Color Insert, C-3

in the Society Islands. This species was apparently quite rare at the time of its discovery. Subsequent searches failed to locate the species and it is presumed to be extinct.

A reported sighting in 1981 has not been confirmed.

Causes for Extinction

Please see Society Islands, page 94.

Adapted from data compiled by the Threatened and Endangered Species Information Institute (Golden, CO) for *Beacham's International Threatened, Endangered, and Extinct Species* published on CD ROM, available from Beacham Publishing.

Black-Fronted Parakeet
Cyanoramphus zealandicus

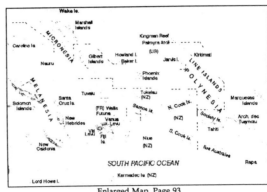

Enlarged Map, Page 93

Description

The black-fronted parakeet, *Cyanoramphus zealandicus*, was about 10 inches (25 centimeters) in length. Adults had a blackish-brown forehead and crown, bright green patches above the eyes and on the cheeks with the rest of the face and head a bright olive-green, and a red stripe between the nostril and the eye. The back and wings were olive green except for the outer edges of the primaries which were violet blue. The rump was red and the underside an olive green with a bluish cast. The bill was bluish gray and the legs and feet were grayish brown. Immatures had a bluish-black forehead, a brown head, a brown and green back, a deep red rump and eye stripe, and a grayish-green underside.

Island inhabitants called the bird "a'a."

Behavior

Little is known about the life history and behavior of this species. The food habits of the black-fronted parakeet are unavailable but other members of the parrot family consume a wide variety of fruits and seeds.

Status	Extinct
Probable Extinction	c.1850
Family	Psittacidae (Parrots and Parakeets)
Description	Black-fronted parakeet with a blackish-brown forehead and crown, bright green patches above the eyes and on the cheeks with the rest of the face and head a bright olive-green, and a red stripe between the nostril and the eye.
Habitat	Forests.
Food	Probably fruits and seeds.
Causes for Extinction	Loss of habitat; introduced predators.
Range	Society Islands
Photo	See Color Insert, C-3

Habitat/Distribution

The black-fronted parakeet probably inhabited the forested areas of Tahiti. It was apparently quite rare at the time of its discovery. The last known specimens were collected in 1844 by Lieutenant Marolles. The species is thought to have become extinct soon after this date.

Causes for Extinction

Please see Society Islands, page 94.

Adapted from data compiled by the Threatened and Endangered Species Information Institute (Golden, CO) for *Beacham's International Threatened, Endangered, and Extinct Species* published on CD ROM, available from Beacham Publishing.

Tahitian Sandpiper
Prosobonia leucoptera

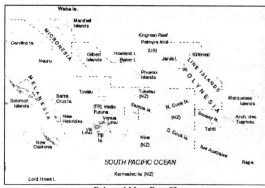

Enlarged Map, Page 93

Description

The Tahitian sandpiper, *Prosobonia leucoptera,* possessed a blackish brown crown with the nape and sides of the face a deeper shade of brown. The lores and ear coverts were reddish with a white spot behind the eye. The cheeks were russet with the chin and upper throat a buffish white. The back and wings were blackish brown with a crescent-shaped patch of white on the lesser wing coverts which continued across the leading edge of the wing. The two central tail feathers were also blackish brown with the rest of the rufous banded with black. The underparts were russet and unbarred. The iris was black along with the bill. The legs and feet were green. The species' wing measured 110 millimeters (4.3 inches) while its tail extended 55 mm (2.14 inches). The culmen was 20 mm (.78 inch) long and the tarsus, 32 mm (1.25 inches).

Habitat/Distribution

The Tahitian sandpiper was a ground nester that inhabited the banks of small streams on the Society Islands of Tahiti and Eimeo (Moorea).

Status	Extinct
Probable Extinction	Not sighted after 1777.
Family	Scolopacidae (Sandpipers)
Description	Sandpiper with a blackish brown crown, and the nape and sides of the face a deeper shade of brown.
Habitat	Banks of small streams.
Reproduction	Ground nester.
Causes for Extinction	Perhaps introduced rats.
Range	Tahiti

The Tahitian sandpiper never interacted with humanity except when it was first collected, and it apparently had no economic value except as it contributed to the ecological stability of its environment.

Causes for Extinction

Predation by the introduced rats during James Cook's visit (1769) to this species' habitat may have been responsible for the extinction of this species.

Please see Society Islands, page 94, for additional information.

Adapted from data compiled by the Threatened and Endangered Species Information Institute (Golden, CO) for *Beacham's International Threatened, Endangered, and Extinct Species* published on CD ROM, available from Beacham Publishing.

Tahitian Red-Billed Rail

Rallus pacificus

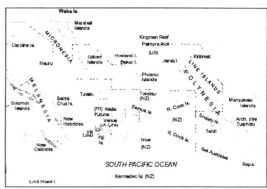

Enlarged Map, Page 93

Description

The Tahitian red-billed rail, *Rallus pacificus*, was a brilliantly colored rail about 9 inches from bill to tail. The top of the head and sides of the face were black with a white stripe running from near the bill to the top of the neck. The back and rump were black and sparsely dotted with white. The throat and abdomen were white and the breast was gray. The short wings were black and variegated with white bands. The bill and the irises were red and the legs pink.

Distribution

Rallus pacificus was discovered during James Cook's second voyage and it is known only from an illustration by George Forster. It once inhabited Tahiti, and it may also have occurred on the nearby island of Mehetia. It is possible that the species survived on Mehetia until the early part of the twentieth century.

Causes for Extinction

Presumably the introduction of rats by Cook's voyages caused the same fate for *R.*

Status	Extinct
Probable Extinction	c. 1900
Family	Rallidae (Rails, gallinules, and coots)
Description	Brilliantly colored rail; head and sides of the face were black with a white stripe running from the bill to the top of the neck; the back and rump were black and sparsely dotted with white; throat and abdomen were white and the breast was gray.
Causes for Extinction	Introduced predators.
Range	Tahiti
Photo	See Color Insert, C-4

pacificus as it did for the Tahitian sandpiper, which was extirpation by predators that attacked young birds and ate the eggs.

Please see Society Islands, page 94, for additional information.

New Caledonia Lorikeet
Charmosyna diadema

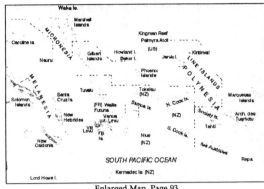

Enlarged Map, Page 93

Description

The New Caledonia lorikeet, *Charmosyna diadema,* was a small (6.5 to 8 inches or 16 to 20 centimeters) member of the parrot family. The description is based on two female specimens taken in the early to mid-1800s. Most of the body was a green to olive-green color. The cheeks and throat were yellow and the crown was violet-blue. The thighs were green tinged with blue, and red and black markings were found around the vent and tail. The tail was long and narrow, colored green above and yellow below. The legs were orange and the bill was deep orange.

Behavior

Little is known about the life history and behavior of this species. Information concerning the food habits of *C. zealandicus* is unavailable, but other members of the parrot family consume a wide variety of fruits and seeds.

Status	Extinct
Probable Extinction	1860
Family	Psittacidae (Parrots and Parakeets)
Description	Small, olive-green parrot with yellow cheeks and throat, and a violet-blue crown.
Habitat	Wet, dense forests.
Food	Probably fruits and seeds.
Causes for Extinction	Habitat destruction, overcollecting, competition with exotic species, the introduction of predators, and diseases.
Range	New Caledonia
Photo	See Color Insert, C-4

Habitat/Distribution

The species was reported to inhabit the forests near Oubatche on the northern end of New Caledonia in the early part of the century.

New Caledonia is a large island (6,221 square miles in area) located over 800 miles to the northeast of Australia. A backbone of mountains run down the center of the island's 250 mile length. The highest elevations (on the northwest end) reach 5,954 feet. Elevations along the southern end rarely exceed 1,500 feet, but this is high enough to affect the prevailing weather patterns. Winds prevail from the east; the island's leeward slopes are arid and are dominated by one species of eucalyptus tree of Australian origin. The windward slopes support a much wetter and denser forest.

The New Caledonia lorikeet apparently inhabited the higher elevation, denser, wet forests in the more northerly parts of the island.

Causes for Extinction

Whalers visiting the island may have relied on this species for food when their rations were short. The extent of such use, if it occurred, is not known. Rumors that the species still may exist have brought offers of large rewards to individuals who find the bird, dead or alive. This indicates the pressure such species have to deal with. Overcollecting may have occurred during the early part of the nineteenth century. Parrots and all their relatives are sought after for the commercial pet trade.

Habitat destruction, overcollecting, competition with exotic species, the introduction of predators and diseases are thought to have been the cause of this species' decline and presumed extinction.

The New Caledonia lorikeet is thought by some experts to still exist. Only two specimens (both females) have been collected; both pre-date 1860. There have been no confirmed sightings, but rumors about the species being sighted periodically occur.

Adapted from data compiled by the Threatened and Endangered Species Information Institute (Golden, CO) for *Beacham's International Threatened, Endangered, and Extinct Species* published on CD ROM, available from Beacham Publishing.

Samoan Wood Rail

Pareudiastes pacificus

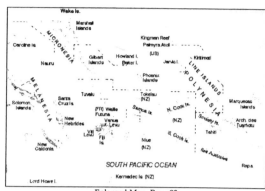

Enlarged Map, Page 93

Description

The Samoan wood rail, *Pareudiastes pacificus*, was a small (6 inches or 15.3 centimeters), mostly flightless member of the rail family, *Rallidae*. This species was described as a gallinule-like bird with a mostly black plumage tinged with olive-green on the back and wings, and a bluish-gray highlight on the breast and throat. The feet, legs, frontal shield, and bill were probably red or reddish-orange. The eyes were notably larger than average which may verify this species' crepuscular or nocturnal habits.

The Samoan wood rail is also referred to as *Gallinula pacifica* and *Pareudiastes pacifica*. The islanders' name for this species was "puna'e".

Behavior

Reproductive data are generally lacking. Reports from islanders indicate this rail used burrows at least for refuge from predators, and possibly for nesting. One nest was reportedly found on the ground.

The Samoan wood rail was described as being primarily nocturnal. The Samoan wood rail, like other rails, was probably

Status	Extinct
Probable Extinction	1873
Family	Rallidae (Rails, Gallinules, and Coots)
Description	Small bird with black plumage, tinge of olive-green on its back and wings, a bluish-gray highlight on the breast and throat, and a red or orange bill.
Habitat	Probably areas with dense undergrowth.
Food	Probably omnivorous, especially insects.
Reproduction	Probably nested in burrows.
Threats	Probably rats and feral cats.
Range	Samoan Islands: Savai'i

omnivorous, but consumed primarily animal matter. Records indicate this rail ate a large quantity of insects.

Habitat

Information concerning this species' habitat preferences is not available. Many other members of the rail family inhabit freshwater, brackish, and saltwater emergent marshes. This species probably inhabited similar areas or areas with dense ground cover to allow this secretive rail a means of escape. The name "wood rail" may indicate the use of scrublands or forested areas.

Distribution

The Samoan wood rail was endemic to the island of Savai'i in the Samoan Islands. The Samoan wood rail may also have been found on the island of Opolu in the same island group but no specimens or confirmed sightings exist. The species is presumed to be extinct since the last sighting and specimen collection occurred in 1873. Some authorities believe the species may still exist.

Causes for Extinction

Predation by exotic mammalian species, especially rats and feral cats, was probably one of the primary factors leading to the decline and extinction of Samoan wood rail.

Also, the Samoan wood rail was probably hunted by islanders for food. Hunting and scientific collecting may have played a part in the decline of this species since it was apparently quite rare when discovered.

Adapted from data compiled by the Threatened and Endangered Species Information Institute (Golden, CO) for *Beacham's International Threatened, Endangered, and Extinct Species* published on CD ROM, available from Beacham Publishing.

Wake Island Rail

Rallus wakensis

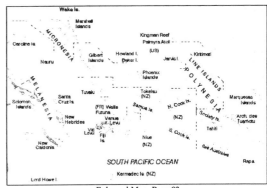

Enlarged Map, Page 93

Description

The Wake Island rail, *Rallus wakensis*, was about 9-10 inches (22-25 centimeters) in length. The male's wing was 85-100 millimeters (3.3-3.9 in) long, the tail 45 mm (1.75 in), the culmen 25-29 mm (.975-1.13 in), and the tarsus 33-37 mm (1.29-1.44 in). The rump, back, neck, top of the head, cheeks, and lores were a dark grayish-brown. A light gray line extended from the lore above the eye back and down to meet the light gray chin, throat, and upper breast. The central lower breast and abdomen were white with the sides covered with alternating white and dark brown stripes. The bill, legs, and feet were brown. The species was probably not sexually dimorphic but the females may have been slightly smaller.

R. wakensis and *R. philippensis*, the banded rail, are considered to be closely related. *R. wakensis* was slightly smaller, paler in color, flightless, and lacked the distinctive spotting of *R. philippensis*. The differences between these two species are few, barely enough to consider *R. wakensis* a separate species.

R. wakensis was a member of the rail, gallinule, and coot family, Rallidae. This species was described and named *Hypotae-nidia wakensis* by Rothschild in 1903. *R. wakensis* is also referred to as *Gallirallus wakensis*.

Status	Extinct
Probable Extinction	c.1945
Family	Rallidae (Rails, Gallinules and Coots)
Description	Dark grayish-brown rail about 9-10 inches in length.
Habitat	Tall, dense shrubs.
Food	Crustaceans, mollusks, insects and worms; probably seeds and other plant matter.
Reproduction	Breeding July and August; possibly other months.
Causes for Extinction	Overcollecting for food.
Range	Pacific Ocean: Wake Island
Photo	See Color Insert, C-4

Behavior

Breeding was known to occur in July and August and it may have occurred during other months as well.

Like other rails, the Wake Island rail was probably omnivorous, with animal matter making up the majority of the diet when available. The species was observed probing mud and drier areas for crustaceans, mollusks, insects and worms. Seeds and other plant matter were probably consumed in varying amounts.

Habitat

Wake Island is several hundred miles west of the western-most part of the Hawaiian Island archipelago. It is volcanic in origin but is much eroded. The island's highest point is only 20 feet (6 meters) above sea level. Tall, dense shrubs (*Pandanus* sp.) cover a large portion of the 9 square mile (23 square kilometer) island. The rail may have occurred throughout the island.

Distribution

The species was considered to be fairly abundant prior to World War II. Post-war surveys failed to find the species and it is believed extinct from Wake Island after approximately 1945. *R. wakensis* was the only land species endemic to Wake Island.

Causes for Extinction

Japanese troops occupying Wake Island during World War II are believed to be responsible for the extinction of the endemic flightless rail. Often on tight rations, many men may have avoided starvation by hunting and eating *R. wakensis*. The species could not be located during post-war surveys of the island.

Adapted from data compiled by the Threatened and Endangered Species Information Institute (Golden, CO) for *Beacham's International Threatened, Endangered, and Extinct Species* published on CD ROM, available from Beacham Publishing.

Red-Moustached Fruit Dove

Ptilinopus mercierii

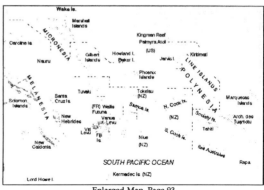

Enlarged Map, Page 93

Description

The red-moustached fruit dove, *Ptilinopus mercierii*, was a small dove (7 inches or 18 centimeters long) with a plump, compact body. The forehead and crown were a bright purplish-crimson color. A bright yellow band circled the head just below the crimson cap. The breast, neck, and nape were a silvery gray color with a slight green tinge, and the throat was a pale yellow. The belly and undertail coverts were a brighter yellow. The legs were gray and the bare feet a grayish-purple. The remainder of the upperparts were a deep golden-green color. The dark green tail had a wide white terminal band. When the wings were closed, the visible portions of the primary and secondary feathers were a glimmering green to bluish-green. The scapulars and inner secondaries had yellowish-green edges and blue to greenish-blue centers. The sexes were similar in appearance but the females' grayish areas had a stronger hint of green.

Status	Extinct
Probable Extinction	After 1970
Family	Columbidae (Doves and Pigeons)
Description	Small dove with a plump, compact body and a bright purplish-crimson forehead and crown.
Habitat	Canopy of forested or brushy habitats and the adjacent open areas.
Food	Primarily fruits and berries; also buds, new-growth vegetation, and invertebrates.
Reproduction	Probably 1 egg per clutch after incubation of 14-18 days.
Causes for Extinction	Possibly competition and predation from exotic species.
Range	Marquesas Islands

Behavior

Information on the reproductive characteristics of this species is limited. Other fruit doves generally lay 1 egg per clutch. Nesting may occur in most months of the year, but probably is concentrated between December and June. In many species both sexes incubate. Incubation lasts from 14 to 18 days and fledglings may emerge in about 14 days.

Ptilinopus sp. are primarily frugivorous, consuming mostly fruits and berries. Buds, new-growth vegetation, and invertebrates are also consumed to some extent.

Although the periodicity is unknown for this species, most pigeons and doves are primarily diurnal.

Habitat

Many fruit doves inhabit the canopy of forested or brushy habitats and the adjacent open areas. Most fruit doves nest above the ground in trees and shrubs. The Red-Moustached fruit dove probably inhabited the forest/brushy areas on Hiva-oa and Nuku Hiva, the two largest islands in the Marquesas Island group. Hiva-oa is about 95 square miles in area and is mostly made up of mountainous areas covered with forest habitats. Nuku Hiva is also mountainous and forested with elevations that reach almost 4,000 feet.

Distribution

The Red-Moustached fruit dove was endemic to the Marquesas Islands. Subspecies were found on the islands of Nuku Hiva and Hiva-oa. The Marquesas Islands are about 1,000 miles northeast of Tahiti in the Pacific Ocean. This group is composed of 13 islands that together are less than 480 square miles in area. Nuku Hiva and Hiva-oa are the largest islands and are found near the center of the island group.

Causes for Extinction

Reasons for the decline of this species are unknown. Its recent demise indicates that habitat loss and possibly the introduction of exotic birds and predators (e.g., rats) may have impacted the species. Competition from introduced species, the introduction of new diseases, and increases in predation in conjunction with the increase in human related development (urban, recreational, and agricultural) and associated habitat loss are common factors that have led to the decline and extinction of other Pacific Island species.

This species was probably hunted by island residents and may have provided an important source of food. Hunting for sport may also have occurred, but this has not been documented.

Adapted from data compiled by the Threatened and Endangered Species Information Institute (Golden, CO) for *Beacham's International Threatened, Endangered, and Extinct Species* published on CD ROM, available from Beacham Publishing.

Choiseul Crested Pigeon
Microgoura meeki

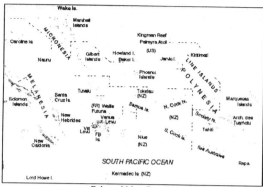

Enlarged Map, Page 93

Description

The Choiseul crested pigeon, *Microgoura meeki*, had a black forehead and face, with the top of the head, crest, mantle and breast dark bluish gray, shading to brown on the lower back. The wings and rump were olive brown, the tail dark brown with purple hues. The abdomen was chestnut; the upper mandible black, and the lower mandible red. It had brown irises and purplish red legs. The wingspan of the male measured about 195 mm (7.6 inches) and the tail about 100 mm (3.9 inches). The culmen was 34 mm (1.3 inches) and the tarsus 60 mm (2.34). The female was about the same size.

Behavior

The birds could easily be caught by hand at their roosts, or by imitating the low trilling sound of their call. Stones were frequently found in their gizzards, indicating a diet similar to other pigeons, which would include seeds and fruits.

Habitat

Natives who remembered the bird said that it resided in lowland, swampy forests

Status	Extinct
Probable Extinction	c.1930?
Family	Columbidae (Doves and Pigeons)
Description	Bird with black forehead and face, with the top of the head, crest, mantle and breast dark bluish gray, shading to brown on the lower back; the wings and rump were olive brown, the tail dark brown with purple hues.
Habitat	Lowland, swampy forests.
Food	Seeds and fruits.
Causes for Extinction	Introduced predators; loss of habitat.
Range	Solomon Islands: Choiseul

but not in mangroves. It was mostly terrestrial but roosted in small parties on low branches, which could easily be discovered because of the droppings the birds left below the roost.

Distribution

A. S. Meek collected the first specimens (6 or 7) skins and a single egg of a large ground pigeon on the island of Choiseul in the Solomon Islands in 1904. The natives of the island told Meek that the bird also existed on Santa Isabel Island and Malaita but no evidence of their existence was ever discovered. English voyagers to Choiseul in 1927 and 1929 were able to gain information about the species, and were told that the bird was rare but alive. A small group was allegedly sighted in the Kolambangara basin during World War II.

Causes for Extinction

Cats introduced to control the rat population were responsible for killing many birds, and the habitat around Choiseul Bay, where Meek probably collected his specimens, was completely destroyed by the clearance of land for coconut plantations by 1920.

EXTINCT BIRDS OF THE HAWAIIAN ISLANDS

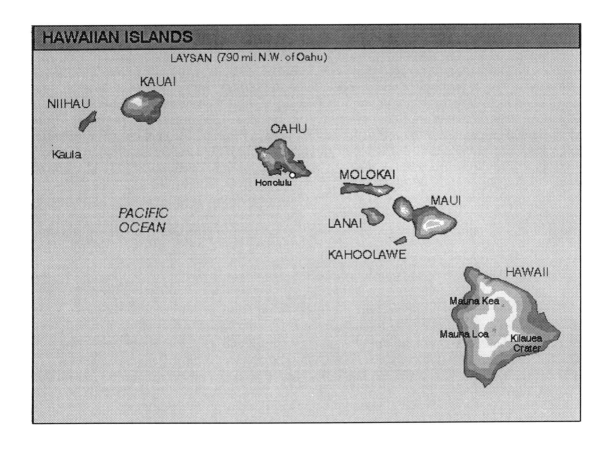

HAWAIIAN ISLANDS

LAYSAN (790 mi. N.W. of Oahu)

KAUAI

NIIHAU

Kaula

OAHU

Honolulu

MOLOKAI

MAUI

PACIFIC OCEAN

LANAI

KAHOOLAWE

HAWAII

Mauna Kea

Mauna Loa

Kilauea Crater

The Hawaiian Islands

The Hawaiian archipelago includes eight large volcanic islands (Niihau, Kauai, Oahu, Molokai, Lanai, Kahoolawe, Maui, and Hawaii), as well as offshore islets, shoals, and atolls set on submerged volcanic remnants at the northwest end of the chain (the Northwestern Hawaiian Islands). The archipelago covers a land area of about 16,600 square kilometers (6,400 sq miles), and ranging in elevation from sea level to 4,200 meters (m) (13,800 feet). The regional geological setting is a mid-oceanic volcanic island archipelago set in a roughly northwest to southeast line, with younger islands to the southeast. The youngest island, Hawaii, is volcanically active. The older islands are increasingly eroded, so that the basaltic portions of many of the northwesternmost islands (such as Laysan, Necker, and Nihoa) are entirely submerged, and coralline atolls and shoals are often all that remain above sea level.

The topography of the Hawaiian Islands is extremely diverse. On the younger islands, Hawaii and Maui, gently sloping unweathered shield volcanoes with very poor soil development are juxtaposed with older, heavily weathered valleys with steep walls, well-developed streams, and gently sloped flood plains. The older islands to the northwest (i.e., Niihau, Kauai, Oahu, and Molokai) are generally more weathered. On a typical older island, sea cliffs and large amphitheater-headed valleys on the windward (northeast) side contrast with erosionally younger, dissected slopes on the leeward (southwest) side.

The climate of the Hawaiian Islands reflects the tropical setting buffered by the surrounding ocean. The prevailing winds are northeast trades with some seasonal fluctuation in strength. There are also winter storm systems and occasional hurricanes. Temperatures vary over the year on an average of only 5 deg. Celsius (C) (11 deg. Fahrenheit (F)) or less. Annual rainfall varies greatly by location, with marked windward to leeward gradients over short distances. Minimum average annual rainfall is less than 250 millimeters (10 inches); the maximum average precipitation is well in excess of 11,000 mm (450 in) per year. Precipitation is greatest during the months of October through April. A dry season is apparent in leeward settings, while windward settings generally receive tradewind-driven rainfall throughout the year.

The native-dominated vegetation of the Hawaiian Islands varies greatly according to elevation, moisture regime, and substrate. The most recent classification of Hawaiian natural communities recognizes nearly 100 native vegetation types. Within these types are numerous island-specific or region-specific associations, comprising an extremely rich array of vegetation types within a very limited geographic area. Major vegetation formations include forests, woodlands, shrublands, grasslands, herblands, and pioneer associations on lava and cinder substrates.

There are lowland, montane, and subalpine forest types in Hawaii, extending from sea level to above 3,000 m (9,800 ft) in elevation. Coastal and lowland forests are generally dry or mesic and may be open- or closed-canopied. The stature of lowland forests is generally under 10 m (30 ft). Montane forests, occupying elevations between 1,000 and 2,000 m (3,000 and 6,000 ft), are dry to mesic on the leeward slopes of the islands of Kauai, Maui, and Hawaii. On those islands, as well as on Oahu, Molokai, and Lanai, mesic to wet montane forests occur on the windward slopes and summits. The dry and mesic forests may be open- to closed-canopied, and may exceed 20 m (65 ft) in stature. Montane wet forests are usually dominated by several species of native trees and tree ferns. At high montane and subalpine elevations, at and above 2,000 m (6,500 ft) elevation, are subalpine forests, usually open-canopied and forming a mosaic with surrounding grasslands and shrublands. Subalpine forests are known only from Haleakala on East Maui and from Hualalai, Mauna Kea, and Mauna Loa on Hawaii.

Hawaiian shrublands are also found from coastal to alpine elevations. The majority of Hawaiian shrubland types are in dry and mesic settings, or on cliffs and slopes too steep to support trees. Wet montane shrublands are typically dominated by Metrosideros ('ohi'a). Hawaiian grassland types are found from coastal to subalpine settings. Coastal and lowland grasslands are known from the Northwestern Hawaiian Islands, Kauai, Oahu, Molokai, Lanai, Maui, and Hawaii.

Habitat Conditions on the Island of Hawaii (the Big Island)

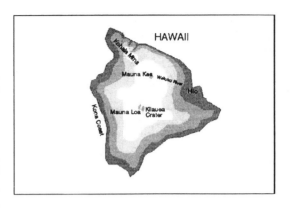

The island of Hawaii is the southernmost, fartherest east, and the youngest of the eight major Hawaiian Islands. This largest island of the Hawaiian archipelago comprises 4,038 square miles, giving rise to its common name, the "Big Island."

The Hawaiian Islands are volcanic islands formed over a "hot spot," a fixed area of pressurized molten rock deep within the Earth. As the Pacific Plate, a section of the Earth's surface many miles thick, has moved to the northwest, the islands of the chain have separated. Currently, this hot spot is centered under the southeast part of the island of Hawaii, which is one of the most active volcanic areas on Earth.

Five large shield volcanoes make up the island of Hawaii: Mauna Kea at 13,796 feet and Kohala at 5,480 feet, both inactive; Hualalai at 8,271 feet, which is dormant and will probably erupt again; and Mauna Loa at 13,677 feet and Kilauea at 4,093, both of which are currently active and adding land area to the island. Compared to Kauai, which is the oldest of the main islands and was formed about 5.6 million years ago, Hawaii is very young, with fresh lava and land up to 0.5 million years old.

Because of the large size and ranges of elevation of the island, Hawaii has a great diversity of climates. Windward (northeastern) slopes of Mauna Loa have rainfall up to 300 inches per year. The leeward coast, shielded by the mountains from rain brought by trade winds, has areas classified as desert and receiving as little as 8 inches of rain annually. The summits of Mauna Loa and Mauna Kea experience snowfall each year, and Mauna Kea was glaciated during the last Ice Age.

Plant communities on Hawaii include those in various stages of primary succession (initiated on newly produced bare areas) on the slopes of active and dormant volcanoes, some in stages of secondary succession (initiated by the disruption of a previously existing community by some major environmental disturbance), and relatively stable climax communities (one that has reached a state of equilibrium). On Hawaii, vegetation is found in all classifications of habitat: coastal; dryland; montane; subalpine and alpine; dry, mesic and wet; herblands, grasslands, shrublands, forests, and mixed communities.

The vegetation and land of the island of Hawaii have undergone much change throughout the island's development. Since it is an area of frequent volcanic activity, vegetated areas are periodically replaced with bare lava. Polynesian immigrants, first settling on Hawaii by 750 A.D., made extensive alterations in lowland areas for agriculture and habitation. European contact with the island brought intentional and inadvertent introductions of alien plants and animal species. By 1960, 65 percent of the total land area of the island of Hawaii was used for grazing, and much land has also been converted to modern cropland.

Habitat Conditions on
the Island of Maui

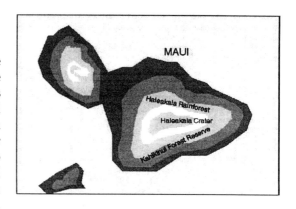

Maui, the second largest island in the state, is 48 miles long and 26 miles wide. The land area is 465,920 acres. This island was formed from the remnants of two large shield volcanoes: the older West Maui volcano on the west and the larger but much younger Haleakala volcano on the east. These two volcanoes and the connecting isthmus formed by lava flows make up the three main areas: West Maui, East Maui, and Central Maui. Steam erosion has cut deep valleys and ridges into the originally shield-shaped West Maui volcano, and created a deeply dissected volcano that rises to 5,788 feet at Puu Kukui. With an average annual rainfall of 400 inches, Puu Kukui is the second wettest spot in Hawaii.

Having erupted just 200 years ago, East Maui's Haleakala (10,023 feet in elevation) has retained its classic shield shape and lacks the diverse vegetation typical of the older and more eroded West Maui mountain. Annual rainfall on Haleakala is about 350 inches, with its windward slope receiving the most precipitation. However, Haleakala's crater is dry cinder desert because it is below the level at which the precipitation develops and is sheltered from moisture-laden winds.

The central part of West Maui consists of canyons and steep ridges and is not easily accessible. It is surrounded by a moderately sloping, smooth narrow belt.

Central Maui is the isthmus that connects West and East Maui. This area is smooth and nearly level. It is used mainly for sugarcane. Much of the isthmus is covered with alluvium. Most of the soils are Andepts, Ustolls, and Humults. Andepts formed in regoliths consisting of volcanic ash or pumice. The soils have a low bulk density and therefore are light and fluffy. Most are acid, and some are strongly acid. Although not all these soils are well drained, none of them is hydric. Humults are the freely drained Ultisols that have a high content of organic matter. Ustolls are well drained and moderately well drained Mollisols of subhumid and semiarid regions. The moisture regime is predominantly ustic.

Along with this area's large mass is its vast number of resource areas and subsequent land uses. Eight total, these resource areas comprised a variety of activities including urban development, military installation, crops, tourism, heavily vegetated native rain forests, wildlife, and pasture.

Maui supports a wide range of vegetation communities (shrublands, forests and bogs), elevation zones (lowland to alpine), and moisture regimes (dry to wet).

The *lowland dry vegetation* type occurs on the leeward side of the main Hawaiian Islands at an elevation of 15 to 2,000 feet. The climate of this vegetation is distinctly seasonal, with hot, dry summers and winter rainfall, usually less than 40 inches but sometimes ranging up to 80 inches annually. The soils range from weathered silty loam to stony clay; rocky ledges with very shallow soil and recent, little-weathered lava are present.

The *lowland mesic shrubland* and forest habitats on West Maui and other Hawaiian islands occur mainly at elevations between 100 and 5,300 feet in areas topographically unsuitable for agriculture. Annual precipitation ranges from less than 40 to 150 inches, falling mostly in the winter months. This community occurs on diverse, well-weathered and well-drained substrates, ranging from rocky, shallow, organic muck soils to steep, rocky talus slopes, shallow rocky soils on steep slopes, to deep soil over soft weathered rock and gravelly alluvium in gulches and erosional plains.

The *lowland wet forest* habitat is composed primarily of native vegetation with canopies from 10 to 130 feet high in sheltered, well-drained, leeward slopes at elevations between 300 and 3,900 feet. Annual rainfall ranges from 60 to 200 inches. The substrate ranges from clay or organic muck over lava to volcanic ash beds or young lava flows.

The windward slopes contain the *montane wet communities*, which includes bogs characterized by thick peat overlaying an impervious clay substrate with hummocks of sedges and grasses, stunted trees, and shrubs. The montane wet forests occur on Molokai, Maui, and Hawaii (the Big Island) at elevations between 3,900 and 7,200 feet, mainly on steep windward valley walls. The vegetation type is characterized by rich soil development, high rainfall of 100 inches annually, high diversity, and a rich understory.

The *subalpine dry vegetation* type occurs on East Maui (and the Big Island) between 5,600 and 9,800 feet. The substrate is of cinder or weathered volcanic ash or bare lava with little or no soil development, partly due to the low annual precipitation of 15 to 40 inches. Periodic frost and occasional snow cover occur on the upper limits.

The *alpine dry shrubland* community occurs above 9,800 feet. The precipitation is only 30 to 50 inches annually. The community is subjected to frequent frosts and arid extremes, limiting vegetation (grasses, mosses, and alpine-adapted shrubs) to near the lower boundary of the community on bare gravel, debris, and cinders.

Habitat Conditions on the Island of Molokai

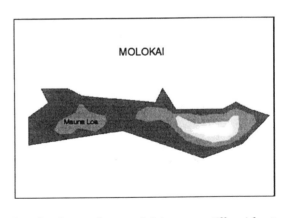

Cattle ranching on Molokai has played a significant role over most of the past 150 years in reducing areas of native vegetation to vast pastures of alien grasses. In 1960 about 61% of Molokai's lands were devoted to grazing, primarily in West and central Molokai. Cattle degrade the habitat by trampling and feeding on vegetation, eventually exposing the ground cover, and increasing soil vulnerability to erosion. Red erosional scars resulting from decades of cattle disturbance, exacerbated by other feral ungulate activities, are still evident on West Molokai and the upper elevations of East Molokai. Cattle facilitate the spread of alien grasses and other plants.

Alteration of vegetation limits natural areas. It was here on the upper elevation mesic to wet forests of East Molokai, where the State designated a single protected area: the Molokai

Forest Reserve. This reserve accounts for 30% of Molokai land area. Cattle ranching was succeeded in the 1920s by pineapple cultivation. Most of the land used for this agricultural activity had already been altered through the decades of cattle ranching. However, pineapple cultivation contributed to a high degree of erosion until its decline in the 1970s.

Habitat Conditions on the Island of Oahu

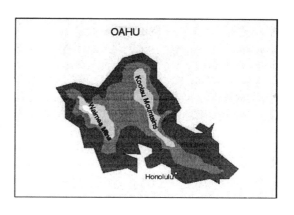

Oahu, the third largest island in the State, is 44 miles long and 30 miles wide. The land area is 386,560 acres. The island is formed from the remnants of two large shield volcanoes, the older Waianae Volcano on the west and the younger Koolau Volcano on the east. Their original shield volcano shape has been lost as a result of extensive erosion, and today these volcanoes are called "mountains" or "ranges." The island is divided into four main areas — the Waianae Range, the Koolau Range, the Schofield Plateau, and the coastal plains.

The Waianae Mountains were built by eruptions along three rift zones. The two principal rift zones run in a northwestward and south-southeastward direction from the summit, and a lesser zone runs to the northeast. The range is approximately 40 miles long, and the caldera lies between the north side of Makaha Valley and the head of Nanakuli Valley. The Waianae Mountains are in the rain shadow of the parallel Koolau Mountains and except for Mt. Kaala, the highest point on Oahu (4,020 feet), receive much less rainfall. The median annual rainfall for the Waianae Mountains varies from 20 to 75 inches, with only the small summit area receiving the highest amount.

The 'ilima shrubland community of the coastal dry shrublands vegetation type occurs on sand dunes and poorly consolidated volcanic soils near shore environments, and is exposed to salt-laden winds. Coastal dry shrublands occur on all of the northwestern Hawaiian islands and along the coastlines of all the main islands, extending to about 1,000 feet in elevation. Because of the effects of the rain shadows, these communities are most extensively developed on the leeward sides of the higher islands. Annual rainfall is less than 45 inches and occurs primarily during the winter months of October to April. Much of the vegetation dies back during a prolonged drought that lasts most of the rest of the year.

The lowland dry vegetation comprises several plant comunities that occur at an elevation of 15 to 2,000 feet on the leeward side of all the main Hawaiian islands. The climate of this vegetation is distinctly seasonal, with hot, dry summers and winter rainfall, usually less than 40 inches but sometimes ranging up to 80 inches annually. The soils range from weathered silty loam to stony clay; rocky ledges with very shallow soil and recent, little-weathered lava are present.

The diverse lowland mesic shrubland and forest habitats on all the main Hawaiian islands occurs mainly at elevations between 100 and 5,300 feet in areas topographically unsuitable for agriculture. Annual precipitation ranges from less than 40 to 150 inches., falling mostly in the winter months. This community occurs on diverse, well-weathered and well-drained substrates, ranging from rocky, shallow, organic muck soils to steep, rocky talus slopes, shallow rocky soils on steep slopes, to deep soil over soft weathered rock and gravelly alluvium in gulches and erosional plains. In the Waianae Mountains, this vegetation community is found in sheltered areas and comprises a rich diversity of native plants with no clearly dominant species.

Most of the area is steep to very steep and is broken by numerous drainageways. There are no perennial streams and the area consists primarily of rough, broken, well drained land. The soils are gently sloping to very steep, and fine textured to moderately fine textured. Tropohumults are formed in deposits of basic igneous rock with an oxidic mineralogy and occur on the narrow ridges at the upper elevations. They have a surface layer and subsoil of reddish-brown silty clay and are underlain by soft weathered rock. Dystrandepts occur in concave positions on the steep side slopes and were derived primarily from volcanic ash mixed with colluvium. They are dark colored and have a surface layer of silt loam or silty clay loam.

Habitat Conditions on the Island of Kauai

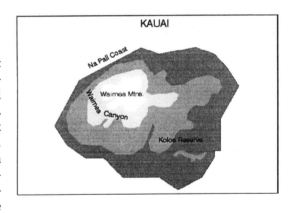

The island of Kauai is the northernmost and oldest of the eight major Hawaiian Islands. This highly eroded island, characterized by deeply dissected canyons and steep ridges, is 553 square miles. It was formed about six millions years ago by a single shield volcano. Its caldera, once the largest in the Hawaiian Islands, now extends about ten miles in diameter and comprises the extremely wet, elevated tableland of Alakai Swamp. Because the highest point of Kauai, at Kawaikini Peak, is only 5,243 feet in elevation, it lacks the contrasting leeward montane rainfall patterns found on the other islands that have higher mountain systems. Rainfall is, therefore, distributed throughout the upper elevations, especially at Mount Waialeale, Kauai's second highest point at 5,148 feet. Mount Waialeale is one of the wettest spots on Earth, where annual rainfall averages 450 inches.

To the west of Alakai Swamp is the deeply dissected Waimea Canyon, extending 10 miles in length and up to a mile in width. Later volcanic activity on the southeastern flank of the volcano formed the smaller Haupu caldera. Subsequent erosion and collapse of its flank formed Haupu Ridge.

Kokee State Park lies just north of Waimea Canyon, and has the Alakai Swamp to the east, the steep cliffs of the Na Pali coast to the north, and drier leeward ridges to the west. The park is surrounded by forest reserves, another state park, and a natural area reserve. In the Kokee region, the annual rainfall ranges from 45 to 80 inches; the average temperature is about 62 degrees F.

One of the island's most famous features is the Na Pali Coast, where streams and wave action have cut deep valleys and eroded the northern coast to form precipitous cliffs as high as 3,000 feet.

Because of its age and relative isolation, levels of floristic diversity and endemism are higher on Kauai than on any of the other Hawaiian Islands. However, the vegetation of Kauai has undergone extreme alterations because of past and present land use. Land with rich soils was altered by early Hawaiians, and more recently converted to agricultural use and pastures. Intentional and inadvertent introduction of alien plant and animal taxa has also contributed to the reduction of native vegetation. Native forests are now limited to the upper elevation mesic and wet regions within Kauai's conservation district.

The lowland dry forests, which extend into mesic forests, are characterized by annual rainfall of 20 to 80 inches, which falls between November and March, and a well-drained, highly weathered substrate rich in aluminum. Lowland mesic forest communities lie between 100 and 3,000 feet in elevation, and are characterized by a 6.5 to 65 foot tall canopy and a diverse understory of shrubs, herbs, and ferns. The annual rainfall of 45 to 150 inches falls predominantly between October and March. The mesic community often grades into lowland wet forests, which are typically found on the windward side of the island or in sheltered leeward situations between 330 and 3,940 feet in elevation. The rainfall in this lowland wet community may exceed 200 inches per year. These forests were once predominant vegetation on Kauai but now exist only on steep rocky terrain or cliff faces. The substrate is generally of well-drained soils that may support tree canopies up to 130 feet in height. The montane forest communities typically occur above 3,000 feet in elevation, where the annual rainfall may exceed 280 inches.

Habitat Conditions on the Island of Lanai

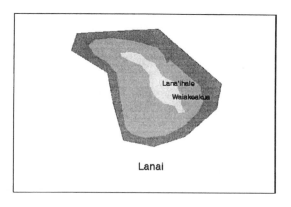

Lanai

Lanai was formed by the extinct volcano Palawai, with the highest peak at 3,370 feet. It was first settled by Mormon elders in 1854, but the colony failed ten years later. Lanai, meaning "hump" was used for cattle grazing until 1922, during which time much of the native vegetation was destroyed. It was purchased by the Dole Corporation for use as a pineapple plantation in 1922, and making Lanai the largest privately owned island in the Hawaiian chain. Ranching and farming have basically desecrated habitats for plants and birds, but as the result of conservation efforts by George C. Munro, a New Zealand naturalist who arrived on Lanai in 1911, scattered patches of dryland forest survive on the western slopes of the island. One of these is Kanepu's Preserve, six miles northwest of Lanai City. Munro erected fences and removed stray cattle to preserve a grove of lama (native persimmon) and olopu'a (a native olive). For 30 years he worked to protect the site, but he managed to save only a token of the many native plants that covered the forested island.

Habitat Conditions on the Island of Laysan

Laysan Island, located 790 miles northwest of Oahu, is about 2.0 kilometers (1.8 miles) long and 1.7 km (1.1 miles) wide; a total of about 1,005 acres. Sand dunes are found around the periphery of this coral sand island. There is a salt-water lagoon inland which covers about 20 percent of the island.

Laysan Island is one of the older volcanic islands in the Hawaiian Island (formerly Sandwich Island) chain. Erosion over time has eroded the volcanic peak; it is now below sea level. The island itself is the result of a buildup of coral, other marine invertebrates, and calcareous algae on top of the remaining portion of the inactive volcano. The island's maximum elevation is 56 feet above sea level. There is an abrupt rise to 15 to 18 feet along the coast, then a gradual rise to an average elevation of about 40 feet.

The vegetated area occupies about half the island. A number of exotic plant species have become established on Laysan over the last 80 years, including a few coconut palms.

Causes for Extinction on Laysan

Introduction of rodents, cats, exotic insects, birds and plants were and continue to be major threats to bird populations on Laysan Island. Rodents prey on eggs and chicks, and destroy vegetation. It is difficult to prevent the accidental introduction of new exotic organisms to these islands. This problem suggests these species will always be threatened with extinction to some degree.

Natural disasters, hurricanes/tidal waves, could destroy some portion of any or all of the remaining endangered populations inhabiting these islands.

The introduction of rabbits to Laysan Island in 1903 led to the destruction of the dense grass and scaevola thickets inhabited by Laysan rail and resulted in the extirpation of the rail from Laysan Island by 1923.

Several transplants were attempted; all failed. Laysan rails were relocated to Midway Island (in 1891 and 1904). Japanese troops stationed on Midway during the latter part of the war killed the rails for food. Although this was not the primary factor leading to the elimination of the rail from Midway, it probably disrupted the reproductive capability of the population and left it more vulnerable to extinction. The Midway introduction was successful until 1944, when rats were accidentally introduced to the island. The Laysan rail was also relocated to Lisianski Island (1913), and Pearl and Hermes Reef (1929). The Lisianski and Pearl/Hermes Reef transplant failures were blamed on the introduction of rabbits and a major storm, respectively.

Introduction of Destructive Species to the Hawaiian Islands

Both Hawaiian bird and plant life have been devastated by introduced species. Bird life in Hawaii (and in most other places) is inextricably linked to plant life, and the decline and extinction of bird species is often caused by the destruction of habitat that provides food and shelter. The introduction of predators is another powerful disrupting factor to the survival of birds. On the Hawaiian islands, rats that came ashore from the ships of explorers were able to prey on birds' nests, devouring both eggs and hatchlings. Rats also consume seeds and flowers, and damage the bark of native plants. In some instances, rats are thought to be significant threats to certain Hawaiian plants.

When Polynesian immigrants settled the islands about 400 A.D., they introduced junglefowl, dogs, pigs, rats, snails and wild seed. By 1,600, the population had peaked at about 200,000 residents, and most of the islands were more heavily populated than they are today. These Polynesians adopted farming techniques such as water control and slash-and-burn systems of agriculture. Their use of the land resulted in erosion, changes in the composition of native communities, and a reduction of biodiversity. Many forested slopes were denuded by the mid-1800s to supply firewood to whaling ships, plantations, and Honolulu residents. Sandalwood and tree fern harvesting occurred in many areas, changing forest composition.

The 1848 provision for land sales to individuals allowed large-scale agricultural and ranching ventures to begin. So much land was cleared for these enterprises that climatic conditions began to change and the distribution of rainfall altered. Plantation owners supported reforestation programs that resulted in many alien trees being introduced. Beginning in the 1920s, water collection and diversion systems were constructed in upland areas to irrigate lowland fields, which opened new routes for the invasion of alien plants and animals into native forests.

Past and present activities of introduced alien animals are the primary cause of altering and degrading vegetation. Feral goats (*Capra hircus*), originally native to the Middle East, were successfully introduced to the islands in 1792. Pigs (*Sus scrofa*) were introduced by Polynesians, with additional introductions by Captain James Cook in 1778. Feral goats and pigs are managed in Hawaii as a game animal, but significant damage to native ecosystems and endangered species occur. Goat and pig hunting is allowed year round, or during certain months, depending on the area. These animals eat native vegetation, trample roots and seedlings, cause erosion, and promote the invasion of alien plants. They are able to forage in extremely rugged terrain and have a high reproductive capacity.

Cattle (*Bos taurus*) native to Europe, North Africa and southwestern Asia, were introduced to the islands in 1793. Large feral herds developed as a result of restrictions on cattle killing. Cattle eat native vegetation, trample roots and seedlings, cause erosion, create disturbed areas which alien plants invade, and spread the seeds of alien plants in their feces. The forest, in areas grazed by cattle, eventually becomes degraded to grassland pasture. Plant cover is reduced for many years following the removal of cattle from the area. Several alien grasses and legumes purposely introduced for cattle forage have become noxious weeds. Feral mountain sheep, mule deer, and axis deer cause the same problems as feral cattle and goats.

The black twig borer is a small beetle that burrows into branches, introduces a pathogenic fungus as food for its larvae, and lays its eggs. Twigs, branches, and even the entire plant can be killed from such an infestation. The black twig borer has many hosts, disperses easily, and is especially prevalent in *Melicope* and *Malvaceae* species.

The introduction of alien weeds has significantly affected dry and mesic forest systems and some wet forests. Species such as *Clidemia*, blackberry, fountain grass, and kukuyu grass pose major threats to the general endangered species populations and have contributed to the extinction of many plants.

Because Hawaiian plants were subjected to fire during their evolution only in areas of volcanic activity, and from occasional lightning strikes, they are not adapted to recurring fires and are unable to recover well from them. Alien plants are often better adapted to fire, and some fire-adapted grasses have become widespread. The presence of such vegetation increases the intensity, extent, and frequency of fire, and fire-adapted alien plants can reestablish a burned area, choking out the native plants.

Fire is an immediate threat in drier areas of Hawaii, Molokai and Oahu, especially during drier months. Most of the fires there are caused by people pursuing recreational activities; prevailing winds spread fires to inland areas. The introduction of alien plants that promote fire intensity has exacerbated the problem.

Laysan Millerbird
Acrocephalus familiaris familiaris

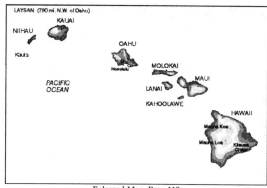

LAYSAN (790 mi. N.W. of Oahu)

Enlarged Map, Page 119

Description

The Laysan millerbird, *Acrocephalus familiaris familiaris,* was a small bird, measuring 4 to 4.5 inches, somewhat like a flycatcher in shape and behavior. The back feathers were grayish brown and it was brownish white below.

Behavior

A. f. familiaris apparently laid its eggs in May and June with chicks being observed in early summer. Clutch sizes were 2 to 3 eggs. Incubation may have lasted about 17 days. The chicks were altricial.

A. f. familiaris was non-migratory. The species was entirely insectivorous, feeding on insects, moths, flies, small beetles, and caterpillars. This bird was named for its affinity for miller moths.

Several sources indicate that *A. f. familiaris* is a crepuscular species. Some accounts report that Laysan millerbirds retired to shade of bushes or tall grass tussocks in the hot part of the day. Other sources reported that Laysan millerbird activity on Laysan Island peaked in the morning and late afternoon, but in the warmer part of the day

Status	Extinct
Probable Extinction	c.1923
Family	Muscicapidae (Thrushes)
Description	Small grayish-brown bird with a brownish-white under side.
Habitat	Salt water lagoon
Food	Insects, moths, flies, beetles and caterpillars.
Reproduction	Nested in tall grass clumps along a lagoon.
Causes for Extinction	Introduced animals, natural disaster.
Range	Hawaii: Laysan Island
Photo	See Color Insert, C-5

Laysan millerbirds took shelter in the bushes and grass. The bird was not shy of humans and would land on people if they remained quiet.

Habitat

A. f. familiaris is reported to have nested a couple of feet above the ground in tall grass clumps of *Eragrostis* along the lagoon. The abundance of the grass *Eragrostis* on Laysan and the paucity of it on Nihoa probably accounts for the apparent difference in nest site preference between the Nihoa millerbird and the extinct Laysan millerbird. Laysan millerbird nests were reportedly made of rootlets, grass, and white albatross feathers.

Distribution

The decline of *A. f. familiaris* occurred within a fairly short period of time. It was considered plentiful in 1891, abundant in 1902, common in 1915 (possibly as many as 1,500 birds remained), and became extinct sometime between 1915 and 1923.

A. f. familiaris was endemic to Laysan Island.

Causes for Extinction

A. f. familiaris belongs to a group of Old World warblers demonstrating an amazing ability to colonize small islands over vast distances of water. Two millerbirds once inhabited the leeward Hawaiian Islands. *A. f. familiaris* became extinct when feral rabbits devoured all living vegetation on Laysan Island.

Introduction of rodents, cats, alien insects, birds and plants are major threats to bird populations on Laysan Island. Rodents prey on eggs and chicks, and destroy vegetation. It will be difficult to prevent the accidental introduction of new alien organisms to these islands. This problem suggests these species will always be threatened with extinction to some degree.

Natural disasters, hurricanes and tidal waves could destroy some portion of any or all endangered populations inhabiting these islands.

Adapted from data compiled by the Threatened and Endangered Species Information Institute (Golden, CO) for *Beacham's International Threatened, Endangered, and Extinct Species* published on CD ROM, available from Beacham Publishing.

Kioea

Chaetoptila angustipluma

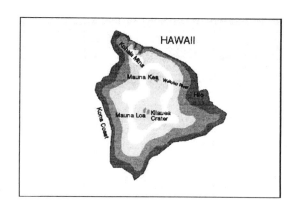

Description

The kioea, *Chaetoptila angustipluma*, possessed a striped head of blackish-brown with a grayish-white stripe above the eyes. Lores, the sides of the face, and the ear coverts were dull black with a patch of feathers immediately below the eye which were mottled with grayish-white. The chin and throat were a dull white tinged with yellow. The feather shafts and whiskers were colored black while the wing coverts and back were a greenish-brown tinged with ochraceous color on the rump. The feathers of the mantle showed a white shaft streak which widened to a tear-shaped spot near the tip. The tail was a deep brown with outer margins green. The breast and abdomen were a dull white, striped longitudinally with darkish-brown. The flanks were strongly tinged with ochraceous and the bill, legs, and feet were dark brown.

The wing measured 140 millimeters (5.46 in) while the tail was 153 mm (5.97 in) long. The culmen was 34 mm (1.33 in) long and the tarsus, 45 mm (1.75 in). The call of this species was a loud chuck.

The common name of the species is kioea. This comes from the Hawaiian Annual from 1879 which was written by a Mr. Dole,

Status	Extinct
Probable Extinction	c.1850
Family	Meliphagidae (Honey-eater)
Description	Small bird with a blackish-brown striped head, dull white chin and throat tinged with yellow, greenish-brown wing coverts and back, and an ochre-colored rump.
Habitat	Possibly the high plateau and edges of the forest near 4,000 ft.
Food	Possibly nectar and insects.
Causes for Extinction	Habitat alteration, predators.
Range	Hawaii: Hawaii
Photo	See Color Insert, C-5

who claimed the species also lived on the island of Molokai despite slim evidence. The meaning of the name in the native Hawaiian is "standing high on long legs".

Behavior

Little is known about this species' diet. However, other honeycreepers of the Hawaiian Islands fed on the nectar from the flowers of ohias, lobelias, and other plants. They possessed a long, tubular tongue. They also ate introduced bananas, and insects in larvae.

The species was active during the day when flowers were in full bloom.

Habitat

The species inhabited the mountain forests of Hawaii. It is assumed to have had many of the habits common to the honeycreepers, the Meliphaga family. It was endemic to the island of Hawaii, but exactly what parts of the island and whether it ranged to other islands is not certain. It is suspected that the species inhabited the high plateau between the mountains and the edges of the forest. Its cousin, the Hawaiian o'o, appeared over the entire island at an altitude of up to 1,220 meters (4,000 feet). It was once recorded at 1,830 m (6,000 ft). *M. nobilis* frequented the high tree tops about 30.5 m (100 ft) off of the ground.

Distribution

Little is known of the biology of this species. Only 4 skins remain as evidence of its life and history. The species thrived in its heyday, probably common over the entire island of Hawaii and may have lived on other islands of Hawaii. The species was the first of the honeycreepers to disappear after alteration of the habitat by Europeans. It became extinct in 1859.

Causes for Extinction

With Europeans came the beginning of the process that altered the species' habitat. Although scientists are not sure of the precise cause of the species' extinction, they suspect a variety of reasons all relating to the change in the environment. The introduction of cattle, cats, and rats have been discussed as possible causes. By eating forest undergrowth, cattle may have changed the habitat in a subtle way still unknown. Cats were often found devouring individuals of the species. Black rats were often found moving in the trees at night hunting for prey, of which the kioea could have been one.

Adapted from data compiled by the Threatened and Endangered Species Information Institute (Golden, CO) for *Beacham's International Threatened, Endangered, and Extinct Species* published on CD ROM, available from Beacham Publishing.

Kona Finch =
Kona Grosbeak
Chloridops kona

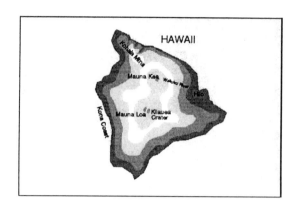

Description

The Kona finch, *Chloridops kona*, was the smallest (6 inches) of the extinct members of the honeycreeper family, *Drepanididae* (now *Fringillidae*), subfamily *Psittirostrinae*, but it had the largest bill. *C. kona* was brownish-olive green to bright olive green on the head and back with a golden green breast and a white to off-white belly. The bill was a dull beige color, the legs and feet were dark brown to blackish, and the irises were dark hazel. This species was not sexually dimorphic. *C. kona* has been described as a slow-moving bird.

C. kona is also referred to by the common names Chloridops, Kona grosbeak, and grosbeak finch.

Status	Extinct
Probable Extinction	1894
Family	Fringillidae (Honey-creepers)
Description	Small bird with a large, thick, beige bill, brownish-olive green head and back, a golden-green breast and white belly.
Habitat	Naio trees in koa forests on the Kona Coast.
Food	Seeds, caterpillars and leaves.
Causes for Extinction	Unknown
Range	Hawaii: Hawaii

Behavior

C. kona was non-migratory and was probably granivorous for the most part. Its large bill had evolved to crack seeds that other species could not use because of the seed's hardness. This bird was observed feeding in the naio tree which has very hard and dry seeds. It was also observed feeding on caterpillars and green leaves.

Information pertaining to periodicity is unknown. Activity levels probably increased during the breeding season. Daily activity levels most likely decreased during the summer as temperatures rose.

Members of this family (Fringillidae, formerly Drepanididae) are thought to have descended from one species. This species spread through the remote Hawaiian Islands and evolved to fill the empty niches that would have been filled by members of other bird families (found in other parts of the world) if those species had reached the Hawaiian Islands. The honeycreepers developed a wide variety of bill sizes and shapes to take advantage of the various food resources, including: short, thick, finch- to parrot-like bills; long, thin, recurved (sickle-shaped) bills; bills where the upper and lower mandibles are different lengths; and bills that are slightly crossed. Several species and subspecies are now considered to be extinct and many others are Federally listed as endangered. The extinct species are the koa finch (*Rhodacanthis palmeri*); Kona grosbeak finch (*Chloridops kona*); greater amakihi (*Hemignathus sagittirostris*); ula-ai-hawane (*Ciridops anna*); mamo (*Drepanis pacifica*); and black mamo (*D. funerea*). The extinct subspecies are the Oahu akialoa (*Hemignathus obscurus ellisianus*); Hawaiian akialoa (*H. o. obscurus*); Lanai akialoa (*H. o. lanaiensis*); Laysan honeycreeper (*Himatione sanguinea freethi*); Oahu nukupu'u (*Hemignathus lucidus lucidus*); and the Lanai creeper (*Paroreomyza maculata montana*).

Habitat

C. kona inhabited the same koa forests on the Kona Coast, island of Hawaii, where *Rhodacanthis palmeri* and *R. flaviceps* were found. It was found more often in naio (bastard sandalwood tree, *Myoporum* sp. rather than koa. Naio often grows in old lava flows. *C. kona* was observed foraging up to 1,350 meters (4,500 feet) in elevation for this tree's seeds. These seeds are hard and dry and it requires a great deal of crushing power to open the seed, which the bird's very thick, large bill could accomplish. *C. kona* may have preferred mid-sized naio in somewhat newer lava flows. These areas have little or no undergrowth.

Distribution

C. kona was considered a rare species when it was discovered. Palmer and Munro collected several specimens in 1891 and Perkins collected some specimens in both 1892 and 1894. This species has not been seen since 1894.

C. kona was endemic to the Kona Coast, island of Hawaii. It was found in the koa forests on Mauna Loa. All but 2 birds were collected or sighted in a 4 square mile (10 kilometer square) area on Mauna Loa's southwest slopes between the elevations of 3,500-5,500 feet; the area is covered by an open naio woodland and rough, fairly new lava flows. A pair of *C. kona* was also found near Honaunau in 1891; this area is about 10 miles south of the above site.

Causes for Extinction

See Introduction of Destructive Species to the Hawaiian Islands, page 128.

Adapted from data compiled by the Threatened and Endangered Species Information Institute (Golden, CO) for *Beacham's International Threatened, Endangered, and Extinct Species* published on CD ROM, available from Beacham Publishing.

Ula-ai-hawane

Ciridops anna

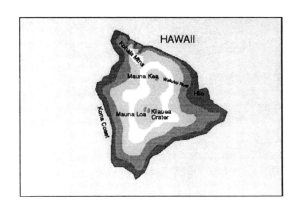

Description

The ula-ai-hawane, *Ciridops anna*, grew to a length of about 4.25 inches. It was black to silvery gray and white on the crown and the nape of the neck; the back was tinged with brown. The tail, wing flight feathers and coverts, breast, and rump were black. A bright red patch occurred on its lower abdomen and the underside of its tail coverts were a brownish buff. Its eyes were dark hazel and its feet were pinkish brown.

The Hawaiian name "ula-ai-hawane" means "The red bird that feeds upon the Hawane palm".

Behavior

The species fed exclusively on the nectar of the Hawane palm tree (*Pritchardia* sp.) Information pertaining to periodicity is unknown. Activity levels probably increased during the breeding season. Daily activity levels most likely decreased during the summer as temperatures rose.

Habitat

The species was endemic to the island of Hawaii. It was known from the Kana and

Status	Extinct
Probable Extinction	c.1892
Family	Fringillidae (Honey-creepers)
Description	Small bird with black to silver-gray crown and neck, black tail, coverts, breast and rump, and a bright red patch on its lower abdomen.
Habitat	Near areas with Hawane palms.
Food	Nectar of the Hawane palm tree.
Range	Hawaii: Hawaii
Photo	See Color Insert, C-6

Hilo districts as well as the Kohala Mountains where it was primarily associated with the Hawane palm (*Pritchardia* sp.).

Distribution

Ula-ai-hawane was endemic to Hawaii where it is speculated that it was once widely distributed. It was known from the windward and leeward sides of the island in the district of Hilo and the Kohala Mountains. It was rare in Kona but often reported.

Even as the species was being described in 1859, its numbers were limited by restricted food requirements and small population numbers. The last specimen was collected on Mount Kohala at the headwaters of the Awini River on February 20, 1892. Ula-ai-hawane may have been sighted in 1937 at Kahua but this was not confirmed.

Ula-ai-hawane occupied a very narrow feeding niche; it was dependent on the various species of the Hawane palm tree (*Pritchardia* sp.) for nectar. Several of the palms are rare or endangered; some are near extinction.

Causes for Extinction

Information concerning the economic value of this species is unknown. It was not a commercially important species but may have been taken for food by island natives.

Adapted from data compiled by the Threatened and Endangered Species Information Institute (Golden, CO) for *Beacham's International Threatened, Endangered, and Extinct Species* published on CD ROM, available from Beacham Publishing.

Black Mamo
Drepanis funerea

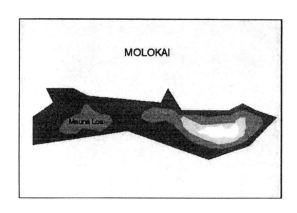

MOLOKAI

Mauna Loa

Description

The black mamo, *Drepanis funerea*, had an average wingspan of 102 millimeters (3.94 inches) with a tail extending about 70 mm (2.73 inches). It possessed lusterless black plumage with a buffy white shade on the outer webs of the primaries. Its bill was black and strongly decurved with a patch of yellow at the base of the maxilla. Its iris was colored yellowish brown and its feet and legs were black. Although the sexes were similar in appearance, the male's beak was longer and the female may have been smaller on average. Its upper mandible was longer than the lower.

Its Hawaiian names are Oo-nuku-umu and Hoa which mean "the o'o with the sucking beak."

Behavior

The black mamo's voice was loud like a cry and very clear. Yet, it also possessed a milder call note. The species was tame and often followed those observing them with curiosity.

The black mamo was nectivorous; it fed exclusively on the nectar of the lobelias and other flowers. It was a "true honey-sucker"

Status	Extinct
Probable Extinction	c.1910
Family	Fringillidae (Honey-creeper)
Description	Small bird with black plumage, black bill with a patch of yellow, black feet and yellow-brown eyes.
Habitat	Underbrush and lower trees in koa forests.
Food	Nectar.
Causes for Extinction	Habitat loss, hunting.
Range	Hawaii: Molokai
Photo	See Color Insert, C-6

and during observations, the species' tongues darted in and out of the beak so fast that they were described as "liquid streaks".

Information pertaining to periodicity is unknown. Activity levels probably increased during the breeding season. Daily activity levels most likely decreased during the summer as temperatures rose.

Habitat

The black mamo was endemic to Molokai; it inhabited the underbrush and lower trees in the koa forest areas. It was associated with the lobelias and other flowers that were its primary food source. The species kept mostly to the forest underbrush; it was rarely seen above 3.6 meters (12 feet). It occurred at an elevation of 1,525 meters (5,000 feet).

Distribution

The black mamo was endemic to Molokai where it is speculated that it was once widely distributed. It was known from the Pelekunu Valley and first described in 1893; even then its numbers were limited and it was considered rare. The species was last collected in 1907 and this is believed to be the date when the last sightings occurred.

Causes for Extinction

A large percentage of Molokai's koa forests have been converted to agricultural use (pastureland and cropland), urban development, and recreational facilities. Habitat loss and alteration, along with hunting for feathers, were probably the primary causes of the decline and extinction of this bird.

The black mamo and its relative, *D. pacifica* (mamo), were hunted for their feathers, which were used to decorate cloaks worn by Hawaiian royalty.

Adapted from data compiled by the Threatened and Endangered Species Information Institute (Golden, CO) for *Beacham's International Threatened, Endangered, and Extinct Species* published on CD ROM, available from Beacham Publishing.

Lanai Akialoa

Hemignathus obscurus lanaiensis

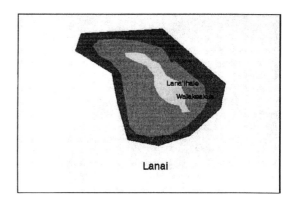

Lanai

Description

The Lanai akialoa, *Hemignathus obscurus lanaiensis,* was a member of the Hawaiian honeycreeper subfamily, *Drepanidinae* (formerly *Psittirostrinae* — the insect and seed eaters), family *Fringillidae* (formerly *Drepanididae*).

This small bird, measuring about 6.5 inches or 16.5 centimeters, was a bright olive green on the head, shoulders, and back; the breast and belly were a duller yellowish-green; the undertail coverts were creamy white; and the wings and tail were brown. The females were a more grayish olive color on the back and a yellower green on the underparts. The male and female bills averaged lengths of 1.85 and 1.45 inches, respectively.

The common name is also spelled akihialoa. The common name is the Hawaiian or Polynesian word describing the bird's long, curved bill. The generic name also describes the bill's shape.

Behavior

H. o. lanaiensis was non-migratory. The species was presumably omnivorous. The long slender bill was used to extract nectar

Status	Extinct
Probable Extinction	c. 1894
Family	Fringillidae (Honey-creeper)
Description	Small bird with a bright olive-green head, shoulders and back, duller yellowish-green underside, and brown wings and tail.
Habitat	Dense, wet areas of ohia-koa forests.
Food	Nectar, insects and spiders.
Causes for Extinction	Deforestation leading to the establishment of predators.
Range	Hawaii: Lanai

from flowering trees including ohia trees and lobelias. This bill shape was also adapted to probing crevices in tree bark and under lichens for insects and spiders. More than one observer noted that this species and other birds seemed to be more active and "happy" (singing more) during or after feeding on nectar, and speculated that the nectar was a stimulant.

Activity levels probably increased during the breeding season. Daily activity levels most likely decreased during the summer as temperatures rose.

Habitat

H. o. lanaiensis inhabited the forested areas on the island of Lanai. It was apparently restricted to the dense, wet habitats of the ohia-koa forests.

Distribution

The last positive sighting and collection was in 1894. This species may have been collected in 1911 but this has not been confirmed. *H. o. lanaiensis* was endemic to the island of Lanai.

Causes for Extinction

Habitat loss resulting from deforestation and conversion to agricultural cropland and pastureland and habitat degradation are the primary factors believed to have led to the decline and extinction of this subspecies. Habitat degradation occurred in areas where exotic plants, insects, birds, and predators were allowed to become established.

Adapted from data compiled by the Threatened and Endangered Species Information Institute (Golden, CO) for *Beacham's International Threatened, Endangered, and Extinct Species* published on CD ROM, available from Beacham Publishing.

Oahu Akialoa

Hemignathus obscurus lichtensteinii

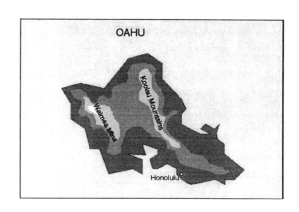

OAHU

Koolau Mountains

Waimea Mtns

Honolulu

Description

The Oahu akialoa, *Hemignathus obscurus lichtensteinii*, was a member of the Hawaiian honeycreeper family, Drepanididae (now Fringillidae), subfamily Drepanidinae (nectar-feeders). This sickle-billed honeycreeper was scarcely studied, and until 1950 'akialoas from all islands were considered one species, and their names remain in dispute. When this species was finally singled out for study, locating the bird was made somewhat easier by its conspicuous trappings and calls.

This small bird (about 6.5 inches or 16.5 centimeters) was olive green on the head, shoulders, and back, the breast and belly were a duller yellowish-green, the undertail coverts were creamy white, and the wings and tail were brown. The females were a more grayish olive color on the back and a yellower green on the underparts. This subspecies had a duller green back than the other subspecies. The male and female bills averaged lengths of 1.85 and 1.45 inches, respectively.

The common name is also spelled akihialoa. The common name is the Hawaiian or Polynesian word describing the bird's long, curved bill. The generic name also describes the bill's shape. The Hawaiian names "iwi"

Status	Extinct
Probable Extinction	1940
Family	Fringillidae (Honey-creepers)
Description	Small bird with an olive-green head, shoulders and back, and a duller, yellowish-green underside.
Habitat	Dense, wet ohia-koa forests on the island of Oahu.
Food	Nectar, insects and spiders.
Causes for Extinction	Deforestation resulting in establishing predator species.
Range	Hawaii: Oahu
Photo (relative)	See Color Insert, C-6

and "iiwi" are also used in reference to this subspecies on Oahu. "Iiwi" is also used in reference to a completely different species on Oahu.

Behavior

The Oahu akialoa was non-migratory and restricted to dense, wet ohia forests. The species was presumably omnivorous. The long slender bill was used to extract nectar from flowering trees including ohia trees and lobelias. This bill shape was also adapted to probing crevices in tree bark and under lichens for insects and spiders. More than one observer noted that this species and other birds seemed to be more active and "happy" (singing more) during or after feeding on nectar, and speculated that the nectar was a stimulant.

Activity levels probably increased during the breeding season. Daily activity levels most likely decreased during the summer as temperatures rose.

Habitat

The Oahu akialoa inhabited the forested areas on the island of Oahu. It was apparently restricted to the dense, wet habitats of the ohia-koa forests.

Distribution

This species occupied Lanai, Oahu, and the island of Hawaii; fossils have been found on Molokai. It is presumed to be extinct but remains on the Federal list as endangered despite the lack of sightings. It apparently was considered to be rare by the latter part of the nineteenth century. Unconfirmed sightings were reported in 1937 and 1940.

Causes for Extinction

Habitat loss resulting from deforestation and conversion to agricultural cropland and pastureland and habitat degradation are the primary factors believed to have led to the decline and extinction of this subspecies. Habitat degradation occurred in areas where exotic plants, insects, birds, and predators were allowed to become established.

Adapted from data compiled by the Threatened and Endangered Species Information Institute (Golden, CO) for *Beacham's International Threatened, Endangered, and Extinct Species* published on CD ROM, available from Beacham Publishing.

Greater Amakihi
Hemignathus sagittirostris

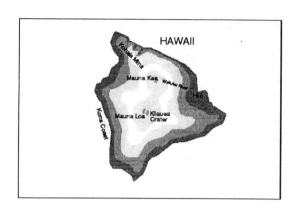

Description

The greater amakihi, *Hemignathus sagittirostris,* possessed upperparts of bright olive-green which showed more of a yellow tinge on the forehead, the sides of the head, and the upper tail coverts. The throat, breast, and abdomen were a yellowish olive-green. The wings were blackish brown with primaries margined with yellowish green. The undersurface of the wing was ash-colored. The bill was black becoming bluish or gray toward the base. The species' irises were hazel with a reddish tinge and its legs and feet were black.

Both male and female appeared identical. The wing measured 83 millimeters (3.24 in) with the tail 53 mm (2.1 in) long. The culmen was 23 mm (.89 in) and the tarsus, 24 mm (.9 in) long. The song of the species was similar to its near ally, the amakihi (*Hemignathus virens*). However, Greater amakihi differed in its singing by introducing 2 or 3 additional whistles at the end of each trill.

Status	Extinct
Probable Extinction	c.1950
Family	Fringillidae (Honey-creeper)
Description	Small bird with bright olive-green upper parts, a yellow-tinged forehead and upper tail coverts, yellowish-green throat, breast and abdomen, blackish wings with an ash-colored undersurface, and a black beak.
Habitat	Dense, wet forests between 1,000-3,000 feet.
Food	Crickets, caterpillars, spiders and beetles.
Causes for Extinction	Probably habitat alteration and ferral animals.
Range	Hawaii: Hawaii
Photo	See Color Insert, C-5

Behavior

The species fed on crickets found on ohia trees or in the foliage growing upon them. Their diet was also made up of caterpillars, spiders, and beetles. The species was also observed feeding upon the nectar of ohia. It had a fairly straight bill and probably did not forage by creeping.

Greater amakihi was active during the day when flowers were in full bloom.

Habitat

Greater amakihi inhabited a narrow band of dense dripping forest on either side of the Wailuku River on the island of Hawaii, possibly between the elevations of 300 and 900 meters (1,000 and 3,000 feet). The species was often seen creeping along the branches of ohia trees, or in the foliage that grew upon them.

Distribution

Easily overlooked, the Greater 'Amakihi was first recorded in 1892. Three years later a researcher, apparently unaware that the bird had been discovered earlier, undertook a two-week study to announce his findings. Even before scientists discovered the bird, it was known to native Hawaiians who were disinterested in its rather plain green plumage.

The species was probably limited by restricted habitat requirements. It is possible the species was uncommon even in the 1700s since native Hawaiians were unaware of its existence.

Causes for Extinction

With Europeans came the beginning of the process that altered the species' habitat. Although scientists are not sure of the precise cause of the species' extinction, they suspect a variety of reasons all related to the change in the environment. The introduction of cattle, cats, and rats has been discussed as possible causes. By eating forest under-growth, cattle may have changed the habitat in a subtle way. Cats were observed devouring individuals of the species, and black rats were often seen moving in the trees at night hunting for prey, of which the greater amakihi could have been one. The last individual was recorded in the early 1900s and the last specimen was taken in 1901. In 1950, D. Amadon reported that the species' restricted habitat was gone; the area was completely covered with sugar-cane. In the very unlikely event that the species has survived, it could only occur in the forests along Hawaii's Hamakua coast.

Adapted from data compiled by the Threatened and Endangered Species Information Institute (Golden, CO) for *Beacham's International Threatened, Endangered, and Extinct Species* published on CD ROM, available from Beacham Publishing.

Apapane = Laysan Honeycreeper
Himatione sanguinea freethii

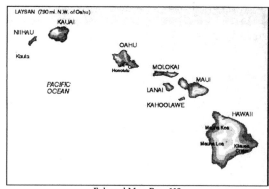

Enlarged Map, Page 119

Description

The Apapane or Laysan honeycreeper, *Himatione sanguinea freethii*, was a member of the Hawaiian honeycreeper family, Drepanididae (now Fringillidae), subfamily Drepanidinae (nectar-feeders). This subspecies was similar in size to other subspecies (about 4.25 to 5.25 inches in length). The bill was about as long as the head and was thin and moderately decurved. The other subspecies have crimson bodies, black wings, tails, legs, and bill, and white bellies and undertail coverts. The Laysan honeycreeper was a duller red color with brown wings and tail and brown irises. Other characteristics are similar. Immature birds were light brown. This bird's stiff feathers created a whirring sound in flight. It has been described as a weak flier.

The Laysan honeycreeper is also referred to as "redbird".

Status	Extinct
Probable Extinction	1923
Family	Fringillidae (Honeycreepers)
Description	Small bird with a long, thin, black bill, dull-red body, brown wings and tail, and white belly.
Habitat	Nested in tall grass and low bushes around lagoons on Laysan Island.
Food	Nectar of flowers and some insects.
Reproduction	Clutch of 3 eggs.
Causes for Extinction	Loss of vegetation on the island by feral rabbits.
Range	Hawaii: Laysan Island
Photo	See Color Insert, C-6

Behavior

H. sanguinea on Laysan built a bowl type nest hidden in shrubby ohia trees (*Metrosideros* sp.). Observed clutches contained 3 eggs.

The Laysan honeycreeper was non-migratory. It was probably primarily nectarivorous but also consumed insects including caterpillars and noctuid miller moths. This bird was observed feeding from the flowers of Nohu (*Tribulus* sp.) and Pohuehue (*Ipomoea* sp.).

Activity levels probably increased during the breeding season. Daily activity levels most likely decreased during the summer as temperatures rose.

Habitat

This species appears to have nested in areas with tall grass and low bushes around the lagoon.

Distribution

The species was endemic to the island of Laysan. The Laysan honeycreeper was considered to be fairly common is 1891 when it was discovered by the manager of the North Pacific Phosphate and Fertilizer Company, which was mining the island. The numbers had dropped to a fairly low level by 1906 and 1915. Only 3 remained in 1923; these birds were apparently killed during an intense sandstorm in 1923.

Causes for Extinction

The Laysan honeycreeper became extinct when feral rabbits devoured all virtually all living vegetation on Laysan Island. The rabbits were introduced around 1904 by employees of a fertilizer company with a mining site on Laysan Island. The rabbits were intended to establish a canning business. Relatively few birds were left in 1906 and the last 3 birds were seen in 1923 just before an intense sandstorm that presumably killed them.

Introduction of rodents, cats, alien insects, birds and plants were and still are major threats to bird populations on Laysan Island. Rodents prey on eggs and chicks, and destroy vegetation. It has been difficult preventing the accidental introduction of new organisms to these islands. This problem suggests the remaining species may always be threatened with extinction to some degree.

Natural disasters, hurricanes/tidal waves could have destroyed some portion of any or all endangered or extinct populations that inhabit or did inhabit these islands.

Adapted from data compiled by the Threatened and Endangered Species Information Institute (Golden, CO) for *Beacham's International Threatened, Endangered, and Extinct Species* published on CD ROM, available from Beacham Publishing.

Oahu 'Akepa = 'Akopeu'ie

Loxops coccineus rufus

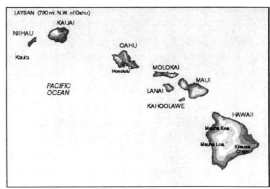

Enlarged Map, Page 119

Description

The Oahu 'akepa or 'akopeu'ie, *Loxops coccineus rufus*, was a member of the Hawaiian honeycreeper family, *Drepanidinae* (now *Fringillidae*), subfamily *Psittirostrinae* (insect- and seed-eaters). This small finch-like bird, measuring 4 to 4.5 inches, was a rufous-orange color sometimes dulled by a brownish cast on the back with brown-black wings, a reddish-orange breast, and lighter red-orange coloring on the belly and undertail coverts (male). Females and immatures were a fairly uniform greenish gray. The tail was long and forked. The bill, if examined closely, was a distinguishing characteristic. The lower mandible was a bit shorter than the upper one and was twisted slightly to the right or left and up across the upper mandible. *L. c. rufus'* tongue was long and tubular in shape.

The common Hawaiian name is also spelled 'akepeuie. Members of this family (*Drepanididae* or *Fringillidae*) are thought to have descended from one species. This species spread through the remote Hawaiian Islands and evolved to fill the empty niches that would have been filled by members of other bird families (found in other parts of the world) if those species had reached the Hawaiian Islands. The honeycreepers developed a wide variety of bill sizes and shapes to take advantage of the various food resources, including short, thick, finch- to parrot-like bills; long, thin, recurved (sickle-shaped) bills; bills where the upper and lower mandibles are different lengths; and bills that are slightly crossed.

Status	Extinct
Probable Extinction	1891
Family	Fringillidae (Honey-creepers)
Description	Small, finch-like bird with brown-black wings, a reddish-orange breast, and lighter red-orange on the underside.
Habitat	Koa forests at elevations of 3,000-6,000 feet.
Food	Insects
Reproduction	Nested in tree cavities, probably in March.
Causes for Extinction	Unknown
Range	Hawaii: Hawaii, Maui, Kauai
Photo	See Color Insert, C-3

Behavior

L. c. rufus most likely nested in tree cavities as the other members of this species do. Nesting may have begun in March. *L. c. rufus* was non-migratory.

L. c. rufus was omnivorous. It consumed insects (many caterpillars), spiders, and ohia, and other plant species' nectar. Insects were found and removed from buds, galls, leaf clusters, and seed pods. The long, tubular tongue may have aided in the removal of insect larvae from the terminal buds of trees. The specialized jaw musculature and asymmetrical bill allowed it to capture insects by twisting aprat bulbs, galls, small green seed pods, and leaf clusters.

Activity levels probably increased during the breeding season. Daily activity levels most likely decreased during the summer as temperatures rose. *L. c. rufus* was often observed in small flocks.

Habitat/Distribution

L. coccineus inhabits koa forests and areas dominated by Ohia and other native tree species between the elevations of 3,000 to 6,000 feet on Hawaii, Maui, and Kauai. *L. c. rufus* most likely inhabited similar habitat types on Oahu.

First collected in 1825, *L. c. rufus* was considered to be a rare species in the 1800s. It has been presumed extinct since 1891. A 1976 siting was not confirmed.

Causes for Extinction

Reasons for the decline and extinction of this species are unknown. Factors affecting other forest birds (e.g., forest destruction, disease) on Oahu probably affected *L. c. rufus*. See Introduction of Destructive Species to the Hawaiian Islands, page 128.

Adapted from data compiled by the Threatened and Endangered Species Information Institute (Golden, CO) for *Beacham's International Threatened, Endangered, and Extinct Species* published on CD ROM, available from Beacham Publishing.

Oahu O'o

Moho apicalis

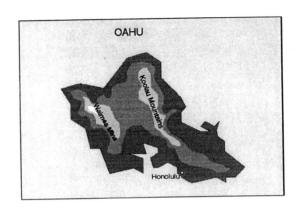

Description

The Oahu o'o, *Moho apicalis*, presented a plumage of sooty black with a brown tail, and outer feathers tipped with large patches of white. Two of the central tail feathers lacked white tipping and were narrower than the others as they tapered to a fine filamentous point. The sides and under tail coverts were yellow with under wing coverts white. The bill and legs were black. Both male and female appeared similar but the female was smaller. The male's wing measured 114 millimeters (4.45 inches); its tail, 165 mm (6.43 inches). The female was slightly smaller.

Behavior

The call of this species was harsh, but distinctive, formed from a double syllable, from which natives of Hawaii derived the name O'o. Its wings, when flapped quickly, produced a continuous buzzing sound not heard from any birds other than *Moho*.

The species fed on the nectar of ohias, lobelias, and other plants. It possessed a long tubular tongue. It also ate bananas and insects.

The species was active during the day

Status	Extinct
Probable Extinction	c.1837
Family	Meliphagidae (Honey-eaters)
Description	Small bird with a sooty-black plumage, brown tail and outher feathers tipped with white, yellow sides and under tail coverts, and black bill and legs.
Habitat	High mountain (3,000-4,000 ft) forests.
Food	Nectar, bananas and insects.
Reproduction	Nested in high trees.
Causes for Extinction	Hunting, introduced predators, habitat alteration.
Range	Hawaii: Oahu

when flowers were in full bloom.

Habitat

The species inhabited the mountain forests of Oahu in the Hawaiian Islands. It appeared over the entire island at an altitude of up to 1,220 meters (4,000 feet). The species frequented the high tree tops about 30.5 m (100 ft) above the ground. The species' nest and eggs have never been found.

Distribution

Little is known of the biology of this species. Only its skins remain as evidence of its life and history. The species was once common over the entire island of Oahu. The species has not been recorded since 1837.

Causes for Extinction

Scientists are not sure of the precise cause of the species' extinction. The introductions of cattle, cats, and rats probably contributed to both habitat loss and direct predation.

Another possible cause may have been overhunting. The species was hunted by native Polynesian Hawaiians for their beautiful brown, black, and yellow feathers. The amount of feathers needed to make just one garment was enormous. The species was easily caught; often, they responded to imitated calls and rushed to the caller, who would either kill the bird or capture it to use as a decoy to attract other birds.

Adapted from data compiled by the Threatened and Endangered Species Information Institute (Golden, CO) for *Beacham's International Threatened, Endangered, and Extinct Species* published on CD ROM, available from Beacham Publishing.

Molokai O'o

Moho bishopi

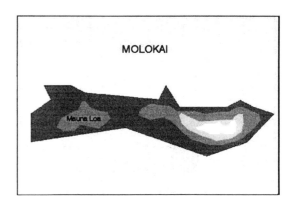

Description

The Molokai o'o, *Moho bishopi*, had a crown with slightly curled feathers and a deep black head with a slightly metallic gloss. The upper parts were black with a brownish tinge on the back. Light shafts were visible on the feathers of the neck. The underparts were brownish black with under-tail coverts, axillary tufts, and a tuft of feathers directed backwards from the ear coverts, all a golden yellow. The tail was black with narrow white fringes to the tips and two middle tail feathers that were long and pointed. The bill and the feet were black. The male and female appeared similar, but the female was smaller. The male's wing measured 102 millimeters (3.98 inches); its tail, 109 mm (4.25 inches). The culmen measured 29 mm (1.13 inches) and the tarsus, 33 mm (1.21 inches). In the female, the wing measured 100 mm (3.9 inches); the tail, 107 mm (4.17 inches). The culmen was 28 mm (1.11 inches) long and the tarsus, 31 mm (1.21 inches).

Status	Extinct
Probable Extinction	c.1837
Family	Meliphagidae (Honey-eaters)
Description	Small bird with a deep black, slightly metallic head, black upper side, brownish-black under parts, golden-yellow coverts, and long, pointed black tail feathers with white fringes.
Habitat	Mountain forests.
Food	Nectar, bananas and insects.
Reproduction	Nested in high trees.
Causes for Extinction	Possibly hunting, ferral animals and habitat alteration.
Range	Hawaii: Molokai

Behavior

The call of this species was harsh but distinctive, formed from a double syllable from which natives of Hawaii derived the name o'o. Its wings, when flapped quickly, produced a continuous buzzing sound not heard from any birds other than *Moho*.

The species fed on the nectar of ohias,

lobelias, and other plants. It possessed a long tubular tongue. It also ate bananas and insects.

The species was active during the day when flowers were in full bloom.

Adapted from data compiled by the Threatened and Endangered Species Information Institute (Golden, CO) for *Beacham's International Threatened, Endangered, and Extinct Species* published on CD ROM, available from Beacham Publishing.

Habitat

This species inhabited the mountain forests of Molokai in the Hawaiian Islands. It appeared over the entire island at high altitudes. The species frequented the high tree tops; nest and eggs have never been found.

Distribution

The species ranged over the entire island of Molokai in the Hawaiian Islands. The species was once common over the entire island of Molokai. It has not been recorded since 1901.

Causes for Extinction

Scientists are not sure of the precise cause of the species' extinction. The introductions of cattle, cats, and rats probably contributed to both habitat loss and direct predation.

Another possible cause may have been overhunting. The species was hunted by native Polynesian Hawaiians for their beautiful brown, black, and yellow feathers. The amount of feathers needed to make just one garment was enormous. The species was easily caught; often, they responded to imitated calls and rushed to the caller, who would either kill the bird or capture it to use as a decoy to attract other birds.

Hawaii O'o

Moho nobilis

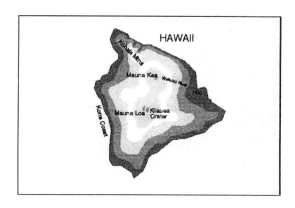

Description

The Hawaii o'o, *Moho nobilis*, presented a plumage of glossy black with shades of dull brown on the abdomen. The axillary tufts and the under tail coverts were a bright yellow with varying amounts of white on two outer pairs of tail feathers. The central pair of tail feathers were elongated and twisted at the tips. The eye of the species was a dark reddish brown with black bill, feet, and legs. Both male and female appeared similar but the female was smaller and had a middle pair of retrices which were not as twisted as the males. The immature bird appeared similar to adults except it lacked yellow axillary tufts. The male's wing measured 150 millimeters (5.85 inches); its tail, 190 mm (7.41 inches). The culmen measured 33 mm (1.29 inches) and the tarsus, 38 mm (1.48 inches). In the female, the wing measured 110 mm (4.29 inches); the tail, 150 mm (5.85 inches). The culmen was 30 mm (1.17 inches) long and the tarsus, 35 mm (1.37 inches).

Status	Extinct
Probable Extinction	c.1904
Family	Meliphagidae (Honey-eaters)
Description	Small bird with glossy-black plumage, bright yellow tufts and under tail coverts, reddish-brown eye, and black bill, legs and feet.
Habitat	Forests between 4,000-6,000 feet.
Food	Nectar, bananas, and insects.
Reproduction	Nested in high trees.
Causes for Extinction	Possibly predators and cattle that altered the habitat.
Range	Hawaii: Hawaii
Photo	See Color Insert, C-5

Behavior

The call of this species was harsh, but distinctive; formed from a double syllable from which natives of Hawaii derived the name O'o. Its wings, when flapped quickly, produced a continuous buzzing sound not heard from any birds other than *Moho*.

The species fed on the nectar of ohias, lobelias, and other plants. It possessed a long tubular tongue, and may have moved on a daily basis into mamane forests to forage on rich nectar resources. It also ate bananas and insects.

The species was active during the day when flowers were in full bloom. An aggressive bird, it dominated other nectarivores.

Habitat

The species inhabited the mountain forests of Hawaii. It appeared over the entire island at an altitude of up to 1,220 meters (4,000 feet). The species frequented the high tree tops; its nest and eggs have never been found.

Distribution

The Hawaii 'O'o was first collected on Captain Cook's third voyage, where it was common in the lower and middle forests, especially in trees growing near lava.

Little is known of the biology of this species. Only its skins remain as evidence of its life and history. The species was once common over the entire island of Hawaii. In 1898, reports said that thousands of the species were taken by hunters in the woods north of the Wailuku. An 1892 attempt to introduce the bird to Kauai failed.

Presumed extinct since 1898, the call of the bird was reported in 1934.

Causes for Extinction

Scientists are not sure of the precise cause of the species' extinction. The introductions of cattle, cats, and rats probably contributed to both habitat loss and direct predation.

Another possible cause may have been overhunting. The species was hunted by native Polynesian Hawaiians for their beautiful brown, black, and yellow feathers. The amount of feathers needed to make just one garment was enormous. The species was easily caught; often, they responded to imitated calls and rushed to the caller, who would either kill the bird or capture it to use as a decoy to attract other birds.

Near the turn of the century more than 1,000 individuals were taken by hunters from a previously overlooked population.

Adapted from data compiled by the Threatened and Endangered Species Information Institute (Golden, CO) for *Beacham's International Threatened, Endangered, and Extinct Species* published on CD ROM.

Lanai Thrush

Myadestes lanaiensis lanaiensis

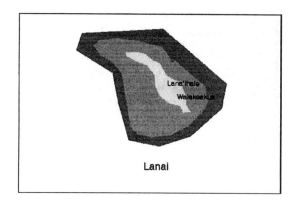

Lanai

Description

The Lanai thrush, *Myadestes lanaiensis lanaiensis*, was about 7 inches (18 centimeters) in length with a dull brown upperside and a grayish-white to white underside. This subspecies had a distinct buff colored patch at the base of the primaries and was thought to be slightly smaller than the other subspecies. Immatures were a darker brown with buffy spots on the back and a pale underside that was streaked with a darker brown. Unlike the other Hawaiian thrushes, this subspecies' vocalizations were limited to a few calls, and it did not have the beautifully melodious song attributed to the other thrushes.

The Hawaiian name 'oloma'o is also used in reference to this species.

Status	Extinct
Probable Extinction	Early 1930s
Family	Muscicapidae (Thrush)
Description	Dull brown upperside, a grayish-white to white underside, and a distinct buff colored patch at the base of the primaries.
Habitat	Montane rain forests.
Food	Fruits, berries and insects.
Reproduction	Nests located in areas of dense ground vegetation or low-growing trees and shrubs.
Cause for Extinction	Agricultural development, predation, disease.
Range	Hawaii: Lanai

Behavior

The Hawaiian thrushes were known for their habit of quivering their wings while perched and sometimes in flight.

Specific information concerning this species' activity patterns are unknown but it was probably diurnal and non-migratory. The Lanai thrush was frugivorous for the most part. Fruits and berries of a wide varie-ty of trees and shrubs were probably the primary food items with insects consumed in smaller amounts.

Habitat

This shy bird was restricted to the forested areas of Lanai. It occasionally flew short distances above the trees but was most often hidden beneath the canopy where it frequently could be heard calling but was rarely seen.

The montane rainforests of Lanai are dominated by ohia-lehua, commonly referred to as ohia. There are only about 5,000 acres of forested lands on Lanai; these areas occur below the elevation of 3,400 feet. These forests support a dense undergrowth of mosses and epiphytes, tree ferns (e.g., hapuu), and climbing vines (e.g., ieie). Ohia forests on parts of the other islands may be considered true "cloud" forests where rain or mist is ever present.

Nests were located in areas of dense ground vegetation or low-growing trees and shrubs (e.g., patches of ieie vine or ferns).

Distribution

The Lanai thrush was endemic to the island of Lanai in the Hawaiian Islands. It was considered to be fairly common in the early 1900s. The subspecies began to decrease in numbers in the 1920s. It was presumed to be extinct by the early 1930s.

The Lanai thrush played an important role in the dispersion of seeds of the trees and shrubs found in its habitat. Seeds were consumed along with the fruits and were passed out intact in various areas throughout the species' range.

Causes for Extinction

The Lanai thrush apparently began to decline in numbers in the 1920s when developments on Lanai accelerated. With development came increased habitat loss, avian diseases and predation. The introduction of mosquitoes which transmit avian malaria

was thought to have been particularly damaging. The call of the Lanai thrush was last heard in 1931 by George Munro, a noted ornithologist.

Adapted from data compiled by the Threatened and Endangered Species Information Institute (Golden, CO) for *Beacham's International Threatened, Endangered, and Extinct Species* published on CD ROM, available from Beacham Publishing.

'Amaui
Myadestes oahuensis

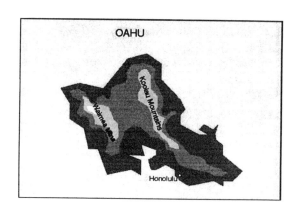

Description

The 'Amaui, *Myadestes oahuensis,* is described as having been about 7.5 inches in length and a dull olive-brown on the upper parts with the tips of the feathers being a paler shade of olive-brown. The underside was grayish. The wings and tail were brown and there were small bristles around the base of the bill. All members of Myadestes in the Hawaiian Islands have (or had) a distinct and beautiful song. The birds were often observed singing throughout the day while perched high in the trees. They were heard singing during all seasons of the year.

Behavior

The Hawaiian thrushes were known for their habit of quivering their wings while perched and sometimes in flight. The breeding season may have run from December through May but specifics about this species' reproduction are unavailable. 'Amaui was non-migratory. Specific information concerning this species' activity patterns is unknown but it was probably diurnal. 'Amaui was probably frugivorous for the most part. The fruits and berries of a wide variety of trees and shrubs were the primary

Status	Extinct
Probable Extinction	1820s
Family	Muscicapidae (Thrush)
Description	Dull olive-brown on the upper parts with the tips of the feathers being a paler shade of olive-brown, grayish underside; brown wings and tail; and small bristles around the base of the bill.
Habitat	Dense, damp to wet edges of forests.
Food	Fruits and berries of a wide variety of trees and shrubs.
Causes for Extinction	Habitat loss, predation.
Range	Hawaii: Oahu

food items.

'Amaui is the Hawaiian name for the thrushes found on the islands of Oahu, Kauai, Molokai, Lanai, Maui, and Hawaii. 'Amaui was also referred to as the Oahu thrush and the omao.

Habitat

'Amaui inhabited the edges of forested areas of the island of Oahu including the dense, damp to wet habitats of the ohia-koa forests.

The montane rain forests of Oahu are dominated by ohia-lehua (*Metrosideros collina*), commonly referred to as ohia. These forests support a dense undergrowth of mosses and epiphytes, tree ferns (e.g., hapuu), and climbing vines (e.g., ieie). Ohia forests on parts of the other islands may be considered true "cloud" forests where rain or mist is frequent.

Distribution

This extinct species was endemic to the island of Oahu in the Hawaiian Islands. All specimens collected have been lost but fossil remains have been discovered on Oahu. Andrew Bloxam, a naturalist who sailed with Lord Byron, recorded in his diary in 1825 that this thrush inhabited the forest fringe of east Oahu, but it has not been reported since the 1820s.

Causes for Extinction

The species may have been hunted for food by island inhabitants. 'Amaui was probably quite rare when it was discovered since it was presumed to be extinct not long after its discovery.

Adapted from data compiled by the Threatened and Endangered Species Information Institute (Golden, CO) for *Beacham's International Threatened, Endangered, and Extinct Species* published on CD ROM, available from Beacham Publishing.

Oahu nukupu'u

*Hemignathus
lucidus lucidus*

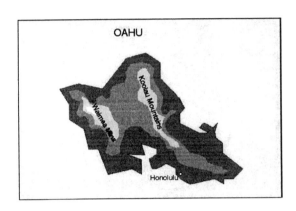

Description

The Oahu nukupu'u, *Hemignathus lucidus lucidus,* was about 5.5 inches (14 centimeters) in length with a bright yellow head (males), black lores, a bright olive-green color on the back and rump, and yellowish on the throat fading to white on the belly. The male's bill was long and strongly decurved; the upper mandible was about two times as long as the lower mandible. The female's and juvenile's bills were shorter and their heads and bodies were a paler yellow and olive-green, respectively. The tail was short and the undertail coverts were yellowish to white (white in the Maui subspecies and yellow in the Kauai subspecies).

Behavior

Oahu nukupu'u was a diurnal, non-migratory bird. Nothing is known of seasonal variation in its habits.

From the limited information known, Oahu nukupu'u was primarily insectivorous, feeding particularly on timber-boring larvae, and on spiders and other invertebrates gleaned and probed from foliage and bark surfaces. Nectar was also consumed. This bird was observed feeding on the nectar of the plantain in the Nuuanu Valley by Deppe in 1837.

Status	Extinct
Probable Extinction	Late 1800s
Family	Fringillidae (Honey-creepers)
Description	Bright yellow head (males), black lores, a bright olive-green color on the back and rump, and yellowish on the throat fading to white on the belly, with a long, strongly decurved bill.
Habitat	Dense, damp forests.
Food	Timber-boring larvae, spiders and other invertebrates.
Causes for Extinction	Destruction of koa forests, predation.
Range	Hawaii: Oahu

Habitat

Oahu nukupu'u inhabited the forested areas of the island of Oahu including the dense, damp to wet habitats of the ohia-koa forests. Areas with large koa trees were apparently preferred.

The montane rain forests of Oahu are dominated by ohia-lehua (*Metrosideros collina*), commonly referred to as ohia. These forests support a dense undergrowth of mosses and epiphytes, tree ferns (e.g., *hapuu*), and climbing vines (e.g., *ieie*). Ohia forests on parts of the other islands may be considered true "cloud" forests where rain or mist is frequent.

Distribution

This extinct species was endemic to the island of Oahu in the Hawaiian Islands.

Oahu nukupu'u was said to be fairly common in the island's lower elevation koa-ohia forests in the 1860s. Surveys between 1893-1902 failed to find this subspecies.

Causes for Extinction

Predation by alien animals and the large-scale destruction of the ohia-koa forests on Oahu in the latter part of the nineteenth century were probably the primary factors leading to the extinction of this subspecies. The introduction of cattle led to the removal of a large percentage of the dense undergrowth once found in the koa-ohia forests; areas where this honeycreeper fed and reproduced.

Habitat destruction limited the availability of food and breeding habitat. These factors, along with this subspecies' limited range, contributed to its decline and extinction.

Adapted from data compiled by the Threatened and Endangered Species Information Institute (Golden, CO) for *Beacham's International Threatened, Endangered, and Extinct Species* published on CD ROM, available from Beacham Publishing.

Lanai Creeper
or 'Alauwahio

Paroreomyza maculata montana

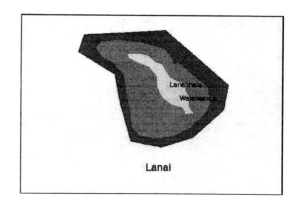

Lanai

Description

The Lanai creeper or 'alauwahio, *Paroreomyza maculata montana,* was a member of the honeycreeper family, Drepanididae (now Fringillidae). It was small (4 to 5 inches), green-gray or yellowish green above and a lemony yellow below, with a sharp, straight, mid-length bill.

This species is referred to by the following common names: Lanai creeper; 'alauahio; Lanai 'alauwahio; and 'alauwahio. The name 'alauwahio is the Hawaiian word for "creeper". It is also classified by some ornithologists as *Paroreomyza montana montana.*

Behavior

The species was non-migratory. The Lanai creeper is thought to have been insectivorous for the most part. Insects were located by probing under tree bark and, at times, were chased and caught during short flights. This species may have consumed nectar to some extent as well.

Habitat

This species is thought to have nested in

Status	Extinct
Probable Extinction	1937
Family	Fringillidae (Honey-creepers)
Description	Small green-gray or yellowish-green bird with a lemony-yellow underside and a sharp, straight bill.
Habitat	Dense, moist brush areas of forests above 2,000 feet elevation.
Food	Insects and perhaps nectar.
Causes for Extinction	Habitat loss, predation, and disease.
Range	Hawaii: Lanai

the island of Lanai's forested areas above 2,000 feet in elevation in areas covered by dense brush. This habitat is often covered by a heavy mist. They were observed probing the bark of koa trees, *Acacia koa.*

Distribution

The Lanai creeper was considered to be quite common in the early part of the twentieth century but the population dwindled and was extremely rare by the 1930s. The last pair was sighted in 1937.

Causes for Extinction

Habitat destruction, predation, and disease probably led to the decline and eventual extinction of this species. Extensive areas of the island of Lanai were deforested in the early part of the twentieth century for conversion to agriculture and rural development. Avian diseases, introducd rats, and the introduction of alien insects may also have contributed to the decline. Alien insects may have competitively excluded many of the native insects consumed by the Lanai creeper.

Adapted from data compiled by the Threatened and Endangered Species Information Institute (Golden, CO) for *Beacham's International Threatened, Endangered, and Extinct Species* published on CD ROM, available from Beacham Publishing.

Laysan Rail
Porzana palmeri

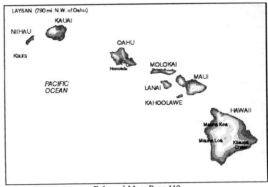

LAYSAN (790 mi. N.W. of Oahu)

NIIHAU

Kaula

KAUAI

OAHU

Honolulu

MOLOKAI

LANAI

MAUI

KAHOOLAWE

PACIFIC
OCEAN

HAWAII

Mauna Kea

Mauna Loa

Kilauea
Crater

Enlarged Map, Page 119

Description

The Laysan rail, *Porzana palmeri*, was a small (15.3 centimeters or 6 inches), flightless, sandy brown member of the rail family, *Rallidae*. It had short, rounded wings and a short tail that lacked flight feathers; yellow-green legs, a light olive-green bill, deep red irises, and pale gray-green eyelids. The female was a bit smaller and lighter than the male; immature birds were lighter on the underparts than on the back.

The Laysan rail is also referred to by the common names "Laysan Island rail" and "Laysan crake".

Behavior

The Laysan rail was a curious, fearless species. There are reports of the species jumping into the laps of military personnel (stationed on Midway during World War II) to eat crumbs and other food offerings.

Their nests were made of grass and were formed into a hollow, ball-shaped cavity with an entrance on the side. Nests were placed in dense stands of grass or in grass under shrubs where they were well hidden. Clutches averaged 2 to 3 eggs.

Status	Extinct
Probable Extinction	c.1944
Family	Rallidae (Rails, Gallinules, and Coots)
Description	Small, flightless, sandy brown bird, with rounded wings, yellow-green legs, olive green bill, and deep-red irises.
Habitat	Dense, low-growing shrubs.
Food	Moths, caterpillars, beetles, spiders and carrion.
Reproduction	Clutch of 2-3 eggs.
Causes for Extinction	Rodents, ferral cats, insects, predator birds, habitat loss, and natural disaster.
Range	Hawaii: Laysan Island
Photo	See Color Insert, C-3

The Laysan rail, like other rails, was omnivorous, but consumed primarily animal matter. Birds were observed eating moths, caterpillars, maggots, beetles, earwigs, spiders, carrion of dead birds, and, at times, eggs that had been broken by other birds (they were capable of breaking the eggs themselves but were rarely observed doing so). A small percentage of the diet was made up of seeds and green plant matter.

Information pertaining to periodicity is generally unknown. Activity levels probably increased during the breeding season. Daily activity levels may have decreased as temperatures rose. The Laysan rail was non-migratory.

Distribution

The Laysan Island population of the Laysan rail was considered to be abundant in 1891 and common in 1915. Only two birds remained in 1923. Those two apparently died in 1923. Transplanted birds on Midway Island survived until 1944.

Causes for Extinction

Naturalists on the U.S.S. *Tanager* expedition reintroduced the Laysan rail to Laysan Island in 1923 when only two birds remained in the island's population. This reintroduction was unsuccessful.

See Causes for Extinction on Laysan, page 127.

Adapted from data compiled by the Threatened and Endangered Species Information Institute (Golden, CO) for *Beacham's International Threatened, Endangered, and Extinct Species* published on CD ROM, available from Beacham Publishing.

Hawaiian Rail
Porzana sandwichensis

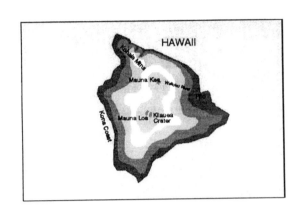

Description

The Hawaiian rail, *Porzana sandwichensis*, was a very small (5.5 inches or 14 centimeters), flightless member of the rail family. Although flightless, it was characterized as a fast runner. Two color phases are described, possibly adult and juvenile plumages, or simply, different color phases. Some authorities believed there were two subspecies which were named *P. s. sandwichensis*, the lighter phase, and *P. s. millei*, the darker phase. The dark phase had a reddish-chocolate brown colored back, the lower back feathers were darker in the center, and a reddish brown throat and breast fading to a grayish-chocolate brown color on the belly, thighs, and under tail coverts. The crown was brown with hints of gray, the feathers covering the ears were gray, and the cheeks were reddish-brown. The feet and legs were an orange-brown color, the bill was bluish toward the tip and yellow near the base, and the iris was reddish-brown. The lighter phase was similar in appearance to the dark phase but paler. The lower back feathers still had a dark center but the outer edges were much lighter, which gave the bird a more mottled appearance.

Status	Extinct
Probable Extinction	1844
Family	Rallidae (Rails, Gallinules, and Coots)
Description	Small bird with two color phases: reddish-chocolate brown back, reddish-brown throat and breast, a grayish brown underside, orange-brown feet, and a blue and yellow beak.
Habitat	Open scrub and grassland areas in forest clearings.
Food	Probably animal matter.
Causes for Extinction	Predators
Range	Hawaii: Hawaii
Photo	See Color Insert, C-7

Behavior

P. sandwichensis was non-migratory. Rails, in general, are somewhat omnivorous, but primarily consume animal matter.

Habitat

P. sandwichensis inhabited open scrub and grassland habitats on hills adjacent to forests or in forest clearings. These areas were primarily found below the rainforest.

Distribution

P. sandwichensis was found on the island of Hawaii, primarily on the eastern or windward side of Kilauea and in the Olaa District. It may have also been found on Molokai but there were no specimens collected from this island and no confirmed sightings. The species was hunted by island residents for food. Reports indicate this rail was served to Hawaiian royalty at feasts. Hunting and collecting for scientific purposes may have had a minor impact on the population as a whole but did not precipitate the decline and extinction of the species. The species, first collected on Captain Cook's final voyage in 1780, was last seen in 1884, possibly 1893; the last specimen was collected in the 1860s.

Causes for Extinction

P. sandwichensis was, no doubt, an extremely rare bird by the time the mongoose was introduced to the islands in the 1880s. Other alien mammalian predators are more likely to have been responsible for the decline and extinction of this rail. Domestic and feral dogs and cats were common in the late 1800s. These animals, along with the introduced rat species, contributed to the extinction of the species.

Adapted from data compiled by the Threatened and Endangered Species Information Institute (Golden, CO) for *Beacham's International Threatened, Endangered, and Extinct Species* published on CD ROM, available from Beacham Publishing.

Lesser Koa Finch
Rhodacanthis flaviceps

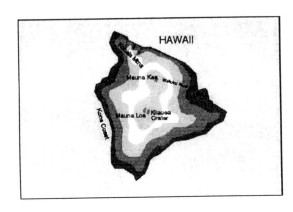

Description

The lesser koa finch, *Rhodacanthis flaviceps*, was similar in appearance to the closely related *R. palmeri* (greater koa finch), except for the smaller body size (*R. palmeri* was 8.0 to 8.5 inches in total length) and a yellowish or golden head and neck (*R. palmeri* had a bright reddish-orange to orange head and neck). The back feathers were a dark olive green, and the underparts were a paler yellow. The bill was short and thick, similar in appearance to an evening grosbeak's bill. Female greater koa finch and probably lesser koa finch, had yellowish heads and greener backs. Juvenile males were similar to females but with a darker belly and breast.

The lesser koa finch was also referred to as the yellow-headed koa-finch.

Status	Extinct
Probable Extinction	1891
Family	Fringillidae (Honey-creepers)
Description	Small bird with a yellowish or golden head and neck, olive-green back, a pale-yellow underside, and a short, thick beak.
Habitat	Koa forests above 4,000 feet.
Food	Koa tree pods, seeds, and insects.
Reproduction	Nested high in koa trees; both male and female fed and cared for young.
Range	Hawaii: Hawaii

Behavior

Nests were probably built by both males and females. Both sexes also appeared to feed and care for the chicks. This species was non-migratory.

Although not confirmed, the lesser koa finch is assumed to have eaten koa tree pods, other seeds, and insects (e.g., caterpillars). The chicks were fed portions of the koa pods and probably insects.

Habitat

The lesser koa finch last inhabited the koa forests above 1,220 meters (4,000 feet) in elevation along Mauna Loa's leeward side (the Kona Coast) on the island of Hawaii.

They were observed in a mixed flock with greater koa finch high in a koa tree.

The species probably placed their nests high in koa trees.

Distribution

Historic (fossil) records indicate the lesser koa finch occurred throughout much of the island of Hawaii. It was also found on Oahu.

In the late 1800s, just prior to its extinction, this species was restricted to the higher elevation koa forests on Mauna Loa's leeward side along the Kona Coast (island of Hawaii).

Causes for Extinction

Reasons for the decline and extinction of this species are unknown. The lesser koa finch was extremely rare when it was discovered. Specimens were collected in 1891 and no subsequent sightings or collections/ specimens exist.

Adapted from data compiled by the Threatened and Endangered Species Information Institute (Golden, CO) for *Beacham's International Threatened, Endangered, and Extinct Species* published on CD ROM, available from Beacham Publishing.

Greater Koa Finch
Rhodacanthis palmeri

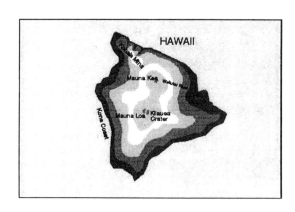

Description

The greater koa finch, *Rhodacanthis palmeri*, was similar in appearance to the closely related lesser koa finch, except for the larger body size (the greater koa finch was 8.0 to 8.5 inches in total length) and a bright scarlet-orange to orange head and neck (the lesser koa finch had a yellowish or golden head and neck). The back feathers were a dark olive green, and the underparts were a paler orange to yellow (moving toward the tail). The bill was short, thick, and bluish grey in color; it was similar in appearance to an evening grosbeak's bill. The female greater koa finch, and probably the lesser koa finch, had yellowish heads and greener backs. Juvenile males were similar to females but with a darker belly and breast.

The greater koa finch is also referred to by the common names "orange koa-finch" and "hopue". Hopue is not the Hawaiian name for this species.

Behavior

The greater koa finch and the lesser koa finch probably placed their nests high in koa trees. Nests were probably built by both males and females. Both sexes also appeared

Status	Extinct
Probable Extinction	1896
Family	Fringillidae (Honey-creepers)
Description	Small bird with a bright orange head and neck, olive green back feathers, and a pale orange to yellow underside.
Habitat	Leeward side of koa forests above 4,000 feet.
Food	Seeds and insects.
Reproduction	Nests were built and young were attended by both parents.
Range	Hawaii: Hawaii
Photo	See Color Insert, C-6

to feed and care for the chicks. The greater koa finch was non-migratory.

Although not confirmed, The greater koa finch is assumed to have eaten koa tree pods, other seeds, and insects (e.g., caterpillars). The chicks were fed portions of the koa pods and probably insects.

Information pertaining to periodicity is unknown. Activity levels probably increased during the breeding season. Daily activity levels most likely decreased during the summer as temperatures rose.

Habitat

The greater koa finch last inhabited the koa forests above 1,220 meters (4,000 feet) in elevation along Mauna Loa's leeward side (the Kona Coast) on the island of Hawaii. They were observed in a mixed flock with the greater koa finch high in a koa tree.

Distribution

In the late 1800s, just prior to its extinction, the greater koa finch was restricted to the higher elevation koa forests on Mauna Loa's leeward side along the Kona Coast (island of Hawaii).

The greater koa finch was first collected by H. C. Palmer and G. C. Munro in 1891. Walter Rothschild described and named this new species *Psittirostra palmeri* in 1892. Greater koa finch specimens were again collected in 1896 by Perkins. This was the last time this species was collected or sighted. Palmer and Munro's collections in 1891 were the only confirmed sightings of the lesser koa finch; in contrast to Rothschild, they believed they had collected variations of one species.

Based on size and male head color (two male and six female specimens), Rothschild determined the specimens represented two species, the lesser koa finch and the greater koa finch. Many other authors believe that the specimens collected by Palmer and Munro represented only one species. They base their assumption on the following: all specimens were taken on the same day and from the same tree; the individuals collecting the birds believed there was only one species; the female specimens assigned to the two species are identical in coloration; speci-

mens labelled as "palmeri" and listed as juvenile or immature are identical to male "flaviceps" in head coloring (technique used to age the specimens is unknown); and size differentiations appear to be based primarily on tail length. The variations in tail length could have been related to tail feather wear. One theory (based on the examination of 4 of the original "flaviceps specimens") asserts that the birds were juvenile or immature "palmeri", that they were born early in the season, and, because of this timing, the feathers were well worn by the time they were collected. Another theory involves the hybridization of the greater koa finch and *Psittirostra psittacea*.

Members of this family (Fringillidae, formerly Drepanididae) are thought to have descended from one species. This species spread through the remote Hawaiian Islands and evolved to fill the empty niches that would have been filled by members of other bird families (found in other parts of the world) if those species had reached the Hawaiian Islands.

The honeycreepers developed a wide variety of bill sizes and shapes to take advantage of the various food resources including short, thick, finch- to parrot-like bills; long, thin, recurved (sickle-shaped) bills; bills where the upper and lower mandibles are different lengths; and bills that are slightly crossed. Several species and subspecies are now considered to be extinct and many others are federally listed as endangered.

Causes for Extinction

Reasons for the decline and extinction of this species are unknown. The greater koa finch was fairly rare when it was discovered. Specimens were collected in 1891 and 1896; no subsequent sightings or collections/specimens exist.

See Introduction of Destructive Species to the Hawaiian Islands, page 128.

Adapted from data compiled by the Threatened and Endangered Species Information Institute (Golden, CO) for *Beacham's International Threatened, Endangered, and Extinct Species* published on CD ROM, available from Beacham Publishing.

EXTINCT BIRDS OF NORTH AMERICA

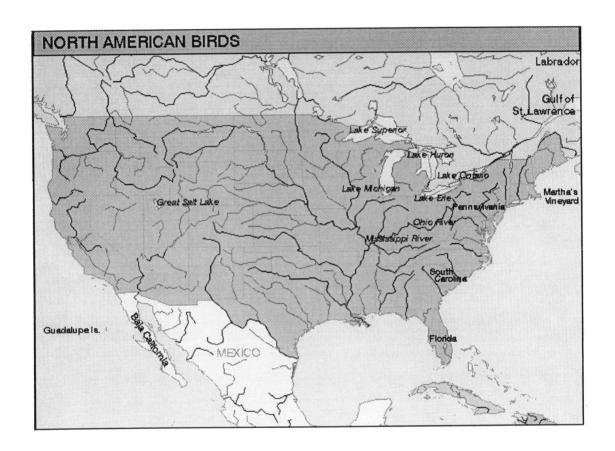

NORTH AMERICAN BIRDS

Threats to North American Birds

While the plumage of many tropical and Hawaiian birds caused their extinction because of overhunting, North American birds were driven to extinction through genocide because they were pests (Guadalupe caracara, Carolina parakeet, passenger pigeon), by destruction of habitat due to human encroachment (Guadalupe storm-petrel, dusky seaside sparrow, heath hen), or because they were vulnerable to predation (great auk, Labrador duck).

Today, North American birds are most threatened by habitat loss and degradation. From forests to wetlands, avian habitats are under severe pressure. Forests have been cleared for timber or converted to agricultural use; wetlands are being drained for crops and pastures; waterfowl habitats are polluted, and many birds die of lead poisoning from shotgun pellets or from oil spills. Until the ban on DDT, pesticides nearly extirpated ospreys, eagles and pelicans, and pesticides remain the primary threat to a fifth of North America's endangered birds.

Guadalupe Storm-Petrel
Oceanodroma macrodactyla

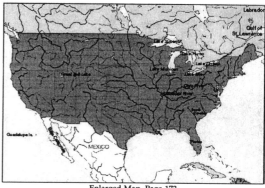

Enlarged Map, Page 173

Description

The Guadalupe storm-petrel, *Oceanodroma macrodactyla*, was similar in appearance to the Leach's or Socorro storm-petrel (*O. leucorhora socorrensis*), another petrel that nested on Guadalupe Island. Guadalupe storm-petrel was black above with a brownish underside and a white rump. The tail was forked. The underside of the wings was a paler brown than that found on *O. l. socorrensis*.

The species is also referred to as the Guadalupe petrel.

Status	Extinct
Probable	
Extinction	1912
Family	Hydrobatidae (Petrels)
Description	Black above with a brownish underside, a white rump, and a forked tail.
Habitat	Open ocean.
Food	Medium-sized-fish, crustaceans, and other invertebrates.
Reproduction	One chick per year.
Causes for	
Extinction	Introduced cats.
Range	Mexico: Guadalupe Island

Behavior

The Guadalupe storm-petrel began breeding in early March; eggs were found in nests from March 2 through July 2 with most observations occurring in late March. Chicks were close to fledgling by late May and the colony was mostly empty by early to mid-June. Most breeding pairs seemed to successfully raise only one chick per year. Chicks were covered with long, thick, light brown down. During the breeding season, adults would leave the chicks unattended during the day while they foraged out at sea. The adults returned in the evening to feed the chicks.

This species apparently did not have a juvenile or subadult plumage; chicks molted directly into an adult plumage.

The Guadalupe storm-petrel migrated between its breeding grounds and the open ocean where it spent most of the year. Migration distances were apparently short; the species' range apparently did not extend very far from Guadalupe Island.

The Guadalupe storm-petrel was a sea-bird which foraged in the open ocean. Small to medium-sized-fish, crustaceans, and other invertebrates were the likely prey items.

Habitat

During the breeding season, the Guadalupe storm-petrel was found on Guadalupe Island off the coast of Baja California, Mexico. The breeding colony was located at about 2,500 to 4,000 feet in elevation in a pine and oak open forest or in cypress habitats. Nests were placed in burrows among the trees; burrows were often placed under rocks. Most burrows had some oak leaves and pine needles near the end of the cavity where the eggs were probably laid.

The Guadalupe storm-petrel inhabited the open ocean during the non-breeding seasons.

Distribution

The Guadalupe storm-petrel's breeding range was restricted to Guadalupe Island, which is 200+ miles west of Baja California, Mexico. The species' non-breeding season range is unknown but it apparently did not stray far from Guadalupe Island.

Causes for Extinction

Cats introduced to the island were responsible for the high mortality rates of Guadalupe storm-petrel chicks. Eggs were also damaged and adults in the vicinity of the nests were attacked and killed by the cats. Overgrazing by goats in the late 1800s may have destabilized the substrates used by Guadalupe storm-petrel to construct the nesting burrows. Some burrows may have collapsed but it is unlikely that this had a major impact on the breeding success of the population.

The breeding population of the Guadalupe storm-petrel on Guadalupe Island was considered to be a fairly good size up until the early 1900s. The last live specimen was seen in 1911. Intensive surveys in the early 1920s failed to find any adults, active nests, or recently used nest burrows.

Adapted from data compiled by the Threatened and Endangered Species Information Institute (Golden, CO) for *Beacham's International Threatened, Endangered, and Extinct Species* published on CD ROM, available from Beacham Publishing.

Guadalupe Caracara
Polyborus lutosus

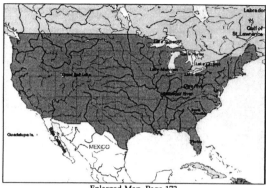

Enlarged Map, Page 173

Description

The Guadalupe caracara, *Polyborus lu-tosus*, was about 54 centimeters (22 inches) long; the wing was 381-418 millimeters (14.86-16.3 in) long and the tail was 260 to 286 mm (10.14-11.15 in) long. This species had a blackish-brown crown and nape, a white throat and buffy cheeks. The bill was a bluish-gray color with a pale reddish cere. The back, middle wing coverts, and most of the tail were a dark brown with blackish-brown and dull white barring. There was a dark terminal tail band. The breast, belly, and thighs were a light brown with blackish-brown barring. The bare legs and feet were yellow and the iris was brown. This species was not sexually dimorphic. Juveniles were distinguished from the adults by their darker brown backs that had little or no visible barring.

Downy young resembled mainland cara-caras; the down was a creamy or buffy to chamois color with darker brown patches/spots on the shoulders, thighs, and rump; the upper part of the head was a darker brown color.

Residents of Guadalupe referred to this species as "queleli".

Status	Extinct
Probable Extinction	1900-1906
Family	Falconidae (Falcons)
Description	Falcon with blackish-brown crown and nape, a white throat and buffy cheeks, and a bluish-gray bill with a pale reddish cere.
Habitat	Arid prairies, grasslands, and desert brushlands.
Food	Carrion, small birds, goat kids, insects, small mammals, worms, and crustaceans.
Reproduction	One brood per year with a clutch of 2-4 eggs.
Threats	Human extermination.
Range	Mexico: Guadalupe Island

Behavior

Little information is available concerning the reproductive characteristics of this species. Mainland caracaras (*P. cheriway*) in Florida begin nesting in February or March, sometimes as early as December. Clutches range from 2 to 4 eggs, with 2 being the more common number. Both sexes incubate the eggs; incubation lasts about 28 days. Only one brood is raised per year but a second clutch will often be laid if the first is destroyed or removed. Reports vary but it appears that fledgling occurs sometime between 7 to 12 weeks after hatching; 8 weeks is probably the average.

The Guadalupe caracara was non-migratory. A large percentage of Guadalupe caracara's diet was made up of carrion. Small birds, goat kids, insects, small mammals, worms, and crustaceans were also captured and consumed. Individuals of this species would join with others to attack and kill larger prey (e.g., goats).

Habitat

Caracaras, in general, are associated with open-country habitats including arid prairies, grasslands, and desert brushlands. The Guadalupe caracara inhabited Guadalupe Island. The island is about 32 kilometers (20 miles) long and 9.6 km (6 miles) wide.

One nest was located on a pile of trash and cacti; it was large and made of sticks. Island residents indicated the nests were generally placed in inaccessible spots, often well hidden, on cliffs.

Distribution

The Guadalupe caracara was endemic to Guadalupe Island which is 200+ miles west of the coast of Baja, California.

The species was considered to be abundant in 1875. By 1887, the population had been dramatically reduced by an extermination program. Few were left by 1900, the last confirmed sighting of the species. An extensive survey of the entire island in 1906 failed

to find even one bird. The bird is assumed to have become extinct between 1900 and 1906.

Causes for Extinction

The Guadalupe caracara was abundant throughout the island when it was discovered by Palmer in 1875. Island residents apparently killed many of the birds with firearms and poison prior to the arrival of Palmer with little obvious effect on the population as a whole. The 1887 field notes of a visiting biologist indicated that he saw only four Guadalupe caracara individuals during a two-day visit to the island's center. The government had instituted an eradication program. The species' unwary nature made it an easy target. A government agent was observed sitting near a commonly used water hole. Birds flying to the hole were systematically shot. When Palmer returned to the island in 1889 he did not see the species. Rollo H. Beck, considered to be a competent ornithologist, collected nine of eleven Guadalupe caracara individuals as they flew over in 1900. He assumed the species was abundant from his limited observations during the visit. An extensive survey of the entire island in 1906 failed to find even one bird.

Goat herders were said to stand over their goats, especially young ones, to protect them from attacking caracaras. Goat herders abandoned the island sometime in the 1880s; the remaining goats were sporadically hunted and killed but some still remained in the early 1900s. Goat carcasses were used as bait (without success) to try and lure the caracaras during the 1906 survey.

Dusky Seaside Sparrow
Ammospiza maritima nigrescens

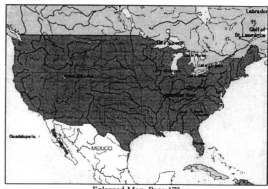

Enlarged Map, Page 173

Description

The dusky seaside sparrow, *Ammospiza maritima nigrescens*, reached lengths of about 15 centimeters. The coloration was black or brown upper parts edged with grayish olive, white venter with heavy black streaking, bright yellow on the lores and at the bend of the wing. The wings and tail of *A. m. nigrescens* were fuscous to fuscous black, edged with light yellowish olive. There was no sexual dimorphism displayed by this species.

Synonyms used for the common name have been black and white shore finch and black shore finch.

Behavior

Nesting was confined to the male's territory, which was defended through song and occasional chasing. The sparrows were observed to breed from March to August, with two egg-laying peaks. Pair formation and copulation is not well known. Parental care is displayed by both parents. The female incubated the eggs for 12 to 13 days and brooded the young for 9 days more. Juveniles would stay in the territory about 2 weeks more after which the male would

Status	Extinct
Probable Extinction	December 12, 1990
Family	Fringillidae (Sparrow)
Description	Small bird with black or brown upper parts, edged with grayish olive, white venter with heavy black streaking.
Habitat	Salt marshes with fluctuating water levels and salinities, and dominated by cordgrass.
Food	Grasshoppers, crickets, spiders; less preferred foods included small snails, dragonfly larvae, butterflies and possibly ants.
Reproduction	Incubation of 12-13 days.
Causes for Extinction	Diking of the marshes for mosquito control; wildfires and drainage of riparian areas for housing, roads and pasture; DDT.
Range	Florida
Photo	See Color Insert, C-8

often drive them away. The fledglings would molt in late August and became indistinguishable from the adults by November.

This subspecies was insectivorous. Studies of stomach contents demonstrated this affinity by producing 37% grasshoppers and crickets and 25% spiders. *A. m. nigrescens* had also been observed to feed on small snails, dragonfly larvae, butterflies and possibly ants.

Habitat

This species was the inhabitant of salt marshes with fluctuating water levels and salinities. *A. m. nigrescens* preferred hydric zones dominated by cordgrass (*Spartina bakerii*), 3 to 5 meters (10-15 ft) in elevation. This species was observed on the St. Johns River marshes. These marshes are savannah-like dotted with small ponds, salt pans, cabbage palms (*Sabal palmetto*), and hammocks. This species utilized dense vegetation for concealment during non-breeding seasons. This species was never found outside the limits of cordgrass (*Spartina bakerii*).

A. m. nigrescens constructed cupped shaped nests from grasses. The nests were formed in tussocks 2 to 35 centimeters (.08 to 1.37 in) above the ground. The nest sites included tussocks of glasswort, black rush, cordgrass, salt grass and wire grass.

Distribution

Prior to 1987, 894 pairs were confirmed on the St. Johns National Wildlife Refuge. All known locations for this species have been determined extirpated.

This species once inhabited the brackish marshes and savannahs in Brevard County, Florida. It bred in salt marshes from New England south to Florida and west across the Gulf Coast. Historically, *A. m. nigrescens* occurred along the Indian River on the northwest coast of Merritt Island, from the Moore Creek-Banana Creek area to Dimmit Creek; and on the mainland in marshes on the east side of the St. Johns River from just south of Salt Lake south to the vicinity of Cocoa. *A. m. nigrescens* is believed to be extirpated throughout its range. The last of this subspecies, fondly referred to as Orangeband by keepers, died in a Florida captive breeding facility in 1987.

Causes for Extinction

This species' limited range and alteration of habitat are the primary factors contributing to its extinction. This species was adapted to narrow, unstable zones of vegetation within salt marshes. Diking of the marshes for mosquito control altered the vegetation, and wildfires and drainage of riparian areas for housing, roads and pasture reduced suitable habitat. Seventy percent of this species' reduction has been linked to aerial spraying with DDT and other insecticides to control mosquitoes from 1942 to 1953.

The establishment of the St. Johns National Wildlife Refuge was an effort to recover *A. m. nigrescens*. Attempts to recover the species on Merritt Island included lowering impoundment water levels and connecting an impoundment to the Indian River. These measures met with no success. Management efforts on the St. Johns National Wildlife Refuge involved land acquisition and controlled burning. In a response for recovery of this species, USFWS allocated $5 million to acquire critical habitat along the St. Johns River.

Adapted from data compiled by the Threatened and Endangered Species Information Institute (Golden, CO).

Carolina Parakeet
Conuropsis carolinensis

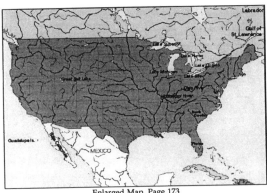

Enlarged Map, Page 173

Description

The Carolina parakeet, *Conuropsis carolinensis*, was a relatively small parrot about 30 centimeters (1.17 inches) long and 280 grams (9.8 ounces) in weight. The forehead, lores, and upper cheeks were orange while the remainder of the head, throat and upper portion of the neck were yellow. Yellow was observed on the outer webs of primaries toward the base, the bend of the wing, the carpal edge and the thighs. Other plumage was green. The eggs of this species were white and 1.4 inches in length.

This species was the only parrot native to the United States. Two subspecies separated by the Appalachian Mountain Ridge persisted in the U.S. The western subspecies, *C. c. ludovician*, was generally paler than its eastern counterpart, *C. c. carolinensis*, which had a bluer tint to its green coloration and more yellow on the wings.

Status	Extinct
Probable	
Extinction	1914
Family	Psittacidae (Parrots and Parakeets)
Description	Small green parrot with orange forehead, lores, and upper cheeks while the remainder of the head, throat and upper portion of the neck were yellow.
Habitat	Cypress swamps.
Food	Variety of fruits, including apple, peach, mulberry, pecan, grape, dogwood, and grains; seeds of grass, maple, elm and pine.
Threats	Agricultural development, hunting, overcollecting.
Range	South Carolina
Photo	See Color Insert, C-7

Behavior

This species' diet consisted of seeds from a variety of fruits: apple, peach, mulberry, pecan, grape, dogwood, and grains. Before this species acclimated to the encroachment of agriculture, its food sources were derived from seeds of grass, maple, elm and pine. In particular this species thrived on seeds of cocklebur (*Xanthium* sp.). This species was exceedingly adaptable and modified its environment to comply with changing food sources. At night this species roosted in a commune and is believed to have been diurnally active.

The Carolina parakeet displayed a typical defensive behavior to parrots in which the flock would noisily swoop or hover over fallen birds. This tactic is assumed to have been used to distract predators from victims and is a common behavior among parrots.

Habitat

The Carolina parakeet inhabited the cypress swamps of the southwestern United States. *C. carolinensis* was extremely common in the eastern deciduous forests, especially in densely wooded river-bottoms. The area in which this species inhabited consists of gently sloping to rolling southern Piedmont and upper Coastal Plain. The average annual precipitation ranges from 1,025 to 1,525 millimeters. Udults, well-drained to moderately well-drained soils with a low content of organic matter, are the dominant soils. Forests are important throughout this region and are the major land use. Cotton, soybeans, small grains, and corn are the main crops grown. This parrot lived primarily in mature forest areas and formed rookeries within hollow tress particularly in stands of buttonwood, cypress or sycamore. This species formed communes within the stumps by crowding and attaching to the sides of the stump.

Distribution

From time to time there continue to be unconfirmed reports of sightings of this bird, but they are doubtful. One known record from the wild is from Brevard County, Florida where specimens were taken in 1901. In the east, the last wild specimen was collected in 1901, and the last sighting was 1904, although parakeets were recorded in Louisiana as late as 1910.

This species' thriving grounds, the Santee Swamp in South Carolina, has been destroyed by development. Other individuals remained alive in captivity until the last one died in the Cincinnati Zoo in 1914. Incidentally, the last passenger pigeon also died in this same zoo and year.

Causes for Extinction

When original forest habitat was cleared to make way for orchards and grainfields, this species adapted to eating the fruit in the orchards. This combined with communal feeding caused the demise of several orchards. For these reasons, farmers exterminated *C. carolinensis*. The instinctive defensive pattern displayed by this species in which a flock would hover over a fallen victim became a disastrous practice. Frequently flocks would continue circling or would come back to the dead on the ground, making it possible to slaughter the entire flock. Overhunting for sport, subsistence and feathers contributed to the decline. This species was also captured and kept as a cage-bird. It was placed in zoos, not for conservation, but simply for show. The captive populations, however, were not bred, and the species eventually became extinct due to the exceeding low population numbers in the wild.

C. carolinensis once flocked by the hundreds. By the 1880s, it became obvious that this species was extremely rare, but little was done to preserve it until it was far too late. Captive birds were studied, but propagation was not stressed, and the reintroduction effort was futile.

Passenger Pigeon

Ectopistes migratorius

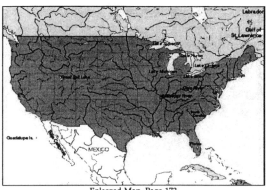

Enlarged Map, Page 173

Description

The passenger pigeon, *Ectopistes migratorius*, possessed a slaty blue head with black blotches around the eyes. The back of its neck was an iridescent bronze that changed to green or purple in differing shades of light. Its back was slate gray and tinged with olive brown. Its lower back and rump was a grayish blue which turned to grayish brown on the upper tail coverts. Two central tail feathers were brownish grey with the rest of the tail white. Its throat and breast were a pale cinnamon which turned paler on the lower breast and merged to white on the abdomen. Its iris was red and it had a black bill with red legs and feet. It measured from 196 to 215 mm (7.64 to 8.38 inches) from wingtip to wingtip.

The females appeared similar to the males except for duller coloring and a shorter tail.

Status	Extinct
Probable Extinction	1914
Family	Columbidae (Doves and Pigeons)
Description	Slaty blue head with black blotches around the red eyes, iridescent bronze neck, slate gray back, and grayish-blue on the lower back and rump.
Habitat	Deciduous forests of the eastern U.S.
Food	Acorns, chestnuts, beechnuts, fruit, grain, insects, worms.
Reproduction	Clutch of one egg laid between March and September.
Causes for Extinction	Genocide
Range	Eastern U.S.
Photo	See Color Insert, C-8

Behavior

The species bred in large colonies in massive districts where they would arrive a short time before they bred. Colonies tended to be long and narrow; some nestings were recorded as large as 64 kilometers (40 miles) in length and one was recorded in 1871 as being 160 km (100 miles) long. A typical nesting would have been 16 km (10 miles) long by 5 km (3 miles) wide. The gatherings were loose and discontinuous. Every tree would be utilized and only when each tree in a general area was filled would individuals begin extending the limits to other areas.

Nests were made of small twigs in a scrappy, flimsy manner. Some nests were so flimsy that observers could view the egg from beneath. They were positioned on strong branches close to the trunk of the tree and despite their shaky appearance, many nests lasted a few years after being used and abandoned.

In the courting ritual of this species, the male appeared pompous and followed the female wherever she went with spread tail and drooping wing. The male's throat swelled, its body elevated, and its eyes sparkled. His notes would sound as he would occasionally rise on the wing dropping down before the female. They caressed by billing, the bill of one crossing the bill of the other.

Eggs were laid between March and September with a peak in April and May. Each pair produced a single white egg measuring 38 by 27 millimeters (1.48 by 1.05 in). Parents took turns incubating, which lasted 12 or 13 days. When hatched, the chick spent two weeks with its parents who would care for it. Then, the old flock left the area. The chick spent some time crying in the nest, too fat and ignorant of how to fly. Then, it dropped to the ground where after a few days it took to the air. The nesting period took only 30 days. Some researchers believe the species nested several times a year while others think it bred only once every summer.

The species migrated in mass numbers in search of food. Migrations were spectacular for their mass numbers and the speed of the species which were as fast as 96 km (60 miles) per hour. For speed, the species was well adapted with a powerfully muscled breast, streamlined body, small head, long tail, and pointed wings.

The patterns in which the species flew in flocks were continuous and uniform. Individuals flew in columns following exactly the movements of those in the front. When one group dipped, those following behind would also dip. This aided the flock when avoiding a preying species such as a hawk. The flock flew high searching for promising areas to feed. When an area was spotted, it would descend and examine the land from a closer perspective. Once it decided to land and forage, the first rank would land followed by the subsequent ranks which flew overhead and landed in the front of the last. These movements occurred so fast that the flock appeared to be constantly on the move.

In order to support its large energy needs when flying, the passenger pigeon was a voracious eater. It fed mainly on acorns, chestnuts, and beechnuts as well as all kinds of fruit when available. It would also eat grain and other cultivated plants, insects, and worms. The species possessed the ability to disgorge food to provide room in its stomach for foodstuffs that were more desirable when and if they became available. After a flock fed, underbrush was cleared completely.

Due to the large number of individuals making up a flock, it has been estimated that the average flock's food intake was close to a million tons daily. To find such stocks of food, a flock would have to fly over 100 miles (161 km) every day. The species usually fed in the morning and early afternoon. The remainder of the day was often spent roosting in the trees. The flock would then depart later in the evening spending much of the night in flight searching for the next feeding ground.

Habitat

The species once inhabited the deciduous

forests of the eastern United States. These forests provided the species with foraging, roosting, and breeding grounds. Roosting sites required large trees with little undergrowth. Dung might lie inches deep beneath roosts and the clearings were needed to make room. Indeed, the vastness of the forests was needed to support the massive flocks in which the species was found. These flocks were estimated in the billions.

Distribution

This species has been described as the "most numerous bird on earth". It existed in flocks of hundreds of thousands over the forests of North America — in virtually every state and in Canada. In its heyday, the species was believed to represent from 25 to 40 percent of the total landbird population of the United States.

Causes for Extinction

Many explanations for the species' extinction have been offered. Some say deforestation or imported avian disease may have been important contributors; others think mass drownings, though these were rare. The principal reason seems to be the mass number of individuals killed by hunters.

Many settlers needed only to walk through a nesting area after the breeding flock had departed and pick up the chicks that had dropped from their nests in search of food and knowledge of flight. These were eaten or used as feed for hogs. Market hunters would lure adults to feed on alcohol-soaked grain on which the birds would become drunk and easy to catch. Other hunters suffocated large numbers in nesting or roosting flocks with grass or sulfur fires lit beneath the trees. Often, captured pigeons

with their eyes sewn shut, were set out as decoys on small perches called stools to attract others of the species. This is how the term "stool pigeon" originated. Chicks were often knocked from nests with long poles or motivated to jump from nests by fire. Such disruption forced whole colonies to abandon nesting sites, thus, reducing breeding success.

The species was collected by market hunters to such an extent that the species became cheap in the market because supply was so great. Live birds were even used as targets at the shooting galleries of local fairs. When the species had been driven from the Atlantic seaboard, it was shipped into eastern cities by train. "Hundreds of thousands were slaughtered year after year, decade after decade".

Since the species associated in vast numbers, it has been suggested that once these numbers had been broken up by hunting and populations dropped, the species could no longer survive despite a large number of survivors. It seems that the evolution of the species favored it to live only in large flocks.

Few individuals remained living in the wild by the last decade of the nineteenth century. One of the species' last strongholds was the State of Michigan where about 3 million birds were shipped east by a single hunter in 1878. By 1889, the species was extinct in the state. In 1896, a flock of about 250,000 — small by the species' standards — was seen and mobbed by hunters. It was estimated that less than 10,000 birds survived. Many sightings were made during the last decade of the nineteenth century and the first decade of the twentieth. In 1909, a $1,500 reward was offered to anyone providing evidence of a nesting pair. But, many of the sightings were not confirmed. The last accepted wild sighting happened on March 24, 1900, when one individual was taken at Sargents in Pike County, Ohio. The specimen was stuffed and now sits in the Ohio State Museum.

Before 1909, many birds still lived in captivity in Milwaukee, Chicago, and the Cincinnati Zoological Gardens. By the spring of 1909, only two individuals — a male and a female — remained alive in Cincinnati. In the summer of 1910 the male died, leaving the female as the only surviving member of the species. She was named Martha and her age was claimed to be 29 years old. She lived another 4 years. At 1:00 p.m. on September 1, 1914, she was found dead on the bottom of her cage.

Her body was stuffed and can be seen at the Smithsonian Institute in Washington, D.C. Of the passenger pigeon, Audubon wrote:

> "When an individual is seen gliding through the woods and close to the observer, it passes like a thought, and on trying to see it again, the eye searches in vain; the bird is gone."

Adapted from data compiled by the Threatened and Endangered Species Information Institute (Golden, CO) for *Beacham's International Threatened, Endangered, and Extinct Species* published on CD ROM, available from Beacham Publishing.

Heath Hen
Tympanuchus cupido cupido

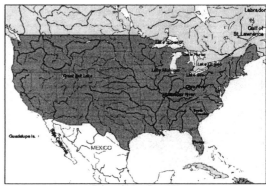

Enlarged Map, Page 173

Description

The heath hen, *Tympanuchus cupido cupido*, was considered an eastern subspecies of the greater prairie chicken, *T. cupido*. *T. cupido* is a chicken-like bird that is 17 inches (43 cm) in length. Its body is heavily barred above and below with dark brown, cinnamon, and creamy white (buff) bars. The tail is short and rounded; males have dark brown tails and females have barred tails. Males have featherless, yellowish-orange eye-combs, golden yellow neck sacs, and elongated dark brown pinnae or neck feathers. The female also has pinnae, but they are not as long or as dark. The pinnae on the heath hen was more pointed than *T. cupido's*. The heath hen's axillaries were banded or heavily patterned versus *T. cupido's* white axillaries.

Downy chicks were a creamy or buffy color underneath; a yellower color on the cheeks and sides of the head with a few dark dots on either side behind the eyes; a tawny-olive color on the back; and they had a reddish-brown rump streaked with black. Juvenile and adult plumages were similar. Juveniles were smaller and they had a slightly rufous cast to the back. The throat was a buffy, light cinnamon color (adult throats

Status	Extinct
Probable Extinction	1933
Family	Phasianidae (Pheasants and Quails)
Description	Chicken-like bird with a heavily barred body above and below with dark brown, cinnamon, and creamy white bars.
Habitat	Grasslands, brushy areas and open pine/scrub oak forests.
Food	Probably fruit, insects, seeds, acorns, and green vegetation.
Reproduction	Clutch of 6-13 eggs.
Causes for Extinction	Overhunting, habitat loss, predation by feral cats.
Range	Massachusetts, Rhode Island, Connecticut, New York, New Jersey, Pennsylvania, Delaware, Maryland, Virginia
Photo	See Color Insert, C-7

were more of a creamy color). Adults continued to molt two times a year, alternating between winter and nuptial plumages.

Behavior

Courtship began in late March or April. Few nests were ever located; those with eggs had from 6 to 13 eggs in the clutch. Incubation probably lasted 24 days and hatching generally occurred in mid-June to early July.

This species' food preferences were probably similar to other prairie chickens. They consumed fruit, insects, seeds, acorns, and green vegetation (buds and leaves). heath hens foraged on bare soil, sand, and vegetated surfaces. In the spring, new green vegetation (grasses, sorrel, etc.) was consumed. They switched their diet to fruits and insects in the summer and fall when the grasses became less palatable. Acorns, seeds, and some berries were the mainstay of the winter diet.

The heath hen was non-migratory.

Habitat

The heath hen preferred grasslands, brushy areas and open pine/scrub oak forests. They avoided densely forested areas. The heath hen inhabited the sandy scrub-oak plains found along the coasts of Massachusetts south through Pennsylvania.

Nests were placed on the ground in a shallow depression in grassy areas intermixed with brushy vegetation. The nests were well hidden in dense stands of grass or under shrubs. Breeding grounds on Martha's Vineyard were located in the grassy areas of the island's interior region. The booming or drumming grounds or leks used by displaying males were located on a more open part of a field.

Distribution

Historic accounts from colonial days seemed to indicate that this subspecies was very common in grassland and brush habitats along the northern Atlantic Coast. The heath hen's population declined dramatically in the late 1800s. By 1900, only 100 individuals remained; all were on Martha's Vineyard, an island off the coast of Massachusetts. Some sources indicate that the Martha's Vineyard population may have been introduced by man in the early 1800s or earlier. This population increased to about 2,000 by 1916 then plummeted to 100 to 150 following a major fire and heavy predation by raptors (goshawks). Another minor increase in numbers occurred around 1920 but the population never fully recovered and the last individual was sighted in 1932 or 1933.

In 1908, a reserve was established on Martha's Vineyard to protect breeding heath hens. Wardens protected the birds from predators and poachers. Six hundred acres were purchased with private money and the state of Massachusetts leased an additional 1,000 acres for the preserve. Attempts to transplant the birds to suitable sites on the mainland during this period all failed. Propagation efforts also failed. These conservation efforts helped to prolong the existence of this subspecies, but all efforts failed and it was declared extinct in 1932 or 1933.

Causes for Extinction

The decline and extinction of this subspecies was precipitated by overhunting, habitat loss, predation by feral cats and other predators, and the introduction of diseases spread by pheasants and domestic poultry. Overhunting was primarily responsible for the extirpation of the subspecies from mainland Massachusetts and Connecticut by the

1840s.

The population fluctuated between 1900 and 1933 when the species was officially declared extinct. Prairie chicken populations appear to fluctuate widely under natural conditions. Ground-nesting birds, as the heath hen was, are susceptible to catastrophic events (e.g., flooding, fire) that decimate a population's yearly reproduction and the habitat required for subsequent reproductive attempts. Fire removes the cover needed to protect active nests and destroys the bird's food supply. Populations plummet following these catastrophic events but increase rapidly once conditions begin to improve. These population explosions are due to the species' large clutch sizes (up to 18 eggs per clutch for *T. cupido*); as conditions improve more chicks survive. If excessive predation, poaching, and disease had been controlled following the fire that devastated the Martha's Vineyard population's habitat, the species might have been able to rebound as it had in the past.

Adapted from data compiled by the Threatened and Endangered Species Information Institute (Golden, CO) for *Beacham's International Threatened, Endangered, and Extinct Species* published on CD ROM, available from Beacham Publishing.

Labrador Duck
Camptorhynchus labradorius

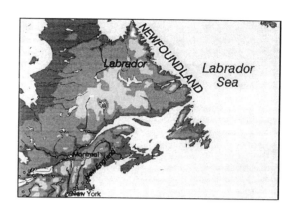

Description

The Labrador duck, *Camptorhynchus labradorius*, was sexually dimorphic. Males had a white head, neck, and scapulars except for stiff yellowish feathers on the cheeks and a black stripe extending from the crown to the nape. A black collar divided the neck from a white breast. Its wings were white with black primaries. The rump and upper tail coverts as well as the tail and upperparts were black. Its iris was a reddish hazel to yellow and its bill was blackish brown for most of its length; a band of yellow-orange or flesh color separated the blackish portion of the bill from a grayish-blue basal area. Its legs and feet were probably grey but could have been yellow.

Females were generally light brownish gray with mantles, scapulars, and wing coverts a bluish-slate tone. The tail was dark with underparts being lighter. Greater secondary coverts and secondaries were white with primaries blackish brown. The color of the soft parts was probably similar to the males. Immature males appeared similar to the adult females during the first year of life, but they had a white feathering on the head, throat, and upper breast which probably increased a little year by year.

The male's wingspan measured an aver-

Status	Extinct
Probable Extinction	c.1875
Family	Anatidae (Ducks and Geese)
Description	Males had a white head, neck and scapulars, and a black stripe extending from the crown to the nape; females were brownish gray with bluish-slate mantles and wing coverts.
Habitat	Sandy bays and inlets along coastal areas.
Food	Shellfish and seaweed.
Reproduction	Breeding grounds were in Labrador or on islands in the Gulf of St. Lawrence.
Causes for Extinction	Perhaps a reduction in food supply.
Range	Canada: Labrador
Photo	See Color Insert, C-7

age of 215 millimeters (8.38 inches). Its tail was 78 mm (3.04 inches) long, the culmen was 44 mm (1.72 inches), and the tarsus was 40 mm (1.56 inches). The female was slightly smaller.

Behavior

The Labrador duck made its nests of large fir twigs lined with dry grass and down.

The species fed on shellfish and perhaps mussels which old records tell us were used as bait by fishermen who accidentally caught this species instead. Its bill resembled that of the Australian pink-eared duck, (*Malacorhynchus membranaceous*). A softness around the edges with a swollen cere and a large number of lamellae inside, seems to indicate that the species' feeding requirements were specialized. The species may have also fed on seaweed.

Activity levels probably increased during the breeding season and decreased during the summer as temperatures rose. The species was a fast flyer.

Habitat

The species' habitat was essentially maritime. Its breeding grounds are thought to have been either in Labrador or on islands in the Gulf of St. Lawrence. It once inhabited maritime areas of Europe and North America where it frequented sandy bays and inlets. The North American population was restricted to the coastal areas and wintered from Nova Scotia south to New Jersey.

Distribution

The species once ranged from as far north as Labrador to as far south as the Chesapeake Bay. It probably kept close to the coast although there is one record of it occurring inland in Michigan. This record is generally discounted among biologists. The species appeared in autumn and winter on Long Island and along the coasts of New Jersey and New England.

By the time of their initial description, the species was already rare. Their numbers may have been dwindling over a period of time or they could have gone down rapidly from human interference across their habitat. From 1840 to 1870, the species experienced a rapid decline during which young males were scarce.

Causes for Extinction

Specific reasons for this species' extinction are little understood. Some speculate that it was over-hunted, yet, other waterfowl species in the same family received far greater hunting pressure with little apparent impact to the population as a whole. The species was fast flying, shy, and wary of humans. Its flesh had a "fishy" taste, but it did appear in the markets of New York and Baltimore on occasion. Its breeding grounds may have been localized and vulnerable to attack. The fact that eggs were harvested by collectors may have had some impact on the species' reproductive capabilities.

It has been hypothesized that the species was a specialized feeder. If this were true, then the species could have been extremely vulnerable to even the slightest alterations in its habitat. Along the Atlantic seaboard after the rapid increase of human populations, a number of subtle changes took place among the molluscan fauna. What was thought to be the last known specimen was shot on Long Island in 1875.

Adapted from data compiled by the Threatened and Endangered Species Information Institute (Golden, CO) for *Beacham's International Threatened, Endangered, and Extinct Species* published on CD ROM, available from Beacham Publishing.

Great Auk
Pinguinus impennis

Description

The great auk, *Pinguinus impennis*, was the first bird humans applied the word "penguin" to. Its upperparts were black with the sides of the head and wings dark brown. A large, oval patch covered the area of the face in front of the eye. Its chin and throat were a blackish brown with the remainder of the underparts white. Its iris was chestnut and its culmen was black with white grooves and black feet.

Adults in winter sported a white chin and throat and lacked the oval patch before the eye. Instead, a gray line ran through the eye to the ear and a broad white band appeared above the eye. Both sexes appeared the same in all seasons except that the females possessed a grayish tinge on the flanks. The overall length was 75 centimeters (29.25 inches); the wing measured from 160 to 178 millimeters (6.24 to 6.94 inches); the tail extended from 83 (3.24 inches) to 95 mm (73.7 inches); the culmen ranged from 82 to 90 mm (3.2 to 3.51 inches) in length; and the tarsus was from 55 to 62 mm (2.14 to 2.42 inches) long.

Behavior

The inside of the great auk's mouth was

Status	Extinct
Probable Extinction	c.1844
Family	Alcidae (Auks)
Description	Large black bird with short brown wings, blackish-brown chin and throat, and white underparts.
Habitat	Rocky platforms in cold climates.
Food	Fish and crustaceans.
Reproduction	Laid eggs on bare ground in June and July, and possibly other times.
Causes for Extinction	Hunting
Range	North Atlantic Islands off Canada and Iceland
Photo	See Color Insert, C-1

a bright yellow in color. Researchers speculate that this coloring may have been used to attract the opposite sex in breeding behavior. The eggs were a dirty yellowish white, and speckled, especially at the bulkier end, with pale gray or brown spots. They measured an average of 124 mm long and 75 mm wide. The eggs were shaped in a pyriform manner which would force the egg to roll in a tight circle when nudged. This helped prevent the eggs from rolling into open areas where they could be smashed. This was an important adaptation since the species did not use nests but laid their eggs on bare or guano-covered rock.

Breeding cycles are not known. However, eggs were often found in June with young sighted in July. Parents probably incubated eggs in an upright position. Chicks spent about 9 days after hatching onshore before entering the sea. The species migrated to specific breeding grounds from areas of feeding and roosting. The species was active during the day.

Marine invertebrates such as fish and crustaceans constituted this species' diet. The species pursued prey in the water with great speed and agility. It sometimes foraged near the sea bottom to a depth of 250 feet (42 fathoms).

Habitat

The species inhabited rocky platforms in latitudes of the far North. It required open seas near islands to provide its food supply. And, it needed rocky island habitat to protect it from rough weather and provide it with breeding grounds.

Distribution

The species is thought to have once occurred widely across the North Atlantic, from the Gulf of St. Lawrence in the west to Norway in the east. It has been recorded as far south as the Channel Islands and northern France. Fossil remains put the species in Gibraltar and Italy. From this fossil evidence, it has been suggested that the species had been brought south with the great ice sheets of the past. The species once numbered in

the tens of thousands; evidence shows that the great auk was an important part of the diet of prehistoric maritime tribes at least as far back as 7,000 B.C.

Though it was widely distributed, it seemed to have bred in only a few locations which included Bird Rocks in the Gulf of St. Lawrence, Fund Island off the Newfoundland coast, Grimsey Island, Geirfuglasker Island (until it was sunk by a volcanic explosion in 1830), and Eldey Island. These last three islands are located near Iceland.

Causes for Extinction

The taking of its eggs and the slaughter of the adults are the generally agreed upon reasons for this species' decline and extinction. The species could not be caught when in the water; however, it was an easy catch when on land. It was clumsy and slow as it waddled with small steps. Wherever humans and the great auk met, the species was harassed, captured, and slaughtered. On Funk Island, the species was herded into pens where they were clubbed to death or until they became immobile. They were then tossed into boiling water to loosen their feathers, which were commercially valuable.

The species was valued for food, bait, fat, feathers, and, ultimately, for its interest to collectors. For many people in the nineteenth century, it was a curiosity and a mystery. By the time the species was well known, it had become so rare that some people considered it a myth. Skins and eggs were especially sought after by collectors. Seamen were contracted to raid the last refuges of the species and were paid high sums by private individuals and institutions. One specimen was purchased for 100 pounds in 1863 by the Dresden Museum. By 1900, long after the last individuals were sighted, a preserved egg fetched a price of

330 pounds. And, in 1970, a stuffed great auk sold for 9,000 pounds in London.

By the end of the eighteenth century, the species was rare. The last verified record occurred on June 3, 1844 in Iceland.

Adapted from data compiled by the Threatened and Endangered Species Information Institute (Golden, CO) for *Beacham's International Threatened, Endangered, and Extinct Species* published on CD ROM, available from Beacham Publishing.

EXTINCT BIRDS OF THE CARIBBEAN ISLANDS

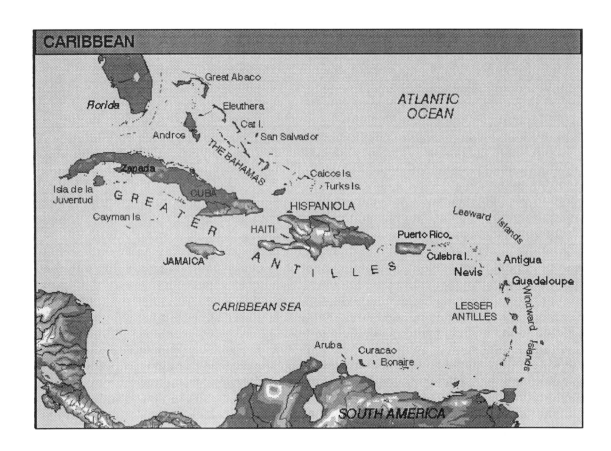

Cuba

Cuba possesses an irregular 3,570 mile coastline with many bays, beaches, mangrove plantations, swamps, coral reefs and rugged cliffs. Cuba's tropical plant life is very rich, with 8,000 plant species, about half of which are endemic. Much of the original vegetation has been replaced by sugarcane, coffee and rice plantations, at the enormous expense and indiscriminate destruction of forests. Cuban animal life is abundant, with more than 7,000 insect species and 4,000 species of land, river, and sea mollusks. Sponges are important off the western coast; arachnids include scorpions and tarantulas. There are 500 edible species of fish and 37 shark species. Only a third of the 300 birds species are endemic, and many of these are migratory. Marine species include the tortoise and endangered hawksbill turtle. Mud turtles and two species of crocodile inhabit the rivers. Mammals include the hutia, manatee, sea cow, and bats, which control the mosquito population.

Jamaica

Jamaica, a part of the Greater Antilles, is the third largest island in the West Indies archipelago; the coast of Honduras (650 km southwest) is the closest mainland area. Current theories postulate that Jamaica was never attached to the mainland or to another island; species colonizing the island must have crossed the wide expanses of water. Most birds appear to have been derived from North American species.

The island is about 11,400 square kilometers in area (230 km long and 80 km wide). A series of mountain chains bisects the island running from east to west. Blue Mountain Peak is the highest point on the island at 2,290 meters.

The island's climate is subtropical. The wettest months of the year are October and May; August, September, November and June are also wet. The John Crow Mountains on the eastern coast receive the most moisture (greater than 500 centimeters). For the most part, the southern to southwestern portions of the island are drier. Because of this, the two sides of the island support different habitat types. There are 3 primary forest types restricted by elevation and moisture regimes. They are 1) the lowland arid limestone forest — primarily in the southern lowlands; 2) wet midlevel limestone forest — most common in the Cockpit Country of west-central Jamaica and the very wet limestone forest — found in the John Crow Mountains; and 3) the montane forest — found in the Blue Mountains. The mostly closed canopy midlevel limestone forests are characterized by *Terminalia latifolia* and *Cedrela odorata* and many other shorter tree species that support a diverse assemblage of lianas and large bromeliads. The montane forests typically grow on the steep slopes of the Blue Mountains. The canopy is closed in the valley areas and on the ridges; more open canopy forests occur on the slopes. There are small areas of "cloud" and "elfin tree" forests on the ridge tops.

Culebra Island, Puerto Rico

Culebra Island lies 20 miles east of the main island of Puerto Rico. About 7 miles long and 2 miles wide, the hilly, almost barren mass of limestone and igneous intrusions rises to 646 feet. It has sparse, thin soils and no permanent streams. It is a bird sanctuary.

Cuban Red Macaw
Ara tricolor

Description

The Cuban Red Macaw, *Ara tricolor*, was a member of the parrot family. Its forehead was red, turning orange on the crown and merging to yellow on the hindneck. Its bare facial area was white while sides of the face, chin, throat, breast, and abdomen along with the thighs were orange. The upper back was a brownish red while the feathers were margined with green. The rump and lower back were pale blue. The lesser wing coverts were brown and the feathers were edged with red. The webs of the primaries and the secondaries were a purplish blue; the upper surface of the tail was a dark red which turned blue toward the tip but was brownish red on the underside. The species was blue beneath the tail coverts. Its bill was a dark brown, growing pale at the tip. Its iris was yellow and its legs were brown. Males and females looked the same. The species' wing measured between 275 and 290 millimeters (10.72 to 11.31 inches) while its tail was between 215 and 290 mm (8.38 to 11.31 inches) in length. The culmen measured between 42 and 46 mm (1.63 to 1.79 inches) long and the tarsus between 27 and 30 mm (1.05 to 1.17 inches).

Status	Extinct
Probable Extinction	1864
Family	Psittacidae (Parrots and Parakeets)
Description	Parrot with a red-to-orange forehead merging to yellow on the hindneck; white facial area; orange chin, throat, breast, abdomen, and thighs; a brownish red upper back; and pale blue rump and lower back.
Habitat	Swamps.
Food	Fruits, seeds, sprouts, and buds.
Reproduction	Nested in the holes of palm trees.
Causes for Extinction	Overhunting.
Range	Cuba

Behavior

The Cuban red macaw is believed to have nested in the holes of palm trees and lived in pairs and families.

The diet of this species consisted of fruit and seeds, sprouts, and buds. They preferred those of the Melia azadarach, a large flowering tree, and palms. The species was active during the day when it fed and foraged.

Habitat

The Cuban red macaw inhabited the Zapata Swamp of Cuba. This is a forested area where the birds nested in the holes of palm trees.

Distribution

This species was highly social in nature. It was important for individuals to remain in constant contact with one another for safety and breeding reasons. Many individuals had been captured and kept as pets by humans. The last known individual was shot at La Vega near the Zapata forest in 1864.

The Cuban red macaw once ranged on the island of Cuba in the region of the Cienaga de Zapata and the Encenada de Cochinos on the south coast.

Causes for Extinction

It is commonly accepted that this species became extinct due to overhunting for commercial and exotic trade. The last living individual seen was shot at La Vega close to the Zapata Swamp during 1864.

Adapted from data compiled by the Threatened and Endangered Species Information Institute (Golden, CO) for *Beacham's International Threatened, Endangered, and Extinct Species* published on CD ROM, available from Beacham Publishing.

Green and Yellow Macaw

Ara erythrocephala

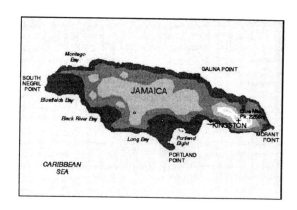

Description

The green and yellow macaw, *Ara erythrocephala*, was described as a parrot-like bird having a red head, light, bright green shoulders, neck, and underparts, blue greater primary coverts, tail feathers that were scarlet and blue on the upper surface and a deep orange yellow on the lower surface and on the undersides of the wings. There is some indication that the person who gave the most detailed description of the bird (a Mr. Hill, an acquaintance of P. H. Gosse) never saw the bird but based his description on a Jamaican resident's observation. Hill believed *A. erythrocephala* was actually *Ara militaris* (the military macaw of Mexico) and assumed it wintered in Jamaica and migrated to its breeding grounds in Mexico.

Status	Extinct
Probable Extinction	1842
Family	Psittacidae (Parrots and Parakeets)
Description	Brightly colored parrot with a red head, bright green shoulders, neck and under parts, blue coverts and tail feathers on the upper side and deep orange on the under side.
Habitat	Isolated forests.
Food	Possibly fruit and seeds.
Reproduction	Possibly migrated to Mexico for breeding.
Causes for Extinction	Unknown
Range	Jamaica

Behavior

Information concerning the food habits of *A. erythrocephala* is unavailable. Other members of the parrot family consume a wide variety of fruits and seeds.

Habitat

The species described as *A. erythrocephala* was observed in isolated forests of the mountain district of Jamaica. No other information concerning the habitat requirements of this species is available.

Distribution

A. erythrocephala may have been hunted by early inhabitants of Jamaica. Because of the limited number of sightings and the lack of specimens, it seems unlikely that this species was collected in great numbers for the commercial pet industry; residents of Jamaica may have captured and domesticated some birds. The population size must have been extremely small by the early 1800s.

A. erythrocephala was described from sightings of a parrot-like bird on Jamaica. Mr. Hill (see Description above) based his description on birds seen in the mountain district in the remote area between St. Anne's and Trelawney and an area called the "Accompong Maroons". Hill believed the bird's breeding grounds were in Mexico. Another possible sighting was made in 1842 by a Reverend Comard near the center of the island at a parish near St. James.

Causes for Extinction

Many factors could have contributed to the extirpation of *A. erythrocephala* from Jamaica, including collecting by residents for food or for domestication as pets, habitat loss/alteration, disturbance during nesting, and natural disasters, especially hurricanes.

Adapted from data compiled by the Threatened and Endangered Species Information Institute (Golden, CO) for *Beacham's International Threatened, Endangered, and Extinct Species* published on CD ROM, available from Beacham Publishing.

Jamaican Least Pauraque
Siphonorhis americanus

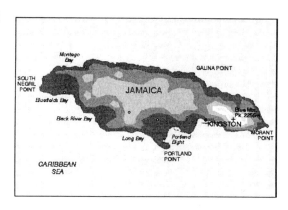

Description

The Jamaican least pauraque, *Siphonorhis americanus*, was a small (9 to 10 inches in length) member of the nightjar family, *Caprimulgidae*. This species had a broad white band that divided the throat from the breast. The upper body was brown with streaks and patches of gray and darker brown. The primaries were irregularly barred with light and dark brown. The nostrils and whiskers were prominent. The tail was strongly rounded.

Behavior

Most nightjars are almost exclusively insectivorous. U.S. species (whip-poor-will and poor-will) are known to consume beetles, moths, flies, grasshoppers, and mosquitoes.

Most members of the nightjar family are mostly crepuscular to nocturnal.

Habitat

The Jamaican least pauraque inhabited the remote lowland forested habitats of Jamaica. Many nightjars feed in more open habitats, but this species' relatively short

Status	Extinct
Probable Extinction	c.1860
Family	Caprimulgidae (Nightjars)
Description	Small nightjar with a broad white band that divided the throat from the breast, and a brown upper body with streaks and patches of gray and darker brown.
Habitat	Remote lowland forests.
Food	Insects
Causes for Extinction	Habitat alteration; exotic rats.
Range	Jamaica

wings indicate it may have hunted among the trees.

Distribution

The Jamaican least pauraque was endemic to Jamaica and may have had a restricted distribution on the island.

This species may never have been very common. It was even more secretive than its relatives, the whip-poor-will and poor-will.

This fact is exemplified by the fact that P. H. Gosse, the noted ornithologist who wrote "The Birds of Jamaica" in the nineteenth century, had never heard of the bird. The last specimen was collected in 1859. This species' secretive nature and its uniquely camouflaging plumage would make it easy to overlook; because of this it is possible that the species still exists in Jamaica. *Caprimulgus vociferus noctitherus*, the Puerto Rican Whip-poor-will, was thought to have become extinct early in the nineteenth century until its rediscovery in the 1960s; since then, census records have indicated the population may exceed 1,000 individuals.

Causes for Extinction

The species was considered to be quite localized and rare in the early 1800s. It is assumed that habitat destruction/alteration and the introduction of rats were responsible for the demise of this species. The mongoose was apparently introduced to the island (1872) after the species had been extirpated (1859).

Adapted from data compiled by the Threatened and Endangered Species Information Institute (Golden, CO) for *Beacham's International Threatened, Endangered, and Extinct Species* published on CD ROM, available from Beacham Publishing.

Culebran Puerto Rican Parrot

Amazona vittata gracileps

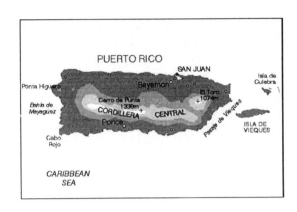

Description

The Culebran Puerto Rican parrot, *Amazona vittata gracileps*, was a subspecies of the Puerto Rican parrot, *A. vittata*, that is quite similar in appearance. *A. vittata* is a small parrot and has an emerald green body with a ruby-red forehead and white eye-rings. The Culebran Puerto Rican parrot may have been slightly smaller and the legs may have been lighter in color.

Behavior

The reproductive characteristics of this subspecies are assumed to have been similar to *A. vittata*. Eggs, averaging 2 to 3 per clutch, are laid deep in old-growth tree cavities. Information concerning incubation and fledgling dates is unavailable. The Culebran Puerto Rican parrot was thought to be extremely gregarious during the non-breeding seasons, but strongly territorial during breeding.

The Culebran Puerto Rican parrot was non-migratory. This species was probably most active during the day. Its diet consisted of fruits, seeds, and leaves. They were observed consuming fruits of the Sierra palm and the tabunoco. Up to 50 different fruits

Status	Extinct
Probable Extinction	c.1900
Family	Psittacidae (Parrots and Parakeets)
Description	Small parrot with an emerald green body and a ruby-red forehead and white eye-rings.
Habitat	Old growth forests.
Food	Fruits, seeds, and leaves.
Reproduction	2-3 eggs per clutch.
Causes for Extinction	Habitat destruction.
Range	Puerto Rico

may have been utilized. Nectar and small animals may have been consumed on occasion.

Habitat/Distribution

The Culebran Puerto Rican parrot inhabited the old growth forests of Culebra Island, off the east coast of Puerto Rico. It most likely nested in deep cavities of large, old growth trees as *A. vittata* does. *A. vittata* prefers to nest in large Palo Colorado trees.

It was last sighted on the island in 1899.

Causes for Extinction

Habitat destruction was the primary factor responsible for the decline of *A. vittata* and the extinction of the Culebran Puerto Rican parrot. Vast areas of the rain forests inhabited by these parrots were cleared in the latter part of the nineteenth century for agricultural and urban development. The large Palo Colorado trees used by *A. vittata* for nesting were cut down for charcoal. Similar activities probably took place on Culebra Island.

Most *Amazona* sp. are popular pet species; the Culebran Puerto Rican parrot may have been overcollected by commercial pet traders. Many of them may have been shot during the extensive pigeon hunts.

Other factors may have contributed to the sudden decline of the species in the late nineteenth century. The *A. vittata* population faces a variety of limiting factors which include nest parasitism, disease/parasites, predation and competition for nest sites from pearly-eyed thrashers and other species, nest vandalism, egg infertility, and an inherently low reproductive rate.

Adapted from data compiled by the Threatened and Endangered Species Information Institute (Golden, CO) for *Beacham's International Threatened, Endangered, and Extinct Species* published on CD ROM, available from Beacham Publishing.

Guadeloupe Burrowing Owl

Speotyto cunicularia guadeloupensis

Description

The Guadeloupe burrowing owl, *Speotyto cunicularia guadeloupensis*, possessed long legs and an upright stance. It had a rounded, dumpy shape, an intense frown, and a look of impatience and even distrust. The white eyebrows were flattened down over large eyes which appeared dark at a distance under the shadow of the brow. The species would sit squat and rounded one moment, and then suddenly become upright, taut, and alert as it bobbed and twisted its head. The species' wing measured between 156 and 164 millimeters (6.1 to 6.4 inches).

Behavior

The species nested in burrows dug out of banksides. Clutch size ranged from 2 to 11 eggs which made the Guadeloupe burrowing owl the biggest of any raptorial bird in North America. Both parents incubated the eggs. Many nesting attempts failed and nests were often deserted. Nests may also have been abandoned due to a large number of nesting birds. The species is colonial occurring in groups of up to 10 or 12 pairs in loose association. Nests were located up to a yard below the ground and were lined with

Status	Extinct
Probable Extinction	Early 19th century
Family	Strigidae (Owls)
Description	Round-shaped owl with long legs, white eyebrows flattened down over large eyes that appeared dark at a distance under the shadow of the brow.
Habitat	Grasslands.
Food	Small mammals, large beetles, frogs, and birds.
Reproduction	Clutch of 2-11 eggs nested in burrows.
Causes for Extinction	Predation by the introduced mongoose.
Range	Antigua, Nevis, St. Christopher (West Indies)

livestock dung, which made the nest less prone to predation.

During the spring, small mammals provided food for the species. Later in the summer, the species switched to eating primarily insects. It consumed large beetles, frogs, and birds.

The species was nocturnal, hunting and foraging during the night and roosting during the day.

Habitat

The species occurred in open grasslands with little or no trees. It required ground holes for nesting. It sometimes utilized the burrows of prairie dogs, ground squirrels, and badgers. Burrows with short grass and good visibility were best to decrease predation.

The species has never held the economic interest of humanity. It had provided amusement with its peculiar behavior and unique looks. Many researchers attributed human emotion to the species' behavior and looks. Yet, its value as a species involved the natural diversity it provided to its habitat in helping maintain a balanced ecological environment.

Distribution

The species once ranged on the islands of Antigua, Nevis, and St. Christopher in the West Indies.

Causes for Extinction

Predation by the introduced mongoose is thought to have been responsible for the extinction of this species. It had never been common. Only 6 specimens were known to exist. The species was preyed upon by badgers and other birds of prey. Eggs were especially vulnerable to theft by ground squirrels. The species was never common since only 6 specimens had been collected and only one has survived to this day.

Adapted from data compiled by the Threatened and Endangered Species Information Institute (Golden, CO) for *Beacham's International Threatened, Endangered, and Extinct Species* published on CD ROM, available from Beacham Publishing.

EXTINCT BIRDS OF THE
SOUTH ATLANTIC ISLANDS

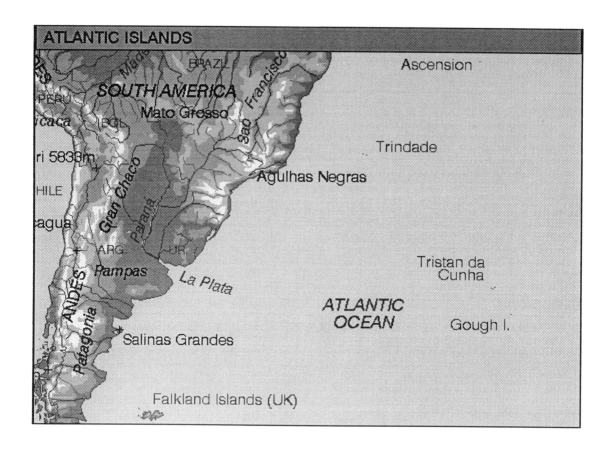

Ascension Island

Ascension is an island of volcanic origin with an area of 34 square miles. It is barren and rocky, almost without vegetation except for some 10 acres atop Green Mountain. A heavy swell breaks on the island's lea shore with great violence. Average annual rainfall varies from 6 inches on the coast to 25 inches on Green Mountain. Sea turtles and sooty terns visit the island. No indigenous vertebrate land animals exist. The U.S. maintains a satellite tracking installation on the island which may have contributed to the disruption of pelican breeding grounds.

Tristan da Cunha

Tristan da Cunha comprises three small volcanic islands: Tristan, Inaccessible and Nightingale. Inaccessible and Nightingale are uninhabited. Inaccessible is 20 miles from Tristan, rises to a height of 1,840 feet, and has a land area of one square mile. A bird peculiar to Inaccessible is the small, flightless land rail.

Nightingale is the smallest island. Its highest point is 1,200 feet; its coasts have low cliffs. Millions of sea birds nest on Nightingale.

Tristan has an area of 38 square miles with a central volcanic core that is usually cloud covered. The climate is wet, windy and mild. The lower parts of the island support dense vegetations of ferns and grasses. Plant and animal life include species that are not found anywhere else in the world. A volcanic erruption in 1961 threatened both human and natural inhabitants; the 198 islanders evacuated to England and returned in 1963.

Ascension Flightless Crake

Atlantisia elpenor

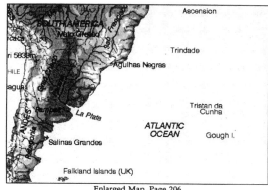

Enlarged Map, Page 206

Description

The Ascension flightless crake, *Atlantisia elpenor*, may have been about 9 inches (22 centimeters) in length. A visitor to Ascension Island described it as gray or mottled (black and white patterned) with much reduced wings that limited the bird to very short flights. They were described as swift runners.

A. elpenor was a member of the rail, coot, and gallinule family, Rallidae. *A. elpenor* was described and named *Atlantisia elpenor* by Olson in 1973, although it probably became extinct in 1656. The Ascension flightless crake is also referred to as Elpenor's rail.

Behavior

Like other rails, The Ascension flightless crake was probably omnivorous but animal matter probably made up the majority of the diet when available. Ascension Island is used by seabirds for nesting. It is possible that the Ascension flightless crake ate seabird eggs and food items brought in by the seabirds for their chicks.

Status	Extinct
Probable Extinction	c.1656
Family	Rallidae (Rails, Gallinules and Coots)
Description	Gray or mottled (black and white patterned) bird with much reduced wings that limited it to very short flights.
Habitat	Possibly nests were placed out in the open, among rocks, among sparse patches of vegetation, or possibly in burrows.
Food	Probably omnivorous.
Causes for Extinction	Probably hunted for food.
Range	Island of Ascension

Habitat

The species' habitat requirements are unknown. Ascension Island is a sparsely vegetated piece of land. Nests would have to have been placed out in the open, among rocks, among sparse patches of vegetation, or possibly in burrows.

Distribution

The Ascension flightless crake was endemic to the island of Ascension, which is located in the southeastern Atlantic Ocean (east of Angola and south of Liberia and Sierra Leon).

The island's avian populations would have been limited by space and by food resources. Other limiting factors are unknown.

Causes for Extinction

The introduction of exotic mammals had a strongly negative impact on the ground nesting and tree nesting avian species found on many remote islands. Black rats (*Rattus rattus*) and brown rats (*R. norvegicus*) were probably common. Their ability to climb trees allowed them to reach most or all bird nests where they probably ate and/or broke the eggs and possibly killed or injured young chicks. Whether rats introduced to Ascension Island had a role in the decline and extinction of this species is unknown.

The Ascension flightless crake was probably hunted for food by early explorers or sailors who stopped on Ascension Island to replenish their food supply. The birds' flightlessness (or nearly so) left them vulnerable to hunters. This was probably one of the primary factors leading to the extinction of this species.

Because Ascension Island lacked predators, a limiting factor for many large land mass species, evolution selected out characteristics necessary to avoid predation. This resulted in a fearless bird that was only capable of limited flight. When predators (including man) were introduced, the species was incapable of adapting to avoid predation.

Adapted from data compiled by the Threatened and Endangered Species Information Institute (Golden, CO) for *Beacham's International Threatened, Endangered, and Extinct Species* published on CD ROM, available from Beacham Publishing.

Tristan Island Gallinule
Gallinula nesiotis nesiotis

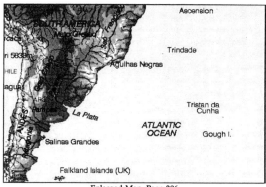

Enlarged Map, Page 206

Description

The Tristan Island gallinule, *Gallinula nesiotis nesiotis*, was a small gallinule sometimes growing up to 10 inches in total length. It had short wings and was almost unable to fly. Its head, neck, and underparts were black while its back and wing coverts were dark olive-brown. Its wings and tail were black with streaks on the sides. The underside of the tail coverts were white with black feathers in the middle. The outer edge of the wings was white, the bill was red with a yellow tip, and the feet and legs were yellow. It possessed a drawn-out call that was shrill and heard all over the island where it lived.

Status	Extinct
Probable Extinction	After 1861
Family	Rallidae (Rails, Gallinules and Coots)
Description	Small wading bird with short wings, black head, neck, and underparts, olive-brown wing coverts; wings and tail were black with streaks on the sides.
Habitat	Marshes.
Food	Carcasses of seals and sea lions.
Causes for Extinction	Possibly predation.
Range	Tristan da Cunha Island

Behavior

The subspecies was omnivorous occasionally feeding on the dead carcasses of seals and sea lions.

Habitat

The subspecies inhabited the marshes and water of Tristan da Cunha Island in the South Atlantic. The only eyewitness account of the subspecies in its habitat was made by Carmichael in 1818: "The Fulica conceals itself in the wood."

The subspecies was found in dense vegetation near stream banks in mountains of about 2,000 feet in elevation. Vegetation consisted of matted and tangled tussock grass (*Sparina arundinacea*) and stunted buckthorn (*Phylica nitida*). The subspecies took refuge in ground holes.

Distribution

The subspecies was known from Tristan da Cunha Island in the South Atlantic. It was never known from nearby islands such as Nightingale or Inaccessible Islands.

Little is known of the biology of this subspecies. Yet, it is known that it was limited by predators natural to the island. The subspecies was occasionally run down by dogs since it was unable to fly and used its wings only for balance when running. Wild hogs hidden in the forest hunted the subspecies.

Causes for Extinction

The subspecies' extinction remains a mystery. The last recorded specimens were taken to London on May 25, 1861. Another expedition by the ship Challenger in 1873 failed to locate further specimens. At this early date in the history of the island's interaction with European influence, there were no introduced animal populations. Yet, if rats accidentally swam ashore from the ships, they might have preyed upon the subspecies. In 1882, a shipwreck may have introduced rats onto the island.

Adapted from data compiled by the Threatened and Endangered Species Information Institute (Golden, CO) for *Beacham's International Threatened, Endangered, and Extinct Species* published on CD ROM, available from Beacham Publishing.

EXTINCT PLANTS OF THE HAWAIIAN ISLANDS

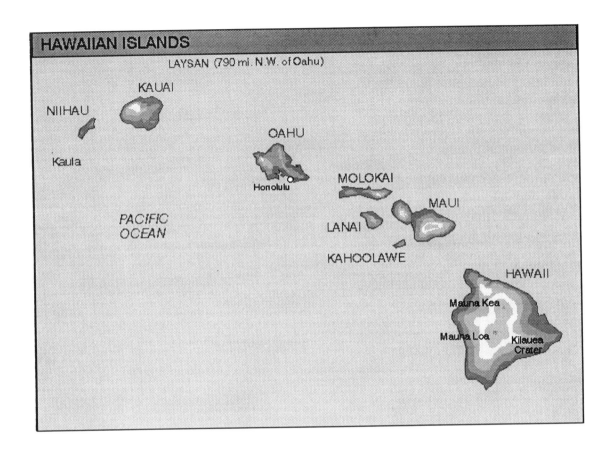

The Hawaiian Islands

Please see pages 119-129 for a discussion of habitat types and conditions on the larger Hawaiian Islands; causes of extinction of species on Laysan; and the introduction of destructive species to the Hawaiian Islands.

Extinction in the Hawaiian Flora

Hawaii is one of the most isolated land masses on Earth. This isolation greatly influenced which species found their way to Hawaii and how they evolved once arriving on these islands. One result of this isolation is that many of the world's most notable predators and herbivores failed to reach Hawaii on their own. Prior to the arrival of humans, Hawaii had no predator mammals (with the exception of two insectivorous bats), no grazing mammals, no rats, no social insects (e.g., ants, termites, or honey bees), no earthworms, no mosquitoes, no cockroaches, no conifer plants (e.g., pine trees), and very few orchids (Hawaii has only three native orchids). The absence of these species has influenced how the Hawaiian flora and fauna evolved and how human activities would eventually affect Hawaiian species. Another result of this isolation has been that Hawaii has evolved one of the most unique assemblages of plants and animals known. The vast majority of Hawaiian plants and animals are found nowhere else on Earth. Unfortunately, many of these unique species have become extinct, and many more are on the brink of becoming extinct. When a Hawaiian species becomes extinct it is truly gone forever — there is nowhere else to look for it.

Beginning with Polynesian colonization over 1,500 years ago, Hawaii has seen a constant increase in the number of native species that have either become extinct or are in danger of becoming extinct. Polynesians had a significant effect on both Hawaii's lowland vegetation and the unique land birds. Approximately half of Hawaii's endemic birds became extinct during the period of Polynesian colonization prior to the arrival of Europeans. Since the arrival of Captain Cook, approximately another quarter of the endemic birds have become extinct. Hawaii's plants and invertebrates have faired equally poorly, though the record of extinctions is not as well recorded. We do know from pollen records that the lowland vegetation of several islands changed dramatically during Polynesian occupation and even more dramatically since European colonization. The most damaging Polynesian effects on Hawaiian plants and animals were probably associated with the hunting of flightless birds, habitat alteration for cultivation, the intentional or unintentional use of fire, and the introduction of alien species such as rats and dogs. It is thought that while Polynesians brought pigs to Hawaii, these highly valued animals were seldom allowed to escape into the forests. European occupation resulted in greatly increased destruction of lowland dry and mesic forests on all islands through conversion to agricultural fields, urban areas, and ranches. The European introduction of cattle, goats, European pigs, deer, additional rat species, mongoose, mosquitoes, ants, alien snails, alien fish, and thousands of alien plant species has had a devastating effect on Hawaiian ecosystems and the species that rely upon those systems. The effects of these alien species have probably caused more extinctions than all other forms of human activities combined.

Many of the historic factors that extirpated Hawaiian species are no longer important threats to endangered species. For example, the hunting of native birds, the large-scale conversion of forests to agricultural lands, the urbanization of native forests are either non-existent or relatively localized threats to endangered species. The on-going threat posed by alien species continues to be the most significant factor in extinction and endangerment. Alien goats, sheep, pigs, and deer continue to destroy native forests and endangered plants. Introduced avian malaria continues to affect native birds. Predatory snails which were released in an attempt to control another alien snail continue to destroy populations of endangered endemic land snails. Numerous introduced insects and diseases afflict remnant populations of endangered plants and invertebrates. Alien weeds continue to out compete endangered plants and increase the risk of catastrophic fires which impact native species more than alien species. The introduction of new alien invertebrates and plants continues at the rate of several dozen per year. In contrast, the direct effects of humans on endangered species have become relatively less important. The combined effect of these threats on Hawaii's unique ecosystems continues to reduce populations of most endangered species, cause additional species to be classified as endangered, and exterminate entire species. Currently, less than ten percent of Hawaii's dry forest remains and most of this remaining forest has been heavily damaged by alien mammals (such as goats, sheep, and rats) and invaded by alien weeds. Mesic and wet forests have been less devastated, but continuing degradation by alien species, especially alien pigs and deer, is placing more and more species at risk of extinction. Analysis of the threats facing Hawaii's 275 currently endangered plants showed that the most common threats were: alien weeds (92%), alien pigs and goats (82%), fire (45%), rats (33%), collecting (33%), and development projects (15%).

Botanists have described 1,162 species of plants native to Hawaii. Of these, approximately 90 percent are endemic to Hawaii and they are found nowhere else. Currently, there are 77 endemic Hawaiian full species that may be extinct (Table 1). None of these species has been seen during recent surveys and biologists do not know of any living plants either in the wild or in cultivation. Species marked with an asterisk are described in the accompanying species accounts. In addition to these species, there are an additional 25 varieties, subspecies, or undescribed taxa that are thought to have also become extinct. Extinctions have not been random among Hawaiian plants. Most extinctions have occurred among species found in low elevation forests, especially dry and mesic forests. Comparatively, species from high elevation wet forests and subalpine areas have had fewer extinctions. Taxonomically, some families such as Campanulaceae, Lamiaceae, and Malvaceae have disproportionally borne the brunt of extinctions. Especially hard hit genera have been *Happlostachys* (4 of 5 species extinct; the 5th species is endangered), *Delissea* (5 of 9 species extinct; all others highly endangered), Cyanea (15 of 66 species), and *Hibiscadelphus* (3 of 7 species extinct; all others are highly endangered).

Unfortunately, additional species will continue to be added to the list of extinct Hawaiian plants.

Table 1. Hawaiian plants that may be extinct. The species listed below have not been seen during recent field surveys and no living representatives are known either in the wild or in cultivation.

Taxon	Family
Acaena exigua	ROSACEAE
Achyranthes atollensis	AMARANTHACEAE
Argyroxiphium virescens	ASTERACEAE
Botrychium subbifoliatum	OPHIOGLOSSACEAE
Clermontia multiflora	CAMPANULACEAE
Cyanea arborea	CAMPANULACEAE
Cyanea comata	CAMPANULACEAE
Cyanea dolichopoda	CAMPANULACEAE

*Cyanea giffardii	CAMPANULACEAE
Cyanea kolekoleensis	CAMPANULACEAE
*Cyanea linearifolia	CAMPANULACEAE
Cyanea lobata	CAMPANULACEAE
*Cyanea longissima	CAMPANULACEAE
*Cyanea parvifolia	CAMPANULACEAE
*Cyanea pohaku	CAMPANULACEAE
*Cyanea profuga	CAMPANULACEAE
*Cyanea purpurellifolia	CAMPANULACEAE
*Cyanea pycnocarpa	CAMPANULACEAE
*Cyanea quercifolia	CAMPANULACEAE
Cyanea truncata	CAMPANULACEAE
Cyrtandra crenata	GESNERIACEAE
*Cyrtandra gracilis	GESNERIACEAE
Cyrtandra kohalae	GESNERIACEAE
Cyrtandra olona	GESNERIACEAE
Cyrtandra pruinosa	GESNERIACEAE
Cyrtandra rivularis	GESNERIACEAE
Cyrtandra waiolani	GESNERIACEAE
*Delissea fallax	CAMPANULACEAE
*Delissea laciniata	CAMPANULACEAE
Delissea lauliiana	CAMPANULACEAE
Delissea parviflora	CAMPANULACEAE
*Delissea sinuata	CAMPANULACEAE
Deparia kaalaana	DRYOPTERIDACEAE
Diellia mannii	ASPLENIACEAE
*Eragrostis hosakai	POACEAE
Eragrostis mauiensis	POACEAE
*Haplostachys bryanii	LAMIACEAE
Haplostachys linearifolia	LAMIACEAE
*Haplostachys munroi	LAMIACEAE
Haplostachys truncata	LAMIACEAE
Hedyotis foliosa (Hillebr.)	RUBIACEAE
*Hibiscadelphus bombycinus	MALVACEAE
Hibiscadelphus crucibracteatus	MALVACEAE
*Hibiscadelphus wilderianus	MALVACEAE
*Kokia lanceolata	MALVACEAE

Lipochaeta bryanii	ASTERACEAE
Lipochaeta degeneri	ASTERACEAE
Lipochaeta perdita	ASTERACEAE
*Lobelia remyi	CAMPANULACEAE
Lysimachia forbesii	PRIMULACEAE
Mariscus kunthianus	CYPERACEAE
Mariscus rockii	CYPERACEAE
Melicope nealae	RUTACEAE
Melicope obovata	RUTACEAE
Melicope wailauensis	RUTACEAE
Ochrosia kilaueaensis	APOCYNACEAE
Peperomia degeneri	PIPERACEAE
Phyllostegia brevidens	LAMIACEAE
Phyllostegia hillebrandii	LAMIACEAE
Phyllostegia rockii	LAMIACEAE
Phyllostegia variabilis	LAMIACEAE
Phyllostegia waimeae	LAMIACEAE
Sanicula kauaiensis	APIACEAE
Schiedea amplexicaulis	CARYOPHYLLACEAE
Schiedea implexa	CARYOPHYLLACEAE
Sicyos hillebrandii	CUCURBITACEAE
Silene cryptopetala	CARYOPHYLLACEAE
Silene degeneri	CARYOPHYLLACEAE
Stenogyne cinerea	LAMIACEAE
Stenogyne haliakalae	LAMIACEAE
Stenogyne kanehoana	LAMIACEAE
Stenogyne oxygona	LAMIACEAE
Stenogyne viridis	LAMIACEAE
Tetramolopium conyzoides	ASTERACEAE
Tetramolopium tenerrimum	ASTERACEAE
Wikstroemia hanalei	THYMELAEACEAE
Wikstroemia villosa	THYMELAEACEAE

▲ *Cyanea arborea* (p.220)

Cyanea giffardii (p. 224) ▲

▼ *Argyroxiphium virescens* (p. 242)

Delissea fallax (p. 237) ▼

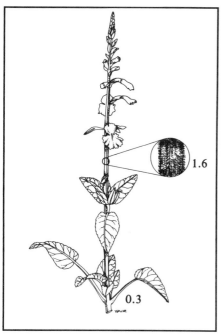

▲ *Haplostachys bryanii* (p. 246)

Cyanea profuga (p. 231) ▲

▼ *Cyanea comata* (p. 222)

Cyanea purpurellifolia (p. 232) ▼

▲ *Delissea laciniata* (p. 238)

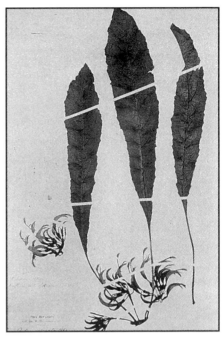

Delissea sinuata (p. 239) ▲

▼ *Lobelia remyi* (p. 240)

Clermontia multiflora (p. 243) ▼

Cyanea arborea
No Common Name

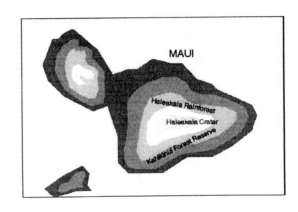

Description

Cyanea arborea was a palm-like tree, 4-8 meters (up to 24 feet) tall. The oblong leaves were clustered at the ends of branches and 65-90 centimeters (up to three feet) long. Inflorescences were pendant and hung below the leaves. The inflorescence consisted of 15-25 creamy-lilac colored flowers, each of which was 40-50 millimeters (two inches) long. The fruits were globose berries, 10-12 millimeters (one half inch) in diameter. Cyanea berries typically contain hundreds of small seeds. Joseph Rock considered this to be one of the most handsome species of Cyanea.

Status	Extinct
Probable Extinction	1928
Family	Campanulaceae (Bellflower)
Description	Palm-like tree with large oblong leaves and clusters of creamy-lilac flowers.
Habitat	Species-rich mesic forests around 5,000 feet in elevation
Causes for Extinction	Cattle grazing and conversion of forests into pastures
Range	Hawaii: Maui
Photo	See Page 217

Habitat

Cyanea arborea formerly occurred in mesic forest on the leeward (western) side of Haleakala, Maui. The species occurred at elevations of 1,520-1,650 meters (approximately 1,800 feet).

Distribution

Cyanea arborea was known only from the island of Maui. Little is known of the population biology of this species. The last re-

cordings of this species mention that there were few individuals left. Given the size that the species attained and the habitat it occurred in, Cyanea arborea was probably slow-growing.

Most of Hawaii's Cyaneas are thought to have been pollinated by birds and the seeds dispersed by birds. Many of Hawaii's nectar-feeding birds have been extirpated from the former range of Cyanea arborea.

Studies of Cyaneas on Oahu indicate that

many species are capable of self-pollinating and producing viable seeds. However, it is not known if *Cyanea arborea* was capable of self-pollination or if successive generations of self-pollinated populations suffered from reduced viability.

Causes for Extinction

Widespread conversion of Maui's mesic forest to pasture probably eliminated this species. Beginning in the early 1800s, these species-rich forests were heavily grazed by cattle and replaced by introduced grasses and Australian Eucalyptus. Joseph Rock commented in 1913 that he could find only a single plant in a narrow ravine which was inaccessible to cattle. The last record of this species was made by George Munro in 1928.

The former range of this species continues to be heavily grazed. Extensive surveys of Maui's remnant patches of mesic forests have failed to locate any specimens of this species. The probability of locating living *Cyanea arborea* is remote.

Cyanea comata
No Common Name

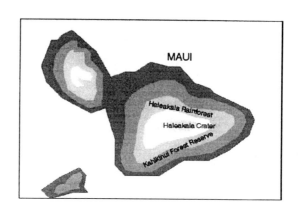

Description

    Cyanea comata was a branched shrub, 1.6-2.6 meters (up to 9 feet) tall. The leaves were oblanceolate to obovate and 15-30 centimeters (5.97-11.9 inches) long. The inflorescence was pendant and up to 1 meter (3.3 feet) long. Each inflorescence consisted of 6-12 strongly-curved, pale lilac-colored flowers that were up to 55 millimeters (2.5 inches) long. The fruits were obovoid berries, 6-14 centimeters (2.36-5.52 inches) wide. *Cyanea* berries typically contain hundreds of seeds. This species was one of the most spectacular Hawaiian lobelias.

Habitat

    Cyanea comata formerly occurred on the leeward (western) side of Haleakala, Maui. This species occurred at elevations of 915-1220 meters. It was known only from a single set of collections made by Hillebrand in the 1870's.

Distribution

    This species was known only from the island of Maui. Little is known of the population biology of this species. Most of Ha-

Status	Extinct
Probable Extinction	1880s
Family	Campanulaceae (Bellflower)
Description	A branched shrub with oblong leaves with long, lilac-colored flowers and in clusters at the end of a long, hanging flowering branch.
Habitat	Mesic forests from 3,000 to 4,000 feet.
Causes for Extinction	Cattle grazing, habitat destruction, and alien species such as feral cattle, goats, and introduced grasses.
Range	Hawaii: Maui
Photo	See Page 218

waii's *Cyaneas* are thought to have been pollinated by birds and seeds dispersed by birds. Given this species' large, curved flowers is likely that birds such as iiwi, oo, or nukuupuu were pollinators.

Causes for Extinction

Widespread conversion of Maui's mesic forest to pasture probable exterminated this species. Beginning in the early 1800's, these species-rich forests were heavily grazed by cattle and replaced by introduced grasses and Australian Eucalyptus.

Native vegetation in the former range of this species has been almost completely eliminated. Extensive surveys of Maui's remnant patches of mesic forest have failed to locate any specimens. The probability of locating an extant population of *Cyanea comata* is remote.

Cyanea giffardii
No Common Name

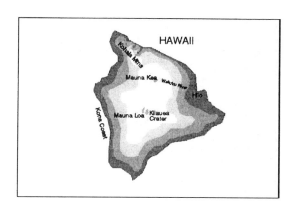

Description

Cyanea giffardii was a spectacular palm-like tree, 5-10 meters (up to 30 feet) tall. The leaves were oblanceolate and 50-60 centimeters (up to 24 inches) long. The inflorescence was pendant and consisted of 5-10 curved, black-purple colored flowers that were up to 80 millimeters (3 inches) long. The fruits were globose berries, 25 centimeters (1 inch) wide. *Cyanea* berries typically contain hundreds of seeds.

Habitat

C. giffardii occurred in wet forests (with ohia, koa, and tree ferns) in the vicinity of Glenwood, Hawaii, with an elevation of 2,000 to 2,500 feet.

Distribution

Cyanea giffardii was known only from a single locality, near Glenwood, Hawaii. Most of Hawaii's *Cyaneas* are thought to have been pollinated by birds and seeds dispersed by birds. Given this species' large, curved flowers is likely that birds such as iiwi, oo, or akialoa were pollinators.

Status	Extinct
Probable Extinction	Early 1900s
Family	Campanulaceae (Bellflower)
Description	Palm-like tree with large oblong leaves and clusters of blackish-purple flowers.
Habitat	Lowland wet forests between 2,000 and 2,500 feet in elevation.
Causes for Extinction	Loss of forest habitat and probably depredation by alien pigs.
Range	Hawaii: Island of Hawaii
Photo	See Page 217

Causes for Extinction

Much of the forest near Glenwood has been destroyed by agricultural and urban development and forest conversion. Alien pigs have degraded most of the remaining relictual patches of forest. This species was probably also affected by alien rats, alien slugs, and competition from alien weeds.

This species was collected from only one site, in 1917. Since then, the wet forests of this area have been destroyed or heavily degraded. Biologists surveying this area have not been able to relocate this and other species that have apparently become extinct.

Cyanea linearifolia
No Common Name

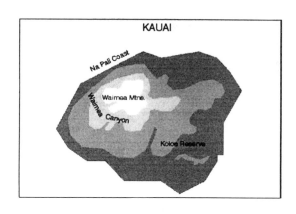

KAUAI

Na Pali Coast

Waimea Mtns.

Waimea Canyon

Koloa Reserve

Description

Cyanea linearifolia was a branched shrub, 1.6-2.6 meters (up to 9 feet) tall. The leaves were oblanceolate to obovate and 15-30 centimeters (5.9-11.8 inches) long. The inflorescence was pendant and up to 1 meter (3 feet) long. Each inflorescence consisted of 6-12 strongly-curved, pale lilac-colored flowers that were up to 55 millimeters (2.5 inches) long. The fruits were obovoid berries, 6-14 centimeters (2.36-5.52 inches) wide. *Cyanea* berries typically contain hundreds of seeds.

Habitat

Cyanea linearifolia probably collected in wet forests of ohia, koa, and tree ferns.

Distribution

Cyanea linearifolia was known only from one site in the Wahiawa Mountains of Kauai. Most of Hawaii's Cyaneas are thought to have been pollinated by birds and seeds dispersed by birds.

Status	Extinct
Probable Extinction	Early 1900s
Family	Campanulaceae (Bellflower)
Description	A small unbranched shrub with linear leaves and flowers less than one inch long.
Habitat	Probably wet forest in the Wahiawa Mountains.
Causes for Extinction	Probably alien plants and pigs.
Range	Hawaii: Kauai

Causes for Extinction

The causes for extinction are unknown, but probably forest degradation by alien pigs and alien weeds.

Cyanea longissima
No Common Name

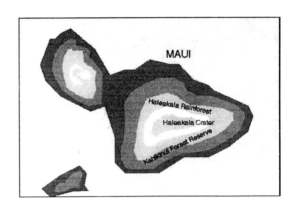

Description

Cyanea longissima was a shrub of unknown size. The oblong leaves were 27-45 cm (18 inches) long. The inflorescence consisted of a cluster of 8-10 white flowers which were 50-60 mm (approximately two inches) long. The fruits were orange ovoid berries, 10-12 mm (.39-.47 inch) wide. *Cyanea* berries typically contain hundreds of seeds.

This species was originally named as a variety of *Cyanea scabra* by Joseph Rock. St. John later elevated this taxon to a full species.

Status	Extinct
Probable Extinction	1927
Family	Campanulaceae (Bellflower)
Description	Shrub with oblong leaves with white flowers and orange ovoid berries.
Habitat	Wet forests on east Maui.
Causes for Extinction	Habitat degradation by alien plants and pigs.
Range	Hawaii: Maui

Habitat

Cyanea longissima occurred in wet forests.

Distribution

Cyanea longissima was known only from the windward side of Haleakala on Maui.

This species was last seen in 1927. While some portions of the species' range has been poorly surveyed, rediscovery seems remote.

Little is known of the population biology of this species. Most of Hawaii's Cyaneas are thought to have been pollinated by birds and seeds dispersed by birds.

Causes for Extinction

The cause of extinction of *Cyanea longissima* is not known. However, this species was probably affected by land conversion, alien pigs, alien rats, alien slugs, and competition from alien weeds.

Cyanea parvifolia
No Common Name

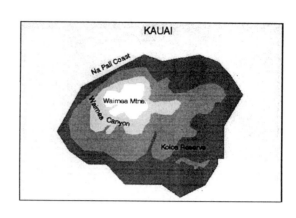

KAUAI

Na Pali Coast

Waimea Mtns.

Waimea Canyon

Koloa Reserve

Description

Cyanea parvifolia was a small shrub, one meter (up to 3 feet) tall. The narrow leaves were somewhat elliptic and 18-22 centimeters (9 inches) long. The inflorescence consisted of 5-6 purplish flowers that were up to 65 millimeters (2.5 inches) long. The fruits are unknown. *Cyanea* berries typically contain hundreds of seeds.

This species was originally collected and named *Rollandia parvifolia* by Forbes. Lammers (1995) later moved this taxon into the genus *Cyanea*.

Habitat

The habitat of *Cyanea parvifolia* is unknown. The description of the original collection only stated that the plant was collected in Waioli Valley of Kauai, Hawaii.

Distribution

Cyanea parvifolia was known only from the original collection by Forbes in 1909 in Waioli Valley of Kauai.

This species has not been seen since the original collection in 1909. While there are areas in the vicinity which may contain suitable habitat, the odds of relocating this species is small. Many of the Kauai valleys

Status	Extinct
Probable Extinction	1909
Family	Campanulaceae (Bellflower)
Description	Small shrub with narrow leaves and purplish flowers.
Causes for Extinction	Probably land development and alien species.
Range	Hawaii: Kauai

have been heavily damaged by human development, agriculture, and alien pigs and weeds.

Little is known of the population biology of this species. Most of Hawaii's Cyaneas are thought to have been pollinated by birds and seeds dispersed by birds.

Causes for Extinction

The causes for extinction of *Cyanea parvifolia* are unknown, but were probably caused by forest degradation by alien pigs and alien weeds.

Cyanea pohaku
No Common Name

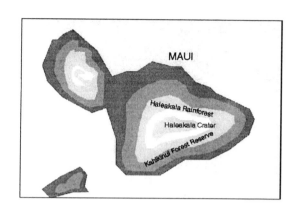

Description

Cyanea pohaku was a branched tree, 6-7 meters (up to 23 feet) tall. The leaves were oblanceolate and 16-30 centimeters (less than one foot) long. The inflorescence was pendant and up to 1 meter (3 feet) long. Each inflorescence consisted of 4-8 gently-curved, greenish-white flowers that were up to 45 millimeters (less than two inches) long. The fruits are unknown. Cyanea fruits typically contain hundreds of seeds.

Cyanea pohaku was originally collected by Joseph Rock in 1910. Rock named this taxon *Clermontia haleakalensis*. Lammers (1988) transferred this taxon to the genus *Cyanea* and renamed it *Cyanea pohaku* in honor of Joseph Rock (pohaku is the Hawaiian word for rock).

Habitat

Cyanea pohaku was collected in a subalpine shrubland at 2,130 meters (7,000 feet) on the northwest side of Haleakala on Maui. The substrate was apparently cinder and/or lava. Associated species included sandalwood and greenswords.

Status	Extinct
Probable Extinction	1910
Family	Campanulaceae (Bellflower)
Description	A small branched tree with oblong leaves and greenish-white flowers.
Habitat	Subalpine shrublands at 7,000 foot elevation on cinder.
Causes for Extinction	Conversion of forest and shrublands to pastures and alien goats.
Range	Hawaii: Maui

Distribution

Known only from the island of Maui, this species was collected only once (in 1910) and in spite of numerous surveys has never been relocated.

Little is known of the population biology of this species. Most of Hawaii's *Cyaneas* are thought to have been pollinated by birds and seeds dispersed by birds.

Causes for Extinction

In 1918, Rock wrote "Unfortunately, only three trees are in existence, and as they are peculiar to the above locality (Puunianiau), it will not be long before they have shared the fate of so many of our native trees, becoming extinct, as cattle have free access and browse on the lower branches with their reach." Rock later confirmed on a subsequent trip that this species indeed had become extinct. Cattle ranching and browsing by introduced feral goats have destroyed much of Maui's unprotected dry and mesic forests and shrublands.

Cyanea profuga
No Common Name

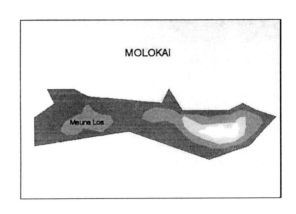

MOLOKAI

Mauna Loa

Description

Cyanea profuga was an unbranched shrub, 1.8-2.4 meters (up to 6 feet) tall. The leaves were elliptic and 18-24 centimeters (less than one foot) long. The inflorescence consisted of 9-12 white flowers that were 30-35 millimeters (less than two inches) long. The fruits are unknown. *Cyanea* fruits typically are fleshy and contain hundreds of seeds.

Cyanea profuga was collected and named by Forbes. St. John later moved this species into the genus *Delissea* as *D. profuga*. Lammers returned the taxon to *Cyanea* in 1990.

Habitat

The habitat of *Cyanea profuga* is unknown.

Distribution

Cyanea profuga was known only from Mapulehu Valley, Molokai. This species has not been seen since it was originally collected over 80 years ago.

Status	Extinct
Probable Extinction	1912
Family	Campanulaceae (Bellflower)
Description	An unbranched shrub with elliptic leaves and white flowers.
Causes for Extinction	Probably invasion by alien pigs and goats, rats, slugs, and alien weeds.
Range	Hawaii: Molokai
Photo	See Page 218

Causes for Extinction

The specific causes for extinction are unknown. Typically *Cyaneas* on the windward side of Molokai are threatened by alien pigs and goats, rats, slugs, and alien weeds.

Cyanea purpurellifolia
No Common Name

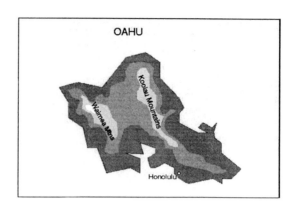

OAHU

Description

Cyanea purpurellifolia was an unbranched shrub, 0.2-0.5 meters (up to 2 feet) tall. The leaves were oblong, had purple undersides, and were 12-35 centimeters (less than 14 inches) long. The inflorescence consisted of 3-6 large dark magenta flowers that were 60-80 millimeters (about three inches) long. The fruits were dark purple berries about 18 millimeters (one-half inch) in size. *Cyanea* fruits typically are fleshy and contain hundreds of seeds.

Habitat

The habitat of *Cyanea purpurellifolia* is unknown. The collection area typically has moist valley bottoms and summit ridges with a diversity of tree types.

Distribution

This species was known only from the area of Kaluanaui Valley (Koolau Mountains) on Oahu.

Cyanea purpurellifolia has not been seen in over 60 years. There is a chance that it may persist in one or more unsurveyed drainages in the north Koolau Mountains.

Status	Extinct
Probable Extinction	1935
Family	Campanulaceae (Bellflower)
Description	Small unbranched shrub with oblong or spatula shaped leaves with the undersides colored purple and large magenta-colored flowers.
Habitat	Probably occurred in moist valley forests at around 2,000 feet elevation.
Causes for Extinction	Invasion of alien pigs, slugs, and rats, and alien weeds. Probably extensive grazing.
Range	Hawaii: Oahu
Photo	See Page 218

Little is known of the population biology of this species. Given the large, curved flowers and the fleshy fruits, it is very likely that this species (like most *Cyaneas*), was bird pollinated and the fruits bird dispersed. *Cyanea* fruits typically contain hundreds of seeds.

Causes for Extinction

The causes for extinction of *Cyanea purpurellifolia* are unknown. However, *Cyaneas* in many Oahu moist forests are frequently damaged by alien pigs, slugs, and rats. Alien weeds compete with young plants. Lower portions of many of these valleys were extensively grazed in the early 1900s.

Cyanea pycnocarpa
No Common Name

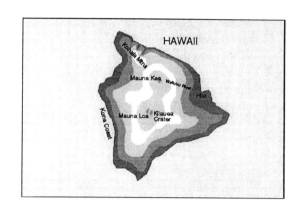

Description

Cyanea pycnocarpa was a palm-like tree of unknown height. Leaves were elliptic and approximately 34 centimeters (14 inches) long. Flowers are unknown. Fruits were ovoid berries about 12 millimeters (one-half inch) wide.

This species was originally collected by Hillebrand in the 1800s. Hillebrand originally called this taxon a variety of *Cyanea arborea* (*C. aborea* var. *pycnocarpa*). F. Wimmer elevated the taxon to full species status, calling it *Cyanea pycnocarpa*.

Habitat

The habitat of *Cyanea pycnocarpa* is unknown. Collection information says that it occurred in the Kohala Mountains, which range from being very wet to very dry.

Distribution

Cyanea pycnocarpa was known only from the type collection from the Kohala Mountains on the island of Hawaii. Nothing is known of the population biology of this species. Like most *Cyaneas*, this species was probably bird pollinated with the fruits dispersed by birds bird. *Cyanea* fruits typically contain hundreds of seeds.

Status	Extinct
Probable Extinction	1880s
Family	Campanulaceae (Bellflower)
Description	A palm-like tree of unknown height with elliptic leaves and flowers of unknown color and size.
Causes for Extinction	Probably destruction of habitat by alien pigs and alien weeds.
Range	Hawaii: Island of Hawaii

Causes for Extinction

The specific causes for extinction are unknown. Lowland and mid-level portions of the Kohala Mountains have been almost completely converted to grazed pastures. The upper elevations of these mountains have been protected from cattle, but have been degraded by alien pigs and alien weeds. Other alien species may have also affected this species.

Cyanea pycnocarpa is known only, and it has not been seen in over 100 years.

Cyanea quercifolia
No Common Name

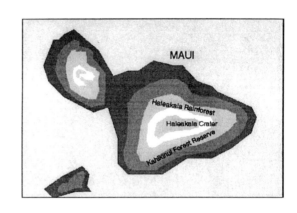

Description

Cyanea quercifolia was a small tree, around 5 meters (16 feet) tall. The stems of this species had small sharp projections and prickles. The obovate leaves were 30-50 centimeters (less than 20 inches) long. Little is known of the flowers. Hillebrand's description states that the flowers were similar to those of *Cyanea solanacea* (white and 48-60 millimeters (a little over 2 inches) long). The fruits were fleshy berries, 16 millimeters (one half inch) wide. Most *Cyaneas* have small to medium sized fleshy fruits with hundreds of seeds.

This species was collected by Hillebrand, who named it *Cyanea solanacea* var. *quericifolia*. F. Wimmer elevated the taxon to full species level.

Habitat

The original collection information identifies an area at 900-1,200 meters (3,000-4,000 feet) on the leeward side of Haleakala as the habitat of this species. Generally, this side of the mountain is dry to mesic.

Status	Extinct
Probable Extinction	1880s
Family	Campanulaceae (Bellflower)
Description	A small tree with large oblong leaves and flowers that were probably white to lilac-colored.
Habitat	Collected from the leeward (western) slopes of Haleakala. This side of the mountain is generally dry.
Causes for Extinction	Loss of land to cattle pastures, habitat destruction by alien goats, feral cattle, and alien weeds.
Range	Hawaii: Maui

Distribution

Cyanea quercifolia was known only from the leeward slopes of Haleakala on Maui from Hillebrand's collection over 100 years ago. Given the extent of habitat loss in this area, there is little likelihood of this species being rediscovered.

Little is known of the population biology of this species. Most of Hawaii's *Cyaneas* are thought to have been pollinated by birds and their seeds dispersed by birds. The presence of small spines on the stem of this species may have been a defense against herbivory from now-extinct birds.

Causes for Extinction

Cyanea quercifolia was known only from the type collection by Hillebrand (ca. 1860s). Most of the dry to mesic forests in this area have been converted to cattle pastures. Most of the remaining areas have been seriously degraded by alien goats, feral cattle, and alien weeds. Many dry and mesic lobelioids are also highly susceptible to wildfires.

Delissea fallax
No Common Name

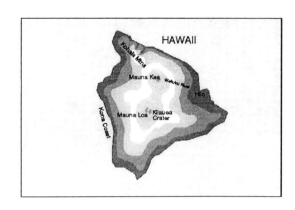

Description

Delissea fallax was a palm-like plant of unknown height. The oblong leaves were 14-24 centimeters (less than 10 inches) in length. The flowers were small, 15-18 millimeters (less than one inch), and of unknown color. The fruits were globose berries 6-8 millimeters (one-quarter inch) in diameter.

Habitat

No specific habitat information is available for this species. The collection of *Delissea fallax* from the forest of the Hilo and Hamaku districts (on the windward side of the island) indicates that it may have occurred in wet or mesic forests.

Distribution

Delissea fallax was known only from the Hilo and Hamaku districts on the island of Hawaii.

This species is known only from the original collections by Hillebrand, over 100 years ago.

Little is known of the population biology of this species. Most of Hawaii's *Deliseas* are thought to have been pollinated by birds and their seeds dispersed by birds.

Status	Extinct
Probable Extinction	1880s
Family	Campanulaceae (Bellflower)
Description	A palm-like tree of unknown height with oblong leaves and small flowers.
Habitat	Collected from forests on the wetter windward side of the island of Hawaii.
Causes for Extinction	Conversion of land to sugar cane and other agricultural production. Probably alien rats and cattle.
Range	Hawaii: Island of Hawaii
Photo	See Page 217

Causes for Extinction

The specific causes for extinction are unknown, but much of the lower elevation forest in this area has been converted to sugar cane and other agricultural production. Cattle and other alien species may have also contributed to the species' extinction.

Delissea laciniata
No Common Name

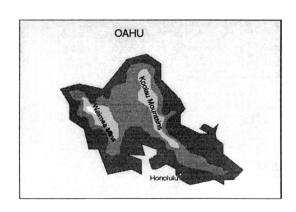

Description

Delissea laciniata was a branched plant of unknown height. The leaves were elliptic and 11-15 centimeters (less than 6 inches) long. The inflorescence consisted of a cluster of 6-10 white flowers that were 35-45 millimeters (less than two inches) long. The fruits were oval berries about 12 millimeters (one half inch) in diameter. *Delissea* fruit typically contain hundreds of seeds.

Habitat

Virtually nothing is known of the habitat of this species. The collection site of Wailupe, Oahu is a region with relatively dry to mesic climate. Presumably, *Delissea laciniata* occurred in lowland mesic or dry forests.

Distribution

Delissea laciniata was known only from Wailupe Valley on the island of Oahu (Koolau Mountains). *Delissea laciniata* has not been seen in over 100 years.

Little is known of the population biology of this species. Most of Hawaii's *Delisseas* are thought to have been pollinated by birds and their seeds dispersed by birds.

Status	Extinct
Probable Extinction	1880s
Family	Campanulaceae (Bellflower)
Description	A branched plant of unknown height with elliptic leaves and white medium sized flowers.
Habitat	Lowland mesic forests
Causes for Extinction	Conversion of forests to urban and agricultural areas, cattle grazing, and alien species.
Range	Hawaii: Oahu
Photo	See Page 219

Causes for Extinction

The lowland portions of Wailupe valley have been almost entirely converted to urban housing. During Hillebrand's time, this area would have been subjected to heavy cattle grazing and agricultural development.

Delissea sinuata
No Common Name

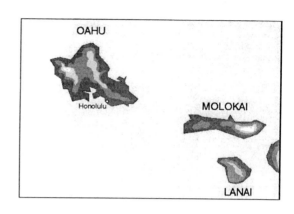

Description

There are two subspecies of this taxon, one from Oahu (*D. sinuata* ssp. *sinuata*) and one from Lanai (*D. sinauata* ssp. *lanaiensis*). *Delissea sinuata* is a somewhat herbaceous plant, with stems 0.6-1.2 meters (less than 4 feet) tall. The leaves were elliptic to spatulate and 15-28 centimeters (up to one foot) long. The flowers were white and 37-40 millimeters (less than two inches) long. The fruits were purple berries, 7-10 millimeters (one-half inch) wide.

Habitat

Delissea sinuata was known to occur in diverse mesic forests on Oahu and Lanai.

Distribution

Delissea sinuata was known only from the islands of Oahu and Lanai.

Little is known of the population biology of this species. Most of Hawaii's *Delisseas* are thought to have been pollinated by birds and their seeds dispersed by birds.

Causes for Extinction

The areas where this species was known from have been extensively modified by

Status	Extinct
Probable Extinction	1937
Family	Campanulaceae (Bellflower)
Description	A small almost herbaceous plant with a curved, white flower.
Habitat	Diverse mesic forests.
Causes for Extinction	Mesic forests have been extensively converted to agricultural purposes and degraded by cattle grazing, alien weeds, and browsing mammals.
Range	Hawaii: Oahu and Lanai
Photo	See Page 219

agricultural and urban development. In addition, alien species such as rats, feral cattle, and weeds may have contributed to the decline or extinction of *Delissea sinuata*.

Delissea sinuata has not been seen for over 60 years. The known sites for this species have been well surveyed during the 1990s and there is little potential unsurveyed habitat remaining.

Lobelia remyi
No Common Name

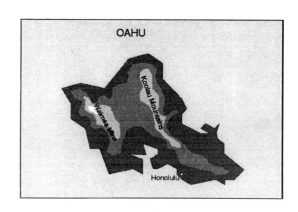

Description

Lobelia remyi was a relatively obscure species. The habit and size of the plant is not known, but the leaves were distinctive. The woolly leaves were elliptic in shape and 12-16 centimeters (up to six inches) long. The inflorescence was an unbranched spike of approximately 30 flowers. Neither the color nor size of the flowers is known. The fruits of *Lobelias* are dry capsules which usually contain hundreds of very small seeds.

Habitat

The specific habitat of *Lobelia remyi* is unknown. The species became extinct before specific habitat information was obtained.

Distribution

Lobelia remyi was known only from the island of Oahu. It has been almost 150 years since this species was last seen.

Little is known of the population biology of this species. Most of Hawaii's *Lobelias* are thought to have been pollinated by birds. However, unlike the fleshy fruited *Cyaneas* and *Delisseas*, the seeds of *Lobelias* were wind dispersed.

Status	Extinct
Probable Extinction	1850s
Family	Campanulaceae (Bellflower)
Description	Leaves were woolly and elliptic; the inflorescence was an unbranched spike with approximately 30 flowers of unknown color and size.
Range	Hawaii: Oahu
Photo	See Page 219

Causes for Extinction

The specific causes for extinction of *Lobelia remyi* are unknown. This species became extinct before either locality information or threat information was obtained.

Achyranthes atollensis
No Common Name

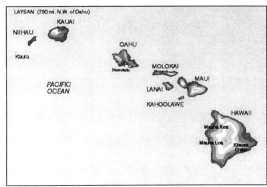

Enlarged Map, Page 120

Description

Achyranthes atollensis was a shrub measuring 1-2 meters (up to six feet) tall with small, hairy obovate to elliptic leaves 2.0-6.2 centimeters (up to two inches) long, densely white or yellow stigose. The leaf surface was completely obscured, with the hairs usually straight and sometimes spreading, and spikes of small flowers partially embedded among the hairs.

Habitat

A. atollensis formerly occurred on low sand islands of the northwest Hawaiian Islands.

Distribution

This species was known only from the islands of Laysan, Midway, Kure Atoll, and Pearl and Hermes Atoll, Hawaii.

The last individuals of *A. atollensis* were observed in 1964. Since then surveys of these islands, including a complete survey by Derral Herbst in 1988, have failed to relocate any individual plants.

Status	Extinct
Probable Extinction	1964
Family	Amaranthaceae (Amaranth)
Description	Shrub (up to six feet tall) with small oval leaves (up to two inches long) and spikes of small flowers.
Habitat	Low sand islands.
Causes for Extinction	Habitat alterations for development and introduction of alien species (weeds and herbivores).
Range	Hawaii: Laysan, Midway, Kure Atoll, Pearl and Hermes Atoll

Causes for Extinction

Habitat alterations from military base development, introduced herbivores, and introduced weeds have destroyed native coastal shrublands.

Argyroxiphium virescens
No Common Name

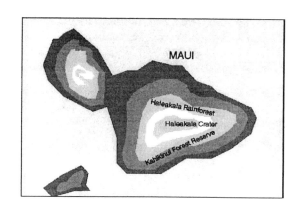

Description

Argyroxiphium virescens was a rosette shrub, usually single stemmed with flowering stems up to 1.5 meters (4 feet) long. Leaves were green and linear-sword-shaped, flattened, and 17-30 centimeters (up to one foot) long. The inflorescence was a spike with 20-120 purplish flowering heads. Flowering occurred in August. Achenes were 8-11 millimeters (one half inch) long.

Habitat

This species formerly occurred in mesic to wet forests at high elevations (1,600-2,300 meters or 5,000-7,000 feet), at Ukulele, Pu'un-ianiau, Ko'olau Gap, and Kuiki, East Maui.

Distribution

Argyroxiphium virescens was known only from the island of Maui.

Little is known of the population biology of this species. The greenswords generally live several years as yucca-like rosettes before accumulating enough energy to produce a flowering stalk. This species, like other monocarpic perennials, probably flowered only once, then died.

Status	Extinct
Probable Extinction	1945
Family	Asteraceae (Aster)
Description	Rosette shrub with sword-shaped leaves (up to one foot long) and a spike-like inflorescene (up to 4 feet tall) with 20-120 white to purplish flowering heads.
Habitat	Mesic to wet forests at high elevations (up to 7,000 feet).
Causes for Extinction	Browsing by goats and cattle.
Range	Hawaii: Maui
Photo	See Page 217

Causes for Extinction

Browsing by cattle and goats were probably significant causes of population decline or extinction.

This species has not been definitively collected since 1947. A plant thought to be a hybrid between this species and another *Argyroxiphium* was found in the 1990s, but its identity has not been verified.

Steller's Spectacled Cormorant (p. 91)

Dodo (p. 19) ▲

▼ Amistad Gambusia (p. 288)

Great Auk (p. 191) ▼

▲ Eastern Hare-Wallaby (p. 328)

New Zealand Quail (p. 61)

▲ Lord Howe Purple Gallinule (p. 48)

Western Barred Bandicoot (p. 334)

▼ Bali Tiger (p. 347)

Black-Fronted Parakeet (p. 104)

Raiatea Parakeet (p. 102) ▲

Oahu 'Akepa, *Loxops coccineus rufus* (p. 148) ▲

Auckland Islands Merganser (p. 70)

Huia (p. 63) ▼

Laysan Rail (p. 164)

Norfolk Island Starling (p. 42) ▼

▲ Tahitian Red-Billed Rail (p. 108)

Wake Island Rail (p. 113)

▲ New Caldonia Lorikeet (p. 109)

Charmosyna wilhelminae ▲

▼ Norfolk Island Kaka (p. 46) *N.m. meridionalis* ▼

▲ Kosrae Rail (left) (p. 98) Black Crake (right)

Laughing Owl (p. 66)

C-4

Greater Amakihi (p. 144)

Laysan Millerbird (p. 130) ▲

Hawaii O'o, *Moho nobilis* (p. 154)

Kioea (p. 132) ▼

▲ Laysan Honeycreeper (p. 146)

Hawaii Akialoa (relative of Oahu Akialoa, p. 142) ◀

Greater Koa Finch (p. 170) ▼

Black Mamo, *Drepanis funerea* (p. 138)

Ula-ai-hawane, *Ciridops anna* (p. 136)

Newfoundland White Wolf (p. 356)

Passenger Pigeon (p. 182) ▲

Texas Red Wolf (p. 356)

Dusky Seaside Sparrow (p. 178) ▼

▲ Heath Hen (p. 186)

▲ Hawaiian Rail (p. 166)

▼ Carolina Parakeet (p. 180)

Labrador Duck (p. 189)

Kona Finch, *Chloridops Kona* (p. 134)

Clermontia multiflora
No Common Name

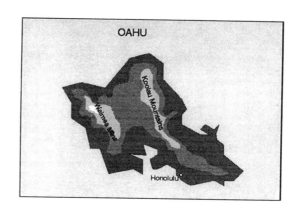

Description

Clermontia multiflora was a branched shrub 2-4 meters (4.5 feet) tall with elliptic leaves 10-12.5 centimeters (5 inches) long. The inflorescence had 7-10 purple flowers 24-32 millimeters (1-1.5 inches) long. The fruits were berries of unknown color and size.

Habitat

Clermontia multiflora formerly occurred in species-rich, lowland mesic forests on Oahu.

Distribution

Clermontia multiflora was known only from the island of Oahu. Little is known of the population biology of this species. Most of Hawaii's *Clermontias* are thought to have been pollinated by birds and the seeds dispersed by birds. Many of Hawaii's nectar-feeding birds have been extirpated from the former range of *Cyanea arborea*. Studies of *Cyanea, Clermontia, and Lobelia* on Oahu indicate that many species are capable of self-pollinating and producing viable seeds. However, it is not known if *Clermontia multiflora* was capable of self pollination or if successive generations of self-pollinated populations suffered from reduced viability.

Status	Extinct
Probable Extinction	1870s
Family	Campanulaceae (Bellflower)
Description	Branched shrub (up to 4.5 feet tall), with medium leaves and small purple flowers.
Habitat	Lowland mesic forests
Causes for Extinction	Habitat conversion for grazing, agriculture, and urban development.
Range	Hawaii: Oahu
Photo	See Page 219

Causes for Extinction

Habitat conversion associated with cattle grazing, agricultural development, and urbanization are the major causes of extinction. Alien weeds may have also been important threats to this species.

Clermontia multiflora has not been seen in over 120 years. The previous collection sites have been extensively altered and little native vegetation remains.

Cyrtandra gracilis
No Common Name

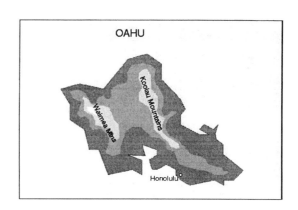

Description

Cyrtandra gracilis was a branched shrub of unknown height with opposite, elliptic leaves 11.5-22 centimeters (less than 9 inches) long. The white flowers were 2.3-2.4 centimeters (1 inch) long and occurred in groups of 1-7. The fruits were white ovoid berries 2.3-2.5 centimeters (1 inch) long.

Cyrtandra gracilis was collected by Hillebrand in the 1880s and named by Clarke. St. John segregated a portion of this species into a new taxon called *C. linearis*. Wagner *et al.* (1990) combined *C. linearis* into *C. gracilis*.

Habitat

Formerly occurring in wet to mesic diverse forest in montane valleys.

Distribution

Cyrtandra gracilis was known only from the island of Oahu, Hawaii. This species has not been seen in over 100 years and there is little likelihood of it being rediscovered.

Status	Extinct
Probable Extinction	1880s
Family	Gesneriaceae (African Violet)
Description	Branched shrub of unknown height. Leaves elliptic and opposite (up to 9 inches long). Flowers and berries white and about 1 inch long.
Habitat	Wet to mesic forests.
Causes for Extinction	Habitat conversion and alien species.
Range	Hawaii: Oahu

Causes for Extinction

Habitat conversion associated with cattle grazing, agricultural development, and urbanization affected the extirpation of this species. Alien weeds may have also had a significant affect on *C. gracilis*.

Eragrostis hosakai
No Common Name

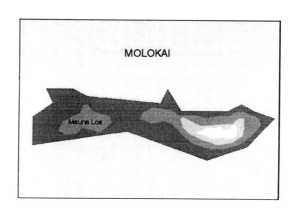

Description

Eragrostis hosakai was collected by Hosaka in 1937 and named by Otto Degener. It was a perennial grass 5-10 decimeters (20-40 inches) tall, somewhat woody at the base, branching at nodes and glabrous. Inflorescence loosely bunched 15-30 centimeters (6-12 inches) long. The branches were 4-8 centimeters (1.6-3.15 inches) long, ascending, with dark green spikelets, becoming gray, 4-8 flowered and oblong. Seeds around 1 millimeter (.04 inch) long.

Status	Extinct
Probable Extinction	1937
Family	Poaceae (Grass)
Description	Perennial grass with loose inflorescences and small seeds.
Habitat	Dry forest
Causes for Extinction	Cattle grazing, fire, and agricultural development.
Range	Hawaii: Molokai

Habitat

E. hosakai formerly occurred in an arid windswept slope at Mauna Loa, Molokai. The elevation was roughly 400 meters (1200 feet).

Distribution

Eragrostis hosakai was known only from the island of Molokai. This species is known only from the type collection made over 50 years ago. The collection area has been heavily modified and is now dominated by alien weeds.

Causes for Extinction

Cattle grazing, fire, and agricultural development have eliminated most of the native vegetation in this part of Molokai.

Haplostachys bryanii
No Common Name

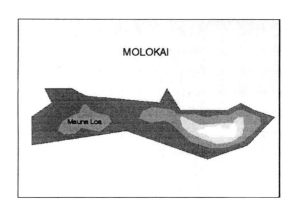

MOLOKAI

Mauna Loa

Description

Haplostachys bryanii was an erect perennial herb 3-5 decimeters (12-18 inches) tall with oblong-cordate leaves 4-7 centimeters (2-3 inches) long. The inflorescence was an erect spike 2 decimeters (8 inches) long with small, white flowers 10-14 millimeters (one half inch) long.

Habitat

Haplostachys bryanii formerly occurred in low elevation dry habitats.

Distribution

Haplostachys bryanii was known only from the Moana Loa area on the island of Molokai.

Causes for Extinction

Cattle grazing, agricultural development, and alien species such as feral goats, feral cattle, and alien weeds were responsible for the extirpation of this species.

The known range of this species has been almost completely eliminated by the above

Status	Extinct
Probable Extinction	1918
Family	Lamiaceae (Mint)
Description	Perennial herb with oblong leaves and small white flowers.
Habitat	Low elevation dry habitats.
Causes for Extinction	Cattle grazing, agricultural development, and alien species.
Range	Hawaii: Molokai
Drawing	See Page 218

threats. There is little likelihood of rediscovering this species in the Moana Loa area.

Haplostachys munroi
No Common Name

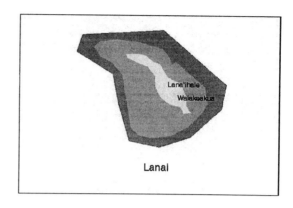

Lanai

Description

Haplostachys munroi was an erect, aromatic, perennial herb with pubescent, ovate leaves 16-24 centimeters (6-10 inches) long. The inflorescence was an erect spike 20-25 centimeters (8-10 inches) long with relatively large, white flowers 20-28 millimeters (one inch) long and a curved corolla tube. Nutlets were dark brown and 6-7 millimeters (one quarter inch) long.

Habitat

This species formerly occurred in dry to mesic forests.

Distribution

Haplostachys munroi was known only from the island of Lanai. Judging from its floral characteristics, this species was probably pollinated by moths.

Causes for Extinction

Cattle grazing, feral deer, feral mouflon, and alien weeds were responsible for the extirpation of this species.

Status	Extinct
Probable Extinction	1935
Family	Lamiaceae (Mint)
Description	Erect, aromatic, perennial herb with ovate leaves and large white flowers.
Habitat	Dry to mesic forests.
Causes for Extinction	Cattle grazing and alien species such as deer, mouflon, and weeds.
Range	Hawaii: Lanai

In the early 1900s, George Munro fenced most of the dry and mesic forests of Lanai in order to protect these species-rich areas from cattle. Unfortunately, these fences were not maintained by subsequent managers and *Haplostachys munroi* along with other species became extinct. Subsequent damage by alien deer and mouflon sheep (which were brought in to provide hunting opportunities) has further damaged Lanai's unique forests.

Hibiscadelphus bombycinus
No Common Name

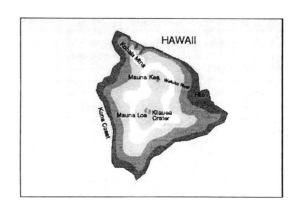

Description

Hibiscadelphus bombycinus was collected by Hillebrand in the 1860s and described by C. N. Forbes. It was a medium sized tree with kidney-shaped leaves 7-9 centimeters (3-4 inches) long. The flowers were borne singly, were 3.5 centimeters (1.5 inches) long, and probably yellowish. The flowers probably produced large quantities of nectar. The fruits were woody capsules about 3 centimeters (1 inch) long with seeds that were densely covered in golden hairs.

Status	Extinct
Probable Extinction	1860s
Family	Malvaceae (Mallow)
Description	Medium tree with kidney-shaped leaves with curved hibiscus-like flowers.
Habitat	Dry forests.
Causes for Extinction	Cattle grazing and alien species.
Range	Hawaii: Island of Hawaii

Habitat

H. bombycinus formerly occurred in dry forests of leeward Hawaii, in the vicinity of Kawaihae.

Distribution

Hibiscadelphus bombycinus was known only from the island of Hawaii, Hawaii. Little is known of the population biology of this species. It is thought that nectar feeding birds pollinated this and other species of *Hibiscadelphus*.

Causes for Extinction

It is likely that cattle grazing, fires, feral goats, and alien weeds affected this species. This species is known only from the original type collection made about 150 years ago. Since then, the Kawaihae area has been extensively modified and little, if any, native vegetation remains. The entire genus of *Hibiscadelphus* is either extinct or in extreme danger of becoming so.

Hibiscadelphus wilderianus
No Common Name

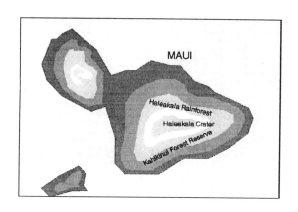

MAUI

Haleakala Rainforest

Haleakala Crater

Kahikinui Forest Reserve

Description

Hibiscadelphus wilderianus was collected and named by Joseph Rock. It was a tree measuring up to 5 meters (15 feet) tall with ovate leaves 7-11 centimeters (3-4 inches) long and with yellow, solitary flowers 3.5-5.0 centimeters (1.5-1.9 inches) long. The flowers somewhat resemble those of *Hibiscus*, except they are narrowed to form a tube and are curved. The flowers probably produced large quantities of nectar. The fruits were woody capsules and the seeds are unknown.

Habitat

Formerly occurring in dry lava forests of leeward Maui at 800 meters (2,500 feet).

Distribution

Hibiscadelphus wilderianus was known only from the island of Maui. Little is known of the population biology of this species. It is thought that nectar feeding birds pollinated this and other species of *Hibiscadelphus*.

Status	Extinct
Probable Extinction	1910
Family	Malvaceae (Mallow)
Description	Tree (up to 15 feet tall) with ovate leaves and yellowish, hibiscus-like flowers.
Habitat	Dry forests on leeward Maui.
Causes for Extinction	Cattle grazing and alien species.
Range	Hawaii: Maui

Causes for Extinction

Habitat conversion for cattle grazing and alien species, especially rats (which eat the flowers and seeds), feral goats, and alien grasses.

Hibiscadelphus wilderianus is known only from the original type collection in 1910. This species has not been seen in 85 years, in spite of searching by biologists. Most of the lower elevation habitat in this area has been completely eliminated.

Kokia lanceolata
No Common Name

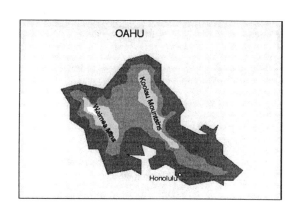

OAHU

Koolau Mountains

Waimea Mtns

Honolulu

Description

Kokia lanceolata was collected by Hillebrand in the 1800s and named by Lewton. Small trees of unknown size with large, lobed leaves 8-12.5 centimeters (3-5 inches) wide. The reddish flowers were about 10 centimeters (4 inches) long and similar to those of Hibiscus, except they were curved. *Kokia* produce large quantities of nectar. The fruits are unknown.

Habitat

Kokia lanceolata formerly occurred in dry forests in eastern Oahu.

Distribution

Kokia lanceolata is known only from the island of Oahu. Little is known of the population biology of this species, though it is presumed that this species was pollinated by nectar feeding birds.

Causes for Extinction

Cattle grazing, urbanization, and alien species (especially weeds) were probably

Status	Extinct
Probable Extinction	Early 1900s
Family	Malvaceae (Mallow)
Description	Small tree of unknown size with large lobed leaves and reddish flowers.
Habitat	Dry forests in eastern Oahu.
Causes for Extinction	Cattle grazing, urbanization, alien species.
Range	Hawaii: Oahu

important factors in this species' decline and extinction.

The collection localities for this species have been extensively altered by grazing, urbanization, and alien weeds. These areas have also been well surveyed, with no plants relocated.

EXTINCT FISHES

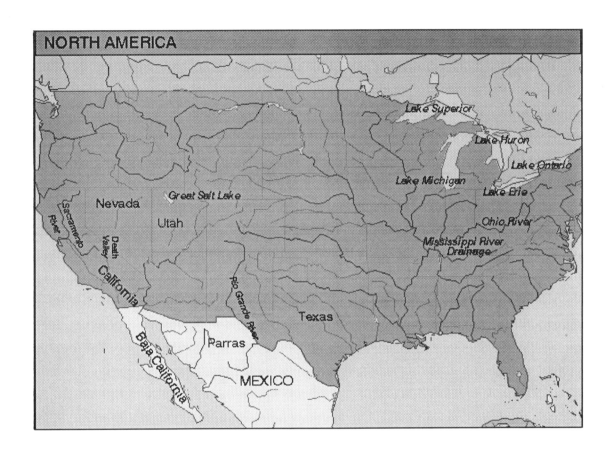

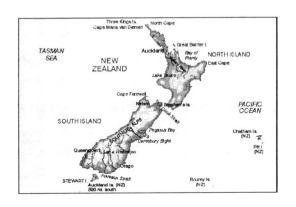

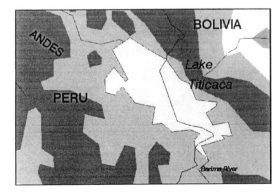

Great Basin, Nevada

The Great Basin area in Nevada is a vast area of mountains and deserts located generally between the western ridges of the Rocky Mountains and the eastern edge of the Sierra Nevada. It is south of the Columbia River basin and north of the Colorado River basin. It is the largest inland drainage in North America. The Great Basin is comprised of over 200 drainages that at one time had individual integrity. There were two great lakes in the basin, Lake Bonneville and Lake Lahontan, and each covered thousands of square miles and were many hundreds of feet deep.

The area is just east of the Death Valley trough that lies along the California-Nevada border. The Death Valley trough is entirely in California, and it presently receives water only from the Amargosa River. The Amargosa rises in Nevada along the Pahute Mesa and flows south and southeast, crossing the state line 110 miles from its origin. In California it turns northward near Tecopa and continues to its terminus in Death Valley. At intervals it is fed by warm springs, the most notable being Saratoga Springs and Devil's Hole in Ash Meadows. Much of the area in the lower two-thirds of Death Valley was previously occupied by Pleistocene Lake Manly.

Causes of Extinction in the Great Basin

Human encroachment and urbanization have taken their tolls on native biotas. Intensive industrialization, rapid urbanization, and water pollution have all adversely affected the environment. Freshwater habitats are particularly vulnerable to ecological changes brought on by human activity. Water demands imposed by the rapidly growing numbers of people have diverted or changed the flow of water throughout many areas. Lowering the water table causes the loss of streams, marshes, and springs, which in turn cause the loss of aquatic species. Diversions for irrigation have also reduced fish populations. Pollution from a variety of domestic and industrial wastes has turned productive habitats into barren ones.

Competition with exotic species was another cause of the extinction of Great Basin fishes. Introduced carp and mosquito-fish (*Gambusia affinis*) successfully dominated native species by predation on young and competition for food and habitat.

General Causes for Extinction of Fish Species

Human intervention was the main cause for the extinction of most fish species. Wetlands for many years have been regarded as worthless and have been drained for agricultural uses, but the drainage has caused enormous waste of the natural resources and the natural inhabitants. The damage caused by such drainage starts with the subsoil water sinking, formally fertile fields lose their productivity, and fish and other wildlife become scarce or disappear completely. These consequences become more pronounced with each passing decade, and it is not until two to three dozen years later that the damage is evident. Remaining lakes and water sources have been shockingly misused by the authorities. When the water has been used for industrial, commercial, or residential uses, it is viewed as a never ending resource with unlimited self-cleansing properties.

The damage done by the resurrection and construction of hydroelectric generating stations is enormous and generally irreparable. The landscape may change rapidly and the flora and fauna is exposed to sudden, fundamental change that many times is fatal in the long run. Spawning runs of fish could be changed or totally eliminated and in many watercourses, the fish cannot move upstream or downstream. To replace the loss of the endemic fish, exotic species, species not native to that specific ecosystem, are introduced.

Introduction of exotic species for various reasons, many for commercial fishing, is most of the time damaging to the native species. Another reason for the introduction could be to replace the original native species that were exploited. The introduction of these exotic species can cause the extinction of the remaining endemic population through competition for food and space and the introduction of disease.

The change in either the physical or biological environment is the key to extinction and sometimes it is the combination of both factors. Species are not equally likely to disappear under the pressure of natural environmental change. The vulnerability of a species depends on a wide variety of such factors as its total population size, geographical distribution, reproductive ability and numbers, ecological relation with other species, and the genetic characteristics.

Pahrump Valley

Pahrump Valley is a moderate sized internal drainage basin separated by Ash Meadows to the northwest and the Amargosa River drainage to the south and west. Three large completely isolated springs, located within a mile of each other, were inhabited by slightly different subspecies of the Pahrump killifish. Each constant temperature spring (24.5 degrees C.) and the more variable outflow environments and irrigation ditches contained large populations of killifishes until all three springs went dry due to excessive ground water pumping and extreme modification of springs for agricultural development. Two of the three subspecies have been extinct for over 20 years. The third, the Manse Ranch killifish, is now maintained in three refuges outside of Pahrump Valley. Its original habitat, a densely vegetated spring, was pumped dry in June 1975.

The Pahrump killifish was an extremely adaptable taxon. It was able to swim actively in water less than an inch deep, it could survive in mud puddles, and it could flip its body between small pools of water. It had the ability to live in water with greatly fluctuating temperatures, and could live in water as hot as 112 degrees Fahrenheit (F). The species usually inhabited springs of 24 degrees Celsius (75 degrees F). It could also tolerate saline concentrations 6 times greater than normal sea water.

The Reproductive Cycle of Pupfish

The social system of all pupfish is based on male spawning territories. During the breeding season, most species of pupfish males vigorously defend territories comprising both vertical and horizontal substrates that are suitable for spawning. Generally, these substrates are a loose mixture of mud, sand, and detritus on which eggs are laid. Spawning lasts 7-8 months, typically from February to September, but in warm springs breeding occurs year round.

Spawning occurs in temperatures between 18 and 35 degrees C. Consequently, the peak of the daily spawning cycle shifts from mid-day to early morning with seasonal temperature changes. In most habitats territories are closely packed due to limited spawning substrate and an excess of mature males.

A receptive female swims into the spawning area, and after pursuit by a male, she nips the substrate signaling her readiness. The male then gives chase with little courtship. The pair move side-by-side along the bottom, ending with simultaneous jerking during which the female releases one or two eggs which the male fertilizes. She may repeat the ritual with the same male or return at a later time to pair with another male. There is no paternal care provided to the eggs or the young.

Males who zealously defend a single territory from intruders are usually so aggressive that they seldom mate, and the reproductive advantage goes to individuals who will spawn in multiple areas.

The Devils Hole pupfish is the exception to the territorial defense. The male is totally non-aggressive and exhibits no territorial behavior of any kind. Pairs spawn throughout the restricted suitable habitat with little courtship and no interference from individuals. Absence of aggression in this pupfish appears to be an evolutionary adaptation to thousands of years of isolation and the energy-deficient and habitat-limiting environment of Devils Hole.

Normally, pupfish, dace and killifish reach maturity in 2-4 months, depending on the time of year they were spawned, water temperature, population density and type of habitat. Fishes in warm springs grow throughout the year at the same rate. Average generation time is 2-4 months due to high mortality rate among the young, but a strong, free-swimming individual lives 6-9 months.

The Diet of Pupfish

All species of pupfish are opportunistic, omnivores that take food particles, both plant and animal, in proportion to the frequency in their habitat. They feed primarily on the substrate. Typically, a pupfish takes a mouthful of algae or other bottom material and vigorously chews it, expelling most material through the mouth or gill covers. These feeding movements appear to be non-selective for particular food items. Another feeding technique is for the fish to stir up the substrate by swimming in place on the bottom, then selecting and snapping at its preferred food. Occasionally, feeding occurs in floating water where food particles drift by.

Where there are large, algae-free areas and minimal currents, pupfish will defend feeding territories by plowing small pits, which the fish occupies for a short time (up to 15 minutes). Under these conditions, the substrate is pock marked with feeding holes; fish will swim from hole to hole and occupy it long enough to feed in that area.

The main foods for pupfish are algae and detritus. Pupfish consume large amounts of detritus, which is quickly passed through the gut. The fish digests only the microbes contained in the detritus, which supplies the caloric value. Animal matter food sources include aquatic insects, crustaceans, snails, and eggs. During the spring pupfish prefer amphipods, ostracods, and insect larvae.

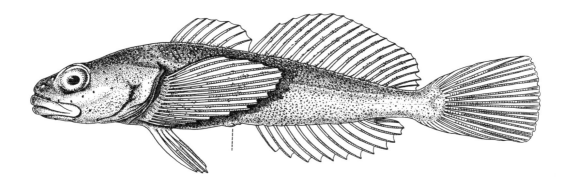

▲ Utah Lake sculpin, *Cottus echinatus* (see page 266), Drawing by Suzanne Runyan

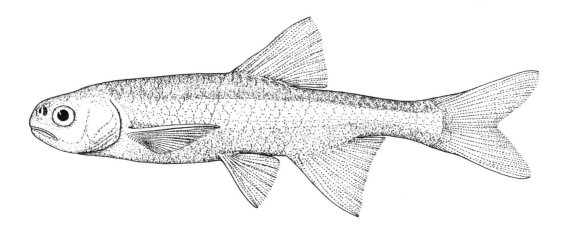

▲ Rio Grande bluntnose shiner, *Notropis s. simus* (see page 288), Drawing by Sara V. Fink

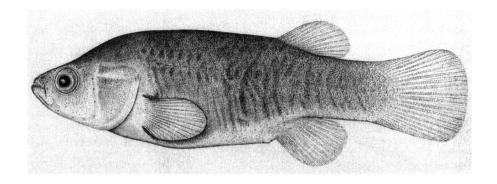

▲ Raycraft Ranch poolfish, *Empetrichthys latos concavus* (see page 268), Drawing by Sara V. Fink

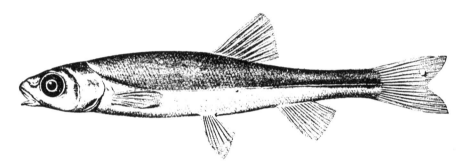

▲ Mexican Dace, *Evarra tlahuacensis* (see page 290)

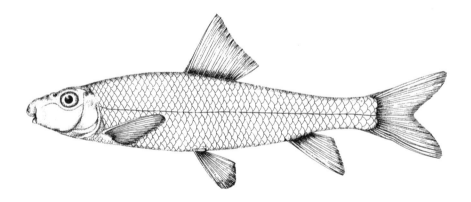

▲ Harelip sucker, *Lagochila lacera* (see page 264), Drawing by H. L. Todd

Longjaw Cisco
Coregonus alpenae

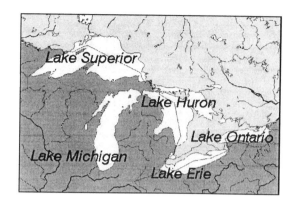

Description

The longjaw cisco, *Coregonus alpenae*, was a member of the salmon and trout family, Salmonidae (whitefish subfamily, Coregoninae). The longjaw cisco was a medium-sized fish (up to 10 inches) that had a silvery body with a greenish or bluish colored back with large scales. The fins contained little or no pigmentation. There were 30 to 46 gill rakers on the first arch. The lateral line contained 68 to 73 scales.

Behavior

Most coregonines spawn in the fall; the longjaw cisco spawned in November. Eggs developed over the winter and then hatched in early spring.

Many coregonines inhabit deep lake waters and feed on plankton and deep bottom organisms. The shortjaw cisco, *C. zenithicus* (a closely related species according to some experts), consumes plankton, including Mysis, as well as midge larvae and the crustacean Pontoporeia.

Habitat

The longjaw cisco was primarily found

Status	Extinct
Probable Extinction	1967
Family	Salmonidae (Salmon and Trout)
Description	Medium-sized fish with silvery body and greenish or bluish colored back with large scales.
Habitat	Deep waters and shoals of the Great Lakes.
Food	Plankton and deep bottom organisms.
Reproduction	Spawned in November; eggs develop over the winter and then hatched in early spring.
Causes for Extinction	Overfishing; deterioration of water quality.
Range	Lakes Michigan, Huron, and Erie.

in the deeper waters (3 to 100 fathoms) of Lakes Huron, Michigan, and Erie. *C. zenithicus* (shortjaw cisco) inhabits near-shore areas between the depths of 60 to 600+ feet. The shortjaw cisco most often spawns in depths between 120 to 200 feet in nearshore areas.

Eggs are deposited on various substrates in shoal areas.

Distribution

The longjaw cisco was one of several closely related species of ciscos that occur in the Great Lakes. It was known to occur in Lakes Michigan, Huron, and Erie.

Despite the considerable effort of the U.S. Fish and Wildlife Service's Great Lakes Fishery Laboratory and the associated states around the Great Lakes, there have been no reported collections of this species in U.S. waters since 1967.

Causes for Extinction

The decline of this species, and the cisco family in general, is usually attributed to fishery and environmental problems. As the ciscos decreased in abundance, there was an increase in the fishery effort along with a decrease in net mesh size. This resulted in further depletion of cisco stocks. In addition to the increased fishing pressure, predation by the sea lamprey and degradation of the habitat further reduced cisco numbers. Hybridization between some species of cisco may also have contributed to the decline.

Extensive industrial and municipal wastes that contributed to an overall deterioration of water quality in Lake Erie may have led to the decline of this species' population.

Sea lamprey predation in Lakes Michigan and Huron along with competition from smaller ciscos, the alewife (*Alosa pseudoharengau*), and rainbow smelt (*Osmerus mordax*) may have exacerbated the decline of the longjaw cisco.

Adapted from data compiled by the Threatened and Endangered Species Information Institute (Golden, CO) for *Beacham's International Threatened, Endangered, and Extinct Species* published on CD ROM, available from Beacham Publishing.

Blackfin Cisco
Coregonus nigripinnus

Deepwater Cisco
Coregonus johannae

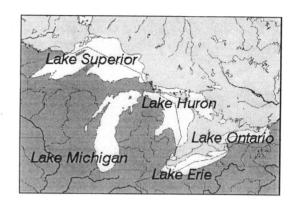

Description

The blackfin cisco, *Coregonus nigripinnus,* and deepwater cisco, *C. johannae,* were members of the *Coregonidae* or whitefish family. The blackfin and deepwater cisco displayed quite unusual characteristics in comparison to other members of its family and many ichthyologists prefer to place it in a separate family, *Leucicthys.* The species possessed both an adipose fin and a process in the angle of each pelvic fin. The premaxillaries at the front of the upper jaw were longer than wide, usually turned forward, giving the front of the snout an angular profile. Maxillary were seldom contained more than three times in the head. The gill-rakers usually numbered 31-33. Individuals in this family can be distinguished from the salmon family by the larger scales (fewer than a hundred in the lateral line), by the smaller mouth with no teeth, or very weak ones, and by internal characters.

Status	Extinct
Probable Extinction	c.1960s
Family	Coregonidae (Whitefish)
Description	Similar to salmon but with larger scales and a smaller mouth with no teeth.
Habitat	Clear cool or cold deep water in the Great Lakes.
Reproduction	Spawned in November, laying eggs on the bottom of shoal areas.
Causes for Extinction	Over-fishing
Range	Great Lakes

Behavior

The blackfin and deepwater cisco generally spawned in freshwater in late November, laying its eggs on the bottom in shoal areas. This species was also able to spawn at various times of the year.

The blackfin and deepwater cisco migrated to deeper water in colder weather.

Habitat

The blackfin and deepwater cisco, and three subspecies, were known from the Great Lakes. They inhabited clear, cold or cool water. The backfin cisco was found in waters deeper than 30 fathoms in Lake Michigan and Lake Huron; in waters 15-100 fathoms deep in Lake Superior; in waters 20-40 fathoms deep in Lake Nipigon of the Lake Superior basin and Long Lake of the Hudson Bay drainage in Ontario; and waters of 60 fathoms or more in depth in Lake Ontario. Deepwater cisco inhabited clear, cold or cool water 30-90 fathoms deep in Lake Michigan, and 16-100 fathoms deep in Lake Huron.

Distribution

The blackfin and deepwater cisco were once wide spread in the Great Lakes area, especially in the waters of Lake Michigan and Lake Huron. Subspecies could also be found in Lake Superior, Lake Nipigon of the Lake Superior basin and Long Lake of the Hudson Bay drainage in Ontario, and Lake Ontario. By World War I the species was on the decline due to commercial over-fishing. Commercial fishing continued until the 1950s, but by this time the species had essentially been fished out. The last blackfin cisco known from Lake Huron was taken in 1926; the last species from Lake Michigan was taken in 1969. The last deepwater cisco was taken from Lake Huron in 1952.

Causes for Extinction

The blackfin and deepwater cisco are believed to have become extinct by the late 1950s. The reason for the species' extinction is overfishing. This species was abundant and available summer and winter and proved to be extremely lucrative to commercial fishermen. Fishermen at this time had no conception of conservation or of an off-season. Intense and consistent fishing pressures were put on these species, and by World War I the species were in decline. When blackfin and deepwater cisco "ran" in November, huge catches were taken. One

lake alone had yielded over 15 million tons in 1885; it was common for one net to take out as much as 10 tons in a day. This huge glut of fish occurred at a time before freezing facilities were available, and wide-scale dumping of unsold catches was not uncommon. Even in the winter when the fish were lying very deep, the fishing continued. Holes were cut in the ice and long lines dropped through. There are records of one man ice-fishing with a pearl-button for bait and hauling up 136 kilograms (300 pounds) of these two species a day.

During this period, the human population of the Great Lakes area was increasing as well, bringing with it the problems of pollution, siltation, drainage of marshes and wetlands, and damming of tributary streams. Compounding the pressures on these fishes were the arrival and establishment in the 1900s of several exotic fishes; and these fishes also contributed to the decline of the Great Lake fishery.

The species became essentially "fished out" and remaining individuals were left alone by the commercial fishermen by the 1950s. The introduced sea lamprey (*Petromyzon marinus*) wiped out the remaining individuals of this species. *P. marinus* became established in the Great Lakes partly by migration up the Saint Lawrence Seaway, but mostly by being flushed off ships using the Seaway into the waters of Lake Michigan and Lake Huron.

Adapted from data compiled by the Threatened and Endangered Species Information Institute (Golden, CO) for *Beacham's International Threatened, Endangered, and Extinct Species* published on CD ROM, available from Beacham Publishing.

Blue Pike
Stizostedion vitreum glaucum

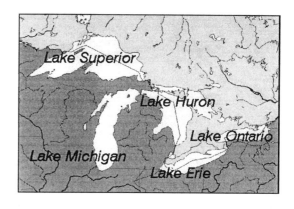

Description

The blue pike, *Stizostedion vitreum glaucum*, was a subspecies of the walleye, *S. vitreum*, a common and popular sport fish. The walleye's color pattern is mottled; there is a dark spot near the spinous dorsal fin. The caudal fin has a white to off-white spot on the lower lobe. This species has several canine teeth. Blue pike were smaller and had a slower growth rate than the walleye. Adult blue pike were 9 to 16 inches long and weighed from a half pound to 1.5 pounds. The blue pike was distinguished from *S. vitreum* by its slate-blue body color that lacked mottling and its bluish-white ventral fins. Fishermen referred to hybrids of *S. vitreum* and the blue pike as "jumbos" or "mules".

Status	Extinct
Probable Extinction	1960s
Family	Percidae (Perch)
Description	Walleye with slate-blue body color that lacked mottling, and bluish-white ventral fins.
Habitat	Shallow to deep-water lakes.
Food	Fish.
Reproduction	35,000-600,000 eggs were deposited over rock, gravel, and/or sand substrates in areas with flowing water or near lakeshores.
Causes for Extinction	Overfishing; competition.
Range	Lakes Erie and Ontario, and the Niagara River.

Behavior

Spawning by the blue pike occurred in a lake's shallow areas or in the lower reaches of tributary streams. Eggs were deposited over rocky substrates in shallow water. The blue pike's reproductive characteristics were similar to those of *S. vitreum*. *S. vitreum* spawn from early April through May when water temperatures average 45 to 50 Deg. F.

Spawning occurs primarily at night; eggs are deposited over rock, gravel, and/or sand substrates in areas with flowing water or near lakeshores where wave action provides the water movement. Females may lay from 35,000-600,000 eggs during the spawning period. Adults return to deep waters after spawning. There is no parental care.

S. vitreum, and probably the blue pike, are carnivorous and prefer to take live prey, but captive fish have eaten carrion. Young fish consume a large volume of insects; once they reach a length of about 2 inches they begin to eat small fish. Adults are almost exclusively piscivorous.

The blue pike was probably most active during the day. Seasonal movements and changes in activity levels may have occurred in response to changes in oxygen levels. Spawning occurred primarily at night.

Habitat

The blue pike was primarily a lacustrine species; it inhabited shallow to deep-water habitats but may have preferred cooler, moderately deep waters closer to shore. Shallow waters along the shoreline and the lower portions of tributary streams were used for spawning.

Distribution

Historically, the blue pike was found in Lakes Erie and Ontario, and the Niagara River and, to some extent, the lower reaches of tributary streams.

Causes for Extinction

The blue pike was abundant in the commercial fishery of the late 1800s but by 1915 landings began to fluctuate extensively. Production peaks in excess of 10,000 metric tons occurred in 1915, 1936, 1944, and 1949, and lows under 2,500 metric tons occurred in 1917-1919, 1929, 1941, and 1946-1947 before the collapse of the fishery in 1958.

Fishery biologists have evidence that an over-intensive fishery, which disrupted the self-stabilizing mechanisms within the population, led to the extreme fluctuations and ultimate crash of the fishery. Since young-of-the-year inhabited the same areas as older members of the populations, they were vulnerable to cannibalism. Overharvesting of adults may have caused an unusually large number of juveniles to escape predation. This would lead to a short population explosion followed by several years of poor recruitment due to over-predation by abundant older fish on the younger fish. An intensive fishery would cause increased amplitude in the fluctuations because the fish would be taken even when they were scarce. In addition, competition with and predation by the newly arrived rainbow smelt, which occupied the same habitat for part of the year, were likely detrimental to the species.

The reasons for the collapse of the fishery in 1958 have not been well defined. Summer oxygen deficiencies in the central basin probably forced the fish into the deeper waters of the eastern basin of Lake Erie where they were more vulnerable to an extensive fishing effort. It has also been suggested that introgressive hybridization with walleye may have been responsible for the final disappearance of the remnant stock.

The blue pike was preyed upon by sea lamprey; this may have contributed to the decline of the species. Competition with the introduced rainbow smelt (*Osmerus mordax*) may also have contributed to this population decline.

The last successful year-class occurred in 1954 and there was virtually no recruitment to the fishery after that date. Production continued at high levels for another 3 years and then collapsed. As growth rates in this period increased, immature fish were exploited which further reduced spawning potential.

Intensive surveys by the U.S. Fish and Wildlife Service and cooperating states occurred in the late 1970s. In 1977, the Blue Pike Recovery Team conducted a survey of all Fish and Game Agencies in the U.S. in an effort to determine if this fish existed in waters under their jurisdiction. All responses were negative and the Recovery Team recommended that the species be removed from the U.S. List of Endangered and Threatened Wildlife because it was believed to be extinct.

Adapted from data compiled by the Threatened and Endangered Species Information Institute (Golden, CO) for *Beacham's International Threatened, Endangered, and Extinct Species* published on CD ROM, available from Beacham Publishing.

Harelip Sucker
Lagochila lacera

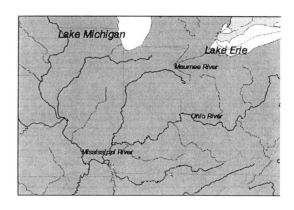

Description

The harelip sucker, *Lagochila lacera*, was a highly adapted bottom-feeder. It had been known to grow to lengths of up to 45 centimeters (18 inches) and weights of 1.4 kilograms (3 pounds). Its back was gray to olive in color and its tail slatey-blue. Its belly was whitish except in mineral-polluted waters where it took on a muddy-green cast. The species had a highly specialized small mouth: down-turned and proboscis-like with a completely divided lower lip. The species was also known from its closely bound gill-covers.

The harelip sucker had several common names throughout the states in which it occurred. It was known as the May sucker in the Columbus and Scioto Rivers, and called the Pea-lip sucker in the state of Indiana.

Behavior

Little is known of the reproductive habits of this species. The Harelip sucker was known to have spawning runs in May in the Columbus and Scioto Rivers.

This species was a highly specialized bottom feeder. Its large optic brain lobes and its highly modified lips with few taste buds indicate that it searched visually for its food. As a sight feeder, it probably seized its prey individually rather than indiscriminately picking up potential food items. Examination of the stomach contents of nine specimens

Status	Extinct
Probable Extinction	c.1893
Family	Catostomidae (Suckers)
Description	Medium-size fish, gray to olive in color with a slate-blue tail, small mouth, and down-turned lower lip.
Habitat	Riverbeds of clear limestone, gravel, sand or clay.
Food	Algae
Reproduction	Spawned in May in the Columbus and Scioto Rivers.
Causes for Extinction	Alteration of habitat by dams, logging and grazing.
Range	Ohio, Maumee and Mississipppi River systems
Drawing	See page 256

revealed that it fed heavily on mollusks (about 90%), supplemented by snails and limpets.

Habitat

The species seems to have been restricted to deep pools between shoal areas with clear water over a bedrock or rocky bottom in moderate to large streams. It was usually found in pool areas of large, clear streams, fifty to a hundred feet wide and three to twelve feet deep. The species' highly specialized mouth was best suited for riverbeds of clear limestone, gravel, sand or clay.

Distribution

The Harelip sucker was widespread in the basins of the Ohio, Maumee and lower Mississippi Rivers, where it occurred in at least eight states. Museum records exist for the Chickamanga River, Georgia; Elk River, Tennessee; Maumee River, Ohio; Tennessee River drainage (Alabama, Tennessee, Virginia); Cumberland River drainage (Kentucky, Tennessee); and Tipppecanoe River, Indiana. It was the most common of the now-extinct species. The species could be found in greatest concentrations in the Columbus and Scioto Rivers. The last individual was caught in 1893 and the species was believed to be extinct by the late 1890s. Logging, grazing and agricultural practices caused erosion which in turn caused the loss of the species' required habitat. The harelip sucker was last collected in 1893, when it was still fairly common.

Causes for Extinction

The main cause of this species' extinction was the alteration of its habitat. This species was once abundant in the central part of the Mississippi valley. Alteration of riverbeds by damming, change in the speed of currents, and erosion contributed to this species' extinction. The most damaging of these alterations was the erosion caused by hillside logging, grazing, and agricultural practices. This erosion converted the clear-water habitat this species prefers to turbid streams. This change caused the decline of mollusks on which the harelip sucker fed, and caused the asphyxiation of individuals from the silt. The highly specialized mouth and the closely bound gill-covers made this species especially susceptible to asphyxiation.

Utah Lake Sculpin

Cottus echinatus

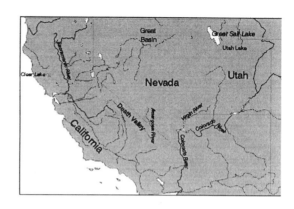

Description

The Utah Lake sculpin, *Cottus echinatus*, was a member of the sculpin family, *Cottidae*. Freshwater cottids typically lack scales and have enlarged, flat heads, large pectoral fins, and slim bodies. The eyes face upward and are set close together. The Utah Lake sculpin was a brownish color and lacked saddles and blotches; it had prickles (reduced, scattered, scale-like appendages) spread over the body, including the breast and belly, 7 (rarely 8) dorsal spines, 16 to 18 pectoral fin rays, and 26 to 29 lateral line pores.

Behavior

Cottus sp. spawn primarily in the spring; some are fall spawners. Spawning by the Utah Lake sculpin may have occurred at the mouths of streams entering Utah Lake or in backwater areas of these same streams further upstream from the lake. Eggs were attached to the lower surface of rocks or logs found adjacent to flowing water. Females were herded into the nest by the male. The male then guarded the nest and eggs.

Other members of the sculpin family are omnivorous, consuming algae, aquatic insects (larvae and adults), and sometimes fish

Status	Extinct
Probable Extinction	1936
Family	Cottidae (Sculpins)
Description	Brownish fish with an enlarged, flat head, large pectoral fins, slim bodies, and eyes that face upward.
Habitat	Deep water in cold water lakes. Known only from Utah Lake.
Food	Possibly algae, insects, smaller fish and fish eggs.
Reproduction	Spawned in the spring.
Causes for Extinction	Drought that altered the habitat.
Range	Utah
Drawing	See page 255

and fish eggs.

The Utah Lake sculpin probably exhibited variations in activity levels associated with season and water temperature. Sculpins are often found hiding under rocks during the day.

Habitat/Distribution

The Utah Lake sculpin was known only from Utah Lake, which is located 30 to 40 miles south-southeast of the Great Salt Lake. The Jordan River drains Utah Lake and empties into the Great Salt Lake. Portions of the Jordan River flow are diverted for irrigation. The river is also used to regulate the water level in Utah Lake. These activities have caused wide variations in stream flow.

The Utah Lake sculpin was a freshwater bottom-dwelling species. Cottids, in general, inhabit shoreline and deep water habitats in coldwater lakes or streams. They are most often found over areas with rocky substrates.

Causes for Extinction

Diversion of inflowing streams to Utah Lake blocked spawning runs, and increased pollution and salinity caused by developing agriculture greatly diminished the water quality in the lake during the late 1800s and early 1900s. In addition, at least eleven non-native fish were introduced and became established in Utah Lake and its tributaries by the 1930s. Extreme drought apparently killed the survivors. During the winter of 1934-1935, the water was so shallow that hundreds of tons of suckers and carp were killed due to freezing and crowding in the few deep holes. Presumably, the last sculpins died as well.

Raycraft Ranch Poolfish
Empetrichthys latos concavus

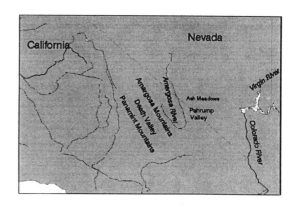

Description

All three subspecies of *Empetrichthys latos* (Manse Ranch poolfish, *E.l. latos*; Raycraft Ranch poolfish, *E.l. concavus*; Pahrump Ranch poolfish, *E.l. pahrump*) had an elongated body with dorsal fins placed far back on the body, complete lack of pelvic fin, a broad upturned mouth, and sides with a longitudinal streak. Dorsal, anal and caudal fins were a bright yellow-orange, with an orange ring around the eye. It was a slender fish with a gently sloping to convex predorsal profile, a relatively short and slender head, a comparatively broad mouth, a weak mandible, and 31-32 scales. The sides were marked by a narrow axial streak. The sides of the head were almost parrallel up to the tip on the mandible. Females were larger with a greenish-brown coloration and conspicuous black mottling. The males were silver blue without mottling.

The Raycraft Ranch poolfish more closely resembled the Pahrump Ranch poolfish. It differed by being much longer and having a more nearly rounded caudal fin, with shorter rays along the upper and lower borders. The anal fin was shorter, and in males the snout was shorter and the body and cheek deeper. The axial streak was finer and less conspicuous.

Status	Extinct
Probable Extinction	c.1950
Family	Cyprinodontidae (Killifishes)
Description	Small fish with a slender body, numerous lateral scales, and a dozen anal fin rays.
Habitat	Hot, freshwater springs and shallow pools.
Food	Algae
Causes for Extinction	Competition with exotic species.
Range	Nevada
Drawing	See page 256

Behavior

Pahrump killifish was an extremely adaptable taxon. It was able to swim actively in water less than an inch deep, survive in mud puddles, and flip its body between small pools of water. The main food source for individuals in this genus was algae, and perhaps nutrients derived from detritus.

Habitat

The Raycraft Ranch poolfish occured in one spring-fed pond, 5-25 feet wide and about 40 feet long, with a water depth of 1.5 feet. The outlet ditch was 1-4 feet wide. In October 1942, when the holotype was collected, the water temperature was 25.3 degrees C., slightly warmer than the pools at Manse and Pahrump ranches. The water in the spring pond and outlet was clear but easily roiled because of silt and trash. The vegetation was water cress. The shore consisted of low banks lined with willows. Beyond the tree line was meadowland. The spring flow was 10 gallons per minute. Carp were present in the pond.

Distribution

E.l. concavus was known only from a single pool on Raycraft Ranch. When Miller collected the holotype in 1942, he noted that the fish were not common. Sokol collected 12 specimens in 1953, which was the last time the fish was seen. Ira La Rivers surveyed Pahrump Valley in 1958 and found only one pool formerly inhabited by the poolfish undisturbed. The Raycraft Ranch pool was filled by bulldozing in 1955 to control mosquitoes.

Causes for Extinction

When Sokol surveyed the Raycraft Ranch pool in 1953, he noted the presence of introduced carp and bullfrogs in larger numbers than Miller had reported in 1942. Presumably, predation and competition from the exotic species caused the decline of the species. The destruction of the pool by land filling certainly confirmed its extinction.

See Causes of Extinction in the Great Basin, page 252, for additional information.

Pahrump Ranch Poolfish
Empetrichthys latos pahrump

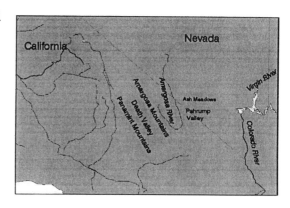

Description

All three subspecies of *Empetrichthys latos* (Manse Ranch poolfish, *E.l. latos;* Raycraft Ranch poolfish, *E.l. concavus;* Pahrump Ranch poolfish, *E.l. pahrump*) had an elongated body with dorsal fins placed far back on the body, complete lack of pelvic fin, a broad upturned mouth, and sides with a longitudinal streak. Dorsal, anal and caudal fins were a bright yellow-orange, with an orange ring around the eye. It was a slender fish with a gently sloping to convex predorsal profile, a relatively short and slender head, a comparatively broad mouth, a weak mandible, and 31-32 scales. The sides were marked by a narrow axial streak. The sides of the head were almost parrallel up to the tip on the mandible. Females were larger with a greenish-brown coloration and conspicuous black mottling. The males were silver blue without mottling.

E.l. pahrump differs from *E. latos* in that there is a longer distance between anal origin and caudal base. It has a more intermediate color pattern, and its paleness may have been influenced by the clay and silt substrate of its habitat. The holotype was 35 mm (1.36 inches) long.

Status	Extinct
Probable Extinction	c.1958
Family	Cyprinodontidae (Killifishes)
Description	Small fish with a slender body, numerous lateral scales, and a dozen anal fin rays.
Habitat	Hot, freshwater springs and shallow pools.
Food	Algae
Causes for Extinction	Competition with exotic species; loss of habitat.
Range	Nevada

Behavior

The Pahrump killifish was an extremely adaptable taxon. It was able to swim actively in water less than an inch deep, it could survive in mud puddles, and it could flip its body between small pools of water. The main food source for individuals in this genus was algae, and perhaps nutrients derived from detritus.

Habitat

The holotype was taken from the marshy overflow of a spring-fed ditch on Pahrump Ranch.

Distribution

E.l. pahrump was known only from two springs located about 180 m (590 feet) east of the ranch house on Pahrump Ranch, Nye County, Nevada. When F. H. Miller collected the holotype in 1942, he noted that the northernmost of the two springs had been greatly altered by dredging and that no poolfish were observed there. The other spring still supported a poolfish population in a marsh formed by the spring outflow.

Causes for Extinction

Sokol surveyed the springs in September 1953 and was unable to find any poolfish, but La Rivers reported that during his survey in 1958 he found evidence of extant individuals. However, he observed that carp and bullfrogs were abundant, and that the springs were periodically pumped dry. Extinction probably occurred in 1958 when one of the springs failed because of excessive pumping.

Ash Meadows Killifish

Empetrichthys merriami

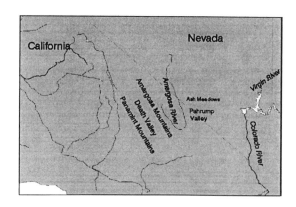

Description

The Ash Meadows killifish, *Empetrichthys merriami,* resembled the mud minnow (*Umbra limi*) but was deeper and more compressed. The species was structurally quite distinct from other cyprinodonts. It was deep-bodied, hump-backed and narrow-mouthed, with a markedly protruding lower jaw. The heavy, chunky head was compressed and its upper surface slightly convex. The mouth was very oblique with a slight, distinct lateral cleft, a conical jaw and somewhat molariform pharyngeal teeth. It had 20 to 30 scales in lateral series, and usually 14 anal fin rays. The maxillary was free only at the tip, reaching slightly behind the front eye. The length was up to 2.5 inches.

E. merriami was dark brown above; the sides and lower parts were lighter and blotched with brown and white. The belly was checkered, the fins dusky, and the scales had a brown center with white margins.

Behavior

The Ash Meadows killifish was known to be an egg-laying species, but little else is known of the reproductive requirements.

Status	Extinct
Probable Extinction	c.1948
Family	Cyprinodontidae (Killifishes)
Description	Deep-bodied, hump-backed, narrow-mouthed fish with a markedly protruding lower jaw.
Habitat	Clear, chalky-blue deep water spring with a sulphurous odor.
Food	Algae
Reproduction	Unknown except that Ash Meadows killifish laid eggs.
Causes for Extinction	Competition with exotic species.
Range	Nevada

The main food source for the Ash Meadows killifish and other individuals in this genus was algae.

Habitat

This species occurred in one thermal,

isolated pool in Ash Meadows. It frequented deeper holes and was usually uncommon in the shallow, spring-fed ditches and marshy areas.

The Ash Meadows killifish was known only from the spring called Deep Spring. It is approximately 9 meters (30 feet) deep; easily the deepest pool in Ash Meadows. The water is described as a clear, chalky-blue, with a distinctly sulphurous odor. The bottom is formed of accumulated silt and mud, and the pool supports a dense growth of algae. The temperature of Deep Springs is about 20 degrees Celsius (68 degrees Fahrenheit).

This species was associated with the Amargosa pupfish and the Amargosa speckled dace. The pupfish was overwhelmingly dominant in the habitat, which may have contributed to the poolfishs' demise.

Distribution

The Ash Meadows poolfish was known from Deep Spring in Ash Meadows in the Nye Valley in Nevada, and was originally known from five springs in Ash Meadows of the Amargosa River drainage, Nye County, Nevada. It appears to have been rare even at the time it was discovered by Gilbert in 1891; only seven specimens were collected as compared to numerous specimens of speckled dace. The next collection was not made until 1930, when only three specimens were taken. Between 1936 and 1942 the Millers surveyed the five springs, Big, Jack Rabbit, Point of Rocks, Forest, and Rogers, and were able to collect a total of only 22 specimens. The last known collection was from Big Spring (= Deep Spring) in 1948. Sokol attempted unsuccessfully to locate a specimen from Big Spring in 1953, and all succeeding efforts to locate the species have failed.

Causes for Extinction

Competition with exotic species appears to be the main cause of this species' extinction. In 1937 exotic bullfrogs, crayfish, and mosquitofish were observed in the habitat, and by 1950 they had become established in several springs in Ash Meadows, including Deep Spring. The introduced species probably removed Ash Meadows killifish by predation and by competition for food and habitat. Habitat alteration may also have contributed to the decline in some springs.

See Causes of Extinction in the Great Basin, page 252, for additional information.

Pahranagat Spinedace

Lepidomeda altivelis

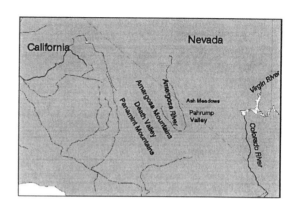

Description

The Pahranagat spinedace, *Lepidomeda altivelis*, was a member of the minnow or *Cyprinidae* family. It, like all members of this family, is a soft-rayed fish with cycloid scales. Like most suckers, Pahranagat spinedace has a toothless jaw and bears only pharyngeal teeth, or teeth in the throat. It had a very oblique mouth, high and sharp dorsal fins, and a compressed head. A line that runs from the uppermost tip of the premaxillary to the middle of the caudal passes below the middle of the pupil. The snout is shorter and the dorsal spines stonger than in other *Lepidomeda* species. Its maximum length is 3.75 inches.

There is almost no pigment on the shoulder girdle in advance of the scapular. There is pigment on the opercles and a band of coarse pigment crossing the chin behind the upper lip.

Behavior

Little is known of the reproductive requirements of this species. Minnows in general exhibit a variety of spawning habits. Most of the species in this family give no parental care to their eggs or their young.

Status	Extinct
Probable Extinction	1938-1959
Family	Cyprinidae (Minnows)
Description	Small, soft-rayed fish with cycloid scales.
Habitat	Small freshwater streams.
Causes for Extinction	Lowering of the water table, competition with exotic species.
Range	Nevada

Habitat

The Pahranagat spinedace was a freshwater species which had been found in Ash Spring and a chain of lakes in Pahranagat Valley in Nevada. This area is within the central basin, which is an area of eastern-central Nevada east of the Lahontan basin bounded on the south by the Colorado River drainage of the White and Virgin rivers. The separation line has been drawn at Lower Pahranagat Lake based on current hydrologic patterns. This area is unique in that it contains no stream of any size (with the exception of the Humboldt River) with permanent flow. It does have numerous small sections of streams and several small lakes and marshes.

The Pahranagat spinedace occurred in the cool, swift outflow from Ash Spring and the upper Pahranagat Lake. The upper waters in the pools in Ash Spring have a temperature of 89 degrees F, but are much cooler below.

The outflow of Ash Spring is a meandering channel 2.5 miles long and 5 to 20 feet wide. It has retained its original bed conditions with only limited diversions. The current is generally swift (rarely quiet and in places very swift). The bottom comprises sand, gravel, mud and boulders. The depth of the water is up to 6 feet. Vegetation consists of abundant bulrushes and submerged weeds, but the stream is partly clear of vegetation. The 5 foot high banks are wooded; beyond the woods are grass and farmland.

When the last specimens were sighted in 1938 the water was dirty green, alkaline to taste, with bottom visibility of two feet. Vegetation included heavy growth of flooded cockleburs. The bottom was firm to soft clay soil. The presence of many carp was noted.

Distribution

The Pahranagat spinedace was originally collected in 1891 in the Pahranagat Valley in the course of Pleistocene White River in the Great Basin in Nevada. It is not known how widespread the species was at that time. The last collections were reported from 1938. It became extinct sometime between 1938-1959.

The Pahranagat spinedace was endemic to the Pahranagat Valley.

Causes for Extinction

The Pahranagat spinedace became extinct between 1938 and 1959. Because the stream feeding the pool has retained its original bed conditions, with only limited diversions, and since the water seems to have remained uniform, it is believed that the main cause of this extinction was competition from introduced species, carp and mosquitofish, and possibly from bullfrogs that may have modified the habitat.

See Causes of Extinction in the Great Basin, page 252, for additional information.

Spring Valley Sucker
Pantosteus sp.

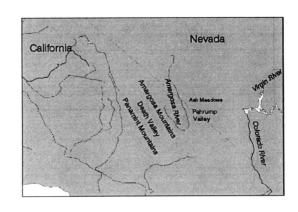

Description

The Spring Valley sucker, *Pantosteus* sp., was a smaller member of the Spring Valley sucker family. This species is only known from one specimen taken in 1938, and has never been fully described.

Habitat

The Spring Valley sucker was endemic to a single small stream in the northern end of Spring Valley in Nevada. Due to the limited data on this species, habitat requirements are not known. The species seemed to be dependent on stream flow.

Distribution

The Spring Valley sucker was known from only one collected specimen (1938) in a single small stream. It is doubtful the species was ever widespread. Deterioration of stream flow and predation by exotic species are believed to be the main causes of the species' extinction.

Due to the undoubtedly small numbers of the species and its limited range, its chances of survival were small from the beginning. With a small genetic pool and a

Status	Extinct
Probable Extinction	c.1950
Family	Catostomidae (Suckers)
Description	Small member of the sucker family; never fully described.
Causes for Extinction	Possibly deterioration of stream flow.
Range	Nevada

limited range, the species was more susceptible to a catastrophic event, such as the deterioration of stream flow in its habitat.

Causes for Extinction

Scientists believe the Spring Valley sucker became extinct due to the deterioration in stream flow. Population growth, urbanization, and expanding agricultural practices have increased the use of water. Lowering of the stream flow in this case is believed to be the main cause of the Spring Valley sucker's extinction.

When studies were conducted of the

stream where the Spring Valley sucker was known, the only two species of fish were a minnow and an introduced trout. There is a chance that the introduced species played a part in the extinction of the Spring Valley sucker. Trout may have preyed on the species or its eggs, and further limited its numbers.

Adapted from data compiled by the Threatened and Endangered Species Information Institute (Golden, CO) for *Beacham's International Threatened, Endangered, and Extinct Species* published on CD ROM, available from Beacham Publishing.

Grass Valley
Speckled Dace

Rhinichthys osculus reliquus

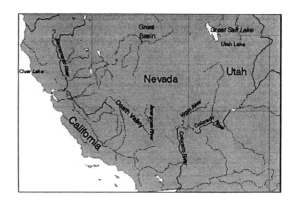

Description

The Grass Valley speckled dace, *Rhinichthys osculus reliquus*, was a soft-rayed fish with cycloid scales and a toothless jaw that bore only pharyngeal teeth. *R. osculus* was grayish-black above with a yellowish or creamy white belly.

Speckled dace can be distinguished from other Death Valley minnows by their slightly overhung snout, dark lateral stripes often running the entire length of the body, speckles and splotches on their sides, small fins, and small size (less than 3 inches long). The avrious isolated populations differ in degree of speckling and completeness of the lateral stripe.

Spawning *R. osculus* males develop fleshy bumps on the rays of the pectoral and anal fins, and an orange-red color around the mouth, above the gill opening, on the base of the anal fin, and along the lower caudal lobe. *R. osculus* live for 3-5 years.

Status	Extinct
Probable Extinction	1938-1959
Family	Cyprinidae (Minnows)
Description	Soft-rayed fish with cycloid scales, grayish-black topside, and a yellowish or creamy-white belly.
Habitat	Warm rivers at low altitudes or cold water stream riffles with fast moving currents in higher altitudes.
Food	Algae, diatoms and invertebrates.
Reproduction	Generally spawned during June and July.
Causes for Extinction	Predation on young and competition for food and habitat by introduction of exotic species.
Range	Nevada

Behavior

Minnows in general exhibit a variety of spawning habits. Most of the species in this family give no parental care to their eggs or their young. *R. osculus* begins to reproduce in its second summer. Spawning peaks in June and July when temperatures average 65 degrees Fahrenheit, but may continue throughout the summer to some extent.

Males clear off small areas, exposing bare rock or gravel. Males surround females as they enter an area. Deposited and fertilized eggs adhere to the lower surface of rocks or on other bottom substrates. Hatching occurs in 6 days; larvae remain in the hatching area's gravel for about a week. Fry emerge from the gravel and congregate near or under large rocks in the shallower, warmer sections of the stream. Fry of lake or spring dwelling subspecies migrate to the quiet, vegetated shoreline or backwater areas in the lakes or springs.

The grass valley specked dace probably exhibited variations in activity levels associated with season and water temperature. *R. osculus* is more or less nocturnal and spends much of the day hidden among or below rocks in shallow to deeper waters.

Speckled dace feed in small schools, foraging primarily on bottom-dwelling invertebrates. Some drifting insects are taken in mid-stream, and during times of low invertebrate food availability, algae are taken. Speckled dace are opportunistic, particulate feeders that typically take the most abundant food species, such as insect larvae in the spring, crustaceans in the fall, and algae and detritus in the winter.

Speckled dace are important as forage fishes for several larger fishes of commercial or recreational importance.

Habitat

The only known collection of *R.o. reliquus* was from a spring-fed creek in a grassy meadow in the partly enclosed southwestern arm of Grass Valley in east Lander County, Nevada.

Distribution

The grass valley speckled dace was known only from a single collection in an enclosed basin in Lander County, Nevada. It was common when it was collected by Hubbs and Miller in 1938, when 474 specimens were taken. Only one trout was observed at this time, but when La Rivers visited the stream in 1959, he found no speckled dace and a stream full of trout. No dace were discovered on the following exploration in 1970. It is believed to have become extinct between 1938-1959.

Causes for Extinction

Economically, introduction of game species into a habitat for sport fishing may at first be profitable and seem successful, but in most cases it results in the demise of native fish. This was true in the case of grass valley specked dace. Introduction of exotic species such as rainbow trout and brook trout probably led to predation on young and competition for food.

Tecopa Pupfish
Cyprinodon nevadensis calidae

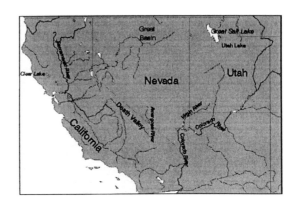

Description

The Tecopa pupfish, *Cyprinodon nevadensis calidae*, was a member of the pupfish or *Cyprinodontidae* family. The body was deep, especially in large males. Breeding males turned bright blue over the entire body, including the caudal peduncle, with a black band at the end of the tail. Vertical bars on females were variable, ranging from 6-10 distinct vertical bands to very few bands. There were 23-28 large scales in lateral series, small pelvic fins (occasionally missing), and central cusps of teeth truncated or pointed. Scales of pelvic fin rays decreased with an increase in water temperatures and salinity. The average length of the species was 2.5 inches.

Status	Extinct
Probable Extinction	c.1960s
Family	Cyprinodontidae (Killifish)
Description	Pupfish 2.5 inches in length, but some grew to be as long as 6 inches with tricuspid teeth.
Habitat	Hot pools of fresh or saline water.
Reproduction	Egg laying.
Causes for Extinction	Competition from exotic species.
Range	California

Behavior

The Tecopa pupfish was an extremely adaptable species. It was able to swim actively in water less than an inch deep, and could survive in mud puddles. It had the ability to flip its body between small pools of water and could live in water with greatly fluctuating temperatures as hot as 40 degrees Celsius (104 degrees Fahrenheit). It could also tolerate saline concentrations 6 times greater than normal sea water.

The Tecopa pupfish was an egg-laying species. Breeding males turned an intensive blue with overlaying black vertical bars and a distinct black terminal band on the caudal fin.

See pages 254-255 for the diet and reproduction of pupfish.

Habitat

The Tecopa pupfish was known only from the South Tecopa Hot Springs in Inyo County in California, about 35 miles east of the southern entrance to Death Valley. The springs are located on the east side of the Armargosa River; the two springs that this fish inhabited are about ten yards apart. They were not found in the head spring where water temperatures are 108-110 degrees F, but downstream in cooler waters (96-102 degrees F).

Tecopa pupfish selected the optimal level in temperature gradient. In the thermal stream near Tecopa, pupfish reached their maximum density at 32-36 degrees C. and moved in response to changing temperatures. On cold, windy days the waters cooled quickly below the spring source, and the fish moved upstream to stay within a comfortable temperature range. Conversely, they moved downstream on hot days.

Distribution

The Tecopa pupfish was discovered in 1942 in the north and south Tecopa Hot Springs in Inyo County, California. It has only been known from this area. It is believed to have become extinct in 1960.

Causes for Extinction

During the early 1940s bath houses were erected around the two springs to take advantage of the hot mineral water. The baths attracted a fairly large seasonal and residential population, which led to trailer parks and landscaping. By 1965 the outflow of the two springs had joined and the remaining channel straightened, causing the rate of flow and temperature in downstream areas to increase, which was unsuitable for the pupfish's reproduction.

The main cause of this extinction was competition with introduced species. Mosquito fish (*Gambusia affinis*) were introduced into this species' habitat and proved to be disastrous to it. The introduced species successfully removed Tecopa pupfish by predation and competition for food and habitat. Other factors affecting the species were its extremely small habitat and low genetic diversity. This localization made the species more vulnerable to a catastrophic event, and its low numbers led to a low genetic diversity which did not allow the species to adapt to change.

Human encroachment and urbanization have also taken their tolls on native biotas. Intensive industrialization, rapid urbanization, and water pollution have all adversely affected the environment. Water demands imposed by rapidly growing numbers of people have diverted or changed the flow of water throughout many areas. Lowering the water table causes the loss of streams, marshes, and springs, which in turn cause the loss of aquatic species. Diversions for irrigation have also reduced fish populations. Pollution from a variety of domestic and industrial wastes has turned productive habitats into barren ones. A nearby bathhouse contaminated the water in the South Tecopa Hot Springs, helping to extirpate the Tecopa pupfish.

Thicktail Chub
Gila crassicauda

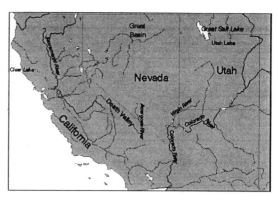

Description

The thicktail chub, *Gila crassicauda*, was a heavy-bodied fish with deep, short, and thick caudal peduncles; a small, cone-shaped head, 8 rays in both dorsal and anal fins, and 9 rays in each pelvic fin. The pharyngeal teeth were sturdy and hooked. It was a soft-rayed fish with cycloid scales. The 8-14 (usually 10-12) gill rakers were stubby and toothlike in appearance. The backs of the fish ranged in color from greenish-brown to purplish-black, while the sides and the belly were yellow. It attained a length of up to 250 mm (9.75 inches). The female was slightly larger.

Status	Extinct
Probable	
Extinction	1970s
Family	Cyprinidae (Minnows)
Description	Soft-rayed fish with a short head, humped back, purplish upper side and yellow under side.
Habitat	Sluggish parts of streams and sloughs.
Food	Probably minnows.
Causes for	
Extinction	Alteration of habitat from dams and urbanization.
Range	California

Behavior

The stubby gill rakers, short intestine, and stout, hooked pharyngeal teeth indicate that the thicktail chub was carnivorous, probably feeding on small fish and large aquatic invertebrates.

The thicktail chub occasionally hybridized, and the hybrids were described as a separate species in 1908.

Most of the species in this family give no parental care to their eggs or their young.

Habitat

The thicktail chub was found in rivers, ponds, marshes and lakes in the Central Valley in California. The species seemed to prefer the sluggish parts of streams and sloughs. It was most commonly taken from Coyote Creek, which ran from Clear Lake into San Francisco Bay. At times of heavy spring flooding it was also caught in the surface waters of the bay itself.

Distribution

Historically, the thicktail chub ranged throughout the Central Valley of California, in lowland areas, as well as in Clear Lake and the the stream tributaries leading to San Francisco Bay. It was one of the most common fish in California, and at the turn of the century was sold in fish markets in San Francisco. Historic Indian middens also revealed an abundance of the species, and it was the most abundant fish in the Sacramento River at the turn of the century, comprising 41% of the fish population. Hybrids of the species are still believed to exist, but the pure-bred species is believed to be extinct.

Causes for Extinction

The primary cause of extinction was the conversion of much of the Central Valley to agricultural use. Many of the sloughs and marshes were drained during the late 1800s, and the remaining streams and rivers were dredged or channelized for navigation or flood control. Most of the species' habitat was destroyed by drainage, dam-building and water-diversion for irrigation. These changes in water flow caused the loss of the sluggish water the species preferred in some areas, and in others it completely dried up the water supply.

Competition with exotic species was another reason for this species' extinction. Introduced species helped to remove the thicktail chub by predation and competition for food and habitat.

Introduced species posed another threat to this species, hybridization. By the 1920s, hybrids between the thicktail chub and the introduced hitch minnow (*Lavinia exilicauda*) had been discovered. This was presumably the final factor in its disappearance as a pure-bred species. It was last collected from Clear Lake in 1938, from the Sacramento River in 1950, and from Steamboat Slough along the San Joaquin River in 1957. Repeated efforts to find the species have failed.

Clear Lake Splittail
Pogonichthys ciscoides

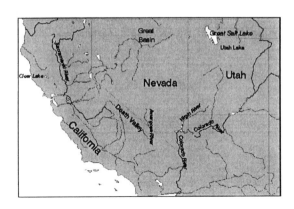

Description

The Clear Lake splittail, *Pogonichthys ciscoides*, was a large minnow that could exceed 40 centimeters (16 inches) in length. Adults were characterized by an elongated body, distinct nuchal hump, and small, blunt head, usually with barbels at the corners of the slightly subterminal mouth. The pharyngeal teeth were hooked and had narrow grinding surfaces. The tail fin was symmetrical and the nuptial tubercles on the head and sides of the breeding male were well developed. The color was a dull silvery gold on the sides; the older the fish, the duller the color. The back was usually dusky olive gray. During breeding season, the paired caudal fins were tinged with red-orange and the general color of the male darkened.

Behavior

Females were highly fecund and produced over 100,000 eggs each year. Populations fluctuated annually depending on spawning success, which was highly correlated with freshwater outflow and the availability of shallow-water habitat with submerged vegetation. Fish usually reached

Status	Extinct
Probable Extinction	1970
Family	Cyprinidae (Minnows)
Description	Large minnow with an elongated body, distinct nuchal hump, and small, blunt head, usually with barbels at the corners of the slightly subterminal mouth.
Habitat	Cool, clear freshwater.
Food	Gnat eggs and larvae.
Reproduction	Spawned in gravel rifles of Clear Lake tributaries in April and May.
Causes for Extinction	Extreme alteration of Clear Lake as a result of agricultural practices; drought; introduction of exotic species and pesticides.
Range	Clear Lake and its tributaries.

sexual maturity by the end of their second year. Some variability in the period of reproduction existed because older individuals reproduce first, followed by younger individuals.

The Clear Lake splittail spawned in the inlet streams in April and May, frequently migrating miles upstream to suitable gravel rifles. The newly hatched fish probably remained in the stream about three weeks before returning to the lake. Once in the lake, they spent the first few months in the littoral zone.

The fish schooled in large numbers over most of Clear Lake, concentrating in the littoral areas. Summer die-offs of large splittail occurred as an annual event, although its causes are unknown.

The Clear Lake splittail depended less on bottom food than the Sacramento splittail. The Clear Lake splittail was recorded feeding on ovipositing gnats and gnat egg rafts on the surface, as well as on bottom-living gnat larvae and on emerging pupae. Much of the diet was zooplankton; the rest was insects or detritus.

Habitat

Clear Lake is the largest freshwater lake in California. Its outlet, Cache Creek, flows through a steep, narrow canyon to join the Sacramento River. Because Cache Creek is impassable for migrating fish, the Clear Lake splittail and the Sacramento splittail have been isolated from each other for a long time, and were finally recognized as distinct species in 1967.

Distribution

P. ciscoides was restricted to Clear Lake and its tributary streams in Lake County, California. During the early and mid-1960s the species was reported from several localities in Clear Lake, and a single specimen washed into Cache Creek. The Clear Lake splittail was abundant until 1942 or 1943, but during three summers of intensive seining from 1946 to 1950, only a few juveniles were collected. The last known specimen was taken from Clear Lake in 1970.

Causes for Extinction

The decline of the once abundant splittail parallels changes in Clear Lake itself. Prior to the 1880s, the lake was cool and clear, and the predominant fish were rainbow trout and Sacramento perch. By the 1940s, it had been transformed into a warm, turbid lake dominated by carp and other introduced fishes. The reasons for the lake's drastic transformation includes the poorly planned development of watershed for agriculture, which washed sediment, fertilizers, and sewage into the lake. The assumption is that the low rainfall during the early 1940s, combined with the diversion of tributary streams for agriculture, eliminated most of the habitat for splittails. The extinction may also have been aided by the large quantities of chlorinated hydrocarbon pesticides used to control swarms of gnats, which was the splittail's main food source. During the 1940s and 1950s, the increased use of DDD caused toxins to appear in Clear Lake fish and fish-eating birds; massive die-offs of western grebes was observed. To compound the problems for the splittail, the abundance of introduced fish, such as bluegills and silversides, probably threatened the weakened population of splittails.

Amistad Gambusia
Gambusia amistadensis

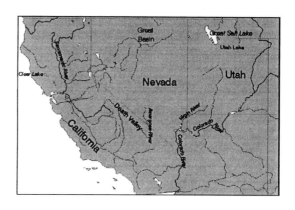

Description

The Amistad gambusia, *Gambusia amistadensis*, is considered an extinct species. *G. amistadensis* was a member of the *G. nobilis* group and appears closely related to *G. senilis* and *G. gaigei* species groups. Preserved specimens indicate that the species' dominant characteristics were a relatively slender body and a terminal mouth with numerous teeth on each jaw. Other observed characteristics were strong crosshatching and numerous darkly pigmented crescent-shaped spots on the scale margins. The mid-dorsal stripe was narrow and the lateral stripe was broad. A short, dusky bar was present under the eye. Adult females had a permanent median dark anal spot.

Common name synonyms for *G. amistadensis* include the Goodenough gambusia and Goodenough Springs gambusia.

Status	Extinct
Probable Extinction	December 4, 1987
Family	Poeciliidae (Livebearer)
Description	Slender-bodied fish with numerous teeth on each jaw and darkly pigmented crescent-shaped spots on the scale margins.
Habitat	Rapidly flowing warm spring waters.
Causes of Extinction	Habitat at Goodenough Springs and its outflow was inundated by waters from the filling of Amistad Reservoir in 1968.
Range	Texas
Photo	See Color Insert, C-1

Behavior

The reproductive behavior of *G. amistadensis* was similar to other members of the *G. nobilis* complex. Male courtship appears to have been similar to other poeciliids.

Little is known concerning the food habits of *G. amistadensis*. No information is available on periodicity of *G. amistadensis*; however, most members of the genus are diurnal.

Habitat

G. amistadensis was restricted to the rapidly flowing warm spring waters of

Goodenough Springs and to the outflow creek which emptied into the Rio Grande. This spring flowed over limestone gravel and sand substrates. Waters originated in the relatively large Edwards-Trinity aquifer. The type locality and habitat for *G. amistadensis* is now behind Amistad Reservoir and the spring flows are greatly reduced.

Distribution

All known populations of *G. amistadensis* are extinct due to the inundation of their only known natural environment and the extirpation of this species in the two artificial cultures by mosquitofish (*Gambusia affinis*). *G. amistadensis* was originally isolated to Goodenough Springs and its outflow stream in Val Verde County, Texas.

Causes for Extinction

G. amistadensis' only known habitat at Goodenough Springs and its outflow was inundated by waters from the filling of Amistad Reservoir in 1968. Captive populations were maintained until the late-1970's at the Brackenridge Field Laboratory of the University of Texas at Austin and Dexter National Fish Hatchery. Both cultures became contaminated with mosquitofish (*G. affinis*) and all species of *G. amistadensis* were extirpated. In relation to this incident, potential hazards have been cited with respect to attempts of "culture-only" populations for reintroduction efforts.

Adapted from data compiled by the Threatened and Endangered Species Information Institute (Golden, CO) for *Beacham's International Threatened, Endangered, and Extinct Species* published on CD ROM, available from Beacham Publishing.

Rio Grande
Bluntnose Shiner
Notropis simus simus

Phantom Shiner
Notropis orca

Description

The general color of these shiners was silvery, with a broad, obscure band of small punctulations along the side. The silvery head was sparsely scattered with small melanophores, and the male had many small nuptial tubercles scattered randomly on his head; the back, abdomen, and peritoneum were silvery. The silver intensified on the sides, with a faint lateral band present. There was a weak mid-dorsal stripe extending to the base of the caudal fin. The deep, spindle-shaped body had a moderately slender caudal peduncle. Its fairly large mouth had no barbels and was overhung by the bluntly rounded snout. The eye diameter was more than half the length of the snout. Fins were moderately pointed. It had 37-38 scales and grew to a length of 3.5 inches.

Notropis orca can be distinguished from *N.s. simus* by its 8 anal fin rays (9 in simus); 38 total vertebra (36-37 in simus); 33-38 gill rakers (25-30 in simus); and a different pharyngeal tooth formula.

Behavior

The spawning period may have begun in the early summer, ending in October, although some accounts place spawning at 4-6

Status	Extinct
Probable Extinction	1964 (Rio Grande) 1975 (Phantom)
Family	Cyprinidae (Minnows)
Description	Silvery fish with a deep, spindle-shaped body, a moderately slender caudal peduncle; its fairly large mouth had no barbels and a bluntly rounded snout.
Habitat	Swift, relatively deep main river channels of the Rio Grande river.
Food	Detritus, algae and terrestrial invertebrates.
Reproduction	May have spawned from early summer through October.
Causes for Extinction	Modification of habitat; competition from introduced species.
Range	Lower reaches of the major tributaries of the Rio Grande river.
Drawing	See page 255

weeks during the early summer.

The S-shaped gut indicates that the

bluntnose shiners were principally carnivorous/ omnivorous, and probably ate detritus, algae and terrestrial invertebrates (mostly adult Diptera).

N. simus and *N. orca* are known to have hybridized in the upper Rio Grande as early as 1891. By 1939, some individuals exhibited introgressive hybridization. It is assumed that hybridization occurred because of the reduction in the number of spawning sites and the rarity of both species. What role hybridization played in the decline of the species is unknown.

Habitat

N.s. simus occupied the swift, relatively deep main river channels of the Rio Grande river, often below obstructions (although it was occasionally taken from irrigation ditches or shallow rifles).

N. orca inhabited the middle and lower segments of the Rio Grande.

Distribution

N.s. simus was found in the lower reaches of the major tributaries from the state line near El Paso, Texas, north to the vicinity of Abiquiu in the Charma River, New Mexico. If the species still survives, the last possible habitat would occur in the Rio Grande between Otowi bridge and Cochiti Lake.

The last known Rio Grande bluntnose shiner was caught in the Rio Grande north of Peña Blanca, Sandoval County, New Mexico, in July 1964. The last Phantom shiner was taken in the lower Rio Grande in 1975.

Causes for Extinction

A number of factors may have contributed to the extinction of the Rio Grande shiner species, including modification of dams and their impoundments, irrigation practices, and channelization. The habitat modifications, along with an abundance of introduced fishes, brought about a significant decline in the abundance of shiners, especially after 1940. Historically, the Rio Grande was characterized by floods and droughts, resulting in an unstable water flow. The now-extinct fishes had adapted to the unstable flows prior to the damn construction which would have stabilized the flow. The introduced fishes, which were vulnerable to floods and droughts, were better able to flourish in the stabilized river flow.

Mexican Dace

Evarra eigenmanni
Evarra tlahuacensis

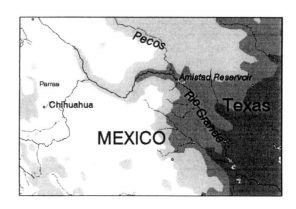

Description

The Mexican dace, *E. eigenmanni*, had an elongated, subteret body growing to a length of 3 inches, with a small head and a bluntish snout. The interorbital area was broad and flatish. The mouth was small, with somewhat thickened lips. The lateral line was decurved anteriorly. All the fins were small. The color was olive green and silvery below. The sides had a faint plumbeous lateral band ending in a small caudal spot.

E. tlahuacensis had an elongated, slender body growing to a length of 2.5 inches. It had a blunt snout; its upper jaw was protractile; the tips of the teeth were hooked and the grinding surface fairly developed. The little mouth was oblique, with the tips of the maxillary reaching the margin of the orbit. The diameter of the eye was 3.6 inches. The lateral line was complete and decurved above the pectorals. The color was dark olive above and white below. The line between the colors was very distinct.

Behavior

Minnows in general exhibit a variety of spawning habits. Most of the species in this family give no parental care to their eggs or

Status	Extinct
Probable Extinction	1983
Family	Cyprinidae (Minnows)
Description	Olive green and silver/white fish with a small head and mouth, thickened lips, and a bluntish snout.
Habitat	Canals.
Causes for Extinction	Loss of habitat.
Range	Mexico City
Drawing	See page 256

their young. *R. osculus* begins to reproduce in its second summer. Spawning peaks in June and July when temperatures average 65 degrees Fahrenheit, but may continue throughout the summer to some extent. Males clear off small areas, exposing bare rock or gravel. Males surround females as they enter an area. Deposited and fertilized eggs adhere to the lower surface of rocks or on other bottom substrates. Hatching occurs in 6 days; larvae remain in the hatching area's gravel for about a week. Fry emerge from the gravel and congregate near or under large rocks in the shallower, warmer sections of the stream. Fry of lake or spring dwelling subspecies migrate to the quiet, vegetated shoreline or backwater areas in the lakes or springs.

Habitat/Distribution

These two species, plus *E. bustamantei*, were described by Woolman in 1895 from specimens taken from canals in the endor-heic Valley of Mexico, where Mexico City and its suburbs now stand. The genus *Evarra* is an Indian name meaning "maker of gods in lands beyond the sea." The genus is presumed to have been derived from the Mexican genus *Algansea*.

Causes for Extinction

Alvarez and Navarro believed all three species to be nearing extinction in the late 1950s, and all were believed extinct by 1983. The extinctions coincided with the dying of lakes, spring-fed ponds, and canals of the valley floor, due to agricultural practices, persistent groundwater removal, and the rapid development of Mexico City.

Parras Pupfish
Cyprinodon latifasciatus

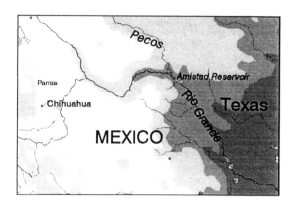

Description

The Parras pupfish, *Cyprinodon latifascia-tus*, had a robust, moderately compressed body, a short head with a bluntish snout, and a small, terminal, slightly convex mouth. The eyes were small, equalling the length of the snout. This pupfish grew to a length of 2.55 inches.

The color of the adult males ranged from very dark to light brown. The caudal fin was plain with a narrow black band at the tip. The ventral and anal fins were plain, tipped with black, and the dorsal fin was dark. The females were much lighter, and the larger females were speckled with small dark dots. There were faint dark bands on the middle of the side along the rows of scales. There was a black blotch on the last rays of the dorsal and anal fins. The smaller females were more or less blotched with darker dots.

Behavior

This species fed on small crustacea and other aquatic animals. The species spawned in spring or early summer.

Status	Extinct
Probable Extinction	c.1930
Family	Cyprinodontidae (Killifishes)
Description	Possessed a lower jaw that protruded with a tilted mouth.
Habitat	Freshwater, desert springs.
Food	Aquatic animals.
Reproduction	Spawned in spring or early summer.
Causes for Extinction	Habitat loss; exotic carp.
Range	Mexico

Habitat

The Parras pupfish was endemic to the Chihuahua Desert, near Parras, Coahuila, Mexico. The Parras springs are relics of a huge Pleistocene watershed, which emerge from a lava hillside and are from the old Rio Nazas Watershed. They are tiny isolated pockets of water.

Distribution

Professor Garman took specimens from Rio Nasas and the headwaters of the Rio Mezquital, the Labor and Durango Rivers in 1881. Jordan and Evermann took specimens from near Durango in Paras, Coahuila in 1896.

In 1903, George Hochderfer took nine Parras pupfish from a stream in Parras Valley, which was the last record of this species. In 1953, Carl and Laura Hubbs investigated this area for any remaining species and found that "there no longer are any natural springs in the immediate vicinity of Parras or anywhere in the Parras basin or in the great desert basin to the North." The habitat of these species, then, has been totally lost. It is thought that this species became extinct around 1930.

Causes for Extinction

Until the 1930s Parras Valley contained magnificent spring systems, but the development of wine factories, a flour mill, a rubber mill, and a textile factory depleted the available surface water. By 1953, when an extensive search was made to locate several rare fish, the springs had dried up.

Pollution and introduced carp also contributed to the extinction of the species.

Also See General Causes for Extinction of Fish Species, page 252.

Parras Roundnose Minnow

Dionda episcopa plunctifer

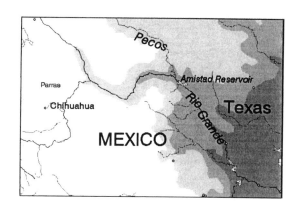

Description

The Parras roundnose minnow, *Dionda episcopa plunctifer*, was a member of the minnow family, *Cyprinidae*. This is the largest family of freshwater fishes in North America, containing more individuals than any other family. The family is closely related to the sucker family, *Catostomidae*, yet it differs in many ways. Minnows do not possess the sucker-like mouth, teeth, and spines. This species, like most in its family, spawned in spring or early summer. It possessed a series of multiple ribs from the posterior margin of the head to the tip of the tail. This made them excessively bony.

The species possessed a dark body with a dark lateral band around the snout, through the eye, and on the sides, extending to a faint caudal spot. Its length was an average of 2.5 inches. Its snout was blunt and the mouth was small.

Status	Extinct
Probable	
Extinction	c.1930
Family	Cyprinidae (Minnows)
Description	Distinguishing characteristic is a series of multiple ribs that made this species excessively bony.
Habitat	Slow flowing springs.
Food	Plants, minute animals, detritus.
Reproduction	Spawns in spring or early summer.
Causes for	
Extinction	Industrialization
Range	Mexico

minute animal life, and detritus.

Behavior

Though the specific food habits of the Parras roundnose minnow remain unknown, the minnow family feed on every type of food which could be found in rivers, streams, and lakes. This includes plants,

Habitat

The Parras roundnose minnow was endemic to the Chihuahua Desert near Parras, Coahuila, Mexico. The Parras springs are relics of a huge Pleistocene watershed which emerge from a lava hillside and are from the old Rio Nazas Watershed. They are isolated pockets of water.

Distribution

The Parras roundnose minnow was found in a small spring in Saltillo, Mexico, as well as Parras, but seems to have disappeared from both localities.

In 1953, Carl and Laura Hubbs investigated this area for any remaining populations and found that "there no longer are any natural springs in the immediate vicinity of Parras or anywhere in the Parras basin of in the great basin to the North." The habitat of this species, then, has been totally destroyed. This species became extinct approximately in 1930.

Causes for Extinction

Human intervention was the main cause for the extinction of this species. Parras Springs has a meager flow which has been combined by tunnels cut into the lava and channeled into a reservoir which first feed a cotton mill — then a series of irrigation ditches. To further hinder this species, the reservoir has been stocked with carp, which would have quickly eaten any surviving small fish.

Also See General Causes for Extinction of Fish Species, page 252.

Adapted from data compiled by the Threatened and Endangered Species Information Institute (Golden, CO) for *Beacham's International Threatened, Endangered, and Extinct Species* published on CD ROM, available from Beacham Publishing.

Stumptooth Minnow
Stypodon signifier

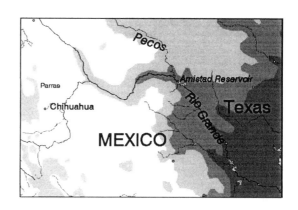

Description

The stumptooth minnow, *Stypodon signifier,* had an oblong, compressed body covered with large deciduous scales; a small, terminal mouth; a trenchant lower jaw without barbels; strong pharyngeal teeth, more or less cylindrical, with round grinding surfaces; a slender, subconical posterior; a decurved lateral line; short gill rakers, and short dorsal and anal fins. The color was brown above and silvery below. It had a broad lateral band bordered by a narrow silvery line.

Status	Extinct
Probable Extinction	1930s
Family Description	Brown and silvery minnow with an oblong, compressed body covered with large deciduous scales.
Habitat	Freshwater spring.
Food	Mollusks.
Causes for Extinction	Loss of habitat.
Range	Parras, Coahuila, Mexico.

Behavior

The stumptooth minnow was named for its large, molariform pharyngeal teeth, which evidently were specialized for feeding on the abundant mollusks.

Habitat/Distribution

Stypodon signifier represents a monotypic genus known only from six specimens: two

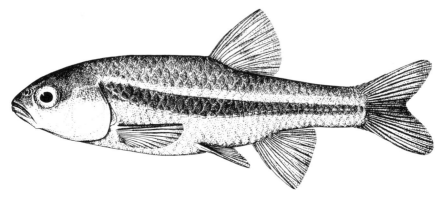

collected by Garman in 1880, and four in 1903, all taken from a spring or spring complex near Parras, Coahuila, Mexico.

Causes for Extinction

Parras Valley had abundant springs and spring water until the 1930s, when industry moved into the area. Habitat modification and loss of springs, and/or water pollution and irrigation practices that carried water into the cultivated fields were important factors in the species' decline. The snails, which were the stumptooth minnows' primary food source, may have been particularly sensitive to changes in the water level and deteriorating water quality. The area was surveyed by C. L. and L. C. Hubbs in 1953, and by Balderas in 1969, and no stumptooth minnows were found.

Parras Characodon
Characodon garmani

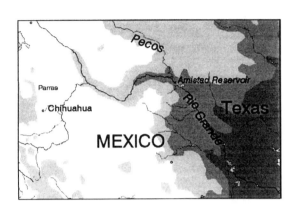

Description

The Parras characodon, *Characodon garmani,* had a robust, somewhat compressed body; a short snout; a longer, prominent lower chin; an eye diameter of 3.6 inches; and a rounded caudal fin.

Its color was olive reddish to light brownish. The males were a uniform color or with bars on the caudal peduncle. The sides of the females were more or less barred or blotched, and lighter in color than the males. The sides usually contained a dark broad lateral band, more broken up on the females. The males' dorsal and caudal fins had a dark band near the tip, bordered with a lighter tone. The larger males were red with only one or two blotches on the sides. Their color varied extensively. The species grew to about 1.5 inches.

Behavior

The fry were born in early June.

Habitat/Distribution

Characodon garmani is known from a single specimen collected by Edward Palmer,

Status	Extinct
Probable Extinction	1900
Family	Goodeid
Description	Red to brownish fish with a robust, somewhat compressed body and a short snout.
Habitat	Freshwater spring.
Reproduction	Fry were born in early June.
Causes for Extinction	Habitat alteration.
Range	Parras, Coahuila, Mexico

probably in the 1880s, from Parras, Coahuila, Mexico. It was classified by Jordan and Evermann in 1895, but was not recognized as a valid species until 1986, when Smith and Miller confirmed its taxon. According to Jordan and Evermann, *C. garmani* was very abundant in the large spring in the city of Durango.

Causes for Extinction

As with the stumptooth minnow and the

Parras pupfish, the decline of this fish was probably caused by the alteration of spring habitats. Parras Valley supported a highly endemic fish fauna, which largely disappeared near the turn of the twentieth century, and which met its final decline with industrialization of the valley during the 1930s.

Lake Titicaca Orestias
Orestias cuvieri

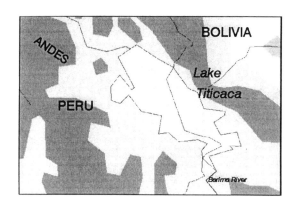

Description

The Lake Titicaca Orestias, *Orestias cuvieri*, was a small, flat-headed, cold-water fish, but comparatively large within its genus. The mouth was upturned so the face appeared almost vertically. The head was concave and took up a full one third of the overall body length. Full grown adults could measure up to 26.5 centimeters (10.5 inches).

Adults were greenish-yellow to amber on the upperside with a black lower jaw and black striped fins. The scales were very light at their center. The juveniles were blotched, spotted, and congregated in the deep, rock bottomed zones in the cold seasons.

Status	Extinct
Probable Extinction	c.1950
Family	Cyprinodontidae (Killifishes)
Description	Small, flat-headed fish with an upturned mouth, concave head, greenish-yellow to umber upperside and black striped fins.
Habitat	High mountain lakes.
Food	Aquatic animals.
Causes for Extinction	Exotic predator trout.
Range	Peru, Bolivia: Andes Mountains

Behavior

This species' upturned mouth allowed it to surface feed on small crustacea and other aquatic animals.

The juveniles congregated in the deep, rock bottomed zones in the cold seasons. The species was said to have gone through seasonal migrations.

Habitat/Distribution

This species was once found in Lake Titicaca in the Andes. The lake lies on the border of Peru and Bolivia and extends 240 kilometers (150 miles) in length. Located in the mountains, its elevation is 4,000 meters (13,000 feet).

This lake is considered small compared to the North American Great Lakes, but it is a massive body of water that is very deep.

Lake Titicaca Orestias, being a deep water fish, was inhibited from migrating via shallow waters and was thus confined to

Lake Titicaca itself. Other members of its family had established themselves in the Bolivian lakes, Poopo and Junim, and in three rivers and connecting waterways.

Selective netting in 1960 failed to procure a single specimen, though all the other Orestias, and numerous lake trout, were collected in the haul.

Causes for Extinction

This species appears to have been destroyed because of the introduction of lake trout, *Salvelinus namaycush,* by the U.S. Fish and Wildlife Service.

Also See General Causes for Extinction of Fish Species, page 252.

Adapted from data compiled by the Threatened and Endangered Species Information Institute (Golden, CO) for *Beacham's International Threatened, Endangered, and Extinct Species* published on CD ROM, available from Beacham Publishing.

New Zealand Grayling
Prototroctes oxyrhynchus

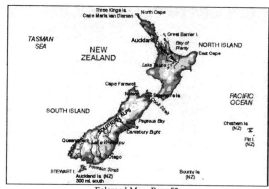

Enlarged Map, Page 52

Description

The New Zealand Grayling, *Prototroctes oxyrhynchus*, was recorded to grow to a length of 50 centimeters (20 inches) and weigh as much as 1.4 kilogram (3 pounds). This species of fish was superficially trout-like, apart from its high dorsal fin.

The exact color of this fish is not known, for when it was caught on its way upstream it was colored a silvery hue with a slate-blue back. After several months in the river, however, this species was often found to be a rich red brown, speckled with gray, with an almost golden hue on its belly.

Behavior

No scientists have ever studied this species and most information is speculative or based on analogy with its only known relative, *Prototroctes maraena*, the Cucumber Herring of southeastern Australia and Tasmania.

It is possible that this species spawned at sea since no individuals were ever taken in fresh water under the size of 12.5 cm (5 inches).

It was reported that this species was often caught on baited fishing hooks but its teeth and intestines suggest that it was primarily an algae eater. Most contemporary reports state that the New Zealand Grayling was a night feeder.

Status	Extinct
Probable Extinction	c.1923
Family	Prototroctidae (Herrings)
Description	Medium-sized fish with a silvery hue and slate-blue back but was also found in a rich red-brown speckled with gray.
Habitat	Swift water in the stony-bedded bottoms of streams and rivers.
Food	Algae
Reproduction	Possibly spawned at sea.
Causes for Extinction	Exotic predators, loss of habitat, industrialization.
Range	New Zealand

Habitat

This species moved in shoals, a large school of fish, and was rarely reported more than 48 kilometers (30 miles) from salt water. It preferred the swift water and the stony-bedded bottoms of streams and rivers.

Distribution

This fish was plentiful in the swift stream waters of both islands in New Zealand when settlers first moved on the islands in the 1980's, but by the end of the century they had all but disappeared. One individual was caught in 1904 and was exhibited in a hotel in Poptiki.

In March 1923, Te Rangi Hiroa, also known as Sir Peter Buck, caught a number of New Zealand Grayling in the Waiapu River, in far eastern North Island, New Zealand. These were the last individuals reliably recorded, though rumors of their survival in the remote lower Westland district of South Island, New Zealand, are still current.

This species became extinct in approximately in 1923.

Causes for Extinction

The introduction of British Brown Trout and Rainbow Trout was almost certainly the main factor in eliminating this species from its habitat; however, it did disappear before the trout took up residence in some areas.

Also See General Causes for Extinction of Fish Species, page 252.

Adapted from data compiled by the Threatened and Endangered Species Information Institute (Golden, CO) for *Beacham's International Threatened, Endangered, and Extinct Species* published on CD ROM, available from Beacham Publishing.

EXTINCT MAMMALS OF SOUTHERN AFRICA

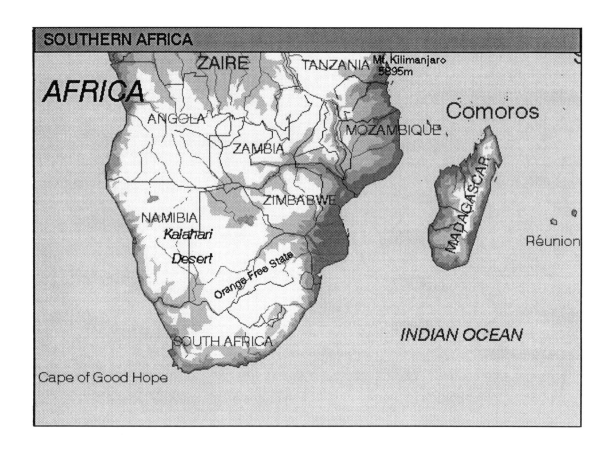

Lion Behavior

Lions in general live in fixed groups called prides — they are the only species of cat which do so. The pride may include up to 25 animals consisting of about 6 adult males with the rest females and cubs. Members of a pride communicate with each other through roaring. A far off lion may roar to call to other pride members. The other members will roar back as a signal of where they are. To non-pride members, the roars are a warning to stay away from the established territory of the pride. The females of the pride are related to each other while the males all leave when they are 3 years old. Brothers may leave together in search of another pride to take over from other males.

Newborns are spotted with woolly fur and their eyes remain closed for a few days after birth. For the first few weeks, they remain hidden in the grass. Nursing for up to 7 months, they nevertheless begin eating meat at 3 months of age. After 8 weeks, they are able to keep up with the rest of the pride in its wanderings. Any female in the pride will nurse the cubs even if the cubs are not their own. Though the cubs will not participate in a kill for up to a year, they spend their time playing games with other cubs that teach them the skills they will need to hunt.

The species hunted for its food. Working together, a pride of lions could kill animals much larger than a single individual. The species would have eaten a wide variety of prey including zebra, wildebeest, antelope, buffalo, and smaller animals. Females did most of the hunting due to their smaller and less conspicuous size. They could stalk better undetected than the males. A pride may have spent an entire day resting near a herd of prey. At night, they began to stalk, fanning out in a circle around the herd. They would then rush at the herd and either bring down a victim themselves or drive the victim into the claws of a fellow pride member.

A number of prey may have been brought down or perhaps just one. Each member of the pride would fight over feeding rights. Individuals would gorge themselves eating as much as they could. If there was enough food, cubs would get a chance to feed. If not, they would starve. When food was scarce, the pride would attempt to steal the kills of other predators such as wild dogs or hyenas.

Lions use the special adaptation of their sharp, rasp-like tongue to crush their food. They possess only sharp, razor-like teeth but no flat teeth for crushing and chewing their food. Thus, they turn their heads to the side when feeding using their sharp tongue to push food around their teeth to cut it into swallowable pieces.

Lions in general are diurnal. Sleeping and resting may occur day or night depending on the availability of food. Often a pride will rest throughout the day near a herd of prey. When night draws near, they will begin to stalk and hunt, feeding and resting the remainder of the night if the hunt is successful.

The home territory of an individual pride may have covered up to 100 square miles. Adult males marked the boundaries of this territory with urine letting other lions know the area had been claimed. Wandering individuals from other prides were chased out of the established territory.

Quagga
Equus burchelli quagga

Burchell's Zebra
Equus burchelli burchelli

Enlarged Map, Page 304

Description

The quagga, *Equus burchelli quagga,* may have been one of the most recognized of the wild horses. This species' markings yielded confusion and many people identified it as the female of *E. b. burchelli,* Burchell's Zebra. This species was brown with white legs and tail. Rather than entirely striped like typical zebras, the quagga possessed stripes only on the head and neck. Below, the species had no distinctive markings. The mane was short and spikey. The quagga possessed a defensive behavior and would attack intruders.

This species was given the name Quahah by the Hottentots. The name was given in honor of this species shrill warning cry 'kwa-ha-ha, kwa-ha-ha'.

Burchell's Zebra, *Equus burchelli burchelli,* was quite similar in appear to the quagga (*E. b. quagga*) and may have even interbred with this species. *E. b. burchelli* had white legs, a white tail and striped markings over its entire body. The mane of this species was short and erect.

Behavior

These species ate grass and other vegetation. Equus species are most active during

Status	Extinct
Probable Extinction	*E.b. quagga* c.1883 *E.b. burchelli* c.1910
Family	Equidae (Horses)
Description	Wild horse resembling a zebra; brown with white legs and tail; with stripes only on the head and neck; mane was short and spikey.
Habitat	Grassland of South Africa.
Food	Grass and other vegetation.
Causes for Extinction	Hunted for food, pelts; exported for display in zoos.
Range	South Africa: Cape Colony veldt and Orange Free State.

the day, but will rest during the hottest parts of the day.

E. b. burchelli and *E. B. quagga* were always associated with wildebeests or hartebeests, and ostriches. This phenomenon is believed to have occurred for mutual protection. With the ostrich's keen eyesight, the antelope's unique sense of smell and *E.b. burchelli*'s acute hearing, a better chance was given for them to flee predators long before they could get close enough to pose any sort of threat. They could be found in herds of thousands.

Habitat/Distribution

Burchell's zebra inhabited the plains and grassland of South Africa until about 1910; the quagga was restricted to the Cape Colony veldt and Orange Free State of South Africa. The quagga was extirpated from this range in about 1883.

Causes for Extinction

The quagga and Burchell's zebra were not particularly singled out for hunting and exploitation but the species' limited range made it particularly vulnerable. The Boers of Cape Colony exploited these animals' defensive behavior and used the quagga to guard their domestic horses.

The Boers' mainstay was that of "Quagga farming." The Boers raised and killed these zebras for their skins, which were used for sacks and other everyday items, and their meat was used for food.

The quagga and Burchell's zebra became a prize and were exported to such places as England. After arriving in its new home the species would be tamed and used for pull horses by the rich or placed in zoos for display.

Adapted from data compiled by the Threatened and Endangered Species Information Institute (Golden, CO) for *Beacham's International Threatened, Endangered, and Extinct Species* published on CD ROM, available from Beacham Publishing.

Photo of a quagga by Russell Norton

Burchell's Zebra

Blue Buck

Hippotragus leucophaeus

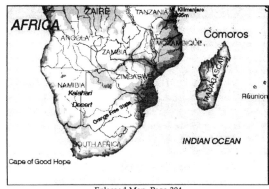

Enlarged Map, Page 304

Description

The blue buck, *Hippotragus leucophaeus*, was the first African species to be extirpated at the hands of man. This mighty antelope had a blue pelt, curved horns and seasonal beard. It is not known whether or not females possessed horns, although it is believed that both sexes did. Being a member of the Bovidae family, this species had no upper canines and the molars were smooth in texture. The stomach of this species was four chambered. From data collected from other *Hippotragus* species (spp. *H. equinus, H. niger*), this animal was probably about 75 to 94 inches from snout to tail base. The tail of this species was 14 to 18 inches long. The blue buck stood 46-57 inches from ground to shoulder and weighed 450 to 660 pounds.

This species was also known as the blue goat.

Behavior

The blue buck most likely traveled in small herds. Females probably gave birth to 1 or 2 young a year. Antelope (and probably this species) are preyed upon by lions, cheetahs, hyenas and wild dogs.

Status	Extinct
Probable Extinction	c.1800
Family	Bovine (Antelopes, sheep, cows)
Description	Antelope weighing 450-660 pounds, with blue pelt, curved horns, and seasonal beard.
Habitat	Wooded areas and savannahs adjacent to woods in South Africa.
Food	Probably grasses, herbs, leaves, twigs, bark, buds, fruit and insects.
Reproduction	Females probably gave birth to 1 or 2 young a year.
Causes for Extinction	Hunted for its unique blue pelt; encroachment by man.
Range	South Africa: Zwellendam

Antelope in general eat grasses, herbs, leaves, twigs, bark, buds, fruit and insects. Most antelope eat during early morning and late afternoon.

Habitat

The blue buck inhabited wooded areas and savannahs adjacent to woods in South Africa. The last recorded population was reported from wooded hills above Soete Melk.

Distribution

The blue buck was known from Zwellendam in South Africa until about 1799.

Causes for Extinction

The Portuguese were the first to inhabit the Cape of Zwellendam in the 1600s. In 1652 the Dutch began to settle South Africa. In the centuries to follow, European countries battled for territory and commercial exploitation. With the invasion of European settlers in South Africa, a malaise came over much of the area. Areas became so populated that animals were forced into other areas. For those species which had created a specialized niche for themselves, overcrowding meant extirpation. In addition to this phenomenon, Blue buck was hunted for its unique blue pelt, and its meat was fed to dogs. Blue buck was no match for the technological advances of the European settlers. Guns determined the ultimate fate for this species.

Adapted from data compiled by the Threatened and Endangered Species Information Institute (Golden, CO) for *Beacham's International Threatened, Endangered, and Extinct Species* published on CD ROM, available from Beacham Publishing.

Cape Lion

Panthera leo melanochaitus

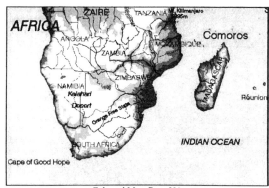

Enlarged Map, Page 304

Description

Once among the largest of all lions, the Cape lion, *Panthera leo melanochaitus,* weighed as much as 227 kilograms (500 pounds) and measured up to 300 centimeters (10 feet) in length. The male of the species was known for its mane, which was thick and black. It extended beyond the shoulders with a fringe of black hair under the belly. The tail was stout and the head was large in the shape of a bull dog. Females were smaller and paler in color.

Species from this family possess a horny papillae on the tongue. They have short faces, forward-pointing eyes, and domed heads. They have successfully adapted to a wide variety of environments due to their binocular vision and unique dentition.

Behavior

See Lion Behavior, page 304.

Habitat

The range of this subspecies stretched across scrub and savanna habitat. Scrub lands are characterized by low, woody perennial vegetation. Summers are normally

Status	Extinct
Probable Extinction	1858
Family	Felidae (Cat)
Description	Among the largest of all lions, weighing up to 500 pounds, with a thick and black mane extending beyond the shoulders and a fringe of black hair under the belly.
Habitat	Scrub and savanna grasslands.
Food	Variety of mammals, including zebra, wildebeest, antelope, buffalo, and smaller animals.
Reproduction	Usually 2-3 cubs every 2 years after gestation of 108 days.
Causes for Extinction	Unknown. Overhunting was a contributing cause.
Range	South Africa

hot and dry and the winters are mild and wet. Total annual rainfall ranges from 250 to 500 millimeters (10 to 20 inches). Average summer temperature is 20 degrees Celsius (68 degrees Fahrenheit).

Savanna grasslands are made up of grass covered plains. There are few and scattered trees across this landscape due to the dry climate. A common tree is the baobab which stores up to 120,000 liters (32,000 gallons) of water in its trunk. Rain falls primarily in the summer months with the remainder of the year being hot and arid.

Distribution

The cape lion once ranged over the southern tip of South Africa.

Causes for Extinction

The extinction of this subspecies remains a mystery to researchers. Soon after the arrival of Europeans, its numbers diminished, but it is likely it was already in decline before European influence. However, already rare, the cape lion was hunted it beyond its numbers by Dutch and English settlers, and this was the final cause of the subspecies' extinction. The last individual sighted was killed in 1858.

Adapted from data compiled by the Threatened and Endangered Species Information Institute (Golden, CO) for *Beacham's International Threatened, Endangered, and Extinct Species* published on CD ROM, available from Beacham Publishing.

Gelada Baboon
Theropithecus darti

Enlarged Map, Page 304

Description

The gelada baboon, *Theropithecus darti*, was a species of *Theropithecus*, of which only one species currently exists, *T. gelada*, and it is endangered. *Theropithecus* seems to have been a divergent species of Papio. Most believe the speciation occurred some time during the Pliocene, when these species invaded grassland habitats.

The gelada baboon was described by Jolly in 1972. Much controversy has resulted over the taxonomic treatment of this species. Many authorities argue that this species is a member of the genus Papio, while others think that it is one of Macaca. This species is not a true baboon, but most recent authorities consider it to be most closely related to Papio and think that it deserves generic distinction.

The gelada baboon was gray to dark brown in color. It was sexually dimorphic. Males had white sideburns and a blackish brown "cape" or mane, consisting of a series of long hairs. Both sexes had pink skin on the front of the neck running down to the chest. This skin was in an hourglass-shape and was surrounded by white fur in males, and by raised vesicles in females. The gelada baboon was rather large and heavily built,

Status	Extinct
Probable Extinction	Unknown
Family	Cercopithecidae (Old World monkeys)
Description	Gray to dark brown baboon with pink skin on the front of the neck, a caved-in snout, and a somewhat bare chest.
Habitat	Central mountains above 2000 meters.
Food	Grass, grass seeds, and grass bulbs.
Reproduction	Gestation period of six months.
Causes for Extinction	Agricultural development, human encroachment.
Range	Southern Africa

had a caved-in snout and was somewhat bare chested. From the tip of the snout to the tip of the tail this species was about 19.7-29.6 inches in length. The tail was 15.8-21.7 inches long and shoulder height was 15.8-25.6 inches. The weight of the gelada baboon was probably between 22-44 pounds. Males are generally much larger than females in *T. gelada*.

Behavior

Communication of primates is most generally displayed with physical color patterns and facial expressions. Gelada communication has been studied recently and the gelada baboon probably used the same sort of communication methods. Male geladas will reveal their white teeth and gums of the upper jaw with a simple eversion of the upper lip; simultaneously, the scalp is retracted to reveal the eyelids. This communication can be observed in rage, fear or jealousy. Males will round up straying females with a barking vocalization along with the previously described "lipflip".

The social system of the gelada baboon was one in which individuals organized themselves into "quasi-military" units, consisting of up to 400 individuals. Within smaller groups the females displayed hierarchy. Those higher on the ladder would protect inferior males. Fights between males for the attention of females may have resulted in a change in the order of command within the troop.

Menstruation lasted for about 32-36 days. Pregnant females were distinguished by a swelling of the chest vesicles and simultaneous brilliant pink coloration of these vesicles. Gestation lasted for about six months and lactation extended through about 18 months. The chest patch became scarlet during lactation. The nipples were located close together on the chest, which allowed for the young to take in both nipples when feeding.

Primates have a primarily omnivorous diet, displayed in the uniform development of the cusps and lack of specialization of

dentition. However, the gelada baboon was strictly herbivorous; as a result the cheek teeth possessed defined ridges used to mince vegetation. The main food of this species was grass, grass seeds and grass bulbs.

This species was diurnally active.

Habitat

The gelada baboon was limited to the central mountains above 2,000 meters (6,562 feet) in southern Africa. At night this species took shelter on cliffs along gorges. During the day the gelada baboon may have been observed feeding on grasses in montane grasslands. The gelada baboon was probably found at altitudes of 6,550-16,400 feet in alpine meadows, rocky gorges and other treeless areas.

Distribution

The gelada baboon is considered to have diverged from Papio in the Pliocene. Fossil evidence from this era indicates Theropithecus ranged from as far north as Ternifine on the Mediterranean coast of Africa to Swartkrans and Makapan in South Africa. The gelada baboon was known to have occupied regions of southern Africa prior to extinction.

Causes for Extinction

The gelada baboon was threatened by agricultural development and human encroachment and settlement. Agricultural practices forced this species into less suitable habitat. Grass density was lower and as a direct result population size decreased. With intense agricultural development this species' habitat was altered by Eucalyptus plantations. Trees were also cut by natives for the use of fuel.

Traditionally, every 8 years Galla tribesmen shoot large numbers of males for their capes. These capes are used to make head-dresses and capes which are worn during ceremonies. The gelada baboon may have been persecuted for similar reasons.

Adapted from data compiled by the Threatened and Endangered Species Information Institute (Golden, CO) for *Beacham's International Threatened, Endangered, and Extinct Species* published on CD ROM, available from Beacham Publishing.

EXTINCT MAMMALS OF NORTH AFRICA

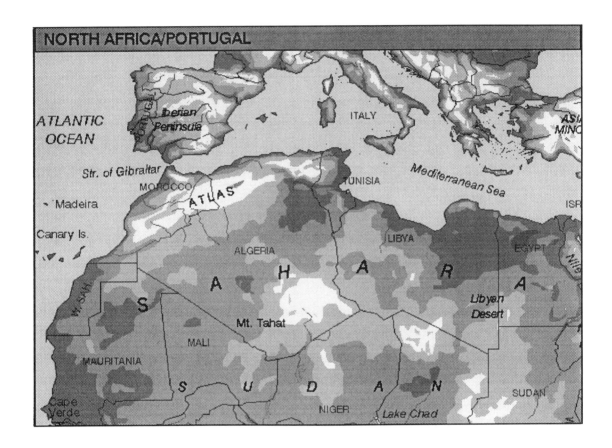

NORTH AFRICA/PORTUGAL

Bear Behavior

In general, adult bears are individualistic in behavior and normally are solitary wanderers. Except when caring for young or breeding, bears have individual patterns of behavior. Individuals probably react from learned experiences. Two individual bears may respond in opposite ways to the same situation. Strict territoriality is unknown, with defense limited to specific food concentrations, defense of young, and surprise encounters.

Each bear appears to have a minimum distance within which another bear or person cannot enter; any intrusion of this distance may evoke a threat or an attack. Surprise is an important factor in many confrontations involving bears and humans. A female with young exhibits an almost reflexive response to any surprise intrusion or perceived threat to her individual distance. Bears will also defend a kill or carrion out of a perceived need.

Bears of all ages will readily congregate at plentiful food sources and form a social hierarchy unique to that grouping of bears. Mating season is the only time that adult males and females tolerate one another and then it is only during the estrous period. Other social affiliations are generally restricted to family groups or mother and offspring, siblings that may stay together for several years after being weaned and an occasional alliance of subadults or several females and their offspring.

Mating generally occurs from late May through mid-July, with a peak in mid-June. Estrus lasts from a few days to over a month. Females in estrus are receptive to practically all adult males. A male may isolate and defend a female in areas of low bear density; but in areas of high density, males and females may both be promiscuous. Age of first reproduction and litter size varies and may be related to nutritional state. Individuals may begin mating anywhere from age 3.5 to 8.5 with an average in the grizzly populations of 5.5. Litter sizes also vary from 1 to 3 cubs with an average of 2. Intervals between pregnancies average 3 years.

The search for food is a prime influence on movements. Upon emergence from the den in the early spring or late winter, bears seek the lower elevations, drainage bottoms, and ungulate winter ranges, where their food requirements can be met. Throughout late spring and early summer, they follow plant phenology back to higher elevations.

Bears, in general, are very adaptable when it comes to eating. They will eat whatever is available or in season. They feed primarily on plants, fruit, and insects. Using their long, curved claws, they dig for roots. They may eat small mammals and carrion. Usually they feed and forage alone. Only females and her cubs will feed together.

Bears must have food rich in protein or carbohydrates in excess of maintenance requirements in order to survive denning and post-denning periods. They are opportunistic feeders and will prey or scavenge on almost any available food including ground squirrels, ungulates, carrion, and garbage. When animal matter is scarce, they will feed on roots, bulbs, tubers, fungi, and tree cambium to meet their protein requirements. High quality foods such as berries, nuts, and fish are also important in some areas for food sources.

Upon emergence from the den in late winter, they seek the lower elevations, drainage bottoms, and ungulate winter ranges where their food requirements can be met. Throughout late spring and early summer, they follow plant phenology back to higher elevations. In late summer and fall, there is a transition to fruit and nut sources, as well as herbaceous materials. However, this is a generalized pattern and it should be kept in mind that bears are individuals trying to survive and will go where they can best meet their food requirements.

The unavailability of food and low ambient air temperatures appear to make winter sleep essential to the bears' survival. When rodents and bats hibernate, they enter into a periodic phenomenon in which body temperature falls to a low level approximating the habitat, and heart rate, metabolic rate and physiologic functions fall to a correspondingly minimum level. By contrast, bears are homeo-hypothermic hibernators whose body temperature drops no more than 5 degrees Celsius (10 degrees Fahrenheit) and is maintained there indefinitely. With normal fat reserves, bears are capable of fasting for six months with only slight reductions in body temperature. They do exhibit a marked depression in heart rate and respiratory frequency, but only a relatively slight drop in body temperature. Day length and inclement weather have been documented as influencing the onset of winter sleep or hibernation.

Digging of dens is probably instinctive. It starts as early as September or may take place just prior to entry in late November. Dens are usually dug on steep slopes where in cold climates wind and topography cause an accumulation of deep snow, and where the snow is unlikely to melt during warm periods. Elevations of dens vary geographically, but generally they are found at higher elevations well away from any development or activity by humans. Finding an isolated area that will be protected well enough to minimize the escape of body-warmed air, and one that will provide a secure environment for a five-month sleep, appears to be a factor favoring survival of the species.

Tiger Behavior

The tiger is thought to have originated in northern Eurasia and moved southward. It's modern range extends from Siberia and Turkistan south to Sumatra. The size, color and striped markings vary according to locality and race. Tigers of the south are smaller and more brightly colored. The Bengal tiger and other tigers of southeast Asia are bright reddish tan, marked with dark transverse stripes; the underparts, inner sides of the limbs, the cheeks, and a large spot over each eye are whitish. Tigers have no mane, but in old males the hair on the cheeks puffs out.

Tigers inhabit grassy and swampy terrain, and forests. They swim well, enjoy bathing, and under duress climb trees. They hunt by night and prey on a variety of animals, including deer, wild hogs and large land birds. Tigers generally avoid stalking healthy large animals, although there are records of tigers attacking elephants and adult buffalo. Tigers will attack domestic animals, and an old or disabled tiger, or a tigress with cubs, will attack any weaker animal, including humans. In general tigers are nocturnal, sleeping and resting during the day and hunting alone at night. Often an individual will rest throughout the day near a herd of prey. Some of the slower tiger subspecies stalk their prey, rush, and pull it to the ground. The tiger camps near a kill for a number of days, eating and resting until all of the meat and most of the bones are consumed. It then grooms, drinks, and rests before hunting again.

Tigers in general live a solitary life away from other individuals. The largest social unit is an adult female with her cubs. They will gather together only if food is plentiful. They do communicate with one another through scents and sounds. When two individuals meet, the encounter is usually friendly. They may rub heads and make puffing sounds.

In warm regions, tigers produce young at any time of year; in cold regions young are born in the spring. Females will give birth at two or three year intervals. Pregnancy lasts an average of 3.5 months. Litter size is usually two or three, although five and six have been recorded. Cubs will nurse for six months although they will be taken on a hunt at two months of age. Cubs gradually spend more and more time on their own, becoming independent by age two. A female tiger will not breed again until her cubs are independent.

Bubal Hartebeest
Alcelaphus buselaphus buselaphus

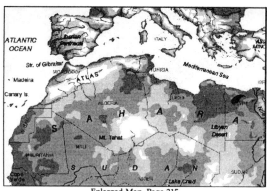

Enlarged Map, Page 315

Description

The bubal hartebeest, *Alcelaphus buselaphus buselaphus,* was a subspecies (ssp.) of *Alcelaphus buselaphus,* the hartebeest. Bubal hartebeest measured 59 to 96 inches from the tip of the snout to the base of the tail. This species stood 43 to 59 inches (about 4 feet) measured from the ground to the shoulder, had a 11.8 to 27.6 inch long tail and weighed 220 to 496 pounds. Males were the larger of the species. Being a member of the Bovidae family, this species had no upper canines and the molars were smooth in texture. The stomach of this species was four chambered.

Behavior

The bubal hartebeest could be found in large herds. This species most likely fed on desert vegetation, as well as leaves, bark and grasses during cooler times of the day, during the early hours and the late afternoon.

Females probably gave birth to 1 or 2 young a year. Antelope (and probably this species) are preyed upon by lions, cheetahs, hyenas and wild dogs.

Status	Extinct
Probable Extinction	c.1923
Family	Bovidae (Antelopes, goats, cattle)
Description	Antelope measuring 59 to 96 inches from the tip of the snout to the base of the tail; stood about 4 feet; tail was 11.8 to 27.6 inches long; weighed 220 to 496 pounds.
Habitat	Mountains of Algeria and the Moroccan High Atlas.
Food	Probably desert vegetation, as well as leaves, bark and grasses.
Reproduction	Females probably gave birth to 1 or 2 young a year.
Causes for Extinction	Massive hunting.
Range	North Africa, Arabia

Habitat

This montane species roamed the mountains of Algeria and the Moroccan High

Atlas. Because the mountains were inaccessible, bubal hartebeests were able to survive for many years, safe from the hands of its newly introduced human predator. This species was also found in the Algerian desert.

Distribution

The bubal hartebeest ranged from Morocco to Egypt and may have extended into Palestine and Arabia.

Causes for Extinction

When the French began their occupation of Morocco, they organized hunting games that resulted in huge massacres of the bubal hartebeest.

Adapted from data compiled by the Threatened and Endangered Species Information Institute (Golden, CO) for *Beacham's International Threatened, Endangered, and Extinct Species* published on CD ROM, available from Beacham Publishing.

Portuguese Ibex
Capra pyrenaica lusitanica

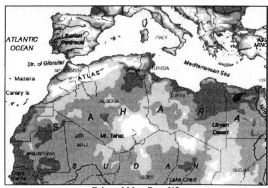

Enlarged Map, Page 315

Description

The Portuguese Ibex, *Capra pyrenaica lusitanica*, was distinguished by its brown markings and its 51 centimeters (20 inches) long, uniquely wide and closely set horns.

Behavior

This species was herbivorous, feeding on grasses, herbs, shrubs, and other plants. This species, like all four-chambered stomached species, would regurgitate ingested food and chew this partly digested food (cud) thoroughly, swallow and digest it entirely.

Habitat

The Portuguese Ibex inhabited rocky and mountainous areas. This area is characterized by a scrub biome with an average annual temperature of 17.3 degrees Celsius and rainfall of 627 millimeters (24.45 inches). The vegetation of this area consists of grass and other herbaceous plants, and broadleaf evergreen trees found in groups or singly.

Status	Extinct
Probable Extinction	c.1892
Family	Bovidae (Antelopes, goats, cattle)
Description	Wild goat with brown markings and long, closely set, wide horns.
Habitat	Rocky and mountainous areas characterized by a scrub biome.
Food	Grasses, herbs, shrubs, and other plants.
Causes for Extinction	Hunted for valuable horns, meat, and pelts.
Range	Portugal: Galicia and Northwest Iberian Mountains

Distribution

The Portuguese Ibex was known from the Galicia and Northwest Iberian Mountains of Portugal.

Causes for Extinction

This species was relatively unharmed until its horns became a trophy item. The villagers also utilized the horns to make trumpets or horns which could carry a call across the valleys of the northwest mountains of the Iberian peninsula. What was a protective device for one species became fashionable decoration or musical instrument for another. The Portuguese ibex was also hunted for its meat, pelt and the stones it carried in its stomach. The meat was used for food. The pelt was made into coverlets. The stones were thought to possess medicinal powers. Many villagers believed these stones provided antidotes to many poisons. Males were killed much more often than females, causing a gender imbalance that pressured the population.

Diseases carried by domestic livestock were transmitted to the Portuguese ibex, creating further pressure on survival rate. This species was also occasionally the victim of avalanches.

Adapted from data compiled by the Threatened and Endangered Species Information Institute (Golden, CO) for *Beacham's International Threatened, Endangered, and Extinct Species* published on CD ROM, available from Beacham Publishing.

Barbary Lion
Panthera leo leo

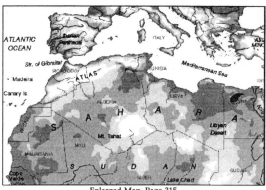

Enlarged Map, Page 315

Description

Once among the largest of all lions, the Barbary lion, *Panthera leo leo*, weighed as much as 227 kilograms (500 pounds) and measured up to 300 centimeters (10 feet) in length. The male of the species was known for its mane, which covered almost half its body and was a dusky ocher color. It extended to the middle of the back and portions of the underparts. Females were smaller and paler in color and the inside of their foreleg was white.

Other species from this family possess a horny papillae on the tongue. They have short faces, forward-pointing eyes, and domed heads. The species has successfully adapted to a wide variety of environments due to their binocular vision and unique dentition.

Behavior

See Lion Behavior, page 304.

Habitat

This species occurred in temperate for-

Status	Extinct
Probable Extinction	1922
Family	Felidae (Cat)
Description	Large lion weighing up to 500 pounds, with a dusky ocher colored mane that covered almost half its body and extended to the middle of the back and portions of the underparts.
Habitat	Scrub and savanna grasslands.
Food	Variety of mammals including zebra, wildebeest, antelope, buffalo, and smaller animals.
Reproduction	Usually 2-3 cubs every 2 years after gestation of 108 days.
Causes for Extinction	Habitat destruction; hunting.
Range	Algeria, Morocco.

ests with rainfall between 300 and 1,200 mm (12 to 48 in) evenly spread over the year. No dry season befell this area. Summer lasted from 4 to 6 months and was productive for all forms of life. Though cold enough for most species of plant to cease growth, winters were mild with an average temperature of minus 2 degrees Celsius (28 degrees Fahrenheit) in the coldest months. Only three months out of the year possessed a mean temperature below zero degrees Celsius (32 degrees F).

Distribution

This species once ranged over all of North Africa. Habitats were destroyed, causing the desert to expand so that its range gradually dwindled to the forest and mountain regions of Morocco and Algeria.

Causes for Extinction

This particular subspecies of lion always held the interest of humanity. In ancient times, the Roman Empire used the subspecies for the arena and gladiatorial combats. In the popularized scenario of feeding Christian martyrs to man-eating lions, Barbary lion were the lions used for these events. Roman emperors — including Julius Caesar and Pompey — captured hundreds of individuals at a time and showed them off in the arena. In more recent times, the subspecies has been hunted by French and Arab sportsmen.

Though the subspecies has been widely hunted and captured for use in various human activities, the primary reason for its extinction lies with the destruction of its habitat, which has been gradually destroyed by humans over a period of 2,000 years.

In ancient times, North Africa was not a desert. Rather it consisted of rich forest lands

capable of supporting large cats and bears. Even pre-Christian Romans knew this area to be mostly forested. Yet, because it fell under Roman rule, this land was ruthlessly plundered and exploited to feed the great consumer economy of the Roman Empire. Timber was cut down at break-neck speed to supply the natives of Rome. Building materials from this area supplied the Empire for centuries. Vast areas were cleared for breeding sheep and goats. Over the years, the habitat began to change.

Sand is characteristic of North African soil. Without covering vegetation, the soil eroded and dune formations began to appear. The Great Sahara Desert had been formed and, once started, would prove impossible to stop. Even today, the desert in this region continues to expand.

The Barbary lion struggled to survive these changes by retreating from the shifting desert sands to the mountains and partially forested regions of Morocco and Algeria. But, by this time, the basis of world power had been shifted from Rome to Europe. Europeans sold firearms to the native people of Morocco and Algeria. The remnant population of Barbary lions was now at risk to the hands of hunters. The species managed to survive into the 1870s though they continued to steadily decline, and hunting was certainly the final blow leading to extinction. The last individual reported was seen in 1922 right before it was shot to death.

Adapted from data compiled by the Threatened and Endangered Species Information Institute (Golden, CO) for *Beacham's International Threatened, Endangered, and Extinct Species* published on CD ROM, available from Beacham Publishing.

Atlas Bear
Ursus arctos crowtheri

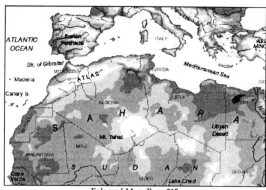

Enlarged Map, Page 315

Description

Africa's only native bear, the Atlas bear, *Ursus arctos crowtheri*, was much smaller in size than the American black bear. However, it was more solidly formed with a shorter face, a broader, pointed muzzle, and short toes and claws. It ranged in color from black to brownish-black and its coat was shaggy, growing to a length between 10 and 13 centimeters (4 and 5 inches). Some individuals sported an orange rufous color on the underparts.

Behavior

See Bear Behavior, page 315.

Habitat

The Atlas bear occurred in temperate forests with rainfall of 300 to 1,200 mm (12 to 48 inches), evenly spread over the year. No dry season befell this area. Summer lasted from 4 to 6 months and was productive for all forms of life. Though cold enough for most species of plant to cease growth, winters were mild with an average temperature of minus 2 degrees Celsius (28 degrees Fahrenheit) in the coldest months. Only three months out of the year possessed a mean temperature below zero degrees Celsius (32 degrees F).

Status	Extinct
Probable Extinction	1860s
Family	Ursidae (Bear)
Description	Smaller but more solid than the American black bear, with a shorter face, a broader, pointed muzzle, and short toes and claws; color is black to brownish-black with a shaggy coat.
Habitat	Temperate forests.
Food	Plants, berries, fruits, roots, some carrion.
Reproduction	1-3 cubs every 2-3 years.
Causess for Extinction	Habitat degradation; hunting.
Range	Algeria, Morocco

Distribution

This species once ranged over all of North Africa. As its habitat was destroyed and turned to desert lands, its range gradually dwindled to the forest and mountain regions of Morocco and Algeria.

Causes for Extinction

This extinct species is believed to have been widely hunted in ancient times, the Middle Ages, and colonial times. The Greek historian Herodotus wrote about the "Libyan Bear". This species was also referred to by ancient Roman writers, Virgil, Juvenal, and Martial. The species was imported to Italy in 61 B.C. by the Roman magistrate, Domitius Ahenobarbus for cruel sports of the arena.

Though the subspecies has been widely hunted and captured for use in various human activities, the primary reason for its extinction lies with the destruction of its habitat, which has been gradually destroyed by humans over a period of 2,000 years.

In ancient times, North Africa was not a desert. Rather it consisted of rich forest lands capable of supporting large cats and bears. Even pre-Christian Romans knew this area to be mostly forested. Yet, because it fell under Roman rule, this land was ruthlessly plundered and exploited to feed the great consumer economy of the Roman Empire. Timber was cut down at break-neck speed to supply the natives of Rome. Building materials from this area supplied the Empire for centuries. Vast areas were cleared for breeding sheep and goats. Over the years, the habitat began to change.

Sand is characteristic of North African soil. Without covering vegetation, the soil eroded and dune formations began to appear. The Great Sahara Desert had been formed and, once started, would prove impossible to stop. Even today, the desert in this region continues to expand.

U.a. crowtheri struggled to survive these changes by retreating from the shifting desert sands to the mountains and partially forested regions of Morocco and Algeria. But, by this time, the basis of world power had shifted from Rome to Europe. Europeans sold firearms to the native people of Morocco and Algeria. The remnant population of *U. a. crowtheri* was now at risk by the hands of hunters. The species managed to survive into the 1860s. In 1867, there were reports of numerous bears near Edough in the Moroccan and Algerian mountain regions. "The animal was said to be small, thickset, and brown, with a white spot on the throat, and to be very fond of honey and fruits." This was the last confirmed report of the species. It has not been seen since.

Adapted from data compiled by the Threatened and Endangered Species Information Institute (Golden, CO) for *Beacham's International Threatened, Endangered, and Extinct Species* published on CD ROM, available from Beacham Publishing.

EXTINCT MAMMALS OF AUSTRALIA AND THE SOUTH PACIFIC

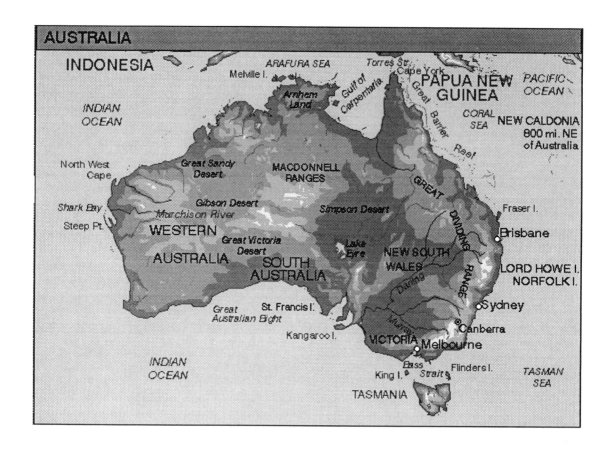

Decline of Wildlife in Australia

Less than 200 years ago, Australian vegetation was still in its primal stage. In the short history of modern Australia, vast changes have come to the native vegetation. Agricultural expansion stripped whole regions, substituting introduced crops, pastures and plantations, while forested areas were cut through for timber. Enormous central and northern areas, too arid for agriculture or too remote for harvesting timber, were stocked with millions of sheep and cattle. Many weeds were introduced, as were rabbits and brush fires, all of which contributed to the degradation of the land. The speed with which Australia's flora and fauna have disappeared is of great concern to the Australian government, which has established reserves — some people fear too late to help — to protect vanishing wildlife. Australia's best known animals, the marsupials, have long been targeted as enemies of agricultural development and ranching, and from time to time many different marsupial species have become the target of systematic eradication by people.

Wallabies

The wallaby is a middle-sized member of the kangaroo family. The 11 species of wallaby are built like the big kangaroos; the head and body length is 18 to 41 inches, and the tail 33 to 75 centimeters (13 to 29.5 inches). The more common red-necked wallaby occurs in the brushlands of south eastern Australia and Tasmania; the pretty-faced wallaby, with distinctive cheek marks, is found in open woods of coastal eastern Australia.

The three species of rock wallabies live among rocks, usually near water. These pretty animals have thin tails; they thump their feet when alarmed. The three-nailed wallabies have a horny growth on the tip of their tail; because they rotate their forelimbs while jumping, they are called organ-grinders.

Hare wallabies are long-eared, thin-legged species native to New Guinea and the Bismarck Islands of Tasmania. They are small and stocky, with short hind limbs and pointy noses, and are hunted for meat and fur.

Bandicoots

Bandicoots are marsupials with a long, pointy nose and snout, and long, rabbit-like ears. They are 12 to 31 inches long, including their 10 to 30 cm (3.94 to 11.82 inches), sparsely-haired tail. The body is stout and coarse, the muzzle tapered, and the hind limbs longer than the front limbs. The teeth are sharp and slender. The pouch opens rearward; unlike other marsupials, bandicoots have a placenta. Gestation takes 12-15 days, producing 2-6 young. Bandicoots are terrestrial, largely nocturnal solitary animals that dig funnel-like pits in their search for insect and plant food, which makes them a pest for farmers and dangerous to cattle. Some species are endangered, a few are extinct, and all species of bandicoot have declined.

Rat Kangaroos

There are nine species of Australian and Tasmanian marsupials that comprise this family, although some authorities separate the potoroo (Pototoidae) as a separate family. The species differs from other kangaroos in skull and urogenital anatomy and in their large, canine teeth. All are rabbit-sized or smaller. Rat kangaroos live in undergrowth; at night they forage for grass, tubers, and underground fungi. Some also eat grubs and worms.

The four species of short-nosed rat kangaroos, also called boodies, have pinkish noses and short ears. The two long-nosed rat kangaroos — the potoroos — have shorter tails and more pointed faces. The rufous rat kangaroo is the largest of the family and has an indistinct, whitish hip stripe. The musky rat kangaroo has a naked tail and retains the first digit of the hind foot.

Eastern Hare-Wallaby
Lagorchestes leporides

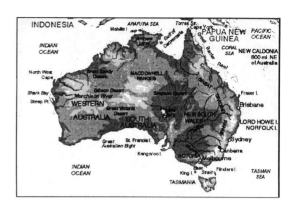

Description

The eastern hare-wallaby, *Lagorchestes leporides,* was distinguished by a conspicuous ring of bright orange around each eye. This species was also uniquely marked with white "elbow-patches". The coat of *L. leporides* was dominantly brown.

Given the natural history of *Lagorchestes,* this species was probably relatively nomadic.

Behavior

The common name "eastern hare-wallaby," was given by colonists due to its behavior of lying among spinnifex tussocks or bushes and when disturbed or frightened bolting off out of its cover. This behavior reminded colonists of brown and Balegian hares of Britain. This species fed on plants and fruits.

Habitat/Distribution

L. leporides occurred in spinnifex tussocks or shrub areas of native open grasslands of southeastern Australia. The climate of this species' past range is generally that of

Status	Extinct
Probable Extinction	c.1890
Family	Macropodidae (Wallabies)
Description	Wallaby with bright orange eye rings; coat was dominantly brown in color, marked with white "elbow-patches".
Habitat	Native open grasslands of southeastern Australia.
Food	Plants and fruits.
Cause for Extinction	Overhunting; predation by foxes.
Range	Australia: New South Wales, Victoria
Photo	See Color Insert, C-2

a savannah, and the average annual precipitation is 840 millimeters (32.76 inches) with an average annual temperature of 18.5 degrees Celsius.

Causes for Extinction

L. leporides was a favorite game animal in southeastern Australia. As British colonists were accustomed to the sport of hunting, this species was shot, snared, netted or coursed with hounds.

Additionally, domestic sheep and cattle began to graze the land this species inhabited. These newly introduced species eroded the soil and promoted the invasion of exotic vegetation which replaced the native flora.

The most prevalent cause for the extirpation of *L. leporides* was the introduction of the European Fox, which was used for lagomorph (rabbits, hares) control and as a game animal. The result, however, was a fox population explosion and native marsupials soon became easy prey to the dominating intruder. *L. leporides* was one of many small mammals included on this fox's menu.

Adapted from data compiled by the Threatened and Endangered Species Information Institute (Golden, CO) for *Beacham's International Threatened, Endangered, and Extinct Species* published on CD ROM, available from Beacham Publishing.

Greater Rabbit-Bandicoot

Macrotis lagotis grandis

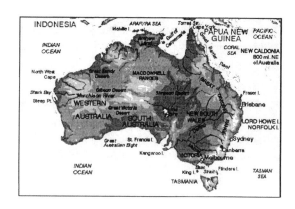

Description

The greater rabbit-bandicoot, *Macrotis lagotis grandis,* had long ears and a long face (contributed primarily from its extended snout). This species had been observed sleeping in a peculiar sort of way, sitting on its tail with its head tucked between its forepaws and ears folded forward along its face. The greater rabbit-bandicoot measured 55 centimeters (21.7 inches) from snout to the tip of the tail. The tail of this species was 26 cm (10.2 inches) long and the ears measured 7.7 cm (3 inches).

M. lagotis species (spp.) had a long, silky coat that was gray above, tinged with reddish-brown or blue along the lateral portions, the underside was white; the middle of the tail was black; the end of the tail was white with long hairs.

Status	Extinct
Probable Extinction	c.1930
Family	Perameidae (Bandicoots)
Description	Rat-like marsupial with a long, silky coat that was gray above, tinged with reddish-brown or blue along the lateral portions, the underside was white; the middle of the tail was black; the end of tail was white with long hairs.
Habitat	Nest-burrowing
Food	Mice and insects.
Causes for Extinction	Hunted for fur; competition from rabbits; predation by foxes.
Range	Southern Australia

Behavior

The greater rabbit-bandicoot was carnivorous and fed on mice and insects. This species was nocturnal.

Habitat

The greater rabbit-bandicoot was a nest-burrowing species that dug extensively. The climate was a temperate grassland with an average annual temperature of 11.5 degrees celsius and precipitation of 309 millimeters (12 inches).

Distribution

The greater rabbit-bandicoot once thrived near Lake Alexandrina in South Australia.

Causes for Extinction

Although the early Australian colonists had a certain affinity for the greater rabbit-bandicoot, the lucrative fur trade resulted in commercial bandicoot exploitation, and the greater rabbit-bandicoot fell victim to senseless slaughter.

Rabbits competed with the greater rabbit-bandicoot for space, especially nesting-burrows. Australians also campaigned against the exploding population of rabbits. Unfortunately, the greater rabbit-bandicoot would get caught in the traps intended for rabbits or would also take poisoned bait set out for dingoes, foxes and marsupial cats.

The most prevalent cause for the extirpation of the greater rabbit-bandicoot was the introduction of the European fox, which was used for lagomorph (rabbits, hares) control and as a game animal. The result, however, was a fox population explosion and native marsupials soon became easy prey to the dominating intruder.

Adapted from data compiled by the Threatened and Endangered Species Information Institute (Golden, CO) for *Beacham's International Threatened, Endangered, and Extinct Species* published on CD ROM, available from Beacham Publishing.

Eastern Barred Bandicoot
Perameles fasciata

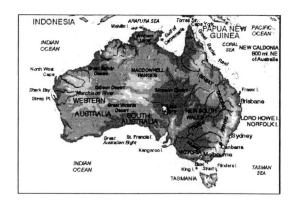

Description

The eastern barred bandicoot, *Perameles fasciata*, was distinguished by its white underparts and yellow flanks. The head and dorsal region of this species appeared to have been penciled in with black and yellow markings. Four vertical stripes could be observed on this species' hind quarters.

Behavior

This species was primarily a vegetarian.

Habitat

The eastern barred bandicoot was non-burrowing and inhabited areas with dense underbrush which provided its food and shelter.

Distribution

The eastern barred bandicoot once inhabited Victoria and New South Wales of Australia.

Status	Extinct
Probable Extinction	c.1940
Family	Perameidae (Bandicoots)
Description	Bandicoot with white underparts and yellow flanks; head and dorsal parts had black and yellow markings.
Habitat	Dense underbrush.
Food	Vegetarian
Reproduction	2-6 young after gestation of 12-15 days.
Causes for Extinction	Competition from introduced species.
Range	Australia: Victoria and New South Wales

Causes for Extinction

Australia separated from Asia near the end of the Reptilian era, a time when mammals where making the first attempts at development. Because of the separation and subsequent isolation, primitive mammalian forms still persisted when Europeans invaded and colonized Australia, bringing with them Western plants, rabbits, foxes, and stoats. These new species proved catastrophic to the well-balanced ecosystem of Australia. Competition between pouched mammals and more advanced placental mammals was disastrous to Australia's native fauna.

As a non-burrowing species, the eastern barred bandicoot was vulnerable to fires, land clearance, and the trampling of cover by domestic sheep and cattle.

Adapted from data compiled by the Threatened and Endangered Species Information Institute (Golden, CO) for *Beacham's International Threatened, Endangered, and Extinct Species* published on CD ROM, available from Beacham Publishing.

Western Barred Bandicoot

Perameles myosura

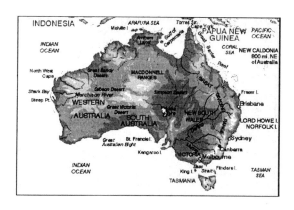

Description

The underparts of the western barred bandicoot, *Perameles myosura*, were a dingy yellow color. This species was black and pale brown above and had one dark band across the lateral portion of its body.

Behavior

The western barred bandicoot probably had 2-3 young per year. *P. myosura* was nocturnal, non-burrowing and primarily insectivorous.

Habitat

The western barred bandicoot occurred in a scrub biome with an average temperature of 17.3 degrees Celsius. The average annual precipitation of this area is 627 millimeters (24.5 inches).

Distribution

The western barred bandicoot ranged from the southwest tip of Western Australia north to Shark Bay.

Status	Extinct
Probable Extinction	c.1910
Family	Perameidae (Bandicoots)
Description	Rat-like marsupial colored black and pale brown above with one dark band across the lateral portion of its body.
Habitat	Scrub biome within the Australian region; non-burrowing.
Food	Primarily insects.
Reproduction	Probably had 2-3 young per year.
Causes for Extinction	Destruction of habitat due to trampling by sheep and cattle.
Range	Western Australia
Photo	See Color Insert, C-2

Causes for Extinction

When Europeans invaded and colonized Australia they also brought Western plants, rabbits, foxes, and stoats. Competition between pouched mammals and more advanced placental mammals was disastrous to

Australia's native fauna.

As *P. myosura* was a non-burrowing species, it became vulnerable to fires and clearance and the trampling of cover by domestic sheep and cattle.

Adapted from data compiled by the Threatened and Endangered Species Information Institute (Golden, CO) for *Beacham's International Threatened, Endangered, and Extinct Species* published on CD ROM, available from Beacham Publishing.

Gilbert's Potoroo
Potorous gilberti

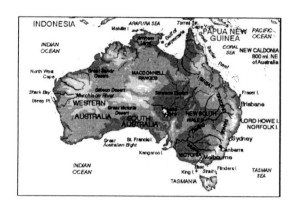

Description

Gilbert's potoroo, *Potorous gilberti*, was a marsupial member of the kangaroo family. Physically, this species resembled a rat, with the exception of its shortened fore limbs, long hind limbs and conspicuously large hind feet. The limb structure was most beneficial to this species, who utilized a hopping motion to get from place to place. Gilbert's potoroo was distinguished by its black tail and the black stripe which ran from its nose to its brow.

Behavior

Given the food habits of a closely related species, *P. tridactylus* (long-nosed potoroo), Gilbert's potoroo probably fed on fungi, roots and other available vegetation, and perhaps insects.

Habitat

Gilbert's potoroo inhabited stank riparian areas characterized by swampy land, dense thickets and running streams.

The climate this species endured was

Status	Extinct
Probable Extinction	c.1900
Family	Macropodidae (Rat kangaroos)
Description	Kangaroo resembling a rat, with the exception of its shortened forelimbs, long hindlimbs and conspicuously large hind feet.
Habitat	Swampy land, dense thickets and running streams.
Food	Probably fed on fungi, roots and other available vegetation, and perhaps insects.
Causes for Extinction	Predation by the European fox.
Range	Western Australia: King George's Sound

most likely one of desert/scrub with an average annual precipitation of 140 to 627 millimeters (5.5 to 24.5 inches) and an average annual temperature of 17.3 to 22.6 degrees Celsius.

Distribution

This species was discovered by John Gilbert in King George's Sound in Western Australia at the turn of the twentieth century. Specimens were sent to the British Museum and the species has not been recorded since.

Causes for Extinction

The most prevalent cause for the extirpation of Gilbert's potoroo was the introduction of the European fox, which was used for lagomorph (rabbits, hares) control and as a game animal. The result, however, was a fox population explosion and native marsupials soon became easy prey to the dominating intruder. Gilbert's Potoroo was one of many mammals included on this fox's menu.

Natives also hunted this species by driving them out of their vegetated safe haven. This hunting was not considered to pressure this species, however.

Adapted from data compiled by the Threatened and Endangered Species Information Institute (Golden, CO) for *Beacham's International Threatened, Endangered, and Extinct Species* published on CD ROM, available from Beacham Publishing.

Broad-Faced Potoroo
Potorous platyops

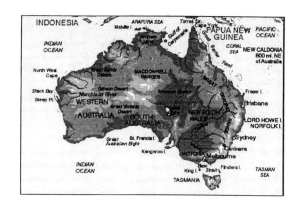

Description

The broad-faced potoroo, *Potorous platyops*, was a marsupial member of the kangaroo family. Physically, this species resembled a rat, with the exception of its shortened fore limbs, long hind limbs and conspicuously large hind feet. The limb structure was most beneficial to this species, which utilized a hopping motion to get from place to place. The broad-faced potoroo was about 48 centimeters (19 inches) long measured from snout to the base of the tail. This species' long tail measured up to 17.7 centimeters (7 inches). The broad-faced potoroo was distinguished from other Potorous species by its wide face with yellowish-white hairs.

Potorous platyops was commonly known as the broad-faced potoroo, mor-da, and warrick.

Behavior

Given the food habits of a closely related species, *P. tridactylus* (long-nosed potoroo), this species probably fed on fungi, roots and other available vegetation and perhaps insects.

Status	Extinct
Probable Extinction	c.1908
Family	Macropodidae (Rat kangaroos)
Description	Kangaroo resembling a rat with the exception of its shortened forelimbs, long hind limbs and conspicuously large hind feet; face was wide with yellowish-white hairs.
Habitat	Riparian areas characterized by swampy land, dense thickets and running streams.
Food	Probably fed on fungi, roots and other available vegetation and perhaps insects.
Causes for Extinction	Predation by foxes.
Range	Western Australia: Margaret River

Habitat

The broad-faced potoroo inhabited stank riparian areas characterized by swampy land, dense thickets and running streams. The climate this species endured was most likely one of desert/scrub with an average annual precipitation of 140 to 627 millimeters (5.5 to 24.5 inches) and an average annual temperature of 17.3 to 22.6 degrees Celsius.

Distribution

The broad-faced potoroo was discovered by John Gilbert in 1908 from the Margaret River area of western Australia. There have been no recorded sightings of the species since then.

Causes for Extinction

The most prevalent cause for the extirpation of the broad-faced potoroo was the introduction of the European fox, which was used for lagomorph (rabbits, hares) control and as a game animal. The result, however, was a fox population explosion and native marsupials soon became easy prey to the dominating intruder.

Natives also hunted this species by driving them out of their vegetated safe haven. This hunting was not considered to pressure this species, however. The colonists were blamed for causing bush-fires which may have also accelerated this species' extirpation.

Adapted from data compiled by the Threatened and Endangered Species Information Institute (Golden, CO) for *Beacham's International Threatened, Endangered, and Extinct Species* published on CD ROM, available from Beacham Publishing.

St. Francis Island Potoroo
Potorous sp.

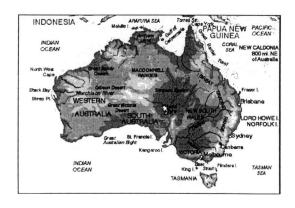

Description

The St. Francis Island potoroo, an undescribed species of *Potorous*, was a marsupial member of the kangaroo family. Physically, this species resembled a rat with the exception of its shortened forelimbs, long hind limbs and conspicuously large hind feet. The limb structure was most beneficial to this species, which utilized a hopping motion to get from place to place. The species had large canine teeth.

Behavior

The *Potorous* species of St. Francis Island were unafraid of people. It foraged in the undergrowth for grass, tubers, and fungi. Once St. Francis Island was settled, these little kangaroos feasted on garden vegetables, and even hopped into homes where they were fed bread crumbs, or devoured whatever edibles were on the floor.

This species of *Potorous* was thought to have been diurnal as it was commonly observed by colonists during the day.

Status	Extinct
Probable Extinction	c.1900
Family	Macropodidae (Rat kangaroos)
Description	Rabbit-size kangaroo resembling a rat with the exception of its shortened forelimbs, long hind limbs and conspicuously large hind feet.
Habitat	Riparian areas characterized by swampy land, dense thickets and running streams.
Food	Grass, tubers, fungi, and garden vegetables.
Causes for Extinction	Cat predation.
Range	Australia: St. Francis Island

Habitat

This species inhabited stank riparian areas characterized by swampy land, dense thickets and running streams. This particular *Potorous* species was not thought to have established any form of burrow, and probably lived in undergrowth. This species' habitat had a climate of temperate rain forests, with an average annual precipitation of 608 millimeters (23.7 inches) and annual temperature of 12.4 degrees Celsius.

Distribution

This *Potorus* species was known from St. Francis Island of the Great Australian Bight in South Australia.

Causes for Extinction

The most prevalent cause for the extirpation of *Potorus* species was the introduction of cats. The colonists of St. Francis Island despised this species for its love of fresh garden vegetables, and the feline predators were deliberately introduced to St. Francis Island to exterminate potoroos. Ultimately, the cats prevailed with no trace of this species to be found.

Natives also hunted this species by driving them out of their vegetated safe haven, but hunting was not considered to pressure this species. The colonists were blamed for causing bush-fires which may have also accelerated this species' extirpation.

Adapted from data compiled by the Threatened and Endangered Species Information Institute (Golden, CO) for *Beacham's International Threatened, Endangered, and Extinct Species* published on CD ROM, available from Beacham Publishing.

Christmas Island Musk Shrew

Crocidura fulginosa trichura

Description

The Christmas Island musk shrew, *Crocidura fulginosa trichura,* was dark gray in color. This species measured 13.5 centimeters (5 inches) in total body length. It had a long-haired tail and was quadruped (using four feet).

Behavior

The Christmas Island musk shrew fed on insects and was nocturnal.

Habitat/Distribution

This species occurred on Christmas Island, which is a 104 square kilometer (64.5 square mile) coral structure with a volcanic core. The elevation of the island ranges from sea level to 366 meters (1,200 feet). The vegetation is jungle and forest. The climate is one of tropical rain forests with an average annual temperature of 26.6 degrees Celsius and annual precipitation of 2,370 millimeters (92.4 inches). Christmas Island was noted for its abundance of food and lack of predatory species.

Status	Extinct
Probable Extinction	c. 1900
Family	Muridae (Rats)
Description	Dark gray in color, measuring 5 inches in total body length with long-haired tail.
Habitat	Jungle and forest of Christmas Island.
Food	Insects
Causes for Extinction	Predation by cats.
Range	Indian Ocean: Christmas Island

Causes for Extinction

Christmas Island provided a rich phosphate reserve for settlers willing to mine it. The establishment of a mining colony resulted in the extinction of this species.

On the ships bringing colonists were rats carrying disease. The disease (thought to be a form of trypanosome) could have wiped out this seemingly stable species, although introduced cats probably were the primary contributor to this species' extirpation.

Captain Maclear's Rat

Rattus macleari

Description

Captain Maclear's Rat, *Rattus macleari*, was a long-tailed rodent. This species measured 48 centimeters (19.8 inches) from its snout to the end of its tail. Dorsally, stiff black hairs stood erect. This species was a reddish color with a lighter colored underside.

Behavior

Captain Maclear's rat was reported to occur in swarms. This species bred all year long. During the day it lived in holes among roots of trees, decaying logs and shallow burrows. Captain Maclear's rat seemed to have been primarily herbivorous and was observed eating fruit, and young tree shoots. It would ascend to the tops of tall trees in search of these young shoots. This species was presumed to be nocturnal.

Habitat/Distribution

This species occurred on Christmas Island, which is a 104 square kilometer (64.5 square mile) coral structure with a volcanic

Status	Extinct
Probable Extinction	c.1900
Family	Muridae (Rats)
Description	Long-tailed rodent reddish in color with a lighter colored underside, measuring 18.9 inches from snout to end of tail.
Habitat	Jungle and forest of Christmas Island.
Food	Fruit, and young tree shoots.
Reproduction	Bred year round.
Causes for Extinction	Loss of habitat due to mining.
Range	Indian Ocean: Christmas Island

core. The elevation of the island ranges from sea level to 366 meters (1,200 feet). The vegetation is jungle and forest. The climate is one of tropical rain forests with an average annual temperature of 26.6 degrees Celsius and annual precipitation of 2,370 millimeters (92.4 inches). Christmas Island was noted for its abundance of food and lack of predatory species.

Causes for Extinction

Christmas Island provided a rich phosphate reserve for settlers willing to mine it. The establishment of a mining colony resulted in the extinction of this species.

On the ships bringing colonists were rats carrying disease. The disease (thought to be a form of trypanosome) wiped out this seemingly stable species. Captain Maclear's rat was observed during the day crawling in what seemed to be agony several years after the invasion.

Adapted from data compiled by the Threatened and Endangered Species Information Institute (Golden, CO) for *Beacham's International Threatened, Endangered, and Extinct Species* published on CD ROM, available from Beacham Publishing.

Bulldog Rat

Rattus nativitatis

Description

The Bulldog Rat, *Rattus nativitatis*, measured 42 centimeters (16.4 inches) and had a very short tail. This species had a fat layer of 1/2 to 3/4 of an inch over its dorsal surface.

Behavior

This species probably bred year round. The bulldog rat was herbivorous and fed on fruit, young shoots and bark of young trees. It was only active at night.

Habitat/Distribution

This species occurred on Christmas Island, which is a 104 square kilometer (64.5 square mile) coral structure with a volcanic core. The elevation of the island ranges from sea level to 366 meters (1,200 feet). The vegetation is jungle and forest. The climate is one of tropical rain forests with an average annual temperature of 26.6 degrees Celsius and annual precipitation of 2,370 millimeters (92.4 inches). Christmas Island was noted for its abundance of food and lack of predatory species.

Status	Extinct
Probable	
Extinction	c.1900
Family	Muridae (Rats)
Description	Rat measuring 16.4 inches with short tail; possessed a fat layer over its dorsal surface of 1/2 to 3/4 inch.
Habitat	Jungle and forest of Christmas Island.
Food	Fruit, young shoots and bark of young trees.
Reproduction	Probably bred year round.
Causes for	
Extinction	Invasion of foreign species and foreigners.
Range	Indian Ocean: Christmas Island

This species lived in small colonies in burrows in the roots of trees, hollow fallen trunks, and half-decayed sago palm.

Causes for Extinction

Christmas Island provided a rich phosphate reserve for settlers willing to mine it.

The invasion of foreigners and foreign species resulted in the extinction of this species.

On the ships bringing colonists were rats carrying disease. The disease (thought to be a form of trypanosome) wiped out this seemingly stable species. The bulldog rat was observed during the day, even though it was a nocturnal species, crawling in what seemed to be agony several years after the invasion.

Adapted from data compiled by the Threatened and Endangered Species Information Institute (Golden, CO) for *Beacham's International Threatened, Endangered, and Extinct Species* published on CD ROM, available from Beacham Publishing.

Bali Tiger

Panthera tigris balica

Description

Once the smallest of all tiger subspecies, the Bali tiger, *Panthera tigris balica,* measured 153 centimeters (60.3 inches) from head to base of tail. Its tail length was 58 cm (23 inches). Its hair was short and dense with white markings over a bright orange coat. Other species from this family possess a horny papillae on the tongue. They had short faces, forward-pointing eyes, and domed heads.

Behavior

Tigers have successfully adapted to a wide variety of environments due to their binocular vision and unique dentition. A solitary hunter, tigers usually prey on such large animals as deer and tapirs, but will also eat birds and fish, and if food supplies are short, cattle and dogs. It is a savage fighter but does not normally attack humans. It is swift and agile and is unafraid of water. The female bears one to four cubs, which will remain with the mother until about two years of age.

Habitat/Distribution

This species inhabited the tropical rain forests of Indonesia.

Status	Extinct
Probable Extinction	1937
Family	Felidae (Cat)
Description	Small tiger with short, dense hair and white markings over a bright orange coat.
Habitat	Tropical rain forests.
Food	Any kind of meat, especially deer, wild cattle and wild pigs.
Reproduction	2-3 cubs every 2-3 years.
Causes for Extinction	Hunting
Range	Indonesia
Photo	See Color Insert, C-2

Causes for Extinction

The subspecies was common in Indonesia. Yet, between the two World Wars, uncontrolled hunting depleted its numbers. Hunters included Dutch colonialists and local people. The last individual was seen in 1937 before it was shot.

EXTINCT WOLVES

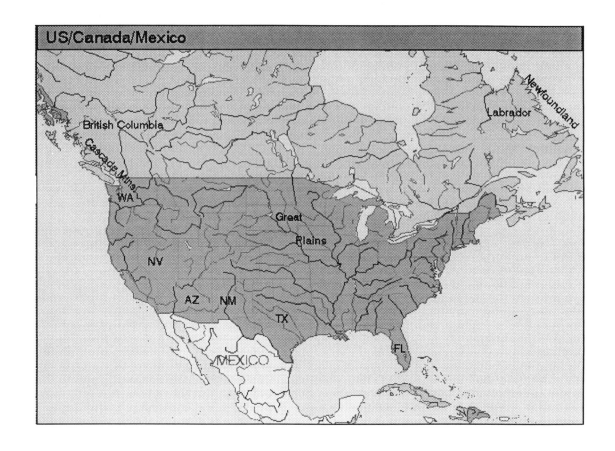

US/Canada/Mexico

Newfoundland
Labrador
British Columbia
Cascade Mtns
WA
Great
Plains
NV
AZ   NM
TX
FL
MEXICO

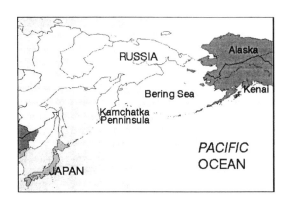

RUSSIA
Alaska
Bering Sea
Kenai
Kamchatka
Penninsula
PACIFIC
OCEAN
JAPAN

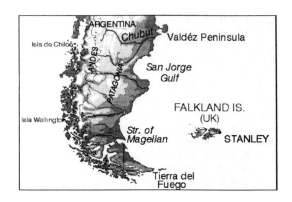

ARGENTINA
Chubut   Valdéz Peninsula
Isla de Chiloé
San Jorge
Gulf
ANDES
PATAGONIA
FALKLAND IS.
(UK)
Isla Wellington
Str. of
Magellan
STANLEY
Tierra del
Fuego

Wolf Behavior

Wolves group themselves into packs with an average of six related individuals. The extinct wolf species followed the same patterns of behavior as their surviving relatives. One male led the entire pack while one female led the females and young. The pack possessed a strict order of dominance that was shown by the behavior of its individuals. The leader, called the Alpha wolf, declared his dominance by holding his head up and raising his tail straight. Subdominant individuals rolled over, wriggled, or crouched in front of the leader. They may also have laid back their ears or tucked their tails between their legs.

Only the Alpha wolf and lead female mated. Birth occurred in the spring when the parents prepared a den 5 meters (15 ft) in length and high enough for the wolf to stand in. Parents may have dug a fresh den or utilized a fox den or a beaver lodge. Five to seven pups made up a typical litter. The eyes of the offspring remained closed for up to two weeks after birth. At three weeks of age, they left the den for the first time and began to eat solid food while continuing to nurse for another month.

The entire pack helped take care of the young pups, especially when the parents were off on a hunt. Returning parents were met with the whines, wags, and licking faces of pups. During the first summer of their lives, the pups rested in safe areas while the rest of the pack was hunting. They spent their time developing hunting skills through play. By fall, they might have joined in on a hunt; perhaps helping to run down prey, but rarely participating in the kill. It took two years for the young to become expert hunters. At that time, they would choose to either stay with the pack or leave to seek out a female and start a pack of their own.

The species ate a variety of items including small mammals, birds, fish, lizards, snakes, and fruit. Yet, dependance centered on larger prey such as moose, elk, caribou, sheep, and deer. In order to successfully hunt and kill these larger prey, the species needed to hunt in packs. To signal the beginning of a hunt, pack members crowded the leader wagging their tails, touching noses, and licking the leader's mouth. Then, the leader would give out a long, low howl in which other members would join. Each member howled on a different note.

The pack then began at an easy, smooth trot, loping for many miles in single file. The pack would have attacked any prey they came across. Often, the chase ended without a kill. Strong, healthy animals often escaped. Usually, only the sick, injured, or very young or old animals were caught.

The hunting method the pack employed varied with the animal hunted. Caribou herds were chased until a weak animal was spotted and then attacked. Mountain sheep often tried to escape by climbing. Thus, the pack would split into those chasing from below and those lying in wait above. Musk-oxen formed a line of defense when attacked. The only way the pack could kill a musk-oxen was to find one that had been isolated from the herd. And, the pack's largest and most dangerous prey, the moose, could have been as large as ten times the size of a wolf. Furthermore, moose could kick at attackers. Yet, the pack could set the moose to running and reduce the risk of being kicked. A running moose could be brought down from hind attacks. In some cases, the pack would come at a prey in two attacking units in pincer fashion.

Wolf species were active during the day; the wolves probably hunted throughout the daylight hours with resting periods in between.

Wolf Habitat Requirements

Historically, wolves utilized a broad spectrum of habitats. These had two specifics in common: an abundance of natural prey and, more recently, minimal conflict with human interests/uses. Present and future requirements necessary on a year-round basis include establishing or maintaining areas of public land that provide these two essential elements.

Key habitat components for wolves are a sufficient, year-round prey base of ungulates (big game) and alternate prey; suitable and somewhat secluded denning and rendezvous sites; and sufficient space with minimal exposure to humans. Wolves are driven to attack domestic animals, and thus bring destruction upon themselves by humans, only when their normal food supply is insufficient. Most of the animals upon which wolves prey are dependent upon vegetation for food or shelter, and the vegetation, especially grassland, is dependent upon climate conditions.

Causes for Extinction of Wolves

All wolf species declined due to intensive human settlement, conflict with domestic livestock, humans' lack of understanding of the animal's ecology and habits that led to fears and superstition, and control programs which attempted to eradicate it. A wolf will not attack a human unless it is sick or threatened. Like any herd of prey, packs would attack domestic cattle when the natural available food supply was limited. As land was cleared for pastures, or as cattle trampled natural vegetation on the prairies, the habitat was degraded for the animals on which wolves preyed, which in turn led to wolf attacks on cattle.

Perceived as a threat rather than a menace, the wolves became targets of federal eradication programs, or ranchers organized hunting parties to slaughter wolves, and these measures were very successful in extirpating wolves from large areas of the United States.

Wolf Recovery Programs

In 1995 the U.S. Fish and Wildlife Service began a pilot project to reintroduce Canadian wolf populations to the western United States. Progress in the effort to recover the gray wolf (*Canis lupus*) in the Rocky Mountains progressed at a pace far better than biologists and managers had expected. In January of 1996 another 37 gray wolves collected from healthy populations in Canada were taken to Idaho and Wyoming, where the species is listed as endangered. Twenty of these wolves were radio-collared and released into a National Forest wilderness area in central Idaho. The remaining 17 were taken to Yellowstone National Park, placed in acclimation pens and released in the spring.

Most of the wolves reintroduced in 1995 adapted well to their new homes. The 15 Canadian wolves released in central Idaho travelled widely, but none left the designated "experimental population" area and all primarily used National Forest lands. No wolf predation on livestock occurred in Idaho. Although several of the Idaho wolves died, losses were well below the level projected when the reintroduction project was planned. One wolf was killed illegally shortly after release, another died of undetermined causes in January 1996, and a third has not been located since March 1995. Of the 12 Idaho wolves released in 1995, five breeding pairs formed.

The wolves released in Wyoming also fared well. Fourteen wolves comprising three packs left their acclimation pens in March 1995; they fed almost exclusively on the park's large elk population and regularly killed coyotes, which the wolves regard as a competitor in their territory. All three packs stayed together after their release and two packs produced a total of nine pups. Four adult wolves had died as of March 1996; two of the wolves were killed illegally, one was struck by a truck, and the fourth was ordered destroyed by the FWS after it went outside the park and attacked livestock for a second time. It had already been moved once for taking two sheep. Defenders of Wildlife, an independent wildlife conservation group, compensated the rancher for the sheep that were killed and for two others reported missing. At the end of 1996, two packs and a new breeding pair (totalling 15 wolves) lived almost entirely within Yellowstone National Park, and another occurred along the park's northwestern border.

Under the terms of the reintroduction program, gray wolves in both Yellowstone and central Idaho are designated as "experimental, non-essential" populations. This classification gives them protection but allows managers additional flexibility in the control of problem animals, although wolf predation on livestock was lower than expected. Defenders of Wildlife maintains a fund to reimburse ranchers for livestock lost to wolves in Wyoming, Idaho, and Montana. The Wolf Education and Research Center (an organization in Boise, Idaho), Defenders of Wildlife, and other organizations also contributed to the recovery program.

In northwestern Montana, where the gray wolf is recovering on its own, the population continues to grow. Biologists have detected 9 or 10 packs in this region, depending on how the wolves are counted.

Shamanu or Japanese Wolf

Canis lupus hodophilax

Status	Extinct
Probable Extinction	1917
Family	Canidae (Wolves, dogs)
Description	World's smallest wolf, with a long tail and a dense, short-haired coat, generally ash-gray tinged with white, russet, and brown.
Habitat	Temperate rain forests.
Food	Large and small mammals, birds, fish, lizards, snakes, and fruit.
Reproduction	5-7 pups born in spring.
Causes for Extinction	Hunting, trapping, superstition.
Range	Japan

Description

The world's smallest wolf, the Shamanu or Japanese wolf, *Canis lupus hodophilax*, measured an average of 84 centimeters (2 feet 9 inches) in length; its height was only 39 cm (14 inches) at the shoulder. This was a miniature wolf with a long tail and a dense, short-haired coat. The subspecies was generally ash-gray in color tinged with white, russet, and brown.

Habitat/Distribution

The species was native to Japan but the extent of the range is not known. Typically, it occurred in temperate rain forests. In these areas, oceanic influences are strong and seasonal factors are subdued. The typical climate is wet and mild but not hot. There are no frost or dry periods, and the majority of the precipitation falls in the winter. As much as 1,000 to 2,000 millimeters (40 to 80 inches) of rain can fall in a single season. The main forest tree is the broad-leaved evergreen. Forests support black bears, and the Asian black bear. Vegetative litter lies thick on the ground in this area due to the cooler climate, which inhibits metabolic activities of the cold-blooded animals that live there.

Causes for Extinction

The subspecies' decline is believed to have been due to the great fear the aboriginal Japanese people, the Ainus, seemed to have had for it. These people called the subspecies the "Howling God," indicating the way in which it howled for hours from hilltops and mountains. In 1885, Henry Faulds, a European traveller, wrote of the charms the Japanese kept over the doors to keep the subspecies away. The subspecies was hunted and trapped all over Japan. The skins of the animal were offered for sale to eager Europeans. Seven yen were paid for an individual by the local government in the region of Honshu, Hokkaido and the Kuriles between the years 1878 and 1882. After 1888, the bounty increased to 10 yen. These regions were the subspecies' last stronghold. In 1905, near Washikaguchi in Hanshu, the last individual seen alive by human eyes was shot, killed, and sold to a European traveller. The subspecies is believed to have become extinct by 1917.

Kenai Wolf

Canis lupus alces

Status	Extinct
Probable Extinction	1915
Family	Canidae (Wolves, dogs)
Description	Unknown, but probably had a pelt with several colored markings, including black, brown, white, and red.
Habitat	Boreal forests.
Food	Small mammals, birds, fish, lizards, snakes, fruit; especially larger prey such as moose, elk, caribou, sheep, and deer.
Reproduction	5-7 pups born in the spring.
Causes for Extinction	Hunting.
Range	Alaska (Kenai Peninsula)

Description

Among the largest of all wolves, the Kenai wolf, *Canis lupus alces,* measured over 180 centimeters (6 feet) in length, and weighed between 45 and 63 kilograms (100 to 140 pounds). This subspecies of the gray wolf is believed to have evolved its large size through hunting the large moose of the Kenai Peninsula. The species is believed to have become extinct in 1915.

Habitat/ Distribution

The species inhabited the Kenai Peninsula in Alaska (see map, page 348). The deciduous habitat of this region consisted of boreal forest lands.

Cascade Mountains Brown Wolf

Canis lupus fuscus

Status	Extinct
Probable Extinction	1950s
Family	Canidae (Wolves, dogs)
Description	Cinnamon to buff-colored medium-large wolf.
Habitat	Temperate grassland and mountainous areas.
Food	Small mammals, birds, fish, lizards, snakes, fruit; especially larger prey such as moose, elk, caribou, sheep, and deer.
Reproduction	5-7 pups born in the spring.
Causes for Extinction	Human settlements; hunting; eradication.
Range	Washington, Canada (British Columbia)

Description

The Cascade Mountains brown wolf, *Canis lupus fuscus,* measured an average of 165 centimeters (5.5 feet) in length, and weighed between 36 and 49 kilograms (80 to 110 pounds). This subspecies of the gray wolf was predominantly cinnamon to buff in color. The subspecies is believed to have become extinct by the 1950s.

Habitat/Distribution

The species inhabited the Cascade Mountain region of Washington and southern British Columbia.

Great Plains Lobo Wolf

Canis lupus nubilus

Status	Extinct
Probable Extinction	1926
Family	Canidae (Wolves, dogs)
Description	Very large wolf with light pelage.
Habitat	Plains and temperate grasslands.
Food	Small mammals, birds, fish, lizards, snakes, fruit; especially larger animals including moose, elk, caribou, sheep, and deer.
Reproduction	5-7 pups born in the spring.
Causes for Extinction	Hunting; human eradication programs.
Range	Great Plains from south Saskatchewan and Manitoba southward to Texas.

Description

The most famous of all North American wolves, the Great Plains Lobo wolf, *Canis lupus nubilus*, measured 165 centimeters (5.5 feet) in length and weighed between 34 and 45 kilograms (75 to 100 pounds). It was colored a light or even white pelage. The subspecies is believed to have become extinct by 1926.

Habitat/Distribution

The species inhabited the Great Plains from south Saskatchewan and Manitoba southward to Texas. The range of this subspecies encompassed the habitat region of the temperate grasslands. Climate in the temperate grassland region is dry with hot summers and cold winters.

Southern Rocky Mountain Wolf

Canis lupus youngi

Status	Extinct
Probable Extinction	1940s
Family	Canidae (Wolves, dogs)
Description	Light, buff-colored medium-sized wolf.
Habitat	Temperate grassland and mountainous areas.
Food	Small mammals, birds, fish, lizards, snakes, fruit; especially larger prey such as moose, elk, caribou, sheep, and deer.
Reproduction	5-7 pups born in the spring.
Causes for Extinction	Human eradication programs.
Range	Colorado, Nevada, Utah

Description

The Southern Rocky Mountain wolf, *Canis lupus youngi*, measured an average of 165 centimeters (5.5 feet) in length, and weighed between 36 and 49 kilograms (80 to 110 pounds). This subspecies of the gray wolf was predominantly light-buff in color. The subspecies is believed to have become extinct by the 1940s.

Habitat/Distribution

The species occurred in Nevada, Utah,

and Colorado. The range of this subspecies encompassed two distinct habitat regions: temperate grassland and mountainous areas.

New Mexican Wolf
Canis lupus mogollonensis

Status	Extinct
Probable Extinction	1920
Family	Canidae (Wolves, dogs)
Description	Darkly colored medium-sized wolf.
Habitat	Temperate grasslands and dry, mountainous areas.
Food	Small mammals, birds, fish, lizards, snakes, fruit; especially sheep, and deer.
Reproduction	5-7 pups born in the spring.
Causes for Extinction	Human eradication programs.
Range	Arizona, New Mexico

Description

The New Mexican wolf, *Canis lupus mogollonensis*, measured between 135 and 150 centimeters (4.5 to 5 feet) in length and weighed between 27 and 36 kilograms (60 to 80 pounds). This subspecies of the gray wolf was darkly colored. It is believed to have become extinct by 1920.

Habitat/Distribution

The species inhabited the dry, mountainous areas of central Arizona and New Mexico. The range of this subspecies encompassed two distinct habitat regions: temperate grassland and mountainous areas. Climate in the temperate grassland region is dry with hot summers and cold winters. This subspecies probably inhabited the middle to lower elevations and rarely ventured as high as the tundra.

Texas Gray Wolf
Canis lupus monstrabilis

Status	Extinct
Probable Extinction	c.1920
Family	Canidae (Wolves, dogs)
Description	Darkly colored, medium-sized wolf.
Habitat	Prairie lands.
Food	Small mammals, birds, fish, lizards, snakes, fruit; especially sheep, and deer.
Reproduction	5-7 pups born in the spring.
Causes for Extinction	Human eradication programs.
Range	New Mexico, Texas

Description

The Texas gray wolf, *Canis lupus monstrabilis*, measured between 135 and 150 centimeters (4.5 to 5 feet) in length and weighed between 27 and 36 kilograms (60 to 80 pounds). This subspecies of the gray wolf was darkly colored. It is believed to have been hunted out by 1920.

Habitat/Distribution

The species inhabited the desert and prairie lands of western Texas and northeastern Mexico. This area is characterized as temperate grassland. Climate in this region is dry with hot summers and cold winters.

Texas Red Wolf
Canis rufus rufus

Status	Extinct
Probable Extinction	1950s
Family	Canidae (Wolves, dogs)
Description	Smallest of all North American wolves, gray-red or gray-tawny in color.
Habitat	Temperate grasslands.
Food	Small mammals, birds, fish, lizards, snakes, fruit; especially larger prey such as moose, elk, caribou, sheep, and deer.
Reproduction	5-7 pups born in the spring.
Causes for Extinction	Human eradication programs.
Range	Texas
Photo	See Color Insert, C-8

Description

The smallest of all North American wolves, the Texas red wolf, *Canis rufus rufus*, measured an average of 72 centimeters (28 inches) at the shoulder and weighed between 18.1 and 27.2 kilograms (40 to 60 pounds). This subspecies of the gray wolf was gray-red or gray-tawny in color. It is believed to have become extinct by the 1950s.

Habitat/Distribution

The species inhabited Texas. The range of this subspecies encompassed the temperate grasslands. Climate in this region is dry with hot summers and cold winters.

Newfoundland White Wolf
Canis lupus beothucus

Status	Extinct
Probable Extinction	1911
Family	Canidae (Wolves, dogs)
Description	Large wolf with a large, slender head that was narrow-skulled, but containing massive teeth; it was pure white in color throughout.
Habitat	Boreal forests.
Food	Small mammals, birds, fish, lizards, snakes, fruit; especially larger animals including moose, elk, caribou, sheep, and deer.
Reproduction	5-7 pups born in the spring.
Causes for Extinction	Hunting; human eradication programs.
Range	Canada (Newfoundland)
Photo	See Color Insert, C-8

Description

The first wolf in North America to become extinct, the Newfoundland white wolf, *Canis lupus beothucus*, measured an average of 180 centimeters (6 feet) in length, and weighed more than 45 kilograms (100 pounds). This subspecies of the gray wolf possessed a large, slender head that was narrow-skulled. Its teeth were in-crooked carnassial and massive. Its coloring was pure white throughout, with the slightest tinge of ivory on the head and limbs.

Habitat/Distribution

The species inhabited Newfoundland,

Canada. The deciduous habitat of this region consisted of boreal forest lands. Precipitation ranged from 400 to 600 millimeters (16 to 24 inches) and may have been as low as 150 mm (6 inches). Yet, water was not limited since the area possessed low evaporation rates which resulted from low temperatures. The region was free of frost only 2 months out of the year with an average low temperature of 60 degrees Celsius (76 degrees Fahrenheit) below zero.

Causes for Extinction

In 1842, the Newfoundland government put a bounty on the subspecies. By 1900, packs were seldom seen. The last recorded sighting of this subspecies occurred in 1911 when a lone individual was shot.

Florida Black Wolf
Canis rufus floridanus

Status	Extinct
Probable Extinction	1917
Family	Canidae (Wolves, dogs)
Description	Medium-sized wolf with black fur throughout, a broad muzzle, and long ears.
Habitat	Temperate forests.
Food	Small mammals, birds, fish, lizards, snakes, fruit; especially sheep, and deer.
Reproduction	5-7 pups born in the spring.
Threats	Human eradication programs.
Range	Florida, Georgia, Tennessee.

Description

More closely related to the red wolf than the gray, the Florida black wolf, *Canis rufus floridanus*, measured a maximum of 150 centimeters (5 feet) in length. It was black throughout and was smaller than the gray wolf. Its muzzle was broader and it had longer ears than its cousin. In 1917, the last known member of this subspecies was shot in Colbert County.

Habitat/Distribution

The Florida black wolf was native to Florida, Tennessee, and south Georgia. This region ranges in character from temperate rain forest to temperate forest. In temperate rain forest habitat, oceanic influences are strong and seasonal factors are subdued. The typical climate is wet and mild, but not hot. There are no frost or dry periods and the majority of the precipitation falls in the winter. As much as 1,000 to 2,000 millimeters (40 to 80 inches) of rain can fall in a single season. Temperate climates are cold enough for most species of plant to cease growth, but winters are mild with an average temperature of minus 2 degrees Celsius (28 degrees Fahrenheit) in the coldest months. Only three months out of the year possess a mean temperature below zero degrees Celsius (32 degrees F).

Warrah or Antarctic Wolf

Dusicyon australis

Status	Extinct
Probable Extinction	1876
Family	Canidae (Wolves, dogs)
Description	Medium-sized wolf with a large head and short legs; its coloring was a mixture of brown, yellow, and black, with black ears, white belly, and white-tipped tail like a fox.
Habitat	Desert or semi-arid shrublands.
Food	Large and small mammals, birds, fish, lizards, snakes, and fruit.
Reproduction	5-7 pups born in the spring.
Causes for Extinction	Hunting; human eradication programs.
Range	Falkland Islands

Description

The only predator to have once inhabited the Falkland Islands, the Warrah or Antarctic wolf, *Dusicyon australis,* grew from 125 to 160 centimeters (4 to 5 feet) in length. Though its head was large and very much wolf-like, its legs were short and it measured only 60 cm (2 feet) at the shoulder. Its coloring was a mixture of brown, yellow, and black while its ears were black, its belly white, and its tail white-tipped like a fox.

Habitat/Distribution

The species was native to the Falkland Islands off the coast of Argentina. The Faulklands are dominated by desert or semi-arid shrublands. Only three months out of the year possess a mean temperature below zero degrees Celsius (32 degrees F).

Causes for Extinction

The species declined due to intensive human settlement, conflict with domestic livestock, a lack of understanding of the animal's ecology and habits, fears and superstition, and control programs which attempted to eradicate it.

During his last visit to the islands, Charles Darwin wrote of the species: "The number of these animals during the past fifty years must have been greatly reduced; already they are entirely banished from that half of East Falkland which lies east of the head of San Salvador Bay and Berkeley Sound; and it cannot, I think, be doubted, that as these islands are now being colonized, before the paper is decayed on which this animal has been figured, it will be ranked among those species which have perished from the earth."

Soon after these words were written, the British colonial government set a bounty on the species. The last known individual was killed in 1876 at Shallow Bay in the Hill Cove Canyon. The species became extinct within Darwin's own lifetime.

All wolf articles were adapted from data compiled by the Threatened and Endangered Species Information Institute (Golden, CO) for *Beacham's International Threatened, Endangered, and Extinct Species* published on CD ROM, available from Beacham Publishing.

EXTINCT MAMMALS OF NORTH AMERICA

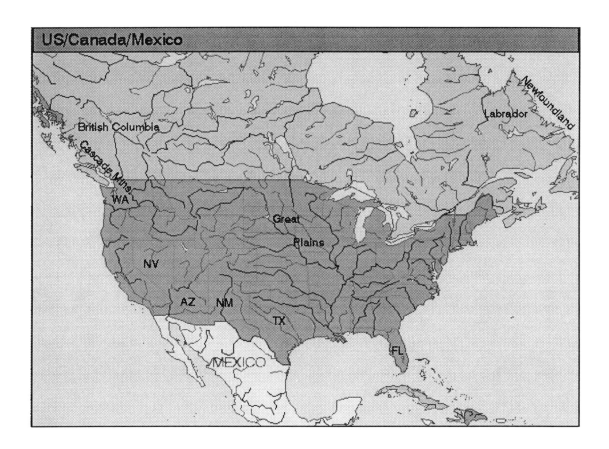

Jaguar Description and General Behavior

Sometimes confused with leopards, the jaguar is the largest New World member of the cat family. It once ranged from the southwest United States to Patagonia but has been extirpated from the U.S.; it usually occurs in swamps, jungles, and other wooded regions in South America. The jaguar resembles the leopard but is larger and more heavily built. The male jaguar can reach a length of 9 feet (including a 2-3 foot tail) and weigh as much as 350 pounds. The ground color varies greatly from white to black, but the typical coloration is orange tan with black spots arranged in rosettes. The tail is marked with black and the nose and upper lip are reddish brown. Except for black spots in the rosettes, the coat pattern of the jaguar is similar to the leopard's spots.

A solitary hunter, the jaguar usually preys on such large animals as deer and tapirs, but will also eat birds and fish, and if food supplies are short, cattle and dogs. It is a savage fighter but does not normally attack humans. It is swift and agile and is unafraid of water. In colder climates it mates toward the end of the year but in the tropics the mating season is unrestricted. After a gestation period of about 100 days, the female bears one to four cubs, which will remain with the mother until about two years of age.

Dawson's Caribou
Rangifer dawsoni

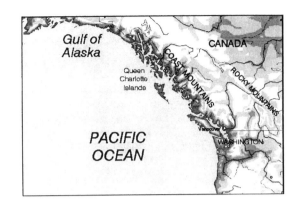

Description

Dawson's caribou, *Rangifer dawsoni*, stood 31.5 to 55.2 inches from hoof to shoulder depending on sex (males were larger than females). Dawson's caribou is considered to have been a rather small species. This deer was 47.3 to 87 inches long measured from snout to the base of the tail. The length of the tail was 2.8 to 8.3 inches. This species may have weighed as little as 132.3 pounds to as much as 701.2 pounds. The pelt of Dawson's caribou was thick and woolly underneath and pale in color. The guard hairs were coarse. *Rangifer* species (spp.) are the only deer species in which both sexes possess horns (antlers). Antlers, unlike horns, are bones which develop and fall off seasonally.

Status	Extinct
Probable Extinction	c.1910
Family	Cervidae (Deer)
Description	Small deer with thick pelts and woolly underneath; pale in color with coarse guard hairs; both sexes possessed antlers.
Habitat	Humid swamp barrens and wooded mesic grounds of Canada.
Food	Probably fed on lichens, leaves, berries, twigs and shoots.
Reproduction	One or two young.
Causes for Extinction	Trapped for fur.
Range	Canada: Queen Charlotte Islands, British Columbia

Behavior

The antlers of Dawson's caribou played an important role in mating. Males displayed their antlers for females and repelled competition by crashing their antlers together with an intruding male and scuffing the ground with their hoofs. The males remained with the female of choice for several days, then would leave and find a new female with which to mate. After a gestation period of six to nine months (unknown for this species), the female would give birth to one or two young.

Dawson's caribou probably fed on lichens, leaves, berries, twigs and shoots (taken from data of a related species *R. tarandus*). This species, like all four-chambered stomached species, would regurgitate ingested food and chew this partly digested food (cud) thoroughly, swallow and digest it entirely.

This species fed in the early morning and evening hours. After feeding, this species would lie hidden and "chew its cud."

Habitat

This species was renowned for its unique habitat: one of great humidity, swamp barrens and wooded mesic grounds. All other genera of Cervidae typically inhabit dry interior lands or arctic lands.

Distribution

This species inhabited the riparian habitat of the Queen Charlotte Islands, British Columbia, Canada. The Queen Charlotte Islands are located west of Canada and just below the Alaskan panhandle. This species was noted from northern Graham Island and Virago Sound. Even given these reports, many naturalists believed Dawson's caribou was from Alaska, and it was not until the species was in total biological distress that its true range was recognized as valid. Dawson's caribou is believed to have become extinct in about 1908, although sightings have been reported from Naden. These reports are credited to the fact the black-tailed deer and wapiti resemble Dawson's caribou very much. Although the fur trade in this species was established in approximately 1878, it was not until 1900 that the species was described. Therefore, many naturalists took for granted that this species was a plentiful Alaskan species of caribou.

Causes for Extinction

Dawson's caribou was left untouched by the anthropogenic inhabitants of the islands, the Haida Indians, for over five thousand years. Then, with the invasion of the Europeans came the exploitation of this species. White explorers convinced these native inhabitants to track down and trap Dawson's caribou for its fur and commercial benefits.

Adapted from data compiled by the Threatened and Endangered Species Information Institute (Golden, CO) for *Beacham's International Threatened, Endangered, and Extinct Species* published on CD ROM, available from Beacham Publishing.

Mexican Silver Grizzly

Ursus arctos nelsoni

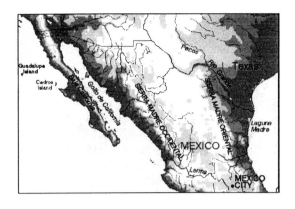

Description

Once the largest animals native to Mexico, the Mexican silver grizzly, *Ursus arctos nelsoni,* weighed an average of 318 kilograms (700 pounds). It measured 183 centimeters (6 feet) from nose to tail. Yet, it was the smallest of the four subspecies of the American brown bear. Its coloring was silver.

Behavior

See Bear Behavior, page 315.

Habitat

The species inhabited the mountain ranges of Mexico.

Distribution

This species once ranged over the entire western half of the North American continent, from the Arctic to northern Mexico and through the entire length of the Rocky Mountains.

Status	Extinct
Probable Extinction	Last sighted in 1964.
Family	Ursidae (Bear)
Description	Medium-size, silver-colored bear resembling the American brown bear.
Habitat	All territories in Mexico including tropical rain forests, temperate grasslands, and mountains.
Food	Plants, fruit, and insects; occasionally carrion and small mammals.
Reproduction	1-3 cubs every three years.
Causes for Extinction	Hunting and trapping.
Range	Mexico

Causes for Extinction

This species has been the victim of steady and gradual extirpation by humanity since the first march of the conquistador Coronado in 1540, which trampled native habitats from Mexico City to the Seven Cities of Cibloa in New Mexico and on into the plains of Texas and Kansas. The subspecies' decline is attributed to hunting, trapping, and poisoning. The subspecies has not been reported since 1964.

The largest threat to bears everywhere is humanity. Before this influence on the species, it was a prolific survivor. Ranging across almost the entire Northern Hemisphere, it inhabited prairies, grasslands, and tundra. Yet, when world conquerors came to the New World, it could not adapt to the destruction of its habitat.

Adapted from data compiled by the Threatened and Endangered Species Information Institute (Golden, CO) for *Beacham's International Threatened, Endangered, and Extinct Species* published on CD ROM, available from Beacham Publishing.

Arizona Jaguar
Felis onca arizonensis

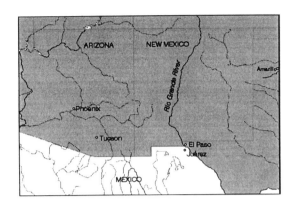

Description

Once the largest cat in the New World, the Arizona jaguar, *Felis onca arizonensis*, measured from 152 to 244 centimeters (5 to 8 feet) in length. It was sandy-red in color marked with large spots encircled by smaller ones.

Behavior

See Jaguar Behavior, page 359.

Habitat

This species inhabited the southwestern United States in two distinct habitat regions: temperate grasslands and mountains. Climate in the temperate grassland region is dry with hot summers and cold winters.

Distribution

This species once inhabited the mountainous areas of eastern Arizona south of the Grand Canyon, the southern half of western New Mexico, and northeastern Sonora.

Status	Extinct
Probable Extinction	c.1905
Family	Felidae (Cat)
Description	Largest cat in the New World, measuring 5 to 8 feet in length; sandy-red color marked with large spots encircled by smaller ones.
Habitat	Temperate grassland and mountains.
Food	Any kind of meat.
Reproduction	2-3 cubs every 2-3 years.
Causes for Extinction	Overhunting
Range	Arizona, New Mexico

Causes for Extinction

The subspecies was hunted beyond its numbers. The last sightings occurred in 1905 when a number of individuals were killed.

The subspecies was the object of game hunters. It was also valued for its skin.

Badlands Bighorn Sheep

Ovis canadensis auduboni

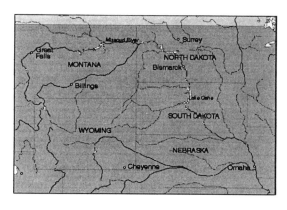

Description

The Badlands bighorn sheep, *Ovis canadensis auduboni,* is a subspecies (ssp.) of *Ovis canadensis,* the bighorn sheep. The Badlands bighorn sheep was about 39.5 inches tall, measured from hoof to shoulder. The tail of this species was 4.3 inches long. The length of this species is thought to have been about 63 inches, measured from the tip of the snout to the base of the tail. This subspecies may have weighed about 320 pounds, but had been reported to weigh up to 350 pounds. The body of this sheep was compact and muscular; the muzzle narrow and pointed, and the tail very short. Both sexes had traversely ribbed large horns that may have exceeded a meter (39 inches) on the outer curvature. The fur was deerlike with a whitish rump patch.

Status	Extinct
Probable Extinction	c.1925
Family	Bovidae (Sheep, cows)
Description	Sheep standing 39.5 inches tall weighing about 320 pounds.
Habitat	Open meadows adjacent to buttes or rock outcrops.
Food	Grasses, herbs, leaves, shoots and twigs.
Reproduction	One lamb in the month of May.
Threats	Hunted for horns; human encroachment.
Range	North Dakota, South Dakota, western Nebraska, eastern Montana, and Wyoming

Behavior

The Badlands bighorn sheep was highly territorial and would utilize its mighty curved horns and muscular build to defend itself from intruders. Males and females were distinctly separate until mating season. In May, the females would give birth to one lamb.

Sheep feed on grasses, herbs, leaves, shoots and twigs.

Habitat

The Badlands bighorn sheep grazed in open meadows adjacent to buttes or rock outcrops.

Distribution

The Badlands bighorn sheep ranged in North Dakota, South Dakota, western Nebraska, eastern Montana and Wyoming.

Causes for Extinction

As settlers encroached on The Badlands bighorn sheep's habitat it fled to the adjacent buttes. This system of survival would ultimately result in the species' demise as it created biological islands for itself. Sustainable populations were dwindling. The closer settlers came, the more isolated populations became. By the 1880s escape routes were limited if at all present. Dogs began to harass the species and it was no time at all before this species' giant curved horns would be discovered. By 1905 most of the population representing this species had been killed for its trophy horns.

Adapted from data compiled by the Threatened and Endangered Species Information Institute (Golden, CO) for *Beacham's International Threatened, Endangered, and Extinct Species* published on CD ROM, available from Beacham Publishing.

Sea Mink
Mustela macrodon

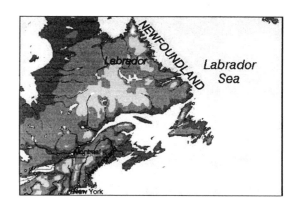

Description

The sea mink, *Mustela macrodon*, was probably the largest Mustelidae species ever to exist. Measurements of 82.6 centimeters (32.5 inches) have been recorded for this species. In comparison, the common mink is only about 57.6 cm (22.7 inches).

Behavior

This species was probably carnivorous and fed on small mammals, insects and any other available food source.

Habitat/Distribution

This species occurred in the coastal waters of New England and the Canadian maritime provinces. Records show that pelts were sold in Maine and Nova Scotia.

Causes for Extinction

The great difference in size between the sea mink and its smaller relatives did not go unnoticed by fur-trappers. This species was commonly available to fur-buyers until the 1860s when the pressure of hunting ex-

Status	Extinct
Probable Extinction	c.1880
Family	Mustelidae (Minks, otters, weasels)
Description	Largest of the minks, measuring 82.6 centimeters.
Habitat	Coastal waters of New England and Canada.
Food	Probably carnivorous and fed on small mammals and insects.
Threats	Hunted for valuable fur.
Range	Coastal waters of New England and the Canadian maritime provinces.

ceeded this species' biological controls. Reproductive rate and longevity were surpassed by traps and commercial exploitation.

It is believed that the Native Americans of the region also killed the sea mink for its pelt. Evidence stems from Indian shell-heaps containing this species' remains. It is not believed, however, that these natives were the primary factor for this species' extirpation. In general, Native Americans were (and still are) respectful of nature and were quite knowledgeable about species abundance, never over-hunting or exploiting.

Adapted from data compiled by the Threatened and Endangered Species Information Institute (Golden, CO) for *Beacham's International Threatened, Endangered, and Extinct Species* published on CD ROM, available from Beacham Publishing.

Glossary

Acaulescent: stemless or nearly stemless.

Achene: a small, thin drywalled one-seeded fruit, such as that of a buttercup or dandelions, that does not split when ripe.

Acicular: pointed or needle-shaped

Actinomorphic: having radial symmetry; divided into two or more planes with similar halves.

Acuminate: tapering to a sharp point.

Acute lobe: a rounded projection ending on a short point.

Adaptation: the features of an animal that enable it to survive in its environment.

Adaxially: relating to or being positioned on the side toward a plant's stem

Adipose: related to animal fat; in fish, a fleshy, finlike, but usually rayless structure lying on the back between the dorsal and caudal fins of certain fishes such as trouts and catfishes.

Adnate: joined to or fused with another part, as parts not normally united.

Adult: sexually mature individual.

Adventitious: appearing in an unusual place or in an irregular or sporadic manner.

Aerial: activities in birds and insects that occur in flight.

Agamospermy: a phenomenon found in plants in which the asexual development of diploid (having genetically similar chromosomes) cells is incomplete due to the abnormal development of the pollen and the embryo sac.

Aggregrate: crowded in a dense cluster.

Agonistic: combative.

Albumin: any of several simple, water soluble proteins that are coagulated by heat and are found in egg white, blood serum, milk, animal tissues, and many plant juices.

Algae: mostly small, one-celled aquatic plants that give water a green or brown color.

Alkali: soluble mineral salts found in natural water and arid soils.

Alkaline: contains soluble mineral salts; opposite of acidic.

Allochthonous: originating elsewhere, or living in a different habitat.

Alluvial deposits: sediment deposited by flowing water.

Alluvion: flow of water against a shore or bank.

Alluvium: sediment deposited by a flowing river.

Alpine: a region that occurs above the tree-line and below the snow-line on temperate and tropical mountains.

Alternate: leaves that do not grow opposite one another on the stem.

Altricial: young birds that are helpless and naked when hatched.

Alveolar: pertaining to the jaw section containing the tooth sockets.

Amblyopsids: The cave fishes; ray fishes distinguished by the structure of the paired fins, supported by the dermal rays.

Amphibian: animal capable of living in both water and land habitats.

Amphipod: a small crustacean of the order Amphipoda, including sand fleas.

Anadromous: fishes that are hatched in fresh water, run to sea to obtain growth, then return to fresh water to spawn, as do shad and Pacific salmon.

Anal fin: the fin on the ventral median line behind the anus.

Andepts: soils with a low bulk density and therefore are light and fluffy; most are acidic.

Androecium: the stamens of a flower considered collectively.

Anestrus: an interval of sexual dormancy between two periods of estrus (period of sexual activity).

Angiosperm: includes the whole range of flowering plants, the most abundant and conspicuous present-day plants, about 250,000 species worldwide.

Angulation: the formation of angles.

Animal: a generically used term to designate all species other than plants.

Antennae: head appendages in invertebrates.

Anterior: in the front of, preceding; opposite of posterior.

Anterior margin: in zoology, toward the forward or ventral end; in botany, inferior or lower; facing away from the axis.

Anthesis: the blooming of a flower or the time the flower is in full bloom.

Aperture: orifice: hole or opening.

Apex: the tip.

Apical: pertaining to or located at the apex (tip).

Apiculate: ending with a sharp, abrupt tip.

Apomixis: a rare reproductive process in which a new individual is produced from a female cell other than an egg cell.

Aquatic: living in water.

Aquifer: a geological formation containing water, especially one that supports wells or springs.

Arachnid: a class of species that includes spiders, scorpions, mites and ticks.

Arboreal: living in trees.

Arboricide: chemicals used to defoliate or kill trees, usually in clearing land for agriculture.

Areoles: the small space between veins in a leaf or insect wings.

Argiustoll: a soil that is darkly colored with an accumulation of silicate clay layers with an average temperature between 5 and 8 degrees Celsius.

Arthropod: invertebrate organism with a horny, segmented external covering and jointed limbs; includes insects, crustaceans, arachnids (such as spiders), and myriapods (such as centipedes).

Association: group of species that are dependent on one another.

Assurgent: slanting or curving upward.

Attenuate: gradually tapering to a point.

Auricular: the feathers covering the opening of a bird's ear; pertaining to hearing.

Awed: having bristles.

Awn: a slender, bristlelike tip, such as those found on spikelets in many grasses.

Axil: the angle between the upper surface of a stalk and its stem or between a branch and its trunk; in fish, the regions under or behind the base of the pectoral or pelvic fins.

Baleen: plates located in the upper jaws of whales that filter plankton from sea water.

Banana poka: woody vine that poses a serious problem to mesic forests on Kauai and Hawaii by covering trees, reducing the amount of light that reaches trees and understory, and causes damage and death to trees by the weight of the vine.

Barbel: a slender, whisker-like sensory organ on the head of a fish or other aquatic animal.

Barred: white or light colored lines; generally refers to barring on the dorsal side of a fish or the breast/belly of a bird.

Basal: located at or pertaining to the base.

Bask: behavior in animals of absorbing sunlight for extended periods.

Basketgrass: perennial grass that is naturalized in shaded mesic valleys and forests, and sometimes in wet forests on most of the main Hawaiian islands.

Beak cavities: a hollow portion in the tip of the umbo of a bivalve mollusk shell.

Beak: the appendage birds use to gather food; the cone-shaped structure in mussels.

Benthic: pertaining to organisms living on the bottom of a lake or sea.

Bicuspid: having two points at the cusp; a tooth with two points.

Biennial-monocarpic: producing a single fruit every other year.

Bifid: divided into two equal parts or lobes.

Bifurcate penis: male sexual organ with two forks.

Bill: the appendage birds use to gather food.

Binomial nomenclature: a taxonomic name consisting of a genus name and a species name.

Bipinnately: having leaflets, lobes or divisions in a feather-like arrangement on every other side of a common axis.

Bivalve: in mollusks, the protective shell composed of two hinged halves.

Bivalve mollusk: a mollusk, such as a clam, whose shell consists of two hinged parts.

Bivoltine: having two adult flights, or generations, per year.

Black twig borer: small beetle which burrows into branches, introduces a pathogenic fungus as food for its larvae, and lays its eggs.

Blowhole: the breathing hole located on the head of a whale.

Blubber: a thick layer of fat beneath the skin of a whale.

Bony fishes: fishes having a hard, calcified skeleton as opposed to a cartilaginous one.

Boreal: a conifer-dominate forest occurring in the northern high latitudes, bounded on the north by tundra (treeless plain) and to the south by broad-leaved, deciduous forests.

Brachial artery: belonging to the pectoral fins or other forelimbs of a vertebrate.

Brachiation: moving through trees by swinging from limb to limb.

Bract: the lifelike part of a plant located below the flower, usually small and sometimes brightly colored; leaves that bracket the flower of a plant.

Branchia: a gill or similar breathing organ.

Breaching: leaping of a whale from the water.

Brood: offspring raised together.

Brood pouch: gill structure in freshwater mussels that is modified to store developing glochidia (larva that have hooks to attach to a host fish).

Brood parasitism: when a bird of one species lays eggs in the nest of a different species to the detriment of the host bird's own young.

Broomsedge: perennial, tufted, fire-adapted grass which is naturalized on Oahu and Hawaii along roadsides and in disturbed dry to mesic forest and shrubland.

Browsing: feeding by plant-eating animals.

Buccal: pertaining to the mouth, or mouthlike.

Bud: a small protuberance (knob) on a stem or branch containing an undeveloped leaf or flower.

Bursa copulatrix: a saclike, bodily cavity used in copulation.

Bursa: a saclike bodily cavity.

Caducous: dropping off or shedding at an early stage of development, as the gills of amphibians or the leaves of plants.

Caespitose: growing in dense tufts or clumps; matted.

Calcareous: composed of calcium carbonate.

Caldera: a large crater formed by a volcanic explosion or by the collapse of a volcanic cone.

Calyx: the outer protective covering of a flower consisting of leaflike, usually green segments called sepals.

Campanulate: bell shaped.

Cannibalistic: the practice among some animals of eating the flesh of their own species.

Canthal: either of two angles formed by the junction of the eyelids.

Carapace: a hard structure covering all or part of the body, such as a turtle's shell.

Cardiform: teeth of some fishes that are arranged like a series of combs.

Carina: a keel-shaped ridge, such as that on the breastbone of a bird or the petal of certain flowers.

Carpel: the central, ovule-bearing, female organ of a plant.

Caryopsis: a one-celled, one-seeded dry fruit, such as wheat, that has its outer covering fused to its surface.

Caudal: near the tail or hind parts.

Caudal fin: the tail fin of a fish.

Caudal peduncle: a narrowing of the body in front of the caudal fin.

Caudex: the woody trunk-like stem, such as that of a tree fern; the thickened base of the stem in some perennial plants.

Caudices: the woody trunk-like stems, such as those of a tree fern; the thickened base of the stem in some perennial plants.

Caulescent: having a stem showing above the ground.

Cauline: growing on a stem.

Cephalic: pertaining to the head or skull.

Cerambycid: a member of the longhorn beetle family, Cerambycidae.

Cere: a fleshy swelling at the base of the upper part of the beak in certain birds, such as parrots and falcons.

Cespitose: growing in dense tufts or clumps; matted.

Channel: the bed or deeper part of a stream, river or harbor.

Channelization: the process of deepening a river bed.

Chaparral: a dense thicket of shrubs and small trees.

Chasmogamous: showy insect-pollinated flowers.

Chela: a pincher-like claw of a crustacean, such as a crab or lobster.

Chelicerae: two pincher-like appendages near the mouth of an arachnid used for grasping.

Chelonian: belonging to the order of Chelonia, which includes turtles and tortoises.

Chemoreception: the reaction of a sense organ to a chemical stimulus.

Chinaberry: small tree widely cultivated and naturalized on most of the main Hawaiian Islands.

Chitin: a semitransparent horny substance forming the principal component of crustacean shells, insect exoskeletons, and the cell walls of certain fungi.

Chlorophylous leaves: producing chlorophyll (green pigment) during photosynthesis.

Chromatophore: a pigment producing cell, or a pigmented animal cell that can change the color of the skin, as in some lizards.

Ciliate: having microscopic, hairlike appendages extending from a cell and often capable of rhythmical motions.

Cilium: microscopic, hairlike appendage extending from a cell and often capable of rhythmical motions.

Circumscissile: splitting or opening along a transverse circular line.

Cirolanid facies: the characteristics or appearance of a population of isopod crustaceans.

Cirri: a slender, flexible appendage, such as tentacles or feelers.

CITES: An international treaty, the purpose of which is to protect endangered species. This is accomplished through the illegalization of trade of these species across international boundaries.

Cladoceran: a small, aquatic crustacean, including water fleas, of the order of Cladocerana.

Class: a taxonomic classification of organisms belonging to related orders. This is the common category by which most animals are referred, such as birds, reptiles, insects, crustaceans, arachnids, amphibians, snails, and mammals; or plants, such as ferns, mosses, and mushrooms.

Clawed: having a narrow petiole-like base.

Cleft: in botany, having deeply divided lobes or divisions.

Cleistogamous: small flowers that lack petals and are self-pollinating; characterized by self-fertilization in an unopened, budlike state.

Cloaca: the cavity into which the intestinal, genital, and urinary tracts open in vertebrates, such as fish, reptiles and birds.

Cloud forest: high-altitude forest with a dense undergrowth of dwarf trees, ferns, mosses, and other plants that grow on the trunks of the trees.

Clump: a thick grouping of plants or trees.

Cluster: a group of similar elements, such as flowers on a plant, occurring closely together.

Clutch: the number of eggs laid in one breeding.

Cocoon: the tough protective covering wherein insect larvae pupate (take their adult form).

Coleopteran: an insect, such as beetles, characterized by fore wings modified to form tough protective covers for the hind wings.

Collembolans: small insects.

Colonial: forming colonies; an inhabitant of a colony.

Colonize: to establish a population in a new territory.

Colony: group of the same species living or growing together.

Commissure: in botany, a surface by which adhering carpels (female organ of a plant) are joined.

Community: a group of plant species that grow in stable association.

Competition: the interaction between different species vying for the same ecological niche, habitat or food supply.

Compound leaf: composed of separate, smaller leaflets.

Congener: a member of the same kind, class or group; an organisim belonging to the same genus as another.

Coniferous forest: comprised primarily of evergreens, usually located in cool, dry climates.

Convective: the transfer of heat or other atmospheric properties by massive motion, especially motion directed upward.

Copepods: small marine and freshwater crustaceans of the order Copepoda.

Copulation: the process by which sperm is transferred from the male to the female.

Coquis: associated with a marine clam of the genus Donax.

Coralline: pertaining to or resembling coral; also red algae covered with a calcareous substance and forming stony deposits.

Cordate: having a heart-shaped outline.

Coriaceous: coarse; leathery.

Corneous: horny, or composed or a hornlike substance.

Corolla: the inner portion of a flower.

Costa: a rib, such as the midrib of a leaf or a thickened anterior vein of an insect's wing.

Costae: ribs, such as the midrib of a leaf or a thickened anterior vein of an insect's wing.

Cotyledon: in botany, a leaf of a plant embryo, being the first or one of the first to appear from a sprouting seed; in anatomy, the lobule of the placenta.

Courtship: behavior in animals prior to mating.

Coverts: one of the feathers covering the longer main feathers of a bird's wing or tail.

Covey: group of birds, usually applied to game birds such as quail.

Crepuscular: becoming active at twilight or before sunrise.

Crest: a tuft or ridge on the head of a bird or other animal.

Cross-blotches: indistinct sequenced specks on a fish.

Crustaceans: invertebrates that include shrimps, crabs and other small marine species.

Ctenoid: having narrow segments or spines resembling the teeth of a comb; fish with ctenoid scales.

Culm: the jointed stem of a grass or sedge.

Cuneate: narrow wedge-shaped leaves that taper toward the base.

Cusp: the fold or flap of a heart valve; also, a pointed end.

Cutaneous: affecting the skin.

Cuticle: the layer of waxlike, water-repellent material covering the epidermis (outer layer) of plants.

Cyathia: small petalless flowers.

Cycle: a series of events that occurs repeatedly in the same sequence.

Cyme: a flat-topped flower cluster that blooms from the center toward the edges, and whose main axis is terminated by a flower.

Cymose: pertaining to a cyme (a flat-topped flower cluster that blooms from the center toward the edges, and whose main axis is terminated by a flower).

Cyprinid: small freshwater fish of the family Cyprinidae, which includes minnows, carps, and shiners.

Cyprinodont: small, soft-finned fish of the family Cyprinodontidae, which includes killifishes and topminnows.

DDT: a pesticide that causes eggshell thinning in birds.

Decapod: ten-legged arthropods.

Deciduous: shedding or losing foliage at the end of a growing season, such as trees losing leaves in the fall.

Decumbent: growing along the ground but erect at the apex (tip).

Decussate: arranged on a stem in opposite pairs at right angels to those above and below.

Deforestation: the process of clearing forests.

Dehiscent: opening at the pores or splitting to release seeds within a fruit or pollen from an anther.

Demersal: eggs that are heavier than water and thus sink.

Dentate: edged with tooth-like projections.

Denticulate: finely toothed.

Depressed: the body form of a reptile that is flattened laterally.

Dermal: pertaining to the skin.

Desert: habitat with low rainfall and sparse vegetation.

Desiccation: the process of drying out.

Desmid: green, unicellular freshwater algae of the family Desmidiaceae that often forms chain-like colonies.

Detritus: debris material (generally plant) that has been deposited on the bottom of an aquatic habitat or is suspended in the water column.

Dextral: pertaining to the right side; in zoology, pertaining to a gastropod shell that has its aperture (opening) to the right when facing the observer with the apex (top) upward.

Diapause: a period during which growth or development is suspended, as in insects.

Diatom: minute unicellular or colonial (living in colonies) algae having siliceous cell walls consisting of two overlapping symmetrical parts.

Dichasium: a flat-topped flower cluster having two lateral stems branching from the main axis.

Dichromatize: to become divided into parts or branches.

Digitate: originating from one point.

Digitigrade: walking so that only the toes touch the ground.

Dimorphic: having two distinct forms.

Dimorphism: the occurrence of two distinct forms of the same parts, such as leaves, flowers or stamens, in a single plant or in plants of the same kind; in zoology, differing characteristics between male and female.

Dioecious: having male and female flowers borne on separate plants.

Diploid: having a homologous (genetically the same) pair of chromosomes for each characteristic except sex.

Disk: the round center of a ray flower, such as a daisy, around which petals are arranged.

Dispersal: migration of individuals from their home range.

Display: a pattern of behavior that serves as communication between species, such as mating rituals.

Distal: anatomically located far from the origin or line of attachment.

Distal: located far from the origin of attachment.

Distichous: arranged in two vertical rows or ranks on opposite sides of an axis.

Disturbed area: habitat whose native vegetation has been altered.

Diurnal: plants that open during daylight and close at night; animals that are active during the day and sleep at night.

Diversity: the number of differing species in a habitat.

Division: in botany, a taxonomic grouping of organisms belonging to similar classes; the equivalent of phylum.

Dorsal: situated at the rear of an animal, such as the dorsal fin in a fish.

Dorsoventral: extending from a dorsal (rear) to a ventral (front) surface.

Dorsum: a part of an organ analogous to the back.

Drupe: fruit with a firm outer layer, a fleshy inner layer, and a stony inner layer surrounding a single seed.

Echolocation: the ability of an animal, such as a bat or dolphin, to orient itself by the reflection of sound it has produced.

Ecology: the study of the relationship of plants and animals to each other and to their habitats.

Ecosystem: a community of organisms that interact with each other and their environment.

Ectocone: an ecological community of mixed vegetation formed by the overlapping of adjoining communities.

Edaphic: pertaining to the soil as it affects living organisms.

Ellipsoid: an ellipse-shaped surface.

Elytral: the thickened, hard fore-wing of a beetle or a platelike respiratory structure on the dorsal surface of a scale worm.

Emarginate: weakly crescent-shaped as opposed to definitely forked, as in the outline of a fin.

Embryo: an organism in the early stages of development; unhatched.

Endangered Species Act of 1973: The purposes of the Act are to determine on the basis of scientific evidence alone whether any species is endangered or threatened and to "list" the ones that are; to prohibit anyone from harming a listed species; protect the species from illegal trade; and to prevent government programs from jeopardizing a listed species.

Endemic: species that are native to a specific region; non-endemic species are called "exotic."

Endocarp: innermost layers of the fruit wall.

Entire: a leaf whose margin is undivided.

Entisols: soils without natural genetic horizons or with weakly developed horizons.

Entomology: the study of insects.

Environment: all the conditions that affect the growth and sustenance of organisms.

Environmental stress: stress on a species caused by the dwindling of resources necessary to sustain an organism's survival.

Epipetalous: united on the petals.

Epiphyseal: part of the bone, often the end of a long bone, that develops separated from the main portion of the cartilage.

Epiphyte: a plant, such as certain orchids and ferns, that grows on another plant for mechanical support but not for nutrients; epiphytes are not considered parasites.

Epiphytic: pertaining to an epiphyte (a plant, such as certain orchids and ferns, that grows on another plant for mechanical support but not for nutrients); not rooted in the soil.

Epiphytically: not rooted in the soil.

Epithet: term used as a descriptive substitute for the name.

Ericoid habitat: occurring in association with an ericaceous (heath family) shrub layer.

Erose: irregularly notched, toothed, or indented.

Estivate: to pass the summer in dormancy.

Estrus: a regularly recurring period of ovulation and sexual excitement in mammals other than humans.

Euphotic zone: occurring in depths less than 4 meters.

Euryhaline: adapted to living in fresh or brackish water.

Eutrophic: pertaining to a body of water in which the increase of mineral and organic nutrients has reduced the dissolved oxygen, producing an environment that favors plant over animal life.

Eutrophication: in a body of water, the process in which the increase of mineral and organic nutrients has reduced the oxygen, producing an environment that favors plants over animal life.

Exocarp: outermost layers of the fruit wall.

Exotic: a plant or organism that is not endemic to a region; non-native, introduced.

Exstipulate: having no stipules.

Extinct: a species that has no surviving individuals.

Extirpate: to eliminate a population.

Faculatatively: adaptive to varying environments.

Falcate: curved and tapering to a point.

Family: a taxonomic category below Order and above Genus based on the grouping of related genera. For example, within the **Class** called birds, the families are grouped into categories such as falcons, sparrows, ducks, and parrots.

Fascicles: a bundlelike cluster of flowers, stems or leaves.

Fasciculate: clustering of flowers, stems or leaves.

Fauna: animal life.

Fecundity: the potential reproductive capacity as measured by the individual production of mature eggs.

Femoral: pertaining to the thigh.

Fen: low, flat, swampy land; a bog.

Fertilization: the union of a sperm and egg that stimulates growth of the embryo.

Filiform: threadlike.

Filter feeding: in marine life, the process of filtering food from water through a siphoning organ.

Fimbriate: fringed, as the edge of a petal or the opening of a duct.

Fin: that portion of a fish's body that propels it or assists in swimming.

Fish ladder: a device constructed by people that assists spawning fish to pass an obstruction, usually a dam.

Flagellum: whip-like extensions of unicellular organisms, usually used for locomotion.

Flank: the side or lateral part of the body.

Fledgling: stage of development in birds when flight feathers are developed.

Flora: plants of a region or period.

Floriferous: bearing flowers.

Foliaceous: having leaves or a leaflike structure.

Follicle: a single-chambered fruit that splits along only one seam to release its seeds.

Fontanelle: the soft membranous intervals between the incompletely ossified cranial bones of a fetus or infant.

Food chain: interdependence of feeding organisms that prey upon lower or more vulnerable species. Frequently, if one species in a food chain is eliminated, all species within the chain are affected. For example, when farmers exterminated prairie dogs in the midwest, a dramatic decline in the black footed ferret occurred.

Fossil: an impression or cast of a plant or animal preserved in rock.

Fossorial: adapted to burrowing or digging.

Fostering: when the young of one species are raised by parents of a related species.

Fountain grass: fire-adapted bunch grass that spead widely over bare lava flows and open areas on the island of Hawaii. It invades Hawaii's dry forests where it interferes with plant regeneration, carries fires into areas not usually prone to fires, and increases the likelihood of fire.

Frog: a smooth-skinned amphibian, usually aquatic or semi-aquatic.

Frontal shield: area covering the forehead of birds.

Fruit dispersal: release of seeds or pollen.

Fuscous: dusky; dark gray or grayish brown.

Fusiform: tapering at each end; spindle shaped.

Galea: a helmet-shaped part, as in the upper part of certain plants and insects.

Gallinaceous: characteristic of the order Galliformes, which includes common domestic fowl, pheasants, turkeys and grouse.

Gallinule: wading bird characteristically having dark, iridescent plummage.

Gamete: a mature sperm or egg capable of participating in fertilization.

Ganglia: in anatomy, a group of nerve cells located outside the brain or spinal cord in vertebrates; in pathology, a cystic lesion resembling a cyst-like tumor.

Gastropods: a mollusk of the class Gastropoda, including snails, slugs, and limpets, characteristically having a single, usually coiled shell and a ventral muscular mass serving as an organ of locomotion.

Genetic: pertaining to characteristics that are passed by chromosomes from one generation to the next.

Genus: principal subdivision of a family, such as rattlesnakes (**genus**) being a type of snake (**family**), which is a type of serpent (**order**), which is a type of reptile (**class**).

Geomorphologic agent: a force causing change in land forms.

Gestation period: amount of time the developing young are carried within the body of the mother.

Gill slits: the openings in the gill that permit water to enter.

Gills: the principal respiratory organ of a fish.

Glabrous: having no hairs; smooth.

Glaciate: to subject to glacial action; to cover with ice or a glacier.

Globose: spherical.

Glochidia: a parasitic larva, produced by freshwater mussels, that have hooks to attach to a host fish.

Glume: a chaffy basal bract on the spikelet of a grass.

Gonad: testicle or ovary; an organ that produces reproductive cells.

Gonopodium: a penetrating organ used in copulation.

Gonopore: a reproductive aperture or pore.

Graminivorous: feeding on grasses, seeds or grain.

Graminoids: the food of graminivorous species that includes grasses, seeds, and grain.

Granivorous: feeding on grain and seeds.

Grasslands: ground dominated by grasses and lacking in trees as a result of the amount of rainfall.

Gravid: said of a female swollen with eggs or embryos.

Group: in the animal kingdom, the division of species into amphibians, arachnids, birds, crustaceans, fish, insects, mammals, mussels, reptiles, and snails.

Gular: pertaining to or located on the throat.

Gynaecandrous: staminate and pistallate flowers that are located on the same spike.

Gynoecium: the female reproductive organs of a flower; the pistil or pistils collectively.

Habit: characteristic appearance, form, or manner of growth of a plant.

Habitat: the locality and conditions which support the life of an organism.

Hacking: to release a captive-bred bird into the wild.

Haploid: having half the number of normal chromosomes.

Haplustolls: a well- to moderately well-drained darkly colored soil that is textured of loamy, very fine sand.

Hatchling: a young animal that has just emerged from its shell.

Head shields: easily identifiable structures which arch over the lip in some nematodes (threadlike worms).

Headpool: headwater pool.

Heads: Dense flower clusters.

Heliothermic: organisms that maintain a comparatively high body temperature by basking in the sun.

Helper: in birds, a bird without young of her own that assists in the nurturing of other young.

Henry's crabgrass: annual grass that forms thick mats, and has been naturalized for lawns and pastures.

Herbaceous: green and leaflike in appearance and texture.

Herbicide: a chemical used to kill plants.

Herbivore: species that feed mainly on plants.

Hermaphrodite: an organism, such as a worm, having male and female reproductive organs in the same individual.

Heteromorphic: possessing two sets of stamens (male reproductive organs in plants) of unequal length.

Heterostylous: a polymorphism of flowers which helps to prevent self-pollination by having various lengths of styles and stamens between individuals of a species.

Hexapod: six-legged arthropods.

Hibernacula: a case, covering or structure in which an organism remains dormant for the winter; the shelter of a hibernating animal.

Hilo grass: one of several grasses introduced for cattle fodder that have become noxious weeds. Hilo grass rapidly forms a dense ground cover in wet habitats. Its small, hairy seeds are easily transported on animals or carried by the wind through native forests.

Hispid: covered with stiff or rough hair, or bristles.

Holostomatous: a minute opening of a leaf or stem through which gases and water vapor pass.

Holotype: the specimen used as the basis of the original published description of a taxonomic species.

Home range: an area defined by the habitual movements of an animal.

Host fish: a fish on which mussel larvae reside until they are capable of surviving on their own.

Host: an organism that harbors and provides nourishment for a parasite.

Hummock: a low mound, ridge or knoll.

Humults: freely drained ultisols which have a high content of organic matter.

Hyaline: a glossy or transparent appearance.

Hybrid: an offspring produced by parents of different species; for example, a donkey and a horse produce a mule.

Hypanthium: the modified, often enlarged floral receptacle of various plants, having a cup-shaped or tubular form; the basal portion of the flower.

Hypogynous: having floral parts or organs that are below and not in contact with the ovary.

Hypothermic: abnormally low body temperature.

Immature: juvenile; in insects, the larval stage of development.

Imperforate: having no opening.

Impoundment: accumulation of water in a reservoir.

Incubation: keeping eggs warm until they hatch.

Indian tribal law: laws that extend to Native Americans certain exceptions to the protective measures of the Endangered Species Act, such as taking for sustenance limited quantities of endangered species.

Individual: a single member of a population.

Indusium: the covering of the sorus of a fern.

Inflated: in botany, hollow and enlarged.

Inflorescence: flower cluster.

Insectivore: an organism that feeds primarily on insects.

Instar: the stage between molts in insects; larval development stages.

Interbrood intervals: period between producing young.

Interneural: in between nerves.

Intersupraocular scales: scales above and between the eyes.

Introduced: a plant or animal that has been brought in from outside a region; also called "exotic" or "non-native."

Invasion: the migration of a species into a new area, usually to the detriment of organisms already living there.

Invertebrate: animals lacking a backbone, such as insects.

Involucre: a whorl of leaflike scales or bracts beneath or around a flower or flower cluster.

Ironwood: large, fast-growing tree that shades out other plants, consumes much of the available nutrients, and possibly releases a chemical agent that prevents other plants from growing beneath it.

Isohyperthermic: an equally high temperature regime of soils (above 25 degrees Celsius at 50 centimeters depth).

Isohypothermic: uniformly low body temperature.

Isolated: a portion of a breeding population that is cut off from the rest of the population.

Isopod: crustacean of the order Isopoda, which includes sow bugs and gribbles.

IUCN Red Data Book: the official listing document of threatened species worldwide by the Swiss organization, International Union for Conservation of Nature and Natural Resources, now known as the World Conservation Union.

Karst: limestone formations.

Keel: a prominent ridge on the back of an animal.

Keratin: a tough, fibrous protein substance that forms the outer layer of epidermal structures (protective covering) such as hair, nails, horns and hoofs.

Keratinized: bifurcated egg tooth.

Kikuyu grass: aggressive, perennial grass introduced as a pasture grass, which chokes out other plants and prevents their seedlings from become established. Declared a noxious weed.

Kingdom: the highest taxonomic division into which organisms are classified, as either animals or plants. Some organisms not readily classified as plants or animals, such as amoebae and paramecium, are sometimes classified in a third kingdom called Protista.

Koa haole: a naturalized shrub which is sometimes the dominant species in low elevation, dry, disturbed areas on all the main Hawaiian islands.

Krill: small marine creatures that serve as an important food supply to fish, whales, and birds.

Kuchler system: An approximation of the potential natural vegetation of the U.S., established by A. W. Kuchler.

Lacustrine: living or growing in lakes.

Lamella: a thin scale, plate or layer, as found in the gills of a bivalve mollusk and the gills of a mushroom.

Lanceolate: narrow and tapering at each end.

Lantana: an aggressive, thicket-forming plant introduced to the Hawaiian islands as an ornamental plant; it grows on all the main islands in mesic forests, dry shrublands, and other dry, disturbed habitats.

Larva: a pre-adult form of a species that does not resemble the adult.

Lateral: pertaining to the side of an animal.

Leaf blade: the flat, extended part of the leaf.

Legume: a pod, such as a pea or bean, that splits into two valves with seeds attached to the lower edge of one of the valves.

Lemma: the outer, lower bract enclosing the flower in a grass spikelet.

Lenticels: small pores on the surface of stems of woody plants that allow the passage of gases to and from the interior tissue.

Lepidopterous: insects with four wings covered with small scales, including moths and butterflies.

Life cycle: the sequence of events in the progression of an organism from birth to death.

Limnetic: pertaining to the deeper, open waters or lakes or ponds.

Linear leaf: long, narrow leaf, characterized by parallel veins.

Lithic: pertaining to stone, or lithium-based.

Littoral: a shore or coastal region.

Live-bearing: giving birth to fully-developed young; ovoviviparous.

Lobed leaf: characterized by rounded projections.

Localized: found within a limited geographic area.

Loculicidal: a small cavity or compartment within an organ or part, such as a plant ovary.

Loess: a buff to gray, fine-grained silt or clay, thought to be a deposit from wind-blown dust.

Lore: the area between a bird's eye and the base of the bill; the area between the snout and eye of a snake or fish.

Lotic: pertaining to or living in moving water.

Lunular: crescent shaped.

Lycaenid: a member of the family Lycaenidae; a heteroneuran lepidopteran insect, including moths and butterflies.

Macrophytes: microscopic plants in an aquatic environment.

Maculation: the spotted markings on a plant or animal, such as the spots on a leopard.

Mamma: an organ of female mammals that contains milk-producing glands.

Mammal: vertebrates that are warm-blooded, usually possess hair, and nourish their young on the mother's milk.

Mandible: the lower jaw in vertebrates; either the upper or lower part of the beak in birds; any one of several mouth parts in insects.

Mandibular: pertaining to the jaw.

Mangabey: a monkey of equatorial Africa, having a long tail and relatively long muzzle.

Mangrove: a tropical tree with exposed roots forming an interlocking mass; often vital to stabilizing shore lines.

Mantle: the cerebral cortex; the wings, shoulder feathers, and back of a bird when colored differently from the rest of the body; in mollusks and brachipods, the membrane between the body and shell.

Manzanita: an evergreen shrub of Pacific North America bearing white or pink flowers in clusters.

Marcescent: withering but not falling off, as a blossom that persists on a twig after flowering.

Margin: the edge of a flower or insect's wing.

Marsupial: a mammal of the order Marsupialia, found mainly in Australia, that includes kangaroos, opossums and wombats; set apart by urogenital and skeletal differences.

Marsupium: an external abdominal pouch in female marsupials that contains mammary glands (breasts) and that shelters the young; also, a temporary egg pouch in animals.

Medial: situation in or extending toward the middle.

Melanistic: darkness of the skin, hair or eyes resulting from high pigmentation (coloration).

Melanophore: a chromatophore (pigment producing cell, or a pigmated animal cell that can change the color of the skin, as in some lizards) that contains melanin (a dark pigment).

Membrane: a thin, pliable layer of tissue covering surfaces or connecting regions, structures or organs of a plant or animal.

Membranous: pertaining to a membrane, a thin, pliable layer of tissue covering surfaces or connecting regions, structures or organs of a plant or animal.

Mesic distichlis meadows: well-drained grassy meadows.

Mesic: between dry and wet.

Mesocone: protrusion in gastropods.

Metabolism: chemical process within an organism to release energy.

Metamorphosis: development from one stage of maturity to the next, usually with marked change in appearance.

Metatarsus: a part of the hind foot in four-legged animals or in the foot of birds.

Microclimate: the conditions immediately surrounding an organism, often differing significantly from the environment as a whole.

Migration: the seasonal movement of animals from one territory to another.

Migratory Bird Treaty Act: This treaty of 1918 provides legal protection of migratory birds; it also paved the way for cooperation in avian management between the U.S. and bordering countries.

Mogotes: small outcrop.

Mollusk: animals that have a muscular foot and a dorsal shell, such as snails and mussels.

Molt: to shed the outer covering.

Monocarpic: producing a single fruit.

Monoclinous: having pistils and stamens in the same flower.

Monoecious: having male and female reproductive organs in separate flowers on the same plant.

Monogamous: having one mate for life.

Monophagous: eating only one kind of food.

Monophyletic: pertaining to a single phylum of plants or animals; derived from one source.

Monotypic: the only member of its genus.

Montane forest: forest located at the middle altitude of a mountain.

Montane: mountainous.

Morph: any individual of a polymorphic (the occurrence of different forms, stages, or color types in organisms of the same species) group.

Morphology: the biological study of the form and structure of living organisms.

Mosaic bones: bone tissue composed of somatic cells of genetically different types; this phenomenon is caused by gene or chromosome mutations.

Mottled: blotched; color spots running together.

Mouth oblique: the mouth lying at an angle to the horizontal axis of the body.

Mouth ventral: the mouth notably located on the ventral side of the head.

Mucronate: a sharp tip of some plants and animal organs.

Mucronulate: having a sharp terminal point or spiny tip.

Mycelium: the vegetative part of a fungus consisting of a mass of branching, threadlike filaments called hyphae.

Mycorrhizae: the symbiotic (mutually beneficial) association of the mycelium (filaments) of a fungus with the roots of a plant.

Myriapod: an arthropod, such as a centipede, with segmented bodies and many legs.

Nacre: Mother-of-pearl.

Native: indigenous; original to the region; not introduced from another region; endemic.

Nectar: secretion from plants that attracts pollinators.

Nectary dish: fleshy, nectar-producing structure.

Nematode: a worm of the phylum Nematoda, having unsegmented, threadlike bodies, many of which are parasitic, as the hookworm.

Nester: a species that nests.

New World Monkey: monkeys inhabiting the tropical forests of the Western hemisphere, primarily South and Central America.

Niche: the adaptive position of a species within the ecosystem.

Nocturnal: active at night.

Non-native: alien to an area; sometimes called "exotic"; not endemic.

Nuchal: pertaining to the neck; in insects, the dorsal region of the thorax.

Nuehal hump: any hump on the nape of the neck.

Nutrient: food substance that promotes growth.

Oblanceolate: broader and rounded at the apex (tip) and tapering at the base.

Obligate lacustrine suckers: fish (suckers) that can survive only in lakes.

Obligate: a type of plant that almost always (greater than 99% of the time), under natural conditions, occurs in wetlands.

Ocellus: a small simple eye found in many invertebrates; a marking resembling an eye.

Ocreolae: sheafs composed of one or more stipules, enclosing the leafstalk.

Off-road vehicle: vehicles designed to travel over rough terrain and, incidentally, often destroy wildlife.

Oligotrophic: lacking in plant nutrients and having an abundance of dissolved oxygen throughout; opposite of eutrophic.

Olivaceous: olive green color.

Omnivore: a species that eats a large variety of foods.

Oostegites: plates on the thoracic limbs of certain crustaceans, forming a brood-pouch in which the young develop.

Operculum: a lid or flap covering an aperture, such as the gill cover in fish or the horny shell cover in snails.

Opportunistic: a species that adapts its feeding habits to the most available food source.

Order: a systematic grouping of organisms belonging to similar families. The order divides the class into animals that share many common characteristics. For example, the **Class** called "reptiles" is further divided into the **Order** of turtles and snakes.

Ossify: to change into bone.

Ostracods: minute, chiefly freshwater crustaceans of the order Ostracoda that have a bivalve carapace (a shell with two hinged parts).

Overgrazing: occurs when animals feed too long in one area, causing destruction of vegetation and erosion of soil.

Oviparous: said of fishes that lay and fertilize eggs outside of the body cavity.

Oviposition: to lay eggs.

Ovipositor: a male organ in live-bearing fishes for depositing sperm in the female; synonymous with gonopodium.

Ovoid: egg shaped.

Ovotestis: the reproductive gland of some hermaphroditic gastropods.

Ovoviviparous: livebearers; said of fishes whose eggs are fertilized, developed, and hatched within the body; the eggs may or may not derive nourishment from the female.

Ovum: the female reproductive cell (eggs) in animals.

Pair bond: a long-term relationship between a male and a female. Pair bond species mate for one or several breeding seasons while monogamous species mate for life.

Palea: small, chafflike bract enclosing the flower of a grass spikelet.

Pallial: pertaining to the mantle (membrane between the body and shell) of a mollusk.

Palmate: having leaflets or lobes radiating from one point; resembling a palm.

Palmate leaf: divided so as to radiate from one point-like a hand.

Panicle: a flower cluster that is loosely and irregularly branched; a complex, branched inflorescence.

Paniculate-cymose: irregularly branched flower cluster blooming from the center.

Papillae: a small, nipple-like projection.

Parasite: an organism that extracts nutrients from another host organism.

Parasitic stage: the period during the development of an organism in which it feeds on and is sheltered by a different organism (host).

Paratypes: A specimen other than the holotype which was collected before the original description but has been deemed one of the specimens upon which the original description was based.

Parietal: in anatomy, relating to either of the parietal bones, which are two large, irregularly quadrilateral bones that form, with the occipital bones, the sides and top of the skull; in botany, attached to the ovary wall.

Parthenogenic: reproduction without contact between the sexual organs.

Parturition: pertaining to childbirth or labor.

Passerines: birds of the order Passerineformes, which includes perching birds and song birds, such as jays, blackbirds, finches, warblers and sparrows.

Paucispiral: growth lines on a snail's operculum occurring as a few, rapidly expanding spirals.

Pectin: colloidal substances found in ripe fruits, such as apples; pectin is used commercially to jell foods, drugs and cosmetics.

Pectinase: a plant enzyme that catalyzes the hydrolysis of pectin.

Pectoral: in animals, pertaining to the chest muscle; in fish, the fin located nearest the head.

Pedicel: small stalks bearing a single flower.

Pedicellate: supported by a pedicel (small stalk).

Pedipalpi: appendages of an arachnid that are modified for sensory functions.

Peduncle: in botany, a stalk or stem bearing a solitary flower; in zoology, a starlike structure in invertebrate animals.

Pelage: the coat of a mammal consisting of hair, fur, wool or other soft covering as distinct from bare skin.

Pelagic: ocean-dwelling.

Pendent: hanging down, dangling or suspended.

Pendulous: hanging loosely so as to swing or sway.

Peraeonal: a segment of a snail's shell.

Percoid: pertaining to the suborder of fish including perches, sunfishes, groupers, and grunts.

Perfect: possessing both male and female flowers.

Perianth: the outer envelope of a flower.

Peridotite: igneous rocks having a granite-like texture.

Periodicity: recurring patterns of behavior.

Periostracum: A protective layer covering the outer portion of a mollusk shell.

Periphyton: stationery organisms that live attached to surfaces projecting from the bottom of a freshwater environment.

Peristone: in botany, a circular row of toothless appendages surrounding the mouth of a moss capsule; in zoology, the area around the mouth in certain invertebrates.

Peritoneum: the membrane that lines the inside of the body cavity.

Petal: a segment of the corolla of a flower.

Petiole: in botany, the stalk by which a leaf is attached to the stem; in zoology, the slender stalk-like connection between the thorax and the abdomen in certain insects.

Petrel: seabirds of the order Procellariiformes, especially the storm petrel.

pH: a measure of the acidity or alkalinity of a solution, numerically equivalent to 7 for neutral solutions; the numerical scale increases with alkalinity and decreases with acidity.

Phacelia: Gastric filament; functions to kill or paralyze live prey taken into the stomach of the species.

Phalanger: a small, arboreal marsupial of Australia having a long tail and dense wooly fur.

Pharyngeal teeth: teeth developed on the pharyngeal bone in many fishes.

Phenology: the study of periodic biological occurrences and behavior, such as flowering, breeding, and migration.

Phenophases: leaf color change.

Phenotype: organisms exhibiting similar environmentally and genetically observable appearances.

Photoperiod: the interval in a twenty-four-hour period during which an organism is exposed to sunlight (or artifical light).

Photosynthesis: the process by which plants convert light to chemical energy and synthesize organic compounds from inorganic compounds, such as carbon dioxide to oxygen.

Phreatic water: ground water.

Phyllite: a green, gray or red metamorphic rock similar to slate.

Phylum: after dividing organisms by their kingdoms–animals and plants–the phylum distinguishes organisms by their bodily structure; for example, sponges form one group within the phylum while mollusks and arthropods form two other groups. Vertebrates (animals with backbones) are grouped into a separate phylum, called a subphylum, which includes mammals and birds; the divisions of the animal kingdom, synonymous to the division of plants.

Phytoplankton: aquatic, microscopic plants.

Pilose: covered with fine hair or down.

Pinna: one of the leaflets in a featherlike leaf.

Pinnae: leaflets in a featherlike arrangement.

Pinnate leaf: compound leaf with leaflets arranged in pairs along a stem.

Pinnate: having leaflets, lobes or divisions in a feather-like arrangement on each side of a common axis, as in many compound leaves.

Pinnatifid: having pinnately (arranged on either side of a common axis) cleft lobes or divisions.

Piscivorous: feeding on fish.

Pistil: the seed-bearing organ of a flower.

Planispiral: having a shell coiled in one plane.

Plastron: the ventral (under) surface of the shell of a turtle or tortoise.

Plate loss: a phenomena experienced in which there is a loss of scutes, lamina or other than flat structure.

Plecopteran nymphs: The immature larval stage of a stonefly.

Pleistocene: belonging to the geologic period characterized by northern glaciation and the appearance of early forms of humans.

Pocosin: a swamp in an upland coastal region.

Poikilothermic: having a body temperature that varies with the external environment, sometimes called "cold blooded."

Pollination: the process by which pollen is transported to the female parts of a flower.

Pollution: the disruption of an ecosystem by contaminants.

Polyandry: having an indefinite number of stamens (male reproductive organs).

Polyembryonic: having multiple embryos.

Polygamy: having more than one mate at the same time. More specifically, the female hatches more than one brood in a nesting season with different mates.

Polymorphism: the occurrence of different forms, stages, or color types in organisms of the same species.

Population: a group of individuals within a defined area that is capable of interbreeding.

Postcleithrum: a membrane-bone between the cleithrum and the supracleithrum in the pectoral girdle of a bony fish. These three bones are of dermal origin and are superimposed upon the original cartilaginous pectoral girdle which consists of the scapulae and coracoids.

Posterior margin: toward the back end; used in reference to mussel/clam anatomy.

Posterior: the rear or tail region of an animal.

Postocular: behind the eyes.

Precambrian: the oldest and most expansive of geological periods characterized by the appearance of primitive life forms.

Precocial: pertaining to birds that are covered with down and capable of mobility when first hatched.

Predator: an animal that hunts other animals for food.

Premaxillae: bones located in front of and between the maxillary bones in the upper jaw of vertebrates.

Prey: animals that are hunted by predators.

Proandrous: condition in which the stamens (male organ) of a flower mature before the pistil (female organ) is receptive.

Proboscis: a long flexible snout or trunk, as of an elephant; the slender, tubular feeding and sucking structure of some insects.

Process: an appendage; a part extending or projecting from an organ or organism.

Progenitor: a direct ancestor or originator of the line of descent.

Proliferous: reproducing freely by means of buds and side branches; freely producing buds or offshoots, sometimes from unusual places.

Pronotum: plates covering the first segment of the thorax in insects.

Propagules: portion of an organism capable of producing a new individual.

Prosoma: the anterior (front) portion of the body of an invertebrate when primitive segmentation is not evident.

Prostrate: growing flat along the ground; similiar to decumbent except that with decumbent growth the plant becomes erect at the apex.

Protozoa: single-shelled, usually microscopic organisms of the phylum or sub kingdom Protozoa, which included the most primitive forms of animal life.

Protractile premaxillaries: bones located in the upper jaw of vertebrates that are capable of being extended.

Psyllid: any of various plant lice of the family Chermidae.

Puberulent: covered with minute hairs or very fine down.

Puberulous: covered with minute or fine hairs.

Pubescent: covered with short hairs or soft down; also, having reached puberty.

Pulmonate: having lungs or a lunglike structure.

Pulvinate: having a swelling at the base; used as a leafstalk; cushionlike.

Punctate: having tiny spots, points or depressions.

Pupa: the inactive stage in the metamorphosis (evolution) of many insects following the larval stage and preceding the adult form.

Pupal stage: the non-feeding period when larval tissues are reformed into adult structure inside a cocoon.

Pupation: to become a pupa (pre adult).

Pustule: a small swelling similar to a blister or pimple.

Quadrate: in zoology, a bone or cartilage of the skull joining the upper and lower jaws in birds, fish, reptiles and amphibians.

Quartzipsamment: sandy, quartz-based soil.

Raceme: the arrangement of flowers singly along a common main stalk, as in the lily of the valley.

Rachis: the main stem of an inflorescence (flower cluster);
the stalk that bears the flowers.

Rack: the antlers of mammals in the family Cervidae, including deer and moose.

Radio tracking: using an affixed transmitter to follow the movements of an animal.

Radipose: a fleshy fin posterior to the dorsal.

Radula: in mollusks, a flexible tongue-like organ with rows of horny teeth on the surface.

Range: geographical area wherein a species resides.

Raptor: a bird of prey.

Rays: the flat blades that encircle a flower disk; in zoology, one of the bony spines supporting the membrane of a fish's fin; also, a description for the color pattern or ridges on a shell.

Receptacle: base of the flowers.

Redds: the eggs deposited in one spawning season in fish.

Refugia: multiple places of protection or shelter (refuges).

Refugial population: the plants or animals protected in a refuge.

Regolith: the layer of loose rock material resting on bedrock, and constituting the surface of most land.

Relict: a localized species or population that has survived from an earlier epoch.

Reproductive phenology: the study of breeding as related to weather.

Reticulate: marked with lines resembling a network, as in the veins of a leaf.

Retrices: stiff tail feathers used for maneuvering during flight.

Revolute: rolled back on the under surface from the tip, as in some leaves before they open.

Rhizomate: a root-like, usually horizontal stem growing under or along the ground that sends out roots from its lower surface and leaves from its upper surface.

Rhomboidal: shaped-like a parallelogram with unequal adjacent sides.

Riffle: a rocky shoal or sandbar lying just below the surface of a river.

Riparian: pertaining to the bank of a natural course of water.

Rosette: a circular cluster of leaves or other plant parts.

Rufous: strong yellowish pink to moderate orange or reddish-brown color.

Rugose: having a rough and ridged surface, as in prominently veined leaves.

Sagittal: relating to the structure that unites the two parietal bones of the skull.

Salamander: type of amphibian characterized by a tail.

Salverform: a phenomenon in which a flower has united petals in which the calyx and corolla
  (perianth) are the same size, shape and texture. The perianth extends from the center of the
flower, and the corolla has an elongated slender tube and a flared flat limb.

Saprophyte: a plant that lives on or derives nourishment from dead or decaying organic matter.

Savanna (savannah): an extensive tropical vegetation dominated by grasses with varying mixtures of
  bushes and trees in open, wet land.

Scabrous: rough-surfaced, bearing short stiff hairs, scales or points.

Scandent: climbing.

Scapular: one of the feathers covering the shoulder of a bird.

Scarious: thin, membraneous and dry.

Scavenger: an animal that feeds on dead animals it did not kill.

Schizocarp: a dry fruit that breaks open at maturity. It is derived from two or more female stalks
  and matures as a single fruit.

Sclerophyllous forest: characterized by thick hard foliage.

Sclerotization: the process by which the cuticle of an insect is hardened.

Scorpiod: curved or curled-like the tail of a scorpion.

Scrape: a shallow depression that serves as a nest.

Scrub: a plant community characterized by scattered, low-growing trees and shrubs, interspersed
  with herbs, grasses, and patches of bare soil.

Sculpture: the ridges or outer markings on a shell.

Scute: a horny, chitinous or bony external plate or scale, such as the shell of a turtle.

Seepage water: water flowing toward stream channels after infiltration into the ground.

Sepal: usually green segments forming the calyx (outer covering) of a flower.

Sericeous: covered with silky hairs.

Serrate: having notched, toothlike projections.

Serrations: a series of teeth or notches.

Serrulate: having small, toothlike notches along the edge.

Sessile: in botany, stalkless and attached directly to the base; in zoology, permanently attached, not free-moving.

Sheath: a protective covering, such as the tubular base of a leaf surrounding a stem.

Shiner: small, often silvery North American fish of the family Cyprinidae.

Silicle: a short, flat pod that is divided by a membranous partition and splits at both seams.

Silique: a long pod that is divided by a membranous partition and splits at both seams, such as the fruit of the mustards.

Siltation: the process of depositing silt.

Sinistral: in zoology, pertaining to a gastropod shell that has its aperture (opening) to the left when facing the observer with the apex (top) up.

Sinuses: in botany, a notch or indentation between lobes of a leaf or corolla.

Siphon: a tubular organ, especially in aquatic invertebrates such as squids and clams, by which water is taken in or expelled.

Slackwater: the period at high or low tide when there is no visible flow of water; an area in a sea or river unaffected by currents.

Solifluction: freezing and thawing soil.

Solitary: individual that lives alone.

Sori: clusters of spore cases borne by ferns on the underside of the fronds; groups of spore-producing bodies.

Sorus: a cluster of spore cases borne by ferns on the underside of the fronds.

Spatulate: shaped like a spatula, having a broad, flat, flexible blade.

Spawning: laying and fertilizing of fish eggs, often involving migration to stream headwaters.

Specialization: evolution of a species so that it occupies a narrow place or niche in the community.

Species: a scientific classification or biological unit subordinate to the genus, the members of which differ among themselves only in the most minor details of structure, color, physiology, and behavior; they are capable of producing fertile offspring like the parents indefinitely.

Spike: a long flower cluster arranged along a stem.

Spikelets: subclusters of flowers.

Spikes: unbranched clusters of unstalked flowers.

Spine: in zoology, the spinal column of a vertebrate; in botany, a sharp-pointed, usually woody part extending from the stem of a plant.

Spinifex: any of a variety of Australian grasses growing in arid regions and having spiny leaves or seeds.

Spiracle: a secondary gill slit positioned in front of the primary gill slits.

Sporangium: a sac-like structure within which fungal spores are formed; spores are released when the sac ruptures.

Spurs: branches with much shortened internodes.

Squamation: an arrangement of scales, as on a fish.

Stamen: the pollen producing reproductive organ (male) of a flower, usually consisting of a filament and an anther.

Staminate: bearing stamens but lacking pistils.

Statoconia: one of the calcareous granules found in the statocyst of certain animals.

Statocysts: small organs of balance in many invertebrates, consisting of a fluid-filled sac containing statoliths that help to indicate position when the animal moves.

Statolith: a small, movable concentration of calcium carbonate.

Stellate: shaped like a star; radiating from a center.

Stipe: a stalk or stalk-like structure, such as the stem-like support of the cap of a mushroom or the main stem of a fern frond.

Stipitate: having a stipe or being supported by a stipe (stalk).

Stipules: one of the usually small paired leaf-like appendages at the base of a leaf or leafstalk.

Stochastic: chance or random events that could lead to the extinction or extirpation of a species.

Stoma: a minute opening of a leaf or stem through which gases and water vapor pass.

Strawberry guava: widely naturalized on all the main Hawaiian Islands, this plant is found in mesic and wet forests in the Koolau Mountains. Strawberry guava develops into dense stands in which few other plants can grow. Feral pigs eat the plant, and disburse its seeds throughout the forest.

Striae: many lines.

Style: a slender, tubular, or bristle-like appendage; in botany, the slender part of a pistal rising from the ovary.

Sub-rhomboidal: less than rhomboidal in shape (like a parallelogram with unequal adjacent sides).

Subalpine: a conifer-dominated forest which occurs in temperate latitudes; related to the boreal forest.

Subgenus: taxonomical category between a genus and a species, such as dogs (**genus**) being divided into spaniels and terriers.

Subphylum: subdivision of phylum composed of closely related groups of animals, such as vertebrates.

Subsessile: attached below the base.

Subspecies: a group of local populations of a species that inhabit a geographic subdivision of the range of the species and that differ taxonomically from other populations of the species; a division of species.

Substrate: composition of stream bed; the surface on which a plant grows or is attached.

Subterminal mouth: located nearly at the end.

Subtropical: regions bordering on the tropics.

Succession: progressive changes in the composition of a plant community.

Succulent: a plant having thick, fleshy leaves or stems that conserve moisture.

Sucker: in zoology, a chiefly North American fish having a thick-lipped mouth adapted for feeding by sucking; in botany, a secondary shoot arising from the base of a trunk.

Suffrutescent: having a woody stem or base.

Sulcus: narrow fissures separating cerebral convolutions (convex folds on the surface of the brain).

Superclass: taxonomic level between phylum and class; a combination of classes, such as fish.

Supralabials: above the lip.

Supraoculars: above the eye.

Sutures: in biology, a seam-like joint or line of articulation, such as the line of dehiscence (an opening that releases seeds) in a seed or fruit; in anatomy, the line of junction between two bones, especially the skull.

Sympatric: occupying the same geographic area without interbreeding.

Synchronous: in biology, the birth of all the young, usually hatching from eggs, at the same time.

Syndactyl: having two or more wholly fused digits (fingers or toes).

Synonyms: a taxonomic name that is equivalent to or replaced by another name.

Tadpole: the larva of a frog or toad.

Taenioglossate: a long narrow tongue-like structure or a ribbon with tooth-like structure.

Talus: a slope formed by the accumulation of debris; a sloping mass of debris at the base of a cliff.

Taproot: the main root of a plant, usually stouter than the lateral roots and growing straight downward from the stem.

Tarsus: the distal segmented structure on the leg of an insect or arachnid; in vertebrates, the section of the foot between the leg and metatarsus.

Tautonym: a taxonomic designation, such as *Gorilla gorilla,* commonly used in zoology in which the genus and species names are the same.

Taxon: a group of organisms with common characteristics constituting one of the categories in taxonomic classification, such as phylum, order or family.

Taxonomy: the science of classifying organisms.

Teeth: notched projects along the edge of a leaf, flower or wing.

Tendril: a long, slender, coiling root-like extension that attaches climbing plants to their surface.

Terete: cylindrical but usually slightly tapering at both ends, circular in cross section, and smooth-surfaced.

Terminal: in biology, appearing at the end of a stem, branch or stalk.

Terrapin: a type of freshwater turtle.

Terrestrial: living on land.

Territory: an area that an animal will defend against intruders.

Tertiary dichasia: the third flower cluster.

Tertiary: the short flight feathers nearest the body on the inner edge of a bird's wing.

Tetradynamous: having four long stamens and two short ones, as in the androecium of the Cruciferea.

Thoracic: situated near the thorax; the second or middle region in insects bearing the true legs and wings; in animals, the part of the body between the neck and the diaphragm.

Thrum: loose ends or fringe.

Toad: a warty-skinned, land frog.

Tolerance limit: physical extremities beyond which a species cannot survive.

Tomentum: covering of closely matted woolen hairs.

Tomial: cutting edge of a bird's bill.

Torpic: lethargic, dormant.

Torpor: a state of inactivity.

Tortoise: a land turtle.

Tribe: taxonomic category between family and genus.

Trichotomous: divided into three parts.

Tridentate: long, three-pronged fork.

Troglobite: a cave-dwelling species.

Troglobitic: cave-dwelling; in animals, a species that lives its completes its lifecyle in openings underground (like a cave), usually with small or absent eyes, attenuated appendages, and other adaptations to the subsurface environment.

Trophic: response to a specified stimulus.

Truncate: shortened.

Tubercle: in mussels a small raised area that limits water loss and prevents entry by microorganisms; a small knobby prominence on a plant or animal.

Tuberculation: having tubercles (small raised area in mussels that limits water loss)

Tundra: a treeless plain of the Arctic and Antarctic, characterized by a low, grassy sward, and dominated by sedges, rushes, lichens, and dwarf-woody species.

Turbid: muddy; having sediment or foreign particles stirred up.

Turtle: any shelled reptile.

Ultisol: a type of mineral soil with an accumulation of silicate clay layers with an average soil temperature of 8 degrees Celsius or higher.

Ultramafic: excessively rich in magnesium and iron.

Umbel: an umbrella-like flower cluster.

Umbilicus: a small opening or depression similar to a navel, such as the hollow base of the shell of a mollusk.

Umbo: knoblike proturbence, such as the prominence near the hinge of a mollusk.

Umbonate: knob-like protuberance.

Umbos: the beak cavity in mussels.

Undershell: plastron.

Undulate: moving in a smooth, wave-like motion.

Ungulate: having hoofs.

Unionids: fresh water mussels.

Uniserial: arranged in one row or in one sequence.

Univoltine: one flight season.

Uronites: part of an abdominal appendage of some crustaceans.

Uropods: one pair of rear abdominal appendages of certain crustaceans, including lobsters and shrimp.

Ustic: a soil temperature regime common to subhumid and semiarid regions; moisture is limited; temperatures range between 5 degrees Celsius and 8 degrees Celsius at 50 centimeters depth.

Utricle: a small, bladder-like, one-seeded fruit.

Valves: one of the paired hinged shells of mollusks; one of the sections into which a seed pod or fruit splits.

Vannal: veins.

Variety: a closer taxonomic relationship than subspecies.

Veliger: a larvae stage of a mollusk characterized by the presence of a hairlike swimming organ.

Venation: the distribution or arrangement of veins.

Vent: the anal opening of the body.

Venter: in anatomy, the abdomen or belly; in biology, a swollen structure or part similar to a belly.

Ventral: located at the lower side of a fish or bird.

Ventrum: anal region.

Vermiculation: worm-like marks; the condition of being worm eaten.

Vertebrate: an animal with a backbone.

Vestigial: a small, degenerate rudimentary organ that is a nonfunction remnant of an organ that was fully developed in earlier generations.

Vesture: a covering, especially cloth.

Vibrissa: feather near the beak of an insectivorous (insect eating) bird.

Villous: covered with fine, unmatted hair.

Viviparous: in zoology, giving birth to living offspring that develop within the mother's body; in botany, producing seeds that germinate before becoming detached from the parent plant.

Wetlands: marshes.

Whorl: three or more leaves radiating from a single point.

Wingbar: white or light colored lines or bars on a bird's wing near the shoulder.

Xeric: adaptable to an extremely dry habitat.

Xeromorphic: adaptable to drought conditions.

Xerophyte: a plant that can grow in very dry conditions and is able to withstand periods of drought.

Zero-plated: lacking scutes, lamina, or other than flat structures.

Zooplankton: small aquatic invertebrates with feeble swimming ability.

Zygomorphic: organisms that are bilaterally symmetrical and capable of being divided along a single longitudinal plane.

Zygotes: the cell formed through sexual union.

FEATURES AND MEASUREMENTS USED FOR IDENTIFYING FISH

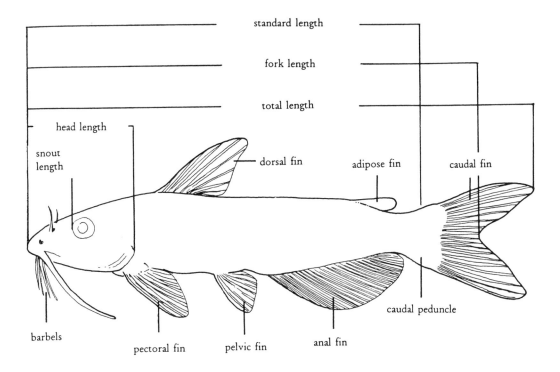

standard length

fork length

total length

head length

snout length

dorsal fin

adipose fin

caudal fin

barbels

pectoral fin

pelvic fin

anal fin

caudal peduncle

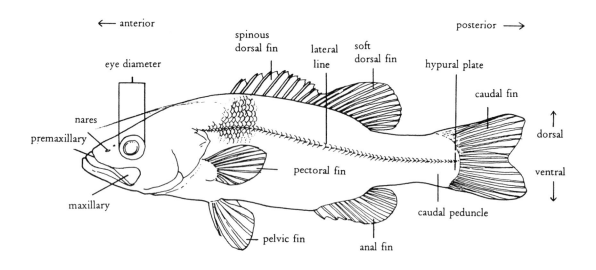

← anterior

posterior →

eye diameter

spinous dorsal fin

lateral line

soft dorsal fin

hypural plate

caudal fin

nares

premaxillary

dorsal

ventral

maxillary

pectoral fin

caudal peduncle

pelvic fin

anal fin

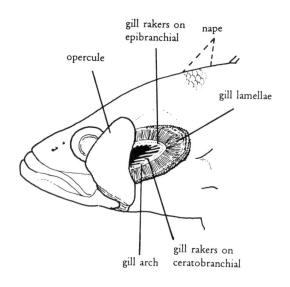

gill rakers on epibranchial

nape

opercule

gill lamellae

gill arch

gill rakers on ceratobranchial

Index

A